Contested Capital

The expansion and transformation of Asian economies is producing class structures, roles and identities that could not easily be predicted from other times and places. The industrialisation of the countryside, in particular, generates new, rural middle classes which straddle the worlds of agriculture and industry in complex ways. Their class position is improvised on the basis of numerous influences and opportunities, and is in constant evolution. Enormous though the total rural middle-class population is, meanwhile, it remains invisible to most scholars and policymakers. *Contested Capital* is the first major work to shed light on an emerging transnational class comprised of many hundreds of millions of people.

In India, the 'middle class' has become one of the key categories of economic analysis and developmental forecasting. The discussion suffers from one major oversight: it assumes that the middle class resides uniquely in the cities. As this book demonstrates, however, more than a third of India's middle class is rural, and 17 per cent of rural households belong to the middle class. The book brings this vast and dynamic population into view, so confronting some of the most crucial neglected questions of the contemporary global economy.

Maryam Aslany is a Postdoctoral Researcher and a Junior Research Fellow at Wolfson College, University of Oxford, and an Associate Researcher at Paris Diderot University. Her research focuses on theories of class, emerging middle classes, rural capitalism and political economy of climate adaptation in South Asia.

Contested Capital
Rural Middle Classes in India

Maryam Aslany

CAMBRIDGE
UNIVERSITY PRESS

University Printing House, Cambridge CB2 8BS, United Kingdom

One Liberty Plaza, 20th Floor, New York, NY 10006, USA

477 Williamstown Road, Port Melbourne, VIC 3207, Australia

314–321, 3rd Floor, Plot 3, Splendor Forum, Jasola District Centre, New Delhi–110025, India

79 Anson Road, #06–04/06, Singapore 079906

Cambridge University Press is part of the University of Cambridge.

It furthers the University's mission by disseminating knowledge in the pursuit of education, learning and research at the highest international levels of excellence.

www.cambridge.org
Information on this title: www.cambridge.org/9781108836333

© Maryam Aslany 2020

This publication is in copyright. Subject to statutory exception and to the provisions of relevant collective licensing agreements, no reproduction of any part may take place without the written permission of Cambridge University Press.

First published 2020

Printed in India by Nutech Print Services, New Delhi 110020

A catalogue record for this publication is available from the British Library

ISBN 978-1-108-83633-3 Hardback

Cambridge University Press has no responsibility for the persistence or accuracy of URLs for external or third-party internet websites referred to in this publication, and does not guarantee that any content on such websites is, or will remain, accurate or appropriate.

They embrace the God that consumes them.

—Albert Camus, *The Myth of Sisyphus (1942)*

Contents

List of Figures and Maps	ix
List of Tables	xi
List of Abbreviations	xv
Foreword	xvii
Acknowledgments	xxi
Introduction: The Problem of the 'Rural Middle Class(es)'	1
1. Trajectory of the Indian Middle Class: Its Size and Geographical Variations	11
2. In Search of the Rural Middle Classes: From Village Stratification to Rural Household Variations	41
3. Marx: Capital, Labour and the Rural Middle Classes	65
4. Weber: Marketable Capital, Status and the Rural Middle Classes	115
5. Bourdieu: Cultural Capital, Self-perception and the Middle-class Identity in Rural India	164
Conclusion: Understanding the Rural Middle Classes	203
Appendices	211
References	272
Index	288

Figures and Maps

Figures

1.1 Factors contributing to 'middle-class-ness'	22
1.2 Income levels across the population: All-India, Urban and Rural (2011–12)	25
1.3 Illustration of relative index decomposition (2011–12)	30
1.4 Categorisation of All-India population into seven classes (2011–12)	31
1.5 Middle classes: rural/urban distributions (2011–12)	35
1.6 Occupational categories of rural classes in India (2011–12)	36
3.1 Changes in the main source of household income, by sector (1993–2012)	79
3.2 Distribution of land in Rahatwade and Nandur (in acre)	86
4.1 Transformation in the housing style of the rural middle class in Nandur	133
4.2 Residence of a middle-class family in Nandur	133
4.3 Typical old style of housing: residence of a farmer in Rahatwade	134
4.4 Typical style of housing of the majority of Dalit agricultural labourers	134
4.5 Lorenz curve for household income distribution between and within different caste groups in rural India (2011–12)	155
5.1 Residence of a Dalit agricultural labouring family in Nandur	187
5.2 Residence of a Dalit agricultural labouring family in Nandur	187
5.3 Residence of a Dalit agricultural labouring family in Rahatwade	188
5.4 Living room of a self-identified *lower-middle-class* family in Nandur	188
5.5 Living room of a self-identified *middle-middle-class* family in Nandur	189
5.6 Living room of a self-identified *middle-middle-class* family in Nandur	190
5.7 Living room of a self-identified *middle-middle-class* family in Nandur	190
5.8 Living room of a self-identified *middle-middle-class* family in Rahatwade	191
5.9 Living room of a self-identified *upper-middle-class* family in Rahatwade	191

x   Figures and Maps

A3.1 Graph illustrating the persistence of caste inequalities in occupational patterns in rural India (1993–94 to 2011–12)   216
A4.1 Annual household income distributions in rural India (2011–12)   218
A4.2 Annual household income distributions in urban India (2011–12)   219
A4.3 Annual household income distributions on logarithmic scaled axes in rural India (2011–12)   220
A4.4 Annual household income distributions on logarithmic scaled axes in urban India (2011–12)   220

Maps

2.1 Map of Rahatwade village   49
2.2 Map of Gāvāta (main village) and Kamble Basti in Rahatwade   50
2.3 Map of Nandur village   55

Tables

1.1	Calculating the size of the middle class based on relative monetary definition (2011–12)	20
1.2	Fixed monetary estimation of the size of the Indian middle class	21
1.3	Household groups based on main source of household income (2011–12)	23
1.4	Income groups: All-India, Urban and Rural (2011–12)	24
1.5	Calculation of housing component (2011–12)	27
1.6	Categorisation of non-labouring households: All-India (2011–12)	28
1.7	Classification of non-labouring households: All-India (2011–12)	28
1.8	Calculating the scores and weight of indices: All-India (2011–12)	29
1.9	Proportions of identified classes: All-India (2011–12)	30
1.10	Categorisation of classes: characteristics, All-India (2011–12)	32
1.11	Calculating the size of all classes: All-India (2011–12)	34
1.12	Distribution of classes in rural India (2011–12)	35
1.13	Self-identification and class (2011–12)	37
2.1	Rahatwade and Nandur: some basic characteristics	46
2.2	Land and home ownership and access to basic amenities in Rahatwade	48
2.3	Land and home ownership and access to basic amenities in Nandur	52
2.4	Caste compositions of Rahatwade and Nandur	56
2.5	List of caste groups in Rahatwade	56
2.6	List of caste groups in Nandur	57
2.7	The two-cluster classification of households	61
3.1	Changes in the main source of household income, by sector (1993–2012)	78
3.2	Distribution of land in Rahatwade (2014–15)	85
3.3	Distribution of land in Nandur (2014–15)	85
3.4	Class structure in villages (capital, labour, surplus and accumulation)	89
3.5	Classification of households in Rahatwade	91
3.6	Classification of households in Nandur	91

xii   Tables

3.7	Classes in Rahatwade: composition and characteristics	105
3.8	Classes in Nandur: composition and characteristics	106
4.1	Changes in the economic condition of non-labouring households over the last 10 years (2015)	130
4.2	Occupational classification of households in Rahatwade and Nandur	137
4.3	Distribution of annual household income among different occupational categories in Rahatwade	138
4.4	Distribution of annual household income among different occupational categories in Nandur	138
4.5	Caste affiliations among the labouring households in Rahatwade	147
4.6	Caste affiliation among labouring households in Nandur	148
4.7	Occupational distribution among caste groups in rural All-India (2011–12)	149
4.8	Descriptive statistics for socio-economic variables among different caste groups in Rahatwade	151
4.9	Descriptive statistics for socio-economic variables among different caste groups in Nandur	152
4.10	Distribution of land ownership (irrigated and dry combined) among Marathas in Rahatwade	153
4.11	Income distribution among the non-labouring Maratha households in Rahatwade	154
4.12	Caste composition of classes in rural India – percentage (2011–12)	157
5.1	Is your household a middle-class household?	174
5.2	Self-identified class distributions of households	175
5.3	Vehicle ownership among Rahatwade's self-identified classes	195
5.4	Vehicle ownership among Nandur's self-identified classes	195
5.5	Possession of domestic appliances among Rahatwade's classes	196
5.6	Possession of domestic appliances among Nandur's classes	196
5.7	Possession of communications devices among Rahatwade's classes	197
5.8	Possession of communications devices among Nandur's classes	197
5.9	Social media use in Rahatwade	198
5.10	Social media use in Nandur	198
5.11	Possession of sofa set among Rahatwade's classes	199
5.12	Possession of sofa set among Nandur's classes	199
A1.1	Non-farm occupations in Rahatwade	211
A1.2	Non-farm occupations in Nandur	212
A2.1	Distribution of main source of income among different caste groups in urban India (2011–12)	213

A3.1	Distribution of main source of income among different caste groups in rural India (1993–94)	214
A3.2	Distribution of main source of income among different caste groups in rural India (2004–05)	215
A4.1	Distribution of annual household income by caste category in rural India (2011–12)	217
A4.2	Distribution of annual household income by caste category in urban India (2011–12)	217
A4.3	Distribution of annual household income by caste groups in rural India (2011–12)	221
A4.4	Distribution of annual household income by caste groups in urban India (2011–12)	221
A4.5	One-way ANOVA in rural India	222
A4.6	Linear regressions: relationship between income in logarithmic scale and caste (categorical)	223
A4.7	Linear regressions: relationship between income (dependent variable) and caste, highest level of adult education, education of head of the household, area of land owned and social network	225
A4.8	Linear regressions: relationship between income (dependent variable) and highest level of adult education, education of head of the household, area of land owned and social network (to compare the reliability of the two models, this model excludes caste)	226
A5.1	Descriptive statistics for socio-economic variables among different caste groups in rural India (2011–12)	228
A5.2	Descriptive statistics for socio-economic variables among different caste groups in urban India (2011–12)	230
A6.1	Caste compositions of identified classes in urban India (2011–12)	231
A7.1	Caste compositions of classes in rural Maharashtra – percentage (2011–12)	232

Abbreviations

ALDH	Agricultural Labour Days Hired-in
ALDS	Agricultural Labour Days Sold-out
ANOVA	analysis of variance
BKU	Bharatiya Kisan Union
CI	composite index
CMC	comfortable middle class
CSDS	Centre for the Study of Developing Countries
DTs	De-notified Tribes
E&TC	electronics and tele-communications
GDP	gross domestic product
HDPI	Human Development Profile of India
IBM	International Business Machines Corporation
ICPSR	Interuniversity Consortium for Political and Social Research
IHDS-I	India Human Development Survey-I
IHDS-II	India Human Development Survey-II
IMF	International Monetary Fund
LC	lowest class
LMC	lower middle class
NALD	net agricultural labour days
NCAER	National Council of Applied Economic Research
NSS	National Sample Survey
NT	Nomadic Tribe
OBCs	Other Backward Classes
PCA	principal component analysis
PCP	petty commodity production
PCPs	petty commodity producers
PMC	Professional and Managerial Class
RCC	reinforced cement concrete
SCs	Scheduled Castes

xvi   Abbreviations

SLC	second lowest class
SMC	straddling middle class
STs	Scheduled Tribes
SD	standard deviation
UC	upper class
UMC	upper middle class

Foreword

While the term 'middle class' has been in currency for almost 300 years, its definition – and thus its size – has always been bathed in vagueness, ambiguity and controversy. Just as the concept of class itself has been the subject of a series of mutually incompatible theories, the question of what might constitute the middle of an economic distribution or a social hierarchy has until now never been resolved by the sizeable industry devoted to it, other than in arbitrary ways. The peculiarities of the statistical evidence that might clarify the concept have made identifying middle classes, let alone comparing them, very difficult. And people have their own views about their class positions: their self-identifications can challenge those of the researcher.

In spite of these difficulties, the importance of what the concept denotes is indisputable, and has several equally indisputable dimensions. One dimension of 'middle-class-ness' involves culture – expressed in particular kinds of housing, social networks, leisure pursuits, style, and aspirations. The hope of upward mobility within the middle class focusses the longing to enjoy a swathe of services, notably health and education, to achieve competences and forms of security, and – in the view of many commentators – to develop and protect an illiberal politics of techno-authoritarian management.

Middle class culture also calls for a certain level of discretionary income – though the range of incomes considered to denote 'middle-class-ness' by scholars varies greatly. For India alone in the last decade this range has varied between an annual household income of US$ 4,300 in rupee equivalents, to one of US$ 27,000. Middle-class-ness may also be measured as the median expenditure group in a distribution of household expenditure; or identified by occupations – though here too there is a huge and debated range of occupations considered by analysts to be middle class.

Aspirational goods and services give rise to a politics of provision and consumption, of acquisition and defence of the status goods expressing discretionary income. The provision of such goods entails vast investments in the

xviii   Foreword

massification of formerly luxury commodities and services, and in the privatisation of facilities, places and spaces.

A further dimension of the middle class is the desire to escape and dissociate oneself from the (lack of) choices of occupation and lifestyle forced on (ever more precarious) manual labourers. This gives rise to tense power relations not only between those who are included, and those who are excluded, but also between exclusivism as a principle of middle-class politics, and the patronage/trusteeship/'speaking for society as a whole' which middle classes are often seen as upholding.

However the middle class is defined, India has contributed conspicuously to its world-wide growth. Whether its middle class is Deutsche Bank's estimated 40 million people or McKinsey's 600 million, India may well be home to a fifth of the world's total. Much has been written about India's middle class, suggesting it is shot through with distinctive barriers to entry and mobility rooted in the differentiating politics of caste, ethnicity, region, religion and patriarchal control over education, income and wealth.

Above all, the middle class has been assumed to be urban – until this book arrived. *Contested Capital: Rural Middle Classes in India* demonstrates that this assumption is false. In fact, as Maryam Aslany argues, about a third of India's middle class is rural.

India's rural economy remains overwhelmingly characterised as a labour sponge of last resort, a repository of poverty with agriculture as the dominant source of livelihoods. And despite decades of evidence of increasing rural inequality (and thus of increasing rural income and wealth), of rural consumption patterns imitating metropolitan ones and of the expansion of the non-farm economy into agrarian regions, debates in political economy and rural sociology about capitalist transformations have made scant mention of the possibility that a rural middle class or classes was emerging. The same is true for village studies. Classes occupying niches between the polar classes of capital and labour have appeared as awkward rather than central in demographic and analytical terms – whether in relation to the peasantry and petty commodity producers, or to merchants and commercial capital. Even in Kalecki's controversial theory of intermediate regimes, taken up by K. N. Raj, in which the ruling class is seen as composed of 'peasants and lower middle classes', and as being numerically powerful enough to make accommodative state-capitalist arrangements with 'upper middle classes', the middle classes are seen as urban. In this book, Dr Aslany has rectified this glaring neglect.

Hers is an ambitious and original contribution in a number of ways. First, given that there is no theory of everything, no single story, and that pluralism is the order of the day in the 21st century, it has required the development of evidence to enable the interpretation of the rural middle class from the perspectives of not one but three great founding fathers of social theory: Marx, Weber and Bourdieu. She has honed hermeneutical skills to trace a nuanced history of ideas that are sometimes inconsistent and unclear even at their points of origin. She has then translated delicate theoretical ideas into schemes and practices for field research, and has drafted, tested and delivered novel and demanding questionnaires. She has completed a unique piece of field research over an 18-month period in two Maharashtrian villages, which have a range of rental arrangements and forms of petty production, wage labour, and commercialised agricultural inputs and marketed surpluses, and most importantly, emerging industries at their peripheries.

Second, she has developed methodological and analytical skills not just for interrogating these theories but also for applying mixed methods for handling large national data bases, quantitative field evidence, qualitative case material and social profiles. This approach is transferable. It enables comparisons at different scales, just as it provides the empirical base for comparisons between the theories through which we understand rural economies.

Third, she has made a substantive contribution to our knowledge of rural transformations through the heterogeneity, fluidity and churning of the elements that form rural middle classes. She has traced the interweaving of oscillating and emergent class positions in agriculture, industry and ancillary professional services, the social ramifications of education and caste in rural economic diversification and the fascination of the rural living room as a significant site of class distinction.

This book will open up new research. It will encourage comparisons and contrasts between a range of theories about class. It will also invite comparisons of the trajectories of middle class formation in Maharashtra with those of other states and indeed other countries whose agrarian and non-agrarian rural economies have developed differently, and in which policy regimes for rural development diverge. From now on the 'rural middle class' will have to be factored into the analysis of agrarian change and rural development.

In this highly original and inter-disciplinary book, Maryam Aslany has addressed an enigmatic phenomenon that is difficult to grasp analytically and has been overlooked by many. She has mainstreamed into rural development a neglected class and its class relations, combining intellectual elegance with a determination forged through curiosity and the inspiration of fieldwork.

Enjoy, criticise and develop the research pioneered here.

Barbara Harriss-White
Emeritus Professor of Development Studies, Oxford University
Emeritus Fellow of Wolfson College, Oxford
November 2019

Acknowledgments

Without the many wonderful people who accompanied it on its journey, this book would never have existed, and I would have been deprived of some of the great pleasures of my life.

First and foremost, I am profoundly grateful to the people of Rahatwade and Nandur for opening their homes to me. The conversations I had with them during fieldwork taught me more than I can say. Throughout the book I have tried to preserve their narratives as closely as possible by using a word-by-word translation of the original interviews, which took place in Marathi. I must thank my research assistant, Raghunath Yadav, who also acted as my interpreter. His enthusiasm and curiosity made these conversations both smooth and enjoyable. My thanks go also to Datta, Amar and Ravi, who assisted me during fieldwork, to Mangesh Dahiwale for the important input he provided during early days of my field research, and to P. Sainath for initial advice on the inner in/formal economic structure of Maharashtrian villages.

I am profoundly grateful to Professor Barbara Harriss-White and Professor Christophe Jaffrelot for the significant roles they both played in the making of this book, which began as a doctoral project. Their lifetime of research on India has been a great source of inspiration to me, and I was extremely privileged to have them as my doctoral supervisors. I want to thank them for their brilliance, vision and guidance – as well as for their encouragement and forbearance. I would not have been able to complete this book without them. Barbara's role far exceeded that of academic supervisor, and was extended to a precious friendship: thank you.

I want to express my deep feelings of gratitude to my dear friend and mentor Dr George Kunnath for his countless stimulating insights and outstanding teaching. I feel deeply indebted to George for introducing me, both to the beauties of ethnographic research and to innovative ways of applying social theories to empirical field studies.

Special thanks go to Dr Judith Heyer for her generous input and perceptive corrections while proof-reading the manuscript. This is also my chance to express

xxii   Acknowledgments

my utmost gratitude to my PhD examiners, Professor Matthew McCartney and Dr Jonathan Pattenden for their invaluable comments during my viva, which proved to be instrumental when I came to refine the manuscript. I am also very appreciative of the helpful criticism and advice provided, during conferences and discussions, by Professor Craig Jeffrey, Professor Jens Lerche, Dr Indrajit Roy, Professor Jairus Banaji, and Dr Alessandra Mezzadri.

I also thank my anonymous reviewers, whose comments have greatly helped in improving this book, as well as the team at Cambridge University Press, whose tireless efforts were important in its publication.

During the long period I spent researching and writing, I benefited from institutional support from various quarters. The King's India Institute at King's College London, where I did my doctorate, provided a stimulating atmosphere of intellectual freedom. My thanks go to Professor Sunil Khilnani, Dr Kriti Kapila, Dr Sunil Mitra Kumar and Dr Louise Tillin for their intellectual contributions during my doctorate.

The Oxford School of Global and Area Studies, where I completed my MSc in Contemporary India, and the Wolfson South Asia Research Cluster, a hub for scholars of various disciplines working on India, both provided nurturing environments where I developed interdisciplinary skills which proved fundamentally helpful during my research. I am particularly grateful to Professor Kate Sullivan de Estrada for her significant contribution to my academic journey, especially during my MSc days.

I feel a great debt to the Gokhale Institute of Politics and Economics in Pune, which generously hosted me as a visiting scholar for three years, offered remarkable encounters with field economists and scholars working on rural Maharashtra, provided me with an office space, and facilitated my research visa. In particular, I feel extremely indebted to its director, Professor Rajas Parchure, who made my research in Maharashtra possible and who advised me throughout my fieldwork.

I am very thankful to Professor Isabelle Guérin who facilitated my association at the Centre for Social Studies on African, American and Asian worlds (CESSMA), at Paris Diderot University.

I must also express my gratitude to Wolfson College, Oxford, which provided me with many remarkable friendships and collaborations, and allowed me to resolve several struggles along the way. Thanks in particular to Yasser Khan, my intellectual twin (for exciting conversations on capitalism's dysfunctionality and our mutual literary idols), Ali Jan, my academic comrade (for our inspiring conversations about Karl Marx and rural capitalism in South Asia), Richard Toppo (for helping to kick start my fieldwork in rural Maharashtra), Niyati Sharma (for her continued encouragement to voice my inner thoughts), and Amogh Sharma and Fahad Rahman (for their generous hearts and ears), all of whose presence

Acknowledgments xxiii

enhanced this intellectual journey. Others whose friendship and inspiring conversations proved to be a great asset in the making of this book were, in no particular order: Adam Mahdi, Taha Yasseri, Jai Bhatia, Hugo Rojas, Victor J. Willi, Zaad Mahmood, Michael Peterer, Ionut Moise, Shannon Brincat, Roham Alvandi, Nasim Fathi, Sejal Inn, Alena Kulinich, Kyo Ikeda, Leonellha Barreto Dillon, Alfred Gathorne-Hardy, Arturo Soto, César Giraldo Herrera, John Francis Davies, Nicolas Lippolis, Yuhan Vevaina, Andreas Winkler, and Theo van Lint.

I cannot thank Steffi Pondini enough for her eternal friendship and encouragement. U has been a great source of courage and curiosity: thank you for believing in the subterranean life that lies within us. This is also my chance to thank Rana whose support has been a wonderful asset, his brilliance a major source of inspiration and creativity. Lastly, I must thank my father for his enduring faith in possibilities, and my dearest, now departed, grandparents for always believing in my future, which, in turn, helped me to live a more fulfilled and hopeful life.

Above all, my greatest debt is to Kaveh Moussavi, without whose encouragement and financial support this project would not have begun, and certainly not have been completed – a mark of generosity and support that is, unequivocally, unequalled: thank you.

Introduction
The Problem of the 'Rural Middle Class(es)'

> Granted, nothing raises the academic red flag faster than the concept of the middle class.
>
> —Diane Davis, 2004

> The epistemic ambition of defining, once and for all, the 'real' boundaries of the middle class is doomed to failure because it rests on a fundamentally mistaken conception on the ontological status of classes: the middle class does not exist ready-made in reality.
>
> —Loïc Wacquant, 1991

On my second visit to Rahatwade, a small village in western Maharashtra, in May 2015, I am talking, through my research assistant, with a group of men, a meeting arranged by the Village Panchayat. They are curious about my work, bemused to hear of my academic interest in their village. I tell them: 'I am here to visit middle class households.' The little of the village that I had seen did not register in my head as qualifying, categorically, to have any middle classes from the conventional theoretical perspectives. So, I threw the question out to them: 'I was wondering if there are any middle-class families in this village? I would like to talk to them.' The village guide's response surprised me. He looked around at the group of men, hands outstretched, and said, 'Don't worry about that madam. We are all middle class!'

This book explores the formation and trajectories of India's rural middle class(es).[1] Studies of the middle class are almost exclusively confined to urban contexts. This is particularly the case in developing countries, where it is assumed that cities, not the countryside, host the process of middle-class formation, effectively eliminating from view large numbers of rural households. Rural societies are rarely analysed in middle-class terms. There are theoretical reasons

2   Contested Capital

to explain this. Most influential social theorists, such as Karl Marx, Max Weber, Georg Simmel, Ferdinand Tönnies and Émile Durkheim, assumed a clear social distinction between 'rural' and 'urban' societies, which in turn created ideal categories that made it possible to theorise the similarities and contrasts between pre-industrial and modernised industrial societies.[2] While cities were assumed to be the chief sites of economic growth, industrial development and modernity, the rural world, embodying something primordial, represented a community that, by virtue of its isolation from the urban-based practices of capitalist development and experiences of modernisation, was considered to be classless by definition, bounded by kinship ties, family lineages, personal networks, and relative isolation.[3] For example, Marx, drawing on colonial reports, popularised the notion of Indian villages as self-sufficient economic units impenetrable by the capitalist mode of production, and described occupations within villages as divisions of labour within a community, rather than class positions. For Marx, the economic landscape of Indian villages remained untouched over time, making the Indian countryside a classless society, characterised as static and economically self-sufficient.[4] Similarly, referring to a component of the division of labour, namely the artisan, Weber agreed with Marx that the stability of the Indian village economy was secured by a fixed payment in kind, and not production for the capitalist market, which in turn made 'class' an irrelevant analytical concept in rural India.[5]

Successive generations of rural development scholars held a strikingly similar visualisation of rural societies. For example, for many, categories of peasantry came to convey a meaningful vision of rural life because they retained within them certain economic, social and cultural relations that, by virtue of their characteristics, protected rural producers from being consumed purely by the accumulation objective. Those who began to view the rural world in class terms limited their categorisations to a polarised class structure, confined to the agrarian bourgeoisie and landless and near-landless agricultural proletariats. Scholars who considered middling types, analysed them in terms of 'peasantries', 'petty bourgeoisie' or 'petty commodity producers', and in later writings 'intermediate classes', without any remark on middle-class formation, as though a different set of cultural, social, market and productive relations rules the rural life which makes the term 'middle class' an irrelevant analytical conception.[6]

In India, from the early 1980s until the early 2000s, the study of the Indian middle class, in both city and countryside, was largely ignored due to the influence of subaltern and postcolonial studies, which had an adverse impact on the use of 'class' as a category of analysis. The development of Indian historiography and other social sciences was, to a great extent, shaped by the influential Subaltern

Studies emerged in 1982 by a group of historians working on South Asia.[7] The Subaltern Studies series had a considerable impact on the study of class in Indian society. Class analysis was pushed into the background as scholars such as Gyan Prakash called for post-foundationalist histories of India, intended to free scholars from the concepts associated with a more straightforward political economy approach, which were thought to rely on essentialised (western) categories of analysis not applicable to the Indian context.[8] Moreover, the subaltern studies collective, and the scholars of postcolonial studies it inspired, gradually moved further away from class analysis. Most notably in the mid-1980s, when Edward Said wrote an introduction to *Subaltern Studies V*, the collective took, in keeping with broader trends in the social sciences, a linguistic turn.[9] Vivek Chibber suggests that the pervasive decline in class analysis across the social sciences since the 1990s was particularly acute in the field of South Asian studies, in which the influence of poststructuralism/postmodernism has been most pronounced. The decline in Marxist analysis was, in many ways, inevitable and was part of broader trends in social science. However, the severity of its decline in South Asian studies was a symptom of it never having a strong foothold in the first place. Chibber points out that South Asian studies is one of the few fields in which senior professors and younger scholars are able to agree on their hostility to class analysis.[10] Particularly, in the Indian context, numerous other analytical categories – such as ethnicity, gender, race and perhaps most significantly caste – came to overtake the explanatory ground that class could occupy.[11] Their dominance and popularity left in their wake a dearth of scholarship on class in India.

However, despite this paucity of studies of class in the last two decades of twentieth century India, in recent years, a comparatively limited body of scholarship on the Indian middle class, particularly the 'new middle class', has emerged. This can be divided into two broad categories. First, the Indian middle class has been examined as an income-based or structurally defined class whose economic opportunities are derived from resources such as managerial authority or the possession of scarce occupational skills, which contrasts with the working class whose labour is reduced to the commodity form.[12] Second, central in representations of beneficiaries from economic liberalisation, this new middle class has been defined as an aspirational cultural class, which is often the product of public discourse. In this account, the middle class is the class most dependent on the ownership and control of cultural capital – social identity, competence, and excludability of others – as well as the mechanism for reproduction, transmission across generations, or inheritance of these resources. Differentiating its position from the rest of the population by translating its cultural hegemony into the language of legitimisation, the middle class produces and maintains a dominant ideology through particular aesthetic means, that regulates the social structure, and the other social classes aspire to consume this ideology.[13] However, this developing body of scholarship does not look beyond the boundaries of urban India.

On the other hand, among development scholars who study the Indian countryside, none really offer accounts in which the notion of 'middle class' is employed. In studies of Indian villages, sociologists and anthropologists have primarily devoted their attention to caste and kinship, gender and marriage, migration and the agrarian transformation. Similarly, political economists – whose studies are devoted to patterns of livelihood and changes in occupational patterns, agrarian change, non-farm economy and class formation – have omitted consideration of middle-class formation in Indian villages. The rural middle class has completely skipped the attention of scholars of various disciplines.[14]

In the subsequent chapters, I take to task this conceptual bias and demonstrate the existence of India's rural middle class, which was revealed in field research in the context of emerging industrialisation in close proximity to rural areas. I then examine its composition, characteristics, and the everyday world and social identification of its members. However, the question of how to probe the development of the rural middle class requires an exploration of who or what constitutes the middle class and how to draw boundaries around it. These are known to be among the most 'contentious' and 'intractable' issues in contemporary sociology.[15] Studies of the middle class are confronted with conceptual complexities. There is considerable debate over what constitutes the middle class, not only in terms of contested theory but also in different global contexts. The boundaries of this class, however defined, are fluid – in turn, reflecting the fuzzy meaning of the term 'middle class', and indeed 'class'. Its slipperiness in large part is the result of the variety of definitions based on wealth, income, occupation, consumption, aspirations and identity. Further complications arise when we throw in diversification and informality that characterise the rural economy, which makes the middle class a constantly moving and unstable category, whose size, composition and characteristics can alter dramatically with changes in the economy and across time and space. Furthermore, as this study reveals, the rural middle class is a class that straddles two 'contradictory class locations', to borrow from Erik Olin Wright – a class that holds elective affinities, as well as disparities, with both capital and labour, making the task of studying it even more haunting.

Three major traditions of class analysis follow from the writings of Marx, Weber and Bourdieu, which conceptualise classes on the basis of, respectively, productive

Introduction   5

capital (relations of production); social and marketable capital (market situation); and symbolic and cultural capital (accumulation of knowledge and appropriation of cultural awareness). These traditions are simultaneously complementary to, and their followers in constant debate and disagreement with, each other about conceptualising 'class'. Moreover, beyond the problem of outer boundaries, there are important internal variations within the middle class. Many Marxist scholars deal with the problem of the middle class by denying its existence altogether, enforcing the simple polarisation of class structure. Those recognising the middle class as a class in its own right tend to define it as an unproductive class, situated between the *proletariat* and *bourgeoisie*, and see its internal differentiations on the basis of relations of *exploitation*, and the extent of ownership of productive capital, or opposing its class 'position', to that of labourers or capitalists, or between the 'old' and 'new' middle classes. Those writing within the Weberian tradition rely on relations of *domination*, and define the middle class on the basis of control of marketable capital such as properties, skills and credentials, while recognising its internal distinctions on the basis of status privileges and the differentiated 'situation' in property and the labour markets. Those inspired by Bourdieu differentiate the middle class by its control and ownership of cultural capital and its physical embodiment. Within this tradition, the class cleavages are produced and reproduced through the hierarchically differentiated nature of taste and *habitus*, a socially constituted system of transposable dispositions that motivates one's perception, conception and expression.[16]

Empirically, deciding who belongs to this class on the ground (during the field research) is often the result of the subjective notions of researchers, whose classifications are based on their perceptions, or usually on a single indicator or a theory, in turn, failing to address the multi-dimensionality of its 'type', 'composition' and 'characteristics'. This methodological insufficiency is perhaps due to the theoretical slipperiness of the concept and ambiguity over where the boundaries should be drawn. In practical terms, this raises the question of how to locate the middle class(es) in a given locality and time. Loïc Wacquant suggests that the only way to study the middle class is through a focus on subjective struggle or the self-construction of middle-class identity.[17] Anthony Giddens, on the contrary, points out the *absence* of class identity or consciousness among the middle classes, suggesting middle-class individuals lack a clear conception of class identity, and as such he rejects the subjective definition of its members.[18] The turn to poststructuralist analysis has put additional confusions over boundary drawing by introducing serious but valid questions about the relative worth of subjective versus objective definitions of the middle class.[19]

6   Contested Capital

There is of course more than one way to study the middle class, and in my view, favouring one theory or definition, or even a discipline, over another, is far from satisfactory. Critical pluralism is useful in overcoming this methodological pitfall and the conceptual murkiness. To do this, I develop a three-part analysis, drawing on the perspectives of the three major class theorists – Marx, Weber and Bourdieu – to offer three related, but theoretically distinct, accounts of the formation of India's rural middle classes. The selection of three theories (as opposed to one) provides a solution to the problem of capturing the conceptual difficulties of the term 'middle class', enables its heterogeneity to be explored empirically, and facilitates a holistic examination of its composition. Furthermore, it was indeed possible to witness, even within one village, the various forms of relations of production, market situations, social relations, symbolic and cultural distinctions, aspirations and identity, all of which constitute a specific kind of middle-class privilege, making each theory operationally relevant, which in turn led me to reject the single theoretical perspective. This is not to say that I have completely ignored self-perception and the local language of middle-class-ness. From the beginning, I was mindful that it is possible that my theoretically identified middle classes may not see or talk about themselves in similar class terms. This possible definitional dichotomy raised and enabled a critique of ethnocentrism in social class theory. Therefore, besides unfolding the untold story of their making through the languages of the three class theorists, my aim in the subsequent chapters is to also find the linguistic silences, and allow rural middle class voices to tell a parallel story about their making and trajectories.

In what follows, I look into the formation of rural middle classes through an extensive case study of two villages. The arguments of this book spread over five empirical chapters that draw on a mixed methodology designed to grasp the various sets of classificatory practices that produce class boundaries through each theory. Each chapter develops from four types of fieldwork data, collected from 490 households – a total population of 2,905 – in villages of Rahatwade and Nandur in western Maharashtra, from April 2015 to September 2016. The data includes two rounds of quantitative socio-economic household surveys, and two rounds of in-depth qualitative semi-structured interviews.[20] Overall, Chapters 3 and 4, on Marx and Weber, are primarily the result of the two rounds of household survey. These chapters are interspersed with qualitative interviews relating to economic transformation at the village and household level. This combination of data enabled the validation of the prescriptive theoretical findings by taking into account the voices of participants. Bourdieu's approach to social classes as a theoretical framework has different implications for knowledge which rejects an inflexible definition of class membership. Following this, Chapter 5 is largely the fruit of qualitative interviews piloted with self-identified middle classes.[21] Interviews sought to employ Bourdieu's approach in the form of a heuristic device, to capture the symbolic and cultural markers in rural India, and were primarily related to self-identification, middle-class status, aspirations and the ways in which middle-class boundaries are produced through mechanisms of social and cultural visibility and excludability of others. In addition to my detailed local field research, the book augments three levels of Indian political economy surveys at the All-India level: *Human Development Profile of India*, 1993–94 (HDPI); *India Human Development Survey I*, 2004–05 (IHDS-I); and *India Human Development Survey II*, 2011–12 (IHDS-II). This was to develop the central arguments and to provide a general understanding of the broader structural changes in rural India since 1991, in the context of which the rural middle class has emerged.[22] This contextual knowledge made possible an understanding of how findings from a micro-study of two villages relate to broader socio-economic transformations at the macro-level.

Chapter 1 reviews the literature on the middle class, with a particular focus on the Indian middle class. Through statistical analysis of the IHDS-II (2011–12), it provides one of the most systematic estimates of size of the Indian middle class, and offers a careful examination of its composition. Additionally, it underwrites a significant finding, for the purpose of this book, which is the discovery of the rural middle class, laying the foundation for what is to follow.

Chapter 2 introduces readers to Maharashtra, and offers a detailed analysis – relevant as background to this research – of the internal arrangement and socio-economic structure of field-sites. Given the vastness of rural India, a systematic selection of sample villages, which were likely to host middle-class households, was of crucial importance. To make this chapter particularly useful for academics and postgraduate students who may wish to undertake village studies, I briefly present a structured method for the selection of sample field-sites.

Chapter 3 extensively engages with various ways in which Marx and his legatees dealt with the concept of 'middle class'. It then enquires into the understanding of the dynamics of agrarian change, labour relations and various modes of accumulation that exist in rural India, to elucidate paths to rural capitalism, and the rural class structure in the current phase of industrialisation, when households can simultaneously belong to a variety of classes-in-themselves. The analysis of household data through a Marxian framework enables us to see how the many attempts to identify agrarian classes all provide an incomplete analysis of class formation in the contemporary phase of rural industrialisation. To compensate

8   Contested Capital

for this shortfall, a composite analytical instrument is developed that draws on Marx's notion of the ownership of the means of production, labour relations and modes of accumulation of surplus to identify seven distinct economic classes, including rural middle classes in India.

Chapter 4 characterises the rural middle class from a perspective influenced by Max Weber's conception of 'life chances', which determine classes in the labour market. It shifts the analysis from an exploitation-centred concept of class to one that is based on the concept of domination to examine class formation through occupational mobility and skill differentials. The primary focus is to discover the diverse ways in which rural households seek upward social mobility in the class hierarchy and negotiate their entry into the middle-class skilled-labour market. Following Weber's discussion on the economic effect of the caste system, it then scrutinises the ways caste relations intervene in the labour market, revealing important caste cleavages relating to patterns of class formation in rural India.

Chapter 5 analyses the formation of the rural middle classes from a perspective influenced by Bourdieu. The fundamental difference, for the purposes of this chapter, is that Bourdieu is critical of abstract conceptualisations, and his studies of class are primarily drawn from empirical investigations. Bourdieu was concerned with symbolic representation, in the realms of culture, art, literature, science and language. Using Bourdieu's approach in the form of an experimental method, this chapter puts forward suggestions on productive ways in which this sociology of class can be applied to the rural Indian context. Prompted by a discussion of interior design and 'living rooms' in rural Rahatwade and Nandur, I aim to unpack how middle classes seek social and cultural visibility, and pursue distinction from lower classes, through particular aesthetic means, spatial and cultural strategies, and the language of middle-class-ness. Although it is difficult to grasp the meaning behind certain forms of consumption in two small villages analytically, my overall attempt has been to unravel the 'economy of cultural goods' in rural India.[23]

In the brief concluding chapter, I aim to demonstrate how critical pluralism is useful in social sciences. Following an overview of some of the central empirical findings of the book and the contributions they make to theories of class, I briefly outline the ways in which the three theories are both complementary to, and at times in contrast with, each other, highlighting the fluidity of 'capital' as an analytical concept.

To sum up, the formation of India's rural middle class rests on a complex, and often contradictory, set of processes that began unfolding with growing industrialisation in the periphery of some villages after the introduction of economic liberalisation. Although still in the making, this class will come to play an important role in economic, social and political landscapes of India, through its social and cultural influence, political prominence, and impact on processes of socio-economic exclusion and unequal access to resources. As economic activities in villages are evolving towards industrialisation, theories of class and stratification become ever more useful for understanding the underlying causes of systematic class inequalities and their social, economic and cultural implications. It is indeed possible that the rural middle classes see their economic interest, political allegiances and commitments, and claims on the state as distinct from the urban middle classes. At the same time, their influence might translate into a different combination of demand for industrial and agricultural policies than those of rural elites or the rural poor, which can shape the economic and development planning of the state.[24] Furthermore, the sheer persistence of the use of the term 'middle class', by the state, scholars of various disciplines, media, and the general public, indicates that this class points to a social phenomenon of persisting significance and we are unlikely to succeed in studying any societies without it. By focusing on urban middle classes to the exclusion of the rural, development scholars gloss over a class that is important for our understanding of forms and practices of rural capitalism, agrarian transformations and rural economy and society.

Notes

1. I use 'middle class' in the singular when referring to the concept or category, and 'middle classes' in the plural when referring to a group of households or individuals.
2. The theoretical reason to explain absence of rural middle class studies is explained by Diane Davis in her examination of middle classes in East Asia and Latin America. See Davis (2004).
3. See Davis (2004).
4. Karl Marx never visited India and his ideas about Indian villages were based on colonial reports, written in the *New-York Daily Tribune*. See, for example, Marx (1853).
5. For Weber's perspective on Indian village economy, see Weber (1958).
6. See Bardhan (1998), Basile (2009), Harriss-White (2003, 2010), McCartney and Harriss-White (2000). These studies have drawn their inspiration from Kalecki's theory of intermediate regimes, taken up by K. N. Raj. See Kalecki (1972).
7. The term 'subaltern' in social science originates from Antonio Gramsci (1971), and became a term applied to those in subordinated social groups.
8. See Prakash (2000).
9. Edward Said wrote a foreword to *Selected Subaltern Studies*. See Said (1988).

10. On the decline of class analysis, see Chibber (2006).
11. Deshpande suggests that the significance of 'new social movements', which mobilise around issues such as the environment and the rise of identity politics, also bear no relation to the concept of class. He argues these trends in writing about South Asia 'have certainly deepened the crisis of class concept and amplified the long-standing complaints about its inadequacies'. See Deshpande (2003: 125).
12. Fernandes and Heller have provided an examination of the middle class in the labour market, in which the middle class is defined as a class that generates its income from exclusive acquisition of marketable skills and credentials. See Fernandes and Heller (2006).
13. For example, see studies by Brosius (2010), Deshpande (2003), Fernandes (2000, 2006, 2011), and Ganguly-Scrase and Scrase (2009).
14. Except for Davis (2004), who broadly looks into the rural middle classes in East Asia and Latin America.
15. See the sociological work of Abercrombie and Urry on the theory of class, based on a distinction between Weberian and Marxist approaches, Abercrombie and Urry (1983).
16. See Bourdieu (1977: 86).
17. See Wacquant (1991).
18. See Giddens (1995).
19. See Davis (2004).
20. Creswell and Plano Clark (2007) suggest that the combination of quantitative and qualitative data provides a better and deeper understanding of any social group, in this case the rural middle class, than a single approach. This is because, they argue, quantitative findings are primarily motivated by the concerns of the researcher (in this case using preselected variables which enabled identification of the rural middle class within the three theoretical frameworks), while qualitative data reveals more subtle features of their characteristics which might not be evident from quantitative findings alone, and can therefore validate the quantitative findings by taking into account the voice of the participants. For discussion on using mixed methods, see Creswell and Plano Clark (2007, 2011).
21. The analysis of the first round of survey revealed that in Rahatwade 90 households and in Nandur 93 households self-identify as middle-class households. A detailed account of the sampling method for semi-structured qualitative interviews is provided in Chapter 5.
22. The IHDS-I and IHDS-II are publicly available through the Interuniversity Consortium for Political and Social Research (ICPSR), located at the University of Michigan. The HDPI is not publicly available but was accessed with permission through the National Council of Applied Economic Research (NCAER), New Delhi.
23. See Bourdieu (1984: 1).
24. See Davis (2004).

1

Trajectory of the Indian Middle Class
Its Size and Geographical Variations*

It is manifest that the best political community is formed by citizens of the middle class, and that those states are likely to be well-administered in which the middle class is large, and stronger if possible than both the other classes, or at any rate than either singly; for the addition of the middle class turns the scale, and prevents either of the extremes from being dominant ... and where the middle class is large, there are least likely to be factions and dissensions. ... And democracies are safer and more permanent than oligarchies, because they have a middle class which is more numerous and has a greater share in the government; for when there is no middle class, and the poor greatly exceed in number, troubles arise and the state soon comes to an end.

—Aristotle, 350 BCE

India's biggest strength is its new middle class.

—Narendra Modi, 2019

The 'middle class' is analysed in a range of different global contexts. The term often refers to a category of people who are somewhere near the middle of an imaginary social spectrum along which income, property, wealth and occupational opportunities are distributed. In the context of developing countries, or countries experiencing rapid economic growth, the middle class holds centre stage in economic and public discourse: its size is often used as an important developmental proxy, a litmus test for socio-economic growth, and an indication of political stability in the face of globalisation (Birdsall, Graham and Pettinato, 2000). In the field of development studies, it is commonly assumed that countries with larger middle classes are able to reach a consensus on public goods and economic development planning and therefore tend to enjoy faster economic growth, higher national income and better public services. In contrast, societies with polarised economic classes incline to focus their economic planning on distribution and

12   Contested Capital

redistribution between polarised factions that alternate in power (Easterly, 2001). In a comprehensive examination of the middle classes in East Asia and Latin America, Diane Davis demonstrates a direct relation between the size of the middle class and the state's economic and development planning, and notes that the middle class envisages its economic and political interests as differentiated from the interests of capitalists and of labourers. Therefore, to safeguard its interests and assert its identity as a distinct class, it attempts to shape the ways in which the state designs its economic planning which *disciplines* capitalists and labourers to generate national prosperity and balanced economic growth. With such disciplinary measures, she argues, 'the economy is less prone to distortion and waste, industrial policy decisions are more likely to be made with long-term frameworks in mind, national industrial growth objectives are more apt to be achieved, and sustained macroeconomic development is more likely to materialize' (Davis, 2004: 2).

As such in countries where the middle class is politically strong, or where the middle class is proportionally larger in number, the state is more inclined to accommodate the economic demands of the middle class, and is more likely to curtail policies which promote 'rent-seeking' and 'short-term profit maximising', which are in the interests of the capitalist class. In countries with a smaller middle class, the state is more in favour of accommodating the demands of either the capitalist class, by imposing 'protectionist measures' to safeguard their interests, or the labour forces, by increasing their wages (Davis, 2004: 2). Davis then puts forward a suggestion that the rural middle classes, who she defines as 'self-employed, salaried, or small-scale producers whose economic livelihood is structured primarily around agricultural activities', are more forceful in their demands from the state to enforce *disciplinary* capacity vis-à-vis capital and labour, and therefore, fundamental to the state's development prospects (Davis, 2004: 3).

Similarly, in the Indian context, Pranab Bardhan points to the ways in which the upper layer of the middle class forms the course of development policies of the state. With ownership and control of economic, social, and cultural capital, the Indian middle class has developed a distinct identity from both the ruling bloc, and classes below them, and its political and economic influence has shaped the direction of state-led development in significant ways in decades following Indian independence. Bardhan depicts the upper tiers of the middle class as a 'rentier' class, or a proprietary class, that controls national development in the service of its own economic interests (Bardhan, 1998: 52). In line with such arguments that point to the centrality of the middle class in shaping the development strategies of the state, this class has come to be a significant indicator, perhaps more in a symbolic way, of developmental success narratives of the Indian state, particularly in the post-liberalisation period. But, what is the origin of the Indian middle class, who constitute it and how big is it? These are the questions this chapter seeks to answer. The first section provides a historical overview of the rise of the Indian middle class. The second examines existing methods and debates relating to the calculation of its size. Using the 'composite indicator' method, the third section provides one of the most systematic estimates of the size of the middle class in India.[1] The final part under-writes the most significant finding of this chapter, which demonstrates that a considerable segment of the Indian middle class resides in rural areas. This chapter draws on data from the *India Human Development Survey* 2011–12 (IHDS-II).

The Middle Class in India

Scholarship on the Indian middle class can be broadly divided into three overlapping eras. The first is centred on the colonial middle class and tends to be more historical, the second focuses on the post-independence middle class and the third on the 'new' middle class which emerged since the introduction of economic liberalisation, and is often anthropological or sociological. It is the review of this literature to which we now turn.

The Colonial Middle Class

The origins of the middle classes in India are often associated with the introduction of British colonial education policy.[2] As in other colonial contexts, education was the primary way in which this middle class was created and the English language became a distinctive tool of the Indian middle class. The British attempted to create a class comparable to their own which would assist them in colonial administration. In 1835, Lord Macaulay, who introduced English-medium education to India, stated:

> We must at present do our best to form a class who may be interpreters between us and the millions whom we govern; a class of persons, Indian in blood and colour, but English in taste, in opinions, in morals, and intellect. To that class we may leave it to refine the vernacular dialects of the country, to enrich those dialects with terms of science borrowed from the Western nomenclature, and to render them by degrees fit vehicles for conveying knowledge to the great mass of the population. (Macaulay, 1835)

14   Contested Capital

Misra provides the most comprehensive study of India's colonial middle class, considering the character and role of the Indian middle classes as they developed from the eighteenth to the early twentieth century. He identifies four internal categories within this class that include the commercial middle class, the industrial middle class, the landed middle class and the educated middle class. In western countries, the middle class emerged as a result of technological and economic transformations following the industrial revolutions of the mid-eighteenth century. Misra argued that the Indian experience was fundamentally different and 'middle classness' was a product of colonial policy, western education and capitalist enterprise. '[The] institutions of a middle class social order were imported to India. They did not grow from within. They were implanted in the country without comparable development in its economy and social institutions' (Misra, 1961: 11). Moreover, this middle class was an elite class concerned with individual advancement and not with economic development or mass education. Members of this class were predominantly educated professionals such as government servants and lawyers, college teachers and doctors, and limited to the cities of Madras, Bombay and Calcutta. These educated Indians of the nineteenth century sought prosperity and social recognition through British patronage. They were a product of colonial rule, culturally invented through colonial-based English education and wanted to see themselves as distinct from the masses, and used education and language to achieve this (Misra, 1961). This intelligentsia then came to monopolise the nationalist movement. Indeed, the creation of the Indian National Congress in 1885 was led by the upper and middle classes, who did not seek freedom from colonial rule (this came half a century later), but attempted to create an organisation which would work to advance the interests of the Indian population within the Civil Service (Fernandes, 2006). As Nehru stated in his autobiography:

> I was not an admirer of my own class or kind, and yet inevitably I looked to it for leadership in the struggle for India's salvation; that middle class felt caged and circumscribed and wanted to grow and develop itself. Unable to do so within the framework of British rule, a spirit of revolt grew against this rule, and yet this spirit was not directed against the structure that crushed us. It sought to retain it and control it by displacing the British. These middle classes were too much the product of that structure to challenge it and seek to uproot it. (Nehru, 1998 [1946]: 57)

This educated middle class dominated the freedom movement. Indian independence did not, after all, result from the mobilisation of the working classes, or from an organised labour movement. Similarly, in his study of the Bengali middle class, Chatterjee emphasises the role of education as a defining feature of the Indian middle class during the colonial period. He argues that the colonial Indian middle class existed in a paradoxical position – it was culturally invented through colonial education policies, but in the colonial economic structure, its members were unable to develop economically (Chatterjee, 1992). Joshi provides a similar account of the making of the colonial middle class in Lucknow. He argues that the power and position of the middle class did not have social and economic foundations; rather, the middle class acted as 'cultural entrepreneurs' through activities in the public sphere (Joshi, 2001: 6). For Joshi, the Indian colonial middle class constituted a body of educated men (and later some women) who undertook a cultural project which took the form of participation in public sphere politics. Similarly, Dobbin shows that in Bombay Presidency the spread of educational institutions resulted in a growing urban middle class, employed in a range of service and professional occupations in law, schools and other educational institutions and government services, who then became financial supporters of the institutions that had trained them in the first place. They came to serve as a 'self-perpetuating class', actively invested in the reproduction of the language of colonial rule – their socio-economic position rested on the social, cultural, and economic capital associated with colonial educational training which resulted in state employment (Dobbin, 1972: 40).

Furthermore, the boundaries of the colonial middle class rested on the reworking of social identities of caste. In general, the formation of this class drew on members of the upper castes (Fernandes, 2006: 8). Religious identity too was an important part of this colonial middle class, the formation of which often excluded Muslims, partly because they did not learn English with the same proficiency as Hindu elites (Sangari, 2002: 140). The ways in which this middle class was formed had a significant impact on the historiography of the Indian middle class. The structural constraints of colonialism restricted access to political and economic power, yet historians have focused on cultural spheres of activity. As such, we know very little of the history of economic structures and the economic position of this class.

The Post-independence Middle Class

Varma's *The Great Indian Middle Class*, which focuses on the colonial and post-independence periods, describes how the middle class evolved from the colonial period to the post 1991 period of economic liberalisation. Varma provides a highly emotive, nostalgic and historical account of India's 'great' middle class. The

16   Contested Capital

dominant members of this class set about building the Indian nation-state after Independence, guided both by a commitment to serve the nation and paternalism towards the lower classes. In the years immediately following independence, the Indian middle class adopted an ideological framework that combined elements of a respect for ethics, social sensitivity, self-restraint and idealism. The main components of this middle class were qualified professionals such as doctors, lawyers, engineers, business entrepreneurs, teachers in large urban schools and journalists. Caste distinctions remained crucial and members of the middle class were primarily Punjabi Khatris, Kashmiri Pandits and south Indian Brahmins (Varma, 1998: 26–27). The collective attitude of this class was shaped by the principle of Nehruvian socialism as well as Gandhian austerity, and dominated by notions of social responsibility towards the poor, anti-materialism and rejection of ostentatious displays of wealth. Varma suggests this middle-class ideology predominated until 1962, after which a number of factors transformed the attitudes and behaviours of the middle class. War with China was the first threat to Indian national security and shook Gandhian–Nehruvian idealism, challenging the moderate peacefulness of the Indian middle class. With the death of Nehru in 1964, the consensual legacy lost its most influential spokesperson. The old ideology started to be replaced by a retreat from idealism and a declining interest in social responsibility for the poor. Varma gives a scathing critique of the impact of liberalisation and condemns the 'new' middle class for its 'excessive' consumption, individualism and the declining importance of social values and moral responsibility for the poor. The historical context he provides is a significant contribution to Indian historiography. His polemical rhetoric, however, obscures any serious analysis of the middle class in the post-independence period. Varma's account of middle-class composition proposes that the post-independence middle class grew out of the 'old' middle class of educated elites. Similarly, Leela Fernandes suggests that the post-independence 'new' middle class, which was the subject of her monograph, had strong continuities with the 'old' educated elite middle class (Fernandes, 2006: 1). However, Jaffrelot and van der Veer suggest that the post-independence Indian middle class does not necessarily have its origins in colonial rule – that an entrepreneurial middle class was created (or at least encouraged) by post-independence economic policy. They illustrate their argument with statistics relating to the number of small factories and enterprises. In 1960, there were 36,460 small factories registered under the Factories Act as having less than INR 500,000 in fixed capital. These small factories employed 38 per cent (1,338,000 people) of the factory-registered workforce, and contributed approximately one-third of total factory production (Jaffrelot and van der Veer,

2008; Ministry of Industry, 1963: 16). These small-scale industries, which were protected by restrictions on imported goods, were successful and created a middle class. Furthermore, they suggest the ideas and institutions of a middle class were not simply imported into India by the British – they were not simply imitators of new values. Jaffrelot and van der Veer recognise that the British made the initial impact, but the 'graft was so successful because the men (and women in much less numbers) had shaped, and fashioned their own culture and identity and even invented new values out of the old materials they had at their disposal' (Jaffrelot and van der Veer, 2008: 15).[3] Similarly, in the context of rural India, there is no evidence that the British were responsible for creating a middle class through educational institutions. We need to look beyond colonialism to find the origins of the rural middle class. Rather, my account of the rural middle class shows that they were formed in the context of industrialisation in close proximity to rural areas in the post-liberalisation period, a trajectory which will be explored in detail in the next four chapters.

The 'New' Middle Class

In the post-liberalisation period, a 'new' middle class emerged, defined mainly on the basis of income and lifestyle, which has been the subject of sustained attention from scholars. Economic liberalisation policies emerged in the early 1990s in India and broadly followed the central tenets of the 'Washington Consensus' espoused by the World Bank and the International Monetary Fund (IMF) for developing countries; it involved dismantling large inefficient parastatals, encouraging fiscal and budgetary discipline, and encouraging foreign direct investment, trade liberalisation and deregulation. In India, businesses were freed from the Licence Raj, foreign direct investment and trade was encouraged, and banking regulations were eased – increasing consumer spending and availability of credit. The beneficiaries of these policies were the middle class 'unleashed from the chastity belt of Nehruvian socialism and Indira-era austerities … the producer as well as the consumer driving the engine of economic growth and prosperity' (Baviskar and Ray, 2011: 2–3). As a result of economic liberalisation, new patterns of consumption and new cultures of taste were created. Many studies have examined the post-liberalisation middle class focusing on themes relating to representation, consumption and aspirations, looking at 'excessive' consumption and cultures of taste as salient features of middle-class identity, and markers of middle-class status in the context of rapid social change.[4] In an examination of the post-liberalisation middle class in Mumbai, Fernandes provides a comprehensive

18   Contested Capital

account of the 'new' middle class, arguing that this class 'represents' the political construction of a social group, made up of predominantly English-speaking urban white-collar workers, which supports and perpetuates liberalisation (Fernandes, 2006: xviii; 2011: 68–69). This class is not 'new' in relation to its structure and its 'newness' does not reflect the entry of a new segment of the population into it, but rather refers to 'a process of production of a distinctive social and political identity that represents and lays claim to the benefits of liberalization' (Fernandes, 2006: xviii). She suggests 'the heart of the construction of this social group rests on the assumption that other segments of the middle class and upwardly mobile working class can potentially join it' (Fernandes, 2006: xviii).

Crucial to Fernandes' account is her understanding of the new middle class as a fluid social group – in simple terms, this means that access to new forms of capital such as education, skills and credentials, and social and cultural resources have created new employment opportunities (particularly private-sector employment). This has provided individuals with access to membership of this social category (Fernandes, 2006: xix). Similarly, Ganguly-Scrase and Scrase provide an ethnographic account of the social and cultural impact of liberalisation policies and globalisation on middle classes in urban Bengal. They challenge the common understanding that liberalisation has been beneficial to the middle classes and argue that such policies have in fact brought few real benefits as far as their living standards are concerned. They offer a broad account of the contradictory and paradoxical effect of liberalisation on the lives of the middle classes and suggest that liberalisation policies have not only undoubtedly created more opportunities for education, jobs and access to consumer goods, but have also resulted in rising prices, and have increased competition in the job market, resulting in a decline in their living standards (Ganguly-Scrase and Scrase, 2009: 3). Another study of the emergence of this class is provided by Brosius, based on fieldwork in urban Delhi. She gives an ethnographic description of the new cultures of taste among the middle class, providing a detailed description of how members of this social group attempt to seek distinction from lower classes, through particular aesthetic means, spatial and cultural strategies and religious rituals (Brosius, 2010). However, her study is not fundamentally about the social or economic structure of this class, but about representation. In keeping with many other social scientists that focus on similar themes relating to consumption, aspiration, social and cultural visibility of the middle class, Brosius does not look beyond the sanitised representations of urban India.[5] As such, this developing body of literature is almost exclusively confined to India's urban middle class, overlooking the formation of its rural counterpart.

The existence of the rural middle class in India was hinted at by Varma in his account of the post-independence middle class discussed above. Varma proposes that there was a numerically small segment of rural middle-class households in the early decades after independence, formed as a result of state rural development policy. He suggests that in the years following independence, as part of the cultural transformation, there was a general trend among agriculturalists within rural communities towards commercialisation and consumerism – disposable goods such as televisions, refrigerators and motorbikes became more popular. These agriculturalists started to consume goods which were previously considered unnecessary in rural households. Through these forms of consumption, they were seeking middle-class status, emulating urban patterns of living. This class of agriculturalists were aspiring to urban middle-class status and lifestyle also by taking their family members out of agricultural fields, investing in their children's private education and seeking urban employment. Therefore, an aspirant consumer middle class began to emerge in the early 1980s (Varma, 1998: 52). However, it is important to recognise that overall there is limited scholarship on cultural transformations in rural India. This will be explored further in Chapter 5.

The other account of the non-urban middle class (although not the rural middle class) in India has been provided by Craig Jeffrey, in his ethnography of unemployment and political participation in a small town in western Uttar Pradesh (Jeffrey, 2010a; 2010b).[6] Jeffrey traces the rise of the small-town middle class back to transformations in the political economy of India in the mid-1960s, when the Indian state shifted the focus of development planning from industrial development to improving agricultural production. Jeffrey argues that in many parts of India, rich farmers (who owned the means of production, holding between 4 and 10 hectares[7] of land) benefitted from agricultural innovation and Green Revolution technology. This expanded their agricultural returns, and subsequently they used their agricultural dominance in the following three decades to diversify out of agriculture and move into small-scale business and white-collar government employment and create 'a "middle class" of sorts' (Jeffrey, 2010a: 38). However, the phrases Jeffrey uses, a 'middle class of sorts', seems to indicate that he is content with this conceptual murkiness, which obscures an analytical account of the composition of this social group.[8]

How Big Is the Indian Middle Class?

Many scholars, policy-makers, financial institutions and economists have attempted to estimate the size of this class in different global contexts, and in India,

20 Contested Capital

using financial indicators.[9] Broadly, there are two monetary approaches used in estimation of the middle class size that can be traced in the existing literature: a *relativist* approach and a *fixed* approach (Bonnefond, Clément, and Combarnous, 2015: 43). They both rely on indicators such as income, consumption expenditure, national poverty lines and national median incomes (summarised in Tables 1.1 and 1.2). If we were to rely on each of these definitions, we would have a large set of outcomes before us.

We now apply each of these approaches to the estimation of the size of the middle class in India, based on data drawn from IHDS-II. Table 1.1 provides us with a wide range of middle class sizes in 2011–12, varying between 0 and 40 per cent of the Indian population (note: on the basis of the IHDS-II, the median per capita income at All-India level in 2011–12 is calculated to be INR 15,200).

Table 1.1 Calculating the size of the middle class based on relative monetary definition (2011–12)

Methods	*Criteria*	*Lower and upper limits (INR)*		*Approximate size (per cent of total population)*		
				Below middle class	*Middle class*	*Above middle class*
Median income	Lower limit = 75% of median income Upper limit = 125% of median income (Birdsall, Graham and Pettinato, 2000)	$L = 75\% \times 15,200 = 11,500$ $U = 125\% \times 15,200 = 19,125$		34	22	44
Poverty line approach	[2 times poverty line; 5 times poverty line][10] (Burkhauser et al., 1996)	Urban (INR)	$L = 2 \times 12,000 = 24,000$ $U = 5 \times 12,000 = 60,000$	47	34	19
		Rural (INR)	$L = 2 \times 9792 = 19,584$ $U = 5 \times 9792 = 48,960$	66.5	24.5	9
Quintile approach	Third and fourth income quintiles (Alesina and Perotti, 1996)	Middle-class income (annual per capita income): Between INR 12,200 and 35,900		40	40	20
Fixed income range	Income of PPP USD10 per person per day but not in top 5% (Birdsall, 2010)	Annual per capita income of purchasing power parity (PPP) INR 182,500 and above		100	0	0

Sources: Alesina and Perotti (1996); Birdsall (2010); Birdsall, Graham and Pettinato (2000); Burkhauser et al. (1996); computed from the IHDS-II.

Although the monetary approach provides a concrete definition of the middle class (both in fixed and relative ways), identifying the lower and the upper bounds remains a highly subjective practice – there is no universal consensus on how to determine an appropriate income or expenditure range. For example, the quintile method, although useful in measuring or comparing income growth among different quintiles, cannot be useful in estimating the size of middle class (or any class), due to its inflexible nature – it does not allow the size of the middle class, or any other classes, to either grow or shrink. Furthermore, the monetary method fails to recognise the compositional variance and nuances underlying the heterogeneity of this class, and fails to provide substantive indications of its social and economic composition. Therefore, at best, this technique can demonstrate the size of the middle-income or middle expenditure groups, which are not necessarily the middle class.

Table 1.2   Fixed monetary estimation of the size of the Indian middle class

Methods	Criteria and definition of the middle class	Size of middle class
Fixed income range	Income of PPP USD 10 to 50 per capita per day (Meyer and Birdsall, 2012).	5.88% of the Indian households, roughly 70 million of Indian population in 2009–10.[11]
Fixed income range	NCAER: Annual income between INR 250,000 and 1,250,000, at 2004–05 prices (Shukla and Purusothaman, 2008).[12] Basis: Market Information Survey of Households, Conducted by NCAER	28 million households in 2009–10, approximately 15% of the total Indian population
Fixed income range	NCAER: Households with household annual income of INR 200,000 to 1,000,000 at 2001–02 prices (Meyer and Birdsall, 2012: 2) Basis: Market Information Survey of Households, conducted by NCAER	50 million people, approximately, 5% of the Indian population
Fixed expenditure range	Households with daily per capita consumption expenditure valued at (PPP) between USD 2 and 4 and those between USD 6 and 10 (Banerjee and Duflo, 2008: 4). Basis: Living Standard Measurement Surveys	They do not provide estimations

Let us now try a non-monetary method that relies on a holistic set of variables that are grounded in the main theories of class and are commonly understood to contribute to one's 'middle-class-ness'. These variables include: primary source of household income (in relation to manual labour power – influenced by Marx, Weber and Bourdieu), skills and credentials (adult formal education – influenced by Weber and Bourdieu), social networks (social connections – taken from Weber and Bourdieu), income (annual per capita income of households – derived from Weber), housing (house ownership, building materials and sanitation facilities – taken from Weber and Bourdieu) and lifestyle (ownership of consumer durables

– from Bourdieu), all of which may constitute a specific kind of class privilege.[13] The variables used to compile the middle-class index, illustrated in Figure 1.1, are self-explanatory and are commonly used in the existing literature as social indices (usually, used one at a time) in examination of the middle class.

Figure 1.1 Factors contributing to 'middle-class-ness'

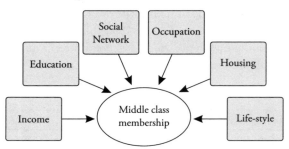

In order to reduce definitional ambiguities and address limitations of composite indices (involving the ad hoc drawing of boundaries and assigning of subjective weights to each component), we start the inquiry with a process of elimination. Instead of identifying the middle class, we first identify groups that structurally cannot be part of the middle class (within the three frameworks of classes: Marxian, Weberian and Bourdieuian). In the first stage, and based on the primary source of household income (which is used as a proxy for occupation), we propose a first-order socio-economic classification of all households in India: manual labouring households, and non-labouring households – the former group consists of those whose main source of income is generated from selling physical labour power (both in agriculture and non-agricultural activities). These households do not hold any position of authority in the labour market and have no control over the means of production. The non-labouring households consist of those whose main source of income are *not* generated from selling manual labour power, and would within them contain the middle class.[14] The IHDS-II classifies the main sources of household income into 11 categories: cultivation; allied agriculture; agricultural wage labour; non-agricultural wage labour; artisan or independent economic activities; petty shop; organised business; salaried employment; profession; pension/rent; and others. The most obvious sources of income that can immediately be recognised as manual labour are agricultural labour and non-agricultural wage labour.

Table 1.3 demonstrates the results of the classifications of households: 35.34 per cent of households in India belong to the manual labouring group, out of which 11.35 per cent earn their living primarily from agricultural wage labour and approximately 24 per cent from non-agricultural wage labour, and hence cannot be situated in the middle class.[15]

Table 1.3   Household groups based on main source of household income (2011–12)

All-India (N = 41,516)	Freq.	Per cent
Manual labouring households	13,739	35.34
Non-labouring households	27,777	64.66
Total	41,516	100

Source: Computed from the IHDS-II.

In the next step, the weighted composite tool is used to further categorise the non-labouring group, as well as to identify the middle class within it, based on the indicators outlined above (see Figure 1.1). Although the selection of weights assigned to each component is subjective, equal weight is given to each composite at this stage.

Constructing Composite Indicators

Income and Poverty Line[16]

In order to limit the arbitrariness of income boundaries for the middle class, and avoid assigning an ad hoc income index, the development of an income index will be undertaken in stages using poverty line, median per capita income and quintile methods. First, non-labouring households are divided into 10 equal income groups. The purpose of this exercise is to identify the segment of the population that falls below the poverty line. Since the poverty line in rural India is different from that of urban, Table 1.4 has divided the income groups into 'All-India', 'Urban' and 'Rural'. The straight horizontal lines in Figure 1.2 illustrate the poverty lines for rural and urban India. Figure 1.2 shows that in both rural and urban India, almost 40 per cent of the population falls below the poverty line. Therefore, the national median per capita income (at 50 per cent annual per capita income) has been chosen as an income threshold to form the income index. The immediate first 10 per cent of the population (All-India) above the poverty line, but below the median annual per capita income, may still be vulnerable, having to face the highest risk of poverty. In order to calculate the income index, Table 1.4 (also depicted in Figure 1.2) was created as a point of reference. The figures for urban and rural poverty lines are provided in the last row of the table.

24 Contested Capital

Table 1.4 Income groups: All-India, Urban and Rural (2011–12)

Income groups	N = 27,777	Annual per capita income (INR)
Bottom 10%	All (Urban + Rural)	Below 4,600
	Urban (N = 14,573)	Below 8,500
	Rural (N = 27,579)	Below 3,870
10%–20%	All (Urban + Rural)	Between 4,600 and 7,160
	Urban	Between 8,500 and 12,150
	Rural	Between 3,870 and 6,000
20%–30%	All (Urban + Rural)	Between 7,160 and 9,500
	Urban	Between 12,150 and 16,000
	Rural	Between 6,000 and 7,975
30%–40%	All (Urban + Rural)	Between 9,500 and 12,120
	Urban	Between 16,000 and 20,000
	Rural	Between 7,975 and 9,900
Median (50%)	All (Urban + Rural)	15,200
	Urban	25,000
	Rural	12,200
50%–60%	All (Urban + Rural)	Between 15,200 and 19,500
	Urban	Between 25,000 and 32000
	Rural	Between 12,200 and 15,100
60%–70%	All (Urban + Rural)	Between 19,500 and 25,300
	Urban	Between 32,000 and 40,800
	Rural	Between 15,100 and 19,400
70%–80%	All (Urban + Rural)	Between 25,300 and35,700
	Urban	Between 40,800 and 56,000
	Rural	Between 19,400 and 26,000
80%–90%	All (Urban + Rural)	Between 35,700 and 57,000
	Urban	Between 56,000 and 84,300
	Rural	Between 26,000 and 40,750
Top 10%	All (Urban + Rural)	Above 57,000
	Urban	Above 84,300
	Rural	Above 40,750
Poverty line	Urban	12,000
	Rural	9,800

Source: Computed from the IHDS-II.

Therefore, the income index for All-India can be calculated as follows:

Income index = 0; if annual per capita income of the household is below the median income.

Income index = 0.2; if annual per capita income of the household is above median income but below that of 60 per cent of the income group. That would be households whose per capita annual income are between INR 15,200 and 19,500 (income group between 50 and 60 per cent of the population).

Income index = 0.4; if annual per capita income falls between INR 19,500 and 25,300 (the income group between 60 and 70 per cent of the population).

Income index = 0.6; if annual per capita income falls between INR 25,300 and 35,700 (the income group between 70 and 80 per cent of the population).

Income index = 0.8; if annual per capita income falls between INR 35,700 and 57,000 (the income group between 80 and 90 per cent of the population).

Income index = 1; if annual per capita income is above INR 57,000 (the income group in the top 10 per cent of the population).

Figure 1.2 Income levels across the population: All-India, Urban and Rural (2011–12)

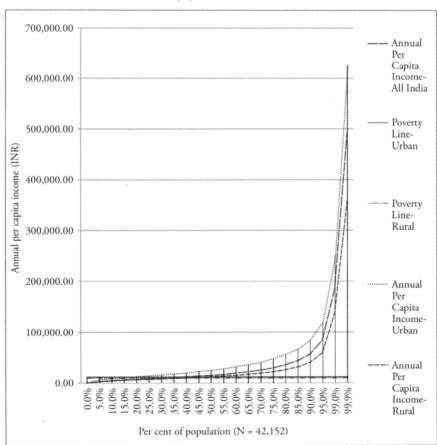

Source: Computed from the IHDS-II.

26   Contested Capital

Skills and Credentials

The formal education level has been a key indicator in several analyses in the middle-class literature (Deshpande, 2003; Fernandes, 2006; Fernandes and Heller, 2006). In order to calculate an index for skills and credentials, and on the basis of the availability of data, the number of years of formal schooling of adults (aged 21 and above) is used. The calibration of this component is as follows:

Education index = 0; if the highest level of adult education in the household is below 12 years of formal schooling.

Education index = 0.5; if the highest level of adult education in the household is 12 years of formal schooling, that is, if any adult member of the households has graduated from higher secondary school, but has not attended college or university.

Education index = 1; if at least one adult member in the household has attended college or university.

Housing and Sanitation

Since the majority of people in India own their dwelling (the analysis of IHDS-II shows 92.14 per cent of total households in All-India own their dwelling/accommodation), the consideration of house ownership is statistically meaningless for our purposes. So, in order to differentiate between classes, a number of other factors are combined to calculate the housing component. These are availability of a flushed toilet within the house; availability of a separate kitchen in the house; access to piped water in the house; and the building materials used for different elements (roof, floor and wall).[17] Some of these components have assumed a lot of importance in the study of the middle class in the current literature (Sheth, 1999). For example, building materials have been used as one of the indicators to differentiate the middle classes by a survey conducted in 2013 by the Centre for the Study of Developing Societies, CSDC-Lokniti. Each of the components qualifies as 0.2 points in the housing component. All sub-components add up to a maximum of one and a minimum of zero. The index is constructed as shown in Table 1.5.

Lifestyle and Consumer Durable Goods

In the extensive literature on the middle class, this social group is often associated with a certain lifestyle and level of consumerism as we saw earlier in the chapter. On the basis of availability of data in the IHDS-II, a total of 17 items (consumer durable goods), which indicate the lifestyle and consumption patterns

Trajectory of the Indian Middle Class 27

Table 1.5 Calculation of housing component (2011–12)

Component	Index	
	Yes	No
Home ownership	0.2	0
Availability of flushed toilet	0.2	0
Availability of separate kitchen	0.2	0
Access to piped water in the house	0.2	0
House material	Pucca = 0.2	Kutcha = 0
Total	1	0

Source: Computed from the IHDS-II.

of households, and their purchasing power have been selected as sub-indices. These items include generator set; motorised two-wheelers; car; mixer; pressure cooker; refrigerator; washing machine; microwave; colour television; cable/dish TV; air cooler or air conditioner; electric fan; chair/table; cot; clock or watch; computer or laptop and cell phone. The weighting assigned to the possession of each of these items is 1/17; all sub-components add up to a maximum of one and a minimum of zero.

Social Networks

Social networks are known to act as resources for gaining access to the skilled labour market in India (Fernandes, 2006). In order to examine the degree of social connections of households, social acquaintance with the members of different professions (either among relatives, friends and caste/community or outside community/caste), have been included. The relevant professions for which data are available in the IHDS-II are: doctors, health workers, teachers, government officers, other government employees, elected politicians, political party officials, police inspectors and military personnel. The weighting for anyone in the household being acquainted with anyone in these professions is 1/9, with all sub-components adding up to a maximum of one and a minimum of zero.

Results

After assigning the composite index for each component, the scores were combined and the households in the non-labouring group were further classified into six

28 Contested Capital

distinct classes, on the basis of their scores. Table 1.6 represents these six classes and their scores within the non-labouring households.

Table 1.6 Categorisation of non-labouring households: All-India (2011–12)

Classes	Composite index score (mean)	
Class 1	$0 \leq CI \leq 1$	0.65
Class 2	$1 < CI \leq 2$	1.49
Class 3	$2 < CI \leq 3$	2.75
Class 4	$3 < CI \leq 4$	3.49
Class 5	$4 < CI \leq 4.5$	4.21
Class 6	$4.5 < CI$	4.66

Source: Computed from the IHDS-II.

Before estimating the size of the middle class or examining its characteristics, we must first decide which of the identified classes within the non-labouring groups of households should be considered middle class. Although the decision is subjective, as long as the middle class falls in the middle of the spectrum, the boundaries are drawn according to the proximity of their scores to the upper and lower classes. These classes are termed as follows: Class 1 (scored 0.65) the *lowest class*; Class 2 (scored 1.49) the *second lowest class*; Class 3 (scored 2.75) the *lower middle class*; Class 4 (scored 3.49) the *comfortable middle class*; Class 5 (scored 4.21) the *upper middle class*; and Class 6 (scored above 4.5) the *upper class*. Classes 3, 4 and 5 are considered middle classes, because they have scored above the average. Class 3 is termed the *lower middle class*, because (as is illustrated in Table 1.7 and Figure 1.3) this class has more similarities to the fourth class than to the second one – the component index score for this group is 2.75, which is much closer to 3 than to 2.

Table 1.7 Classification of non-labouring households: All-India (2011–12)

Classes	Classification of non-labouring population	Score of composite index
Class 1	Lowest class	$0 \leq CI \leq 1$
Class 2	Second lowest class	$1 < CI \leq 2$
Class 3	Lower middle class	$2 < CI \leq 3$
Class 4	Comfortable middle class	$3 < CI \leq 4$
Class 5	Upper middle class	$4 < CI \leq 4.5$
Class 6	Upper class	$4.5 < CI$

Source: Computed from the IHDS-II.

Table 1.8 illustrates the weights scored by each class for each of the indices, and the mean overall score achieved by each class. The first row of Table 1.8 presents the weight of each component – the importance, or weight, of each variable in each of the classes is calculated by Principal Component Analysis (PCA), which is a statistical technique useful for explaining the variance–covariance structure of a set of variables. As evident in Table 1.8, education carries the maximum weight (2.72), which is disproportionately higher than the weight assigned to any other indicators through PCA. The minimum weight has been assigned to the housing index, followed by social network. Although education can be interpreted as the most significant and defining feature of class differentiation in India, it is important to note that this interpretation is only correct in the bottom three classes. In order to avoid any misinterpretation of the PCA result, Table 1.8 has been depicted in Figure 1.3, illustrating the importance of each indicator, in relative terms, as a determinant of class variations. According to Figure 1.3, as we go up the class hierarchy (to the *comfortable middle class* and those classes above it), households begin to score on all indices. So, although education may be the most salient feature of class variation among the lower classes, as we climb the class order, the distinctiveness of education wanes in relative importance. Furthermore, among the top three classes, the social networks factor, followed by lifestyle factor, increase as determinants of class variation. Similarly, when we compare the three middle-class groups, we realise that the major difference between these is income, followed by education (only between the lower and comfortable middle class).

Table 1.8 Calculating the scores and weight of indices: All-India (2011–12)

Non-labouring households (N = 27,255)		Education	Income	Social network	Life style	Housing	Total
Weight applied to each index		2.72	0.78	0.62	0.57	0.31	5
Class 1	Lowest class	0.003	0.031	0.108	0.214	0.297	0.65
Class 2	Second lowest class	0.091	0.224	0.223	0.414	0.536	1.49
Class 3	Lower middle class	0.379	0.501	0.342	0.555	0.697	2.75
Class 4	Comfortable middle class	0.833	0.761	0.444	0.662	0.789	3.49
Class 5	Upper middle class	0.983	0.941	0.661	0.759	0.866	4.21
Class 6	Upper class	1	0.986	0.912	0.83	0.932	4.66

Source: Computed from the IHDS-II.

Figure 1.3 Illustration of relative index decomposition (2011–12)

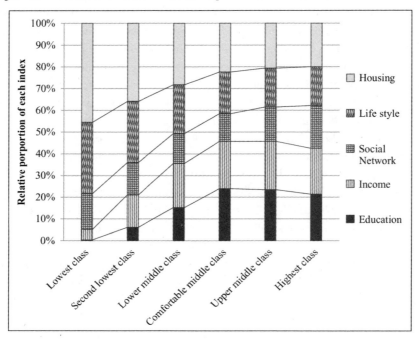

Source: Computed from the IHDS-II.

The Size of the Middle Class in India

On the basis of the composite index, we can now provide a rough estimate of the All-India class structure, represented by the size of each of the classes identified (Table 1.9).

Table 1.9 Proportions of identified classes: All-India (2011–12)

Classes		Proportions of classes (per cent)
Manual labouring households		35.34
Non-labouring classes	Lowest (non-lab) class	15.77
	Second lowest (non-lab) class	20.04
	Lower middle class	14.3
	Comfortable middle class	10.73
	Upper middle class	3.02
	Upper class	0.8
Total		100

Source: Computed from the IHDS-II.

Table 1.9 shows that 35.34 per cent of the All-India population falls in the manual labouring class (agricultural and non-agricultural manual wage workers). Among the non-labouring group of households, a large majority of the population (35.8 per cent) falls into the bottom two classes. The lower middle class consists of 14.3 per cent of the population, the comfortable middle class 10.73 per cent and the upper middle class (also the smallest of the middle classes) consists of 3.02 per cent of the population. Therefore, the three groups of the middle class together constitute 28.05 per cent of the total population in All-India, while the highest class consists of only 0.8 per cent of the population. This result is illustrated in Figure 1.4.

Figure 1.4   Categorisation of All-India population into seven classes (2011–12)

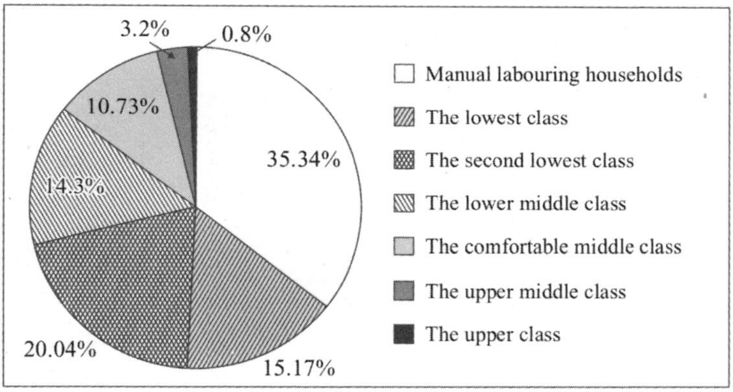

Source: Computed from the IHDS-II.

Features and Characteristics

Table 1.10 represents the various features, characteristics and composition of the identified classes in India, demonstrating the profile of each group in relation to mean annual per capita income, level of education, occupation (the main source of household income), housing status, access to sanitation, ownership of consumer goods (such as computers and cars) and social connections. The caste composition of these classes will be discussed later in Chapter 4. The most distinctive feature of all three middle-class groups is the over-representation of salaried employment as the main source of household income: in all three groups, salaried employment is reported to be the most important main source of household income – 33.47 per cent of the lower-middle-class households, 49.08 per cent among the comfortable middle class and 59.71 per cent of the upper-middle-class households earn their

32   Contested Capital

main source of income from salaried employment, the highest proportion being in the upper middle class. The second significant feature is that entrepreneurship is not the main determinant of middle-class membership. Only a small segment of the middle class is engaged in organised business (slightly greater than 4 per cent among the comfortable middle class, and 4.69 per cent among the upper middle class). Entrepreneurship is more salient among the highest class only. Furthermore, higher education (university-level education) is a very distinctive factor among the middle classes. Almost 90 per cent of the upper-middle-class population have a member in the household who has completed a university degree (46.51 per cent at the bachelor's level, and 44.94 per cent a master's degree and above). However, higher education does not appear to be a decisive factor in membership of the lower middle class.

Table 1.10   Categorisation of classes: characteristics, All-India (2011–12)

Classes of the non-labouring group of households			The middle classes				All (include labouring class)
	LC N = 5,815	SLC N = 8,423	LMC N = 6,704	CMC N = 4,964	UMC N = 1,476	UC N = 395	N = 41,516
Per cent	15.77	20.04	14.3	10.73	3.02	0.8	100
Education							
None (illiterate)	36.99	12.92	2.54	0.15	0	0	19.42
Primary school and below	20.93	14.51	7.66	0.24	0	0	13.73
Secondary school (excluding 12)	41.6	56.27	40.02	6.21	0	0	38.02
12th standard (high school)	0.49	11.34	22.06	17.46	2.93	0	9.56
First or second year post-secondary	0	1.08	5.83	8.92	5.61	5.19	2.78
Bachelor's	0	3.16	16.81	40.08	46.51	43.17	10.1
Above bachelor's	0	0.75	7.62	26.94	44.94	51.65	6.37
Total	100	100	100	100	100	100	100
Primary source of income (per cent)							
Cultivation	58.1	42.67	27.22	14.77	6.67	5.1	24.08
Allied agriculture	2.08	1.88	0.97	0.58	0.28	0	0.95
Artisan/independent	2.85	3.46	2.53	1.74	0.78	0.76	1.75
Petty shop	13.01	19.22	19.69	15.32	10.53	8.49	10.67
Organised business	0.25	0.91	1.98	4.13	4.69	9.64	1.18
Salaried employment	9.04	20.79	33.47	49.08	59.71	55.98	17.8

Contd.

Trajectory of the Indian Middle Class

Contd.

Classes of the non-labouring group of households	LC N = 5,815	SLC N = 8,423	The middle classes			UC N = 395	All (include labouring class) N = 41,516
			LMC N = 6,704	CMC N = 4,964	UMC N = 1,476		
Per cent	*15.77*	*20.04*	*14.3*	*10.73*	*3.02*	*0.8*	*100*
Profession	0.46	0.59	0.77	1.24	1.98	4.23	0.52
Pension/rent	6.68	4.98	8.59	10.59	14.3	14.52	4.97
Others	7.53	5.48	4.78	2.55	1.06	1.24	3.28
Agricultural labour	0	0	0	0	0	0	11.32
Non-agricultural labour	0	0	0	0	0	0	23.48
Total	100	100	100	100	100	100	100
Housing							
Home ownership	96.29	92.24	88.63	86.34	88.51	95.24	92.14
Access to flushed toilet	6.34	35.6	61.04	76.54	88.59	92.98	36.55
Separate kitchen	25.79	58.24	78.05	86.37	94.14	96.27	54.87
Access to piped water	4.68	26.16	43.56	57.07	70.36	82	27.62
Pucca house	12.33	48.57	71.7	83.68	92.85	95.46	45.5
No. of rooms per person	0.59	0.67	0.81	0.88	1	1.1	0.67
Household income (INR)							
Annual per capita income (mean)	8,818	18,077	36,535	64,437	112,540	151,591	26,493
Annual per capita income median	8,042	15,042	27,335	47,318	82,169	114,000	15,000
Life style							
Consumer goods index (mean)	0.214	0.414	0.555	0.662	0.795	0.83	0.39
Owns a car	0.12	1.08	4.33	12.55	31.99	59.3	3.82
Owns computer or laptop	0.01	0.98	6.02	23.19	49.2	68.47	5.77
Social network							
Social network index (mean)	0.108	0.223	0.342	0.444	0.661	0.912	0.25
Geographical distribution							
Urban	8.15	28.69	47.69	66.18	76.86	82.74	31.86
Rural	91.85	71.31	52.31	33.82	23.14	17.26	68.14

Source: Computed from the IHDS-II.

Note: LC: lowest class; SLC: second lowest class; LMC: lower middle class; CMC: comfortable middle class; UC: upper class.

34   Contested Capital

The Rural Middle Class

The most significant finding of this chapter is the identification of rural middle classes in India (evident in the last row of Table 1.10). As the analysis of the IHDS-II demonstrated, contrary to common assumptions in the literature on the Indian middle class, a considerable segment of the middle class resides in rural areas. Among the lower middle class, rural households are heavily represented, that is, slightly more than half the population in this class (52.31 per cent) consists of rural households. Rising through the middle classes, the relative rurality declines but more than 33 per cent of the comfortable middle class and more than 23 per cent of the upper middle class are nevertheless located in rural India. Table 1.11 (also illustrated in Figure 1.5) demonstrates the percentage and proportion of the middle classes in All-India, urban and rural areas separately. Table 1.11 demonstrates that 7.48 per cent out of the total 14.3 per cent All-India lower middle class, 3.63 per cent of the total 10.73 per cent All-India comfortable middle class and 0.7 per cent of the total 3.02 All-India upper middle class are located in rural India. A total number of households that fall into three categories of the middle class in rural India comprise 11.81 per cent of total All-India households.

Table 1.11   Calculating the size of all classes: All-India (2011–12)

Classes		Proportions of classes (per cent)		
		All-India	Urban	Rural
Manual labouring households		35.34	8.13	27.21
Non-labouring classes	Lowest class	15.77	1.29	14.49
	Second lowest class	20.04	5.75	14.29
	Lower middle class	14.3	6.82	7.48
	Comfortable middle class	10.73	7.1	3.63
	Upper middle class	3.02	2.32	0.7
	Upper class	0.8	0.66	0.14
Total		100	32.07	67.93

Source: Computed from the IHDS-II.

Table 1.12 demonstrates the distribution of different classes in rural India. Almost 40 per cent of rural households belong to the manual labouring group, while almost 42 per cent come under the bottom two classes. Approximately 17 per cent of the total households in rural India belong to the three middle-class groups, although the majority belong to the lower middle class, and only 5.34 per cent, and 1.3 per cent belong to the comfortable and the upper middle class respectively. The population of upper classes in rural India is almost negligible.

Figure 1.5 Middle classes: rural/urban distributions (2011–12)

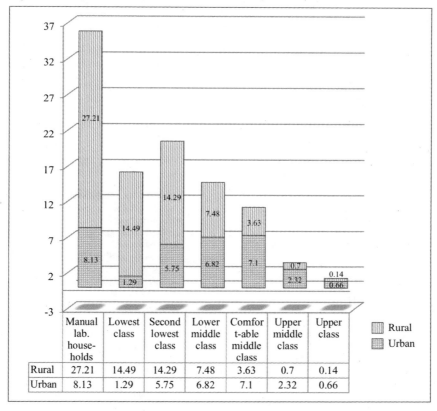

Source: Computed from the IHDS-II.

Table 1.12 Distribution of classes in rural India (2011–12)

Classes in rural India		Per cent
Manual labouring households		40.07
Non-labouring classes	Lowest class	21.3
	Second lowest class	21.03
	Lower middle class	11.01
	Comfortable middle class	5.34
	Upper middle class	1.03
	Upper class	0.1
Total		100

Source: Computed from the IHDS-II.

Figure 1.6 presents the occupational categories of rural classes in India. The most striking feature of India's rural middle classes is the over representation of salaried employment in all three middle class groups, especially among the upper middle class. There is also a negative correlation between the percentage of people engaged in cultivation as a main source of income and class status. As we climb the middle-class ladder in the rural areas, fewer households are engaged in cultivation as their main source of household income, and more are engaged in salaried employment.

Figure 1.6 Occupational categories of rural classes in India (2011–12)

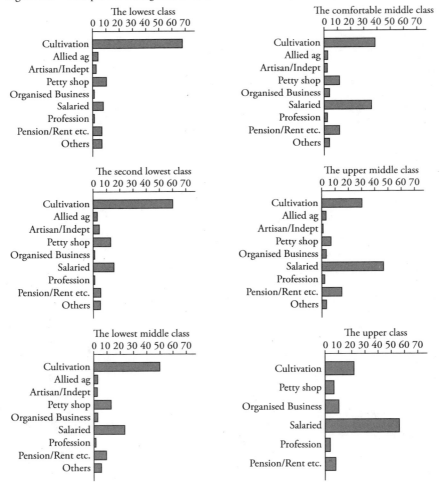

Source: Computed from the IHDS-II.

Self-identification and Middle-Class Status: The Gap in Size

If we go back to the IHDS-II to examine the self-identification of middle classes, it is surprising to see that the size of the self-identified middle classes is much higher than my estimation above. The data suggests that 61.5 per cent of the urban and 48.8 per cent of the rural population identify themselves as middle classes (Table 1.13). Why is there such a big gap between the theoretically driven calculation and self-identification? I was struggling with a similar question that arose from my early fieldwork data from which I learnt that many in both villages claimed to belong to the middle class. This gap, which is much wider in rural than urban India, is partially due to differences between subjective and theoretical definitions of this class, but is also the result of the class aspirations of rural inhabitants. The in-depth interviews about the meanings of middle class will shed some light in understanding this gap. But let us return to this question in the subsequent chapters.

Table 1.13   Self-identification and class (2011–12)

Class categories	Urban N = 14,350	Rural N = 27,165	All-India N = 41,515
Poor	29.48	52.9	45.44
Middle-class	61.59	42.87	48.88
Comfortable	8.93	4.23	5.73
Total	100	100	100

Source: Computed from the IHDS-II.

This chapter challenged the urban bias in studies of the middle class and revealed three significant findings concerning the middle class in India. First, it presented estimates showing that the three groups in the middle class (termed *the lower middle class*; *the comfortable middle class*; and *the upper middle class*) together constitute 28.05 per cent of All-India households. It was noted that previous estimates of the size of the middle class based on the monetary indicators are inadequate, being able at best only to elucidate the size of the middle-income or expenditure group, and failing to recognise the heterogeneous characteristics of the middle class. The new estimate provided in this chapter is the most comprehensive and accurate estimate provided to date. Second, an examination of the occupational composition of the middle class demonstrated that despite the occupational diversity that exists among the middle classes, a large proportion of the middle class are salaried employees. The chapter revealed the over representation of salaried employment in all three middle-class groups, especially the upper middle class. Third, and more significantly for the purposes of this book, it showed that contrary to common assumptions, a considerable

38   Contested Capital

segment of the Indian middle class resides in rural areas. The total number of households situated in the three middle-class groups in rural India constitutes 11.81 per cent of the total Indian population. Among the lower middle class, rural households are heavily represented – 52.31 per cent of the households of this class consist of rural households. More than 32 per cent of the comfortable middle class, and more than 23 per cent of the upper middle class are also located in rural India. We now turn to our field-sites, where a detailed ethnographic account of the formation, size, composition and characteristics of the rural middle class are provided.

Notes

* The main part of this chapter was originally published as an article in *Contemporary South Asia* in 2019 (vol. 27, issue 2). See Aslany (2019).

1. See Aslany (2019).

2. See, for example, Chatterjee (1992), Joshi (2001, 2011), Misra (1961) and Varma (1998).

3. By emphasising Indian agency, Jaffrelot and van der Veer are (implicitly) engaging with debates from colonial historiography. There remains considerable contestation over many features of Indian society, most significantly caste and violence, and whether they were created or exacerbated by British colonial rule – for debates on caste, see Bayly (2001) and Dirks (2003). Similarly, Jaffrelot and van der Veer demonstrate that a class of entrepreneurs already existed in pre-colonial India and the middle class was not simply created by the British colonial rule. See Jaffrelot and van der Veer (2008: 11–34).

4. See, for example, Brosius (2010), Fernandes (2000, 2006, 2011), Ganguly-Scrase and Scrase (2009) and Dasgupta (2014).

5. Many other studies have focused on similar themes relating to consumption and aspirations, examining the ways in which the urban middle class seek social and cultural visibility. See, for example, Donner (2012); Donner and De Neve (2011); Fernandes and Heller (2006); Mawdsley (2004); Mazzarella (2003, 2005); Robinson (2014); Upadhya (2004, 2008, 2011); Varma (1998, 2015).

6. My discussion of Jeffrey's work here refers to a chapter in his *Timepass*, entitled, 'Cultivating Fields: The Rise and Resilience of a Rural Middle Class'. Jeffrey's argument on the formation of middle class is driven from the secondary literature and is not supported by any empirical evidence. In a similar study in Binjor District in western Uttar Pradesh, R. Jeffrey, P. Jeffrey, and C. Jeffrey (2011: 140–63) make a similar argument about the lower middle classes in small towns.

Trajectory of the Indian Middle Class 39

7. One hectare = 2.471 acres.

8. It must be noted that there is considerable literature on class formation in rural India, particularly in the context of the green revolution's agrarian change, of rural industrialisation, and of uneven access to various forms of non-agricultural employment, which will be covered extensively in Chapter 3. However, the existing class categories, identified in the literature on rural class formation, not only have been labelled using different terms but they are also analysed in different theoretical frameworks from that of the middle class, which in turn results in not addressing the issue of a growing middle class in rural India. Moreover, the rural classes identified in the literature have seldom been analysed through the Weberian and Bourdieuian frameworks.

9. In India, the National Council of Applied Economic Research (NCAER) has played a significant role in shaping the debate regarding the size of the Indian middle class. The NCAER estimated the size of the middle class in India, based on their income, at 50 million people (roughly 5 per cent of the Indian population) in 2005, and 142 million people (12 per cent of the Indian population) in 2011. One of their recent definitions, which is based on a fixed income range, identifies the middle class as two sub-groups: 'seekers' – who have an annual household income of between INR. 200,000 and 500,000; and 'strivers' who have an annual household income between INR 500,000 and 1 million at 2001–02 prices (NCAER, 2002; cited in Meyer and Birdsall, 2012: 2). Similarly, in 2009–10, NCAER classified 28.4 million households in India as middle class, whose annual household income was between INR 250,000 and 1,250,000 (NCAER, 2010; cited in Meyer and Birdsall, 2012: 2).

10. According to Planning Commission Report (2011–12), in urban areas poverty line was calculated to be INR 1,000 per capita monthly and in rural areas was INR 816 per capita monthly (Planning Commission, 2012).

11. Meyer and Birdsall estimated that approximately 60 per cent of the Indian population that falls in middle class reside in urban areas.

12. See Jodhka and Prakash (2016: 116–18).

13. Centre for the Study of Developing Countries (CSDS), in their 1996 survey, defined middle class individuals using the following criteria: (1) respondents identifying themselves as middle class, *and*: (2) respondents who had *two* of the following *four* characteristics: (i) 10 years or more of schooling; (ii) residing in a brick and cement house; (iii) having a white-collar occupation; (iv) owning at least three of the following four assets: (a) either a car/jeep/tractor/scooter/motorcycle; (b) television set; (c) electrically operated water pump-set; (d) non-agricultural land (CSDC Survey, 1996). However, some of CSDS criteria are problematic. For example, the first criteria (respondents identifying themselves

40 Contested Capital

as middle class) is given as a necessary condition for middle-class status. This is highly problematic because it privileges the voice of the respondent, requesting a yes or no response to determine a category which may have a different meaning (or no meaning at all) to the respondent. The 'white collar' component of the survey is also inappropriate in the rural context. It ignores the range of occupational diversity among the rural middle class. Moreover, the ownership of non-agricultural land is also urban biased.

14. Many households in India have more than one source of income. To minimise the complication, I use the primary source of household income, the occupation that earns the highest proportion of household income, as the main occupation of the household. A household may partially rely on income from manual labour, but as long as this is not the main source of income, the household would be classified in a non-labouring group at this stage.

15. The missing values (income) have been deleted from the data set. All analyses are adjusted for survey data. All calculations, tables and figures in this book have been computed by Stata software.

16. Similar approach (weighted composite indicator) was taken by Nayeb in estimating the size of the middle class in Pakistan, and here I develop his approach to estimate the size of the middle class in India. Nayeb has used income, ownership of house and various consumer durables, occupation, and education to categorise the households in Pakistan (although his disaggregation of components, sub-indices and weights assigned to each sub-dices differ from the components and weights used in this calculation of the middle class size in India). However, his study suffers from some shortcomings: First, unlike the approach of this book, Nayeb does not exclude the manual labouring households from analysis of the middle class. Nayeb divides the occupations into two distinct categories; manual and non-manual occupations, assigning the weight of zero to manual occupations (without excluding them from analysis of the middle class). Therefore, his middle-class population also includes households that primarily rely on selling their manual labour to generate their living, which is contradictory to the occupational definition of the middle class. Second, Nayeb's calculation of income index on the basis of poverty line is problematic. He does not consider the difference between the poverty line in rural and urban context. See Nayeb (2011).

17. *Pucca* housing refers to solid dwellings that are built of substantial material such as stone, brick, cement or concrete. *Kutcha* housing refer to temporary dwellings that are not durable and are is generally made of materials such as mud, bamboo or leaves.

2

In Search of the Rural Middle Classes
From Village Stratification to Rural Household Variations

> Middle-class people are only those who can fulfil their daily needs. I cannot exactly give the definition of the middle class but can say in our village [Nandur] more than fifty per cent of people belong to the middle class.
>
> —Bala Laxman Ch., personal interview (2016)[1]

This study of the formation of India's rural middle class is undertaken through an extensive case study of two villages, Rahatwade and Nandur, located in Pune District in western Maharashtra. Analysis of the *India Human Development Survey* II (2011–12) indicates that Maharashtra holds the biggest proportion of the self-identified rural middle classes, that is, 8.5 per cent of self-identified rural middle classes are in Maharashtra. Before arriving at the main body of the book, it is crucial to paint a picture – relevant as a background to rural class formation – of research areas. In what follows, I first briefly familiarise readers with the social and economic composition of Maharashtra. Then, I move on to provide a selective history of each village, their physical and social structure, and a more detailed analysis of their internal arrangements and settlement patterns, hamlets, caste composition, cropping patterns and occupational diversities. The last section offers a brief account of rural household stratification and a preliminary examination of class structure, a background necessity for the arguments in the remainder of the book. Beside its contextual purpose, this chapter will also be useful for readers interested in Maharashtra, and academic researchers and graduate students in social sciences with a focus on class formation in agrarian regions and village studies. Let us now turn to a brief overview of the political economy of Maharashtra.

42   Contested Capital

Maharashtra

In 1960, the Marathi-speaking districts of the Bombay Province, the Central Province, Berar and the princely state of Hyderabad were combined to form the new state of Maharashtra.[2] It is divided into five main geographical regions: Vidarbha, located in the east and consisting of the Marathi-speaking districts from the Central Province and Berar; Marathwada, located in the south-eastern part of the state, which was part of the princely state of Hyderabad; Konkan, which includes the coastal districts from the Bombay Province; Khandesh, situated in the northwest of Maharashtra; and western Maharashtra, the district from the Bombay Province, in which Rahatwade and Nandur are located (Vora, 2009).[3] Marathas are understood to be the dominant caste occupying a position of politico-economic dominance in Maharashtra. The rise of Maratha dominance has its origins in the colonial period, specifically in the early part of the twentieth century. One of the major transformations in the economy of rural Maharashtra in that period was the rise in cash crop farming. The most significant cash crops were cotton and sugarcane produced for the world market and Marathas controlled the means of production of both. The rise of the cash economy in Maharashtra also resulted in the rise of the Maratha-led anti-Brahmin movement, which further enhanced the dominance of Marathas in the region (Lele, 1990: 115).

In addition to their relatively advantageous economic position, Marathas were the most numerically significant caste, 31.19 per cent in 1931. However, among the Maratha population, the peasant caste, the Kunbis, accounted for approximately 31 per cent of the total Maratha population (Lele, 1990: 116). Traditionally, Kunbis were considered to be inferior to Marathas in the Hindu caste system, who always claimed Kshatriya status, but the distinction between the two became less significant due to their alliance in the anti-Brahmin movement during 1920s, particularly in western Maharashtra, where many Kunbis sought to be identified as Marathas (Vora, 2009: 215). However, in the 1980s, the Backward Classes Commission listed Kunbis as one of the Other Backward Classes (OBCs). As a result, many Kunbis self-identify as 'Maratha-Kunbi' and seek classification as OBCs in India's system of reservations.[4]

The pattern of Maratha dominance is a unique feature in India because no other state has ever experienced the regional hegemony of any caste group equal to that of the Marathas. This dominance continued into the post-independence period and still persists in contemporary Maharashtra. Lele argues that most state policies concerning rural areas that have been implemented since Independence (relating to land reform, rural educational institutions and agricultural development programmes) were initiated in response to the powerful Maratha lobby (Lele, 1982, 1990: 178). In the post-independence period, Maratha elites throughout Maharashtra maintained their political dominance through a policy of collaboration with the state. State intervention in the agricultural sector opened up new opportunities for rural elites to access newly available state resources. These resources included the establishment of new co-operative societies, banks and agricultural technology. The most significant example of influence of Marathas in state policy can be shown through their dominance in sugar cooperatives.

The origin of sugar cooperatives, with the government as 'stakeholder, guarantor and regulator', goes back to the 1950s (Lalvani, 2008: 1474). In 1954, the Congress government took an initiative to grant industrial licenses for sugar production solely to sugar co-operatives in order to encourage their formation. This gave a major boost to the growth of co-operatives in Maharashtra and they soon became 'means of acquiring political power' for rich Marathas (Lalvani, 2008: 1475). Lalvani suggests that the success of sugar co-operatives is the result of the 'democratic constitution' of India. This, she argues, is because the introduction of universal suffrage after India's independence, which enabled the majority of the village population to vote, resulted in the 'displacement of elite, high-caste urban politicians from state legislatures and led to a strengthening of the nexus between the sugar co-operatives and government' (Lalvani, 2008: 1475). Many co-operative leaders mobilised votes based on caste affiliation in exchange for receiving financial benefits and subsidies from the state. The major expansion of sugar co-operatives took place in the 1970s, when these cooperatives accounted for 32 per cent of total white sugar production in India (Attwood, 1984: 40–41; Dhanagare, 1995: 77–78). This unique agro-industrial development led to the development of the sugar lobby in state politics. Many sugar producers successfully gained high-profile government positions, with two reaching the position of Chief Minister. Therefore, with Marathas as leaders, sugar co-operatives have played a significant role in 'shaping the socioeconomic fabric of Maharashtra' (Lalvani, 2008: 1475). However, the regional dominance of Marathas does not mean that there is socio-economic homogeneity among the Marathas or that this regional dominance affects all Marathas equally. They do not all enjoy the same economic status, privilege and wealth. Lele suggests that elite Marathas maintain their dominance over underprivileged members of their caste group, and over other subordinate castes, through forming alliances with non-elite segments of Marathas or other caste groups, when it is advantageous (Lele, 1982: 55). An example of this caste cleavage, and of elite Marathas using lower status Marathas for their own ends, is the *Shetkari Sanghatana* farmers' movement which rose to its peak in the 1970s. This farmers' movement attempted to secure better prices for farm produce such as onions, cotton, sugarcane, wheat and tobacco; in addition, farmers

44   Contested Capital

with a relatively large marketable surpluses benefitted disproportionately from increases in these prices. Peasants with little or no surplus produce gained very little (Dhanagare, 1995). While this caste group is obviously highly significant, there are important *class* cleavages among the Marathas. The highly successful political manoeuvring and lobbying should be seen as both class and caste domination. Contours and intersections of caste and class in Maharashtra are yet to be examined. The caste structure of Maharashtra and its class cleavages have important implications for rural middle-class formation, and are addressed extensively in this book.

Village Stratification: Rahatwade and Nandur

The selection of sample villages is a crucial part of any field-based study. In some research, the field-site is largely predetermined, for example, if the research is geographically specific, or a specific caste or social group resides in a particular locality.[5] For many research topics, existing scholarship can be suggestive – a particular region may be understudied or relatively poorly understood.[6] In contrast, and in cases such as this topic, the choice of field-site can be relatively open. In such instances, researchers may choose to select the field-site on a random basis, while some adopt a more structured method for their selections. In studies of Indian villages, scholars have used various methods in village classifications. For example, in the study of the effects of the Green Revolution on south Indian villages in 1973, Chinnappa selected eleven sample villages on the basis of stratified random sampling from the villages listed in the 1971 census, using variables such as physical accessibility of the villages, population size and the ratio of agricultural labourers to cultivators (Chinnappa, 1977).[7] Later, in the re-survey of some of the same villages in northern Tamil Nadu, John Harriss (1991) classified the villages on the basis of irrigation facilities, availability of employment and wage rates. Later, Srinivasan attempted to systemise the classification of the set of villages first selected by Chinnappa in 1973, and to introduce village typologies, using two statistical methods – factor analysis (principal component analysis) and cluster analysis (Srinivasan, 2004). Using principal component analysis, he identified four groups of factors that cause village variations. First, factors representing the variables relating to wet and dry land and the development of non-farm employment. Second, variables such as the female literacy rate, the extent of workforce participation by women and per capita income from agriculture were used to represent the backwardness of the village. Third, variables such as the proportion of Scheduled Castes (SCs) to total village population and proximity to urban locations were used to represent social and institutional factors. Fourth, variables such as the area of land owned and cultivated by small farmers, informal activities of landless agricultural labourers and cultivators, liabilities and cropping patterns were used to identify the distribution of means of production. After identifying these factors, five clusters of villages were defined, each having a specific characteristic: (*a*) agriculturally underdeveloped villages; (*b*) suburban villages; (*c*) remote and agriculturally commercialised villages; (*d*) developed villages; and (*e*) SC and poor villages. The first cluster is characterised by households with a high proportion of agricultural assets, moderate cropping intensity and high irrigation concentration. They are generally far from towns, have low work participation rates, with the majority of the population in SC communities, and farmers with very small holdings. Villages in the second cluster are generally suburban and characterised by having dry agriculture. Villages in the third cluster are far from urban centres. In these villages, income from agriculture indicates commercialisation and prosperity in agriculture. Villages in the fourth cluster, that is, developed villages, are more advanced in relation to women's literacy rate and the fertility rate. They are situated close to towns, with an average distance of 10 kilometres, and have higher irrigation and cropping intensity and more small farmers. Villages in the fifth cluster are characterised as those in which social institutions such as gender and caste are most strongly reflected in the economy. These villages are on average 15 kilometres away from towns and have low female literacy rates, but their male and female work participation rates are high compared to those in other clusters. This cluster is also characterised by the highest proportion of SCs in the population (Srinivasan, 2004: 110–11).

Rahatwade and Nandur were not randomly selected. My network of connections at the Gokhale Institute in Pune came to be an important factor in selecting Pune district in Maharashtra, and this turned out to be a good choice because this research, as we shall see, shows a direct relationship between industrialisation and the formation of the rural middle class, and Pune is one of the most industrialised zones of Maharashtra. In terms of selecting the villages, a systematic method was designed on the basis of the availability of information provided in the 2011 population census. The sample villages were chosen according to three criteria: (*a*) population size; (*b*) effective literacy rate; and (*c*) caste diversity.[8] The following steps were taken in village selection: First, research resources (time, transport, funds and research assistance) dictated a total number of two villages, with a population of not more than 2,000. Furthermore, to ensure caste diversity within the village (which would allow examination of the caste/class nexus), single caste villages (for instance, only SC, or only tribal, villages) were eliminated. The effective literacy rate was taken into account because education

46   Contested Capital

is considered to be one of the main markers of middle class status. Villages that had a lower effective literacy rate compared to the average rural India rate were eliminated. From the remaining villages, 10 were randomly selected. The next step involved a visit to each of these villages for further elimination, based on physical accessibility of the villages and cropping patterns (to ensure diversity in the agricultural production). Furthermore, the final selection was determined by the agreement of the village *sarpanch* (village head). If I were to situate Rahatwade and Nandur in Srinivasan's classifications of villages, they would be most similar to villages in the fourth category, that of advanced villages. Basic demographic characteristics of both sample villages are provided in Table 2.1. Data represented in the top rows are from the 2011 population census, and in the bottom rows from preliminary field visits and from Gram Panchayat offices. Let us now turn to some detailed description of these villages.

Table 2.1   Rahatwade and Nandur: some basic characteristics

Village name	Rahatwade	Nandur
Data based on the 2011 Population Census		
Area (acre)	1,613.6	865
Population size	1,818	934
Number of households	347	219
Effective literacy rate	77.23	72.65
Male effective literacy rate	87.04	80.31
Female effective literacy rate	67.13	62.92
Ratio of Scheduled Caste	9.07	18.3
Data based on preliminary field visits and village Gram Panchayat offices		
Caste compositions	Maratha, SCs, STs, OBCs, NT-C, Muslims	Maratha, SCs, STs, OBCs, NT-C, Muslims
Main crops	Rice and onion	Sugarcane
Main mode of irrigation	Rainwater and Bore well	Canals from Mula River
Access to roads	Pucca	Pucca
Distance from Pune	30 km	40 km
Access to drinking water	Yes	Yes
Access to public bus	Yes	No
School availability	Public: up to 7th standard	Public: up to 7th standard
Kindergarten	Yes	Yes
Availability of health care	No	No
Main source of non-agricultural work	Dairy production; factory work (unskilled, semi-skilled and skilled)	Factory work (semi-skilled and skilled)

Source: Census data 2011; Gram Panchayat offices in Rahatwade and Nandur (2015).

Rahatwade is a medium-sized village situated 30 kilometres south of Pune city, in the plain below a series of hills commonly known as the 'Husband and Wife', in the Haveli Taluka. The area of the village is 653 hectares, or 1,613.6 acres, and its 2011 population according to the population census was 1,818 (although in my fieldwork census in 2015, the total population was 1,604 people).[9] There is no recorded history of the village. However, based on discussions with participants on the history of Rahatwade, the earliest settlement in the village goes back to the time of Shivaji in the seventeenth century. The Marathas of Rahatwade claim that their ancestors fought for Shivaji against Muslims, and land on which Rahatwade came to be formed was gifted to them by Shivaji, following a victory. The village is characterised by the cultivation of paddy, the main Kharif season (rainy season) crop, and dairy production, and is commonly understood to be a village of small holdings. At the time of data collection, the average landholding was 2.6 acres, and the average irrigated landholding was 2 acres, and 19 households (7.6 per cent of total households in the village) did not own any land.

There is considerable water scarcity in the village and its agricultural activities, which are primarily dependant on rainwater, are therefore seasonal. The river that separates Rahatwade from its neighbouring village, Kundhanpur, is dry for most of the year. There is no water preservation infrastructure in the village and open wells are the main source of irrigation in the Rabi (dry season). Only 83 households (33 per cent of the total households) had access to a well or borehole in 2014–15. Land tenancy was rare – only 3 households leased agricultural land. The majority of households cultivated more than one crop, the major crops other than rice being onion, wheat and groundnuts, which were mostly cultivated during the Rabi season. The village sold its agricultural produce in an agricultural market yard, a regulated market in Pune city. Insufficient rain had a negative impact on paddy cultivation in 2014–15. According to fieldwork data, almost 60 per cent of the village households depended primarily on agriculture for their livelihood, and 7 per cent depended primarily on agricultural labour, while almost 15 per cent of households were engaged in both cultivation and other non-farm activities (such as plumbing, driving, manual factory labour, and skilled and semi-skilled work in industrial units).[10] Six households (2 per cent of households) had members engaged in low-ranked government employment, and 33 households (13 per cent) had no direct connection to agriculture. Out of these 33 households, 14 were involved only in industrial labour (unskilled work); 4 households had independent businesses (such as a hotel, a restaurant and dairy production); 4 relied on informal independent self-employment (an electrician, two drivers and a street musician); and 2 were agricultural produce brokers.

48   Contested Capital

Furthermore, many households in Rahatwade had members employed as skilled workers and machine operators in industrial plants outside the village. For the list of all non-agricultural activities in Rahatwade, see Appendix A1.

Table 2.2 provides a detailed profile of land ownership, housing (dwelling) and sanitation access. As shown in the table, only 55 per cent of the households had access to a private toilet.[11] The main source of drinking water was Gram Panchayat water, which was provided through pipes, located next to the Panchayat office, and which ran for a few hours every morning. Female residents of the village walked to the water-point each morning to collect water.

Table 2.2   Land and home ownership and access to basic amenities in Rahatwade

Rahatwade (N = 250)	Freq.	Per cent
Land ownership (total)	231	92.4
Irrigated land	230	92
Own house	242	96.8
Own toilet	137	54.8
Access to kitchen	196	78.4

Source: Fieldwork data (2015).

Physical and Social Structure of Rahatwade

The physical structure of Rahatwade is closely related to caste. The village consists of six distinct hamlets (illustrated in Map 2.1), and each has a certain geographic and social identity.[12] This structure has not undergone any substantial change in recent years and reflects the persistence of caste distinctions which govern geographical settlement. The six hamlets comprise:

(i) Gāvāta (the main village) consists exclusively of Maratha households (see Map 2.2). The main village dwellings are packed close each other and there is little room for expansion. In addition to the Maratha houses, the main village *mandir* (temple) is also in this area. The Gāvāta also consists of a *kirana* shop (grocery store), a public primary school (Zilla Parishad school – fourth to seventh standard), a large courtyard for social gatherings and a volleyball court (on which temporary migrant agricultural labourers usually build their plastic shacks). The village Panchayat offices are situated in Gāvāta.

(ii) Kamble Basti or Dalit Basti consists of Mahar and Nav Buddha (formerly Mahar) households (see Map 2.2). This hamlet is named after the surname of its residents all of whom share the surname Kamble. It has its own temple

Map 2.1 Map of Rahatwade village

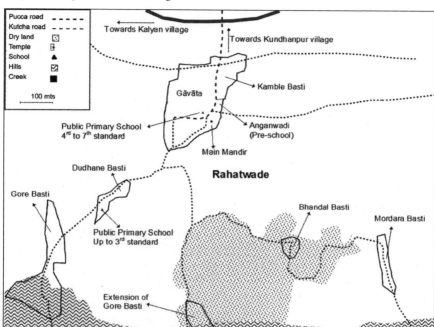

Source: Author.

      and although the main road to the village separates it from the main village, Kamble Basti is the hamlet closest to the main village.

(iii) Dudhane Basti consists of a mixture of different castes and is home to about 10 Maratha households, 4 Dhangars (a Nomadic Tribe population), 2 OBCs and the only Muslim household in the village. There is also a public primary school in this hamlet (first to third standard).

(iv) Gore Basti or Dhangar Basti is named after the surname of the Dhangar residents in Rahatwade all of whom share the surname Gore. This hamlet includes only Dhangar households including the newly elected *sarpanch* of Rahatwade. It is situated approximately 1.5 kilometres from the main village, connected to the main village via a muddy (*kutcha*) road and accessible by cars.

(v) Bhandal Basti is further away from the main village, connected to the village through a *kutcha* road and consists only of Maratha households. The previous *sarpanch* of Rahatwade resides in this hamlet.

Map 2.2 Map of Gãvāta (main village) and Kamble Basti in Rahatwade

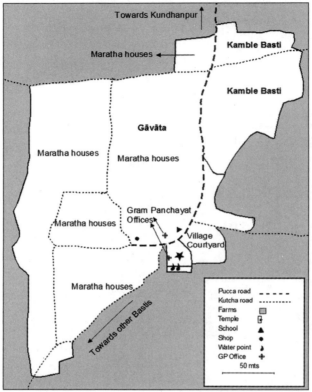

Source: Author.

(vi) Mordara Basti is the furthest away from the village, situated in the foothills, and consists of various farmhouses (that are only occupied as holiday homes) and a few Maratha households. This hamlet is connected to Bhandal Basti and the rest of the village via a muddy *kutcha* road. All these *basti*s are accessible by motorised vehicles, except for Mordara Basti – the road between Mordara Basti and Bhandal Basti is only accessible by motorbikes or on foot during the rainy season.

A cursory analysis of the spatial divisions in Rahatwade suggests that they are largely determined by caste rather than economic status. Village residents from the same caste tend to live together, although they do not necessarily share the same economic status. The significance of caste in relation to economic status is further discussed in Chapter 4. It is possible that this spatial organisation of residential clusters, although based on caste, is a legacy of the historical settlement in the village and does not represent the continued salience of caste. However, we can say for certain that the spatial organisation of Rahatwade is not based on wealth, economic status or class membership.

Nandur is a medium-sized village located in Daund sub-district, approximately 40 kilometres east of Pune. The area of the village is 350 hectares, or 865 acres. According to the 2011 population census, there were 219 families and a total population of 934 in 2011 (although, in my 2015 fieldwork census the enumeration of the village was considerably higher – 240 households and a total population of 1,301 – which is mainly due to the inward migration. I will explore the reasons for this inward migration in Chapter 3). As in the case of Rahatwade, there is no recorded history of Nandur. However, a number of respondents informed me that Dhangars and Malis (OBCs) were the original residents of this village. They also referred to 'some scattered documents of the village, that belong to the year 1818', which concern the early settlement of the village. According to respondents, the documents contain the names of early settlers in Nandur, based on which they conclude that Dhangars and Malis have been residing in Nandur at least since 1818. However, Nandur Gram Panchayat office, established in 1965, was not able to provide such documents or confirm the validity of the narrative of its residents.

One of the major features of Nandur is its proximity to a number of factories and production units. In total, there are 16 large factories surrounding the village. These range from food packaging to car-part production, the largest of which is Fleetguard Filters Pvt. Ltd. (established in 1987) that manufactures hydraulic filters for heavy-duty air and fuel, with a turnover of INR 9,230 million.[13] The first factory outside Nandur was established in 1984. According to village residents, the factories have had an overwhelmingly positive impact on the socio-economic development of the village. Their emergence has resulted in significant diversification out of agriculture by providing employment opportunities for village inhabitants – on average, almost one person in each household was engaged in unskilled, semi-skilled or skilled employment in these factories. It has also led to an improvement in the infrastructure of the village, contributed to a significant rise in land prices and to attracting inward migration.

The distribution of land in Nandur is highly unequal. The average landholding in Nandur was 2.4 acres of irrigated land and 2.9 acres of total land (if dry land is included). However, 75 households (31.25 per cent) did not own any land at all. The detailed distribution of land ownership in Nandur is shown in Chapter 3. As in Rahatwade, agricultural land tenancy is rare in the village (only 2 households).

52   Contested Capital

The village is mainly irrigated and the main source of water for agriculture is the Mula River (depicted in Map 2.3). In addition to the water pipes supplying water from the river, 30 per cent of households own wells. Due to the abundant supply of river water, agriculture in Nandur is not seasonal. Sugarcane is cultivated throughout the year and is the main cash crop in the village. There are many sugarcane factories in the neighbouring towns, which are often directly involved in the harvesting process.

According to fieldwork data, 108 households (45 per cent) depended on agriculture as their primary source of income; 33 households (13.75 per cent) reported agricultural labour as their primary source of income; 49 households (20 per cent) were engaged in both agriculture and non-agricultural activities (ranging from informal self-employment such as plumbing and driving, to factory labour, and skilled work in industrial units); 4 households had members who were labour contractors (providing non-agricultural workers to factories and agricultural labourers to sugarcane factories), and less than 10 households had businesses as their main source of income (leasing tractors, transportation business, workshop owners and poultry farms). Two households earned their household income primarily from government employment. The remaining households only had members working in factories either as unskilled workers (who were termed *company helpers*) or engaged in semi-skilled and skilled activities, such as machine operating. In addition to machine operators, in 17 households, at least one member was engaged in skilled work as a manager, foreman or supervisor in the factories. Skilled industrial economic activities are termed *jobs* in both villages. For the list of all non-farm activities in Nandur, see Appendix A1.

Table 2.3 provides a profile of land ownership, housing and sanitation in Nandur. Almost 91 per cent of households in Nandur own their dwellings and 58 per cent have a kitchen area in the house. The main source of drinking water is the Gram Panchayat water, and privately owned boreholes. Unlike Rahatwade, there is piped water in many of the newly constructed houses, supplying water through water tanks, which is usually connected to a water purifier for drinking.

Table 2.3   Land and home ownership and access to basic amenities in Nandur

Nandur (N = 240)	Freq.	Per cent
Land ownership (total)	165	68.75
Irrigated land	160	66.66
Own house	218	90.8
Own toilet	203	84.6
Separate kitchen	140	58.3

Source: Fieldwork data (2015).

Physical and Social Structure of Nandur

Nandur consists of five distinct hamlets (see Map 2.3). Unlike Rahatwade, and due to industrialisation, the internal physical structure of Nandur carries a less rigid and more heterogeneous spatio-caste division. One of the most striking characteristics of Nandur was the number of large houses under construction at the time of fieldwork. The five Nandur hamlets comprise:

(i) Gāvāta (main village), which has two further sub-divisions next to it, is adjacent to the Mula River on the one side and sugarcane fields on the other. In the centre of Gāvāta, there is a newly constructed Hanuman *mandir*; outside the temple, the men in the village gather, socialise and, more often than not, play cards. Opposite the temple is the Gram Panchayat office. The houses surrounding the centre of Gāvāta consist mainly of Dhangar households, a number of Mali households, and Guravs (OBCs). All the Muslim households of Nandur reside in Gāvāta. Further from the centre, on the outskirts of Gāvāta (towards the east), there are a number of landowning SC households living in a sub-division. Another small sub-section, which is parallel to the Dalit area on the western outskirts of Gāvāta, consists of clusters of corrugated tin houses. These tin houses, which shelter landless SC families, are situated on Gram Panchayat land. Many of these SC households are relatively recent migrants who have settled in Nandur seeking employment as agricultural labourers or unskilled labourers (*helpers*) in factories. In Gāvāta, there is a clear division based on caste and class. Gāvāta also hosts a number of smaller temples, a line of public toilets that remained locked throughout the course of my fieldwork, a public primary school (first to seventh standard), a barber stall, a *paan* shop and a small *kirana* shop. Two former *sarpanch*s of Nandur, including the longest reigning *sarpanch* (from the Dhangar caste), reside in Gāvāta.

(ii) Borate Basti is named after the surname of the Mali families in Nandur, the majority of whom reside in this section. It is located on the main road (*pucca* road) that connects the main village to the factories and the neighbouring village Sahajpur, and hosts the majority of middle-class households. Houses in this cluster are relatively new, and larger than houses in other areas of the village. These newly built houses are constructed in a new style and are usually multi-storey houses with a kitchen and living room on the ground floor and bedrooms on the upper floors, usually with a balcony and a small garden. The interior of these houses (this will be discussed in Chapter 5) is often quite lavish; with extravagant lighting designs, marble flooring,

54 Contested Capital

large flat TVs and sofa sets. This style of housing is very different from the newly constructed houses in Gāvāta. The most remarkable house in this division (and in all of Nandur) is the house of the new *sarpanch*. The house consists of eight bedrooms and is the biggest house in the village. The majority of households in this area are from the Mali caste. There are no SC, Scheduled Tribe (ST), or Muslim households in Borate Basti. There are, however, a number of Dhangars, which, judging by the size of their homes and the four-wheel drive vehicles parked outside their houses, seemed to be in a better economic situation than Dhangars who live in other areas of Nandur (this observation was later confirmed by fieldwork survey data). There are also four Maratha households in this cluster and a number of other households that have migrated to the village as permanent migrants from other parts of Maharashtra (who are semi-skilled and skilled workers in factories in the periphery of Nandur). However, these new arrivals do not own their houses and have tenancy agreements with the owners (who are from Nandur). What distinguishes this section of the village from the rest is not its caste but its class composition. The majority of the households in Borate Basti are among the wealthiest in the village (this observation was also confirmed by fieldwork survey data). Borate Basti is the closest hamlet to Gāvāta and is surrounded by sugarcane fields. It is home to the village labour contractors, families with the largest holdings of land, workshop owners and business owners. Land prices are much higher in this part of Nandur.

(iii) Ghule Basti is a comparatively small area, which is isolated from the rest of the village, and surrounded by sugarcane fields. It consists of only handful of Dhangar households, much less affluent than the Dhangars in Borate Basti. There is also an OBC household in this division. Ghule Basti is connected to Gāvāta via a *kutcha* road.

(iv) Kotemal is located in the most remote part of Nandur, adjacent to a large area of dry land that divides it from the rest of the village. The land in this area is very dry, perhaps due to its distance from the Mula River. During the course of fieldwork, I witnessed frequent deliveries of wet soil to this area. Kotemal suffers from a severe lack of drinking water. Although there are a number of hand-pumped boreholes (one of the main sources of drinking water) in this area, they are dry and therefore the residents of this division have to go to Borate Basti to collect drinking water. There are 12 households living in this area, all from the Dhangar caste, although poorer than other Dhangars in the village. Kotemal also hosts the plastic sheds of the temporary agricultural migrants (sugarcane cutters) who come to Nandur during the sugarcane-harvesting season. Residents of Kotemal usually complain about the lack of attention from the Gram Panchayat office in relation to water supply, roads and other basic amenities.

(v) The fifth division is a neighbourhood which has emerged in recent years, which my research assistant termed 'Migrants Basti'. This is where the majority of permanent industrial migrants live. It is situated between Borate Basti and Kotemal. These households were included in my survey because most of them have been living in Nandur for more than a decade and now consider Nandur as their permanent home. They are mainly from other parts of Maharashtra, and do not own their houses, and have a very modest, basic lifestyle and live in small rented houses.

Map 2.3   Map of Nandur village

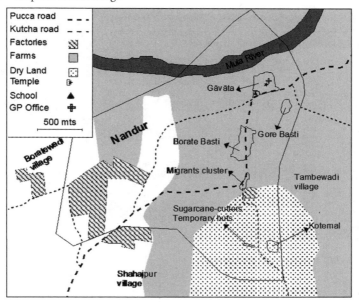

Source: Author.

Caste Composition of Rahatwade and Nandur

Although at the beginning of my fieldwork, I perceived caste to be a sensitive issue of discussion and therefore was hesitant to discuss the caste affiliations of the residents directly, I did not encounter any hesitancy from respondents while

56   Contested Capital

discussing their caste. In any case, the surnames were caste labels. On the basis of my fieldwork survey, Tables 2.4, 2.5 and 2.6 show the caste composition of Rahatwade and Nandur. There are no Brahmins in these villages. In Rahatwade, the majority of households belong to the Maratha caste and SCs are the second biggest caste group. Mahars are the most numerous castes among the SCs in Maharashtra and most have converted to Buddhism under the leadership of Babasaheb Ambedkar in 1956 (Vora, 2009: 218). The third biggest caste group in the village is Dhangar, classified as one of the Nomadic Tribes (NT-C) in Maharashtra. There is one Muslim household, and just one household from the Koli caste which is in the ST category. The population of the Ramoshi caste, which belongs to OBCs, is negligible. Ramoshis are mainly located in Maharashtra, Madhya Pradesh and Karnataka. The term 'Ramoshi' is derived from Rama, 'the legendary hero of Ramayana'. In Maharashtra, the Ramoshis are believed to

Table 2.4   Caste compositions of Rahatwade and Nandur

Caste groups	Rahatwade (N = 250)			Nandur (N = 240)		
	Freq.	Per cent	Population	Freq.	Per cent	Population
Maratha	202	80.80	1,284	8	3.33	31
OBCs	4	1.6	42	90	37.5	501
SCs	25	10	129	34	14.17	178
STs	1	0.4	4	4	1.66	20
DTs & NT-B	-	-	-	12	5	60
NT-C	17	6.80	138	86	35.83	482
Muslims	1	0.40	7	6	2.92	29
Total	250	100	1,604	240	100	1,301

Source: Fieldwork data (2015).

Table 2.5   List of caste groups in Rahatwade

Caste groups (N = 250)	Households	Population
Maratha	202	1,284
Ramoshi (OBCs)	4	42
Mahar/Nav Buddha (SCs)	25	129
Koli (STs)	1	4
Dhangar (NT-C)	17	138
Muslims	1	7
Total	250	1,604

Source: Fieldwork data (2015).

Table 2.6 List of caste groups in Nandur

Caste groups (N = 240)	Households	Population
Maratha	8	31
Mali (OBCs)	75	428
Ramoshi (OBCs)	2	10
Gurav (OBCs)	4	22
Parit (OBCs)	1	3
Lohar (OBCs)	1	6
Sonar (OBCs)	1	7
Jangam (OBCs)	1	5
Lingayat (OBCs)	1	2
Mulani Muslim (OBCs)	4	18
Mahar/Nav Buddha (SCs)	27	143
Mang or Matang (SCs)	6	25
Honar (SCs)	1	10
Koli (STs)	4	20
Vadar (Denotified Tribes, DTs)	2	14
Kanjarbhat (DTs)	7	31
Joshi (NT-B)	2	11
Gopal (NT-B)	1	4
Dhangar (NT-C)	86	482
Muslims	6	29
Total	240	1,301

Source: Fieldwork data (2015).

have been the protectors of Rama. Ramoshis were historically a community of village guards and watchmen, but are settled in villages across Maharashtra as cultivators and shepherds (Dhar, 2004: 1767).

Unlike Rahatwade, where the majority of households are Marathas, in Nandur the share of two caste groups Mali, which is classified as OBCs, and Dhangar, classified as NT-C in Maharashtra, is roughly equal, and together these make up the majority of the village population (see Table 2.6). In addition to Malis, other OBC households in the village include Gurav, Mulani, Jangam, Ramoshi and Sonar. The Malis were traditionally gardeners, engaged in semi-rural cultivation of fruits, vegetables and flowers (O'Hanlon, 1985; Vora, 2009). Because of a large urban market, Malis came to act 'as a medium of contact between rural areas and the growing urban centres' in Maharashtra (O'Hanlon, 1985: 105). Although Malis occupy a *Shudra* position in the traditional caste hierarchy, they appear to have occupied a relatively respectable position, close to that of Maratha-Kunbis, in Maharashtra (O'Hanlon, 1985). The Gurav community is one of the traditional

58 Contested Capital

service providers who act in a priestly role in the village. The Sonars are an artisan community who were traditionally goldsmiths, although at present some work as silversmiths and some are engaged in cultivation (Rao, 2004). Jangam refers to the community of wandering priests who are disciples of Lord Shiva. Parits (also referred to as Dhobis) are a caste group whose traditional occupation was washing clothes (Singh et al., 2004). Furthermore, SCs (consisting of Mahar/ Nav Buddha and Mang/Matang) are the third biggest caste group in the village. The Mang caste, also referred to as Matang, is traditionally associated with low status and ritually impure occupations such as undertakers, midwives and leather workers (Singh, et al., 2004: 1403–09). The Lohar caste is the community of blacksmiths. In Nandur, there are 4 ST households and 12 households belonging to other tribal communities. There are 7 Muslim households, no Brahmins, and a negligible population of Marathas in Nandur.

It is notable that compared to the rest of India, the Dhangar caste group in Maharashtra holds a unique position in the caste hierarchy. The Constitution of India includes the Dhangar community in Schedule two of the Scheduled Tribe list in every state in India except Maharashtra. In Maharashtra, where they have a significant presence, the Dhangar community is listed under the Nomadic Tribes, commonly known as NT-C, and is only entitled to 3.5 per cent reservations in education and government jobs, unlike in other states, where as part of the ST category, they have access to 7 per cent of a set of reservations. In order to have access to a higher reservation percentage, Dhangars in Maharashtra have been seeking classification as STs in India's system of reservations. I have not found any document or scholarship which addresses this or explains the exceptional situation of Maharashtrian Dhangars in the caste reservations system. However, according to a handful of newspaper articles and a number of participants in Nandur, the struggle of the Dhangar community in Maharashtra for reservations as part of the ST category has been on-going for 65 years (Kulkarni, 2014). In the Indian hierarchical caste system, Dhangars are currently placed below the OBCs and above the SCs and STs, and although seeking ST classification would lower their status in the caste hierarchy, it would entitle them to a greater percentage of reservations. Indeed, during the course of my fieldwork, many Dhangar participants informed me that seeking ST status was primarily an economic strategy for gaining access to a higher share of reservation quotas, which would facilitate better economic gains.

As far as religion is concerned, the majority of the households described themselves as Hindu. In Nandur, seven families were Muslim, two of them from the Mulani caste (Muslims from OBCs). In Rahatwade, there was only one Muslim household. It is notable that most of the SC households in both villages described their religion as 'Nav Buddha'.

Social Stratification: In Search of Middle-Class Households

In examining the 'types', 'characteristics', and 'composition' of the middle class in the selected villages, it was important to first determine who belongs to this class. In empirical terms, this raised the question of how to locate the middle class on the ground. During the early days of fieldwork, my attempt to find anecdotal evidence for the existence of middle-class households was unsuccessful. Following various informal discussions with the local residents about the topic of my research, I learnt, to my bewilderment, that a large number in both villages self-identified as middle class. Indeed, during various pilot interviews, I was repeatedly told that the majority of households are middle-class households. This left me quite unconvinced. My scepticism was often met with counter-questions: 'who in the village belongs to this class and why'. Indeed, these questions were the most crucial and important enquiries in my empirical research, and I was not the first person to face such a methodological challenge, fundamental for the validity of this research.

Hidden in the methodological appendix in her study of middle classes and prosperity in East Asia and Latin America, Diane Davis outlines three important methodological and empirical issues one must consider when studying the middle class. First, Davis recognises the need for an 'operational definition' of the 'middle class', which should be used as a 'starting point [rather] than an ending point' (Davis, 2004: 364). She was attempting to move beyond a preoccupation with big capitalists and wage labourers and examine the 'middling' sectors, which are in an intermediate position in relation to income, ownership and autonomy within employment. Having defined her starting point based on occupational categories, she recognises a methodological gap. She states, 'there was no guarantee that the forces I initially chose to examine as middle class would always be seen or see themselves as being in the middle' (Davis, 2004: 364). To address this methodological problem, Davis suggests that it is appropriate to use a more 'objective' criterion to initially locate the groups of people who are of interest, but that as the research project develops both objective and subjective determinants of middle-class status should be examined. Second, she considers what this objective starting point might be, and suggests one should start from the most theoretically consensual and inclusive definition. There tends to be agreement amongst scholars that the middle class consists of three basic occupational categories: (*a*) salaried employees in trade and industry, services and white-collar workers; (*b*) self-employed artisans and craftsmen, and self-employed producers including small farmers, who are often also referred to as 'petty commodity producers'; and (*c*) owners of small enterprises in both industry and agriculture, who also operate

60   Contested Capital

their enterprises (Davis, 2004: 364). Third, she suggests examining middle classes 'through analysis of how they live, how they work, what they aspire to economically and politically....' (Davis, 2004: 368).

Although Davis's approach is one of the most insightful and comprehensive among empirical studies of the middle class, using her starting point in rural India comes with various limitations: categorising the significantly diverse occupations and livelihoods in rural India is an act of simplification and fails to recognise the complexity of labour relations in this most diverse of economies. So, what should be our working definition or 'starting point'? Following Davis, I start from the most theoretically consensual definition, but instead, apply a process of deduction (similar to my method in the previous chapter). That is, instead of identifying who the middle classes are, first the households that objectively cannot be part of the middle class are identified, and then eliminated. There is theoretical consensus that the middle class does not include manual workers, and this is the first stage in addressing definitional ambiguities over who (does not) constitute the middle class. Based on the first round of household survey data, it was possible to propose a rough socio-economic classification of all households based on the main source of household income, and to identify those that belonged to the class of manual workers.[14] These are the households whose primary source of income is agricultural labour and manual non-agricultural wage labour.[15] Each village was divided into two main groups: *manual labouring* and *non-labouring*. Table 2.7 demonstrates the two-group classifications in the sample villages. The manual labouring group includes households which are primarily dependent on selling their physical labour to generate their living – they usually own little or no land. Although some of these households own some land, their income from farming is minimal and insufficient for subsistence – the biggest proportion of their income is generated from agricultural labour, manual unskilled work in non-farm economic activities, including but not limited to, watchmen, cleaners, manual labourers in workshops and factories, company drivers, packers and movers, and people engaged in other physical labouring activities. These marginal farmers are more likely to be situated in the class of labourers, together with wage working landless rural households.[16] Furthermore, in the categorisation of the villages outlined above, the 'company helpers' have been considered as part of the labouring group of households. A total of 131 households in Rahatwade and 121 households in Nandur were identified as manual labouring households and eliminated from further analysis.[17] The non-labouring households consist of the rest of the village who do not depend on selling their physical labour to earn their livelihood.[18]

In Search of the Rural Middle Classes   61

A total of 110 households in Rahatwade and 106 households in Nandur qualified as non-labouring households. In addition, 9 households in Rahatwade and 13 in Nandur had an ambiguous status and further data were required to situate them in either of the groups. These households were put in the non-labouring group of households at this stage of analysis (they are marked as 'Non-labouring households (unclear)' in Table 2.7).

Table 2.7   The two-cluster classification of households

Household groups	Rahatwade (N = 250)		Nandur (N = 240)	
	Frequency	Per cent	Frequency	Per cent
Manual labouring households	131	52.4	121	50.4
Non-labouring households	110	44	106	44.2
Non-labouring households (unclear)	9	3.6	13	5.4
Total	250	100	240	100

Source: Fieldwork data (2015).

Once the manual labouring households were identified and eliminated, the next step was to select an appropriate sample from the remaining households which would be the subject of further examination. A sample of 194 households was selected from the villages for the main data collection exercise. The sample households included 97 households in Rahatwade (88 households out of 110 non-labouring households and all 9 ambiguous households). In Nandur, a total of 97 households were selected as sample households (87 out of the 106 non-labouring households and 10 out of the 13 ambiguous households).[19]

It is notable that the Bourdieuan analysis (Chapter 5) adopted a fundamentally different household sampling method, and relied on the self-ascription of the population who participated in the second round of the survey. This methodological approach of relying on self-identification of middle-class status was influenced by numerous limitations in identifying and understanding cultural markers of class, such as being an outsider and not speaking the local language. Furthermore, this approach also allowed examination of subjective or self-constructed middle class identity. To sum up, the adaptation of this multistage selection of households prevented the inappropriate selection of a sample population (which would have developed from my own subjective observation), and allowed the multi-dimensionality of middle-class characteristics to be examined. To end this section, it is worth underlining the fundamental importance of an operational research method that not only can grasp the various sets of classificatory practices that create middle-class boundaries through each theory but also enables its heterogeneity to be explored empirically.

62   Contested Capital

This chapter has hopefully enabled us to imagine a typical village in present-day India, not only in terms of physical structure, economic and social characteristics, or agricultural patterns, but also in ways in which these villages are changing, and their economy is being integrated into practices of industrialisation, and the implications for their social and cultural fabric. Such depiction is a necessary background for painting a picture of middle-class formation in contemporary Indian villages. Having such detailed information of the internal characteristics of these villages also helps us establish the questions which will guide the subsequent analysis in the remainder of the book: How many classes are there in rural India? What was the extent of economic capability, and social and cultural capital of those rural inhabitants who managed to gain access to the middle-class labour market? Why have some households experienced class mobility while some have remained behind? We look at these questions in the subsequent chapters.

Notes

1. Except for two interviews that were conducted in English, all interviews were conducted in Marathi with the help of my research assistant, who provided me with a brief outline of what was said by the respondents during the interview, confirming my own elementary understanding. The interviews were recorded on a Dictaphone before being translated and transcribed. My research assistant was specifically instructed to undertake a word-by-word translation of the interviews, allowing me to keep as close to the original meaning as possible. Almost all respondents did not have any objection to have their original names – while some encouraged me to use their original name. however, to protect their identity, names have been slightly modified, some have been replaced by pseudonym, and their surnames are not used.

2. I do not propose to give a lengthy or exhaustive account of the political economy of Maharashtra. I refer readers to the autobiography of Sharad Pawar (2015) and Kulakarni (2008), which have fairly comprehensive coverage on society and culture in Maharashtra. For the history of the Marathas, see Chaurasia (2004) and Deshpande (2009).

3. Maharashtra is the second most populated state in India. There are in total 43,665 villages in Maharashtra, out of which 40,960 are inhabited. According to 2011 population census, Pune district has 14 *tehsils*, 35 towns and 1,877 villages (including 25 uninhabited villages).

4. The anecdotal evidence from Rahatwade (where the majority of population belongs to the Maratha caste) suggests many Kunbis seek to be identified as 'Maratha-Kunbi', in order to gain the OBCs certificate, which would facilitate access to government reservations in education and government employment. However, the ways in which such identification and claims of belonging to

In Search of the Rural Middle Classes 63

Kunbi caste takes place was outside the focus of my research, and therefore, is not addressed here. This book does not make any distinction between the two castes of Maratha and Maratha-Kunbi.

5. For example, Kunnath's choice of field-site for examining the Maoist mobilisation of Dalits and Adivasis in Bihar was predetermined by the place where Maoist movement is mostly concentrated. See Kunnath (2012).

6. For extensive discussion on selection of sample sites, see Devereux and Hoddinott (1993).

7. For an extensive discussion on village typology, see Harriss-White and Janakarajan (2004).

8. The 2011 population census data, although limited in scope, provides basic information on all villages in India, including population size, total number of households, literacy rate, caste composition, data on employment rates and patterns of livelihood.

9. The difference between the village population in the 2011 census and my own enumeration of village population in 2015 might be due to migrations – some people have migrated in and out of the village since the time of 2011 census data collection. Furthermore, the members of Gram Panchayat office of Rahatwade informed me that some people keep the village as their main residence formally; while in reality, they have migrated out. Indeed enumerating the households in the sample villages was one of the very early challenges of fieldwork. To overcome these challenges, the Gram Panchayat list of households was used which contained the names of the households' head and the size of the households. The information provided by the Gram Panchayat list was then crosschecked with respondents. Since the time of 2011 census data collections some households in Rahatwade had migrated out of the village, while Nandur had experienced inward migrations. Due to continuous migration and mobility of labour in India, this book is concerned with people whose residence is in the village, who work and live in the village and those who travel to nearby town/cities to work but keep the village as their main residence. Moreover, this research encompasses residents that are not native from these villages but have migrated to these villages (this is not seasonal migration – but is more with the intention with permanent effects).

10. This is not to say the households that primarily depend on agriculture have no other sources of income. Due to the diversity of sources of income and for avoiding misidentification of the primary source of household income, the following steps were taken: (*a*) income from all sources was estimated separately and for each family member. The income sources included agriculture (based on the agricultural year 2014–15); livestock produce; agricultural wage labour; long-term labour in agriculture and allied activities; non-agricultural casual employment; salaried employment in private sectors; salaried employment in the public sector and government employment; business and trade activities; brokerage; remittances; pensions; rent; interest; artisanal work and other sources;

64   Contested Capital

and (*b*) the occupation that earned the highest proportion of household income was identified as its primary source.

11. There are a number of public toilets in the Rahatwade, which did not appear to be used by residents.

12. Hamlet or *basti* refers to a cluster of houses that are located next to each other. There are no available maps of Rahatwade with clear village boundary – the drawn map, however, illustrate the hamlets and the main landmarks – the white areas in the map of Rahatwade are primarily covered with rice fields. All maps are drawn on a basic Google Maps with Free-hand Software, all information included on the maps are from fieldwork data.

13. According to the company's website, Fleetguard Filters Private Limited was established in 1987, and is one of the manufacturers of filters for 'heavy duty Air, Fuel, Lube and Hydraulic filters, Air Intake Systems, Coolants and Chemical Products for On and Off highway applications' (source: http://fleetguard-filtrum.com/home.html); Fleetguard Filters is also the main provider of industrial employment in Nandur.

14. See Appendices A8 and A9 for the first and second rounds of household survey questionnaire.

15. Many households both hire in and hire out labour. In this analysis, if the main source of household income is from selling labour power then they are considered as labouring households.

16. Similarly, Lerche, in classifying rural households based on occupations, situates the marginal farmers in the labouring class. Lerche argues that most marginal farmers receive some of their income from their holdings; however, more than half their income is generated from wage work and therefore they are best characterised as 'de facto wage workers'. See Lerche (2010).

17. Beside hiring in and hiring out labours, many households in Rahatwade and Nandur use family labour, and are also engaged in exchange labour (which takes place without payment of wages). A further analysis of the manual labouring group of households requires a large amount of information on both family labours, labour hired in, and labour hired out.

18. Data from Rahatwade and Nandur are not merged, because these villages, as indicated earlier in this chapter, have a different socio-economic characteristics, cropping patterns and caste compositions. Furthermore, a separate analysis of each village would allow a comparison between the results of the two village analyses.

19. However, subjective self-assessments of individuals within these eliminated households should not be ignored. For this reason, the first survey included the question 'is your household a middle-class household and if so, why?' This enabled examination of the self-perception in relation to middle-classness, even if the household was not objectively defined as a middle class (this will be addressed in full in Chapter 5).

3

Marx
Capital, Labour and the Rural Middle Classes

> The arrival of factories in our village has provided us with many different sources of income. The standard of living of the village population has progressed. Some in the village have started their own business, handling trucks, cranes rentals and transport. Some people have invested in buying and then hiring JCB tractors, and most importantly, many now have industrial jobs. There are many other sources of income too. We still have our farming activities, but working in farms has become less popular because of these factories: with our income from factory employment we are now able to hire labourers to take care of our agriculture. Working in industries and entrepreneurial activities are the new trends now. The average income of factory workers is 20,000 rupees to 25,000 rupees per month [2015]; hence there is no hurdle in the way of developing our standard of living and providing proper education for our children.
>
> —Ramchandra Gh., personal interview (2016)

The statement above by Mr Ramchandra, the former *sarpanch* of Nandur, who described himself as a 'farmer', a 'businessman' and a 'politician', provides anecdotal evidence of the diversified modes of generating livelihoods in rural India. In Rahatwade and Nandur, as in many parts of India, the processes of industrialisation have created new forms of economic diversification and significant class differentiations. This chapter is an attempt to examine the relations of production in the current phase of rural industrialisation, and to locate the middle class. Is rural India a capitalist economy, and if so, how many classes does it contain? These are important questions to have in mind when we talk about class formation in a Marxian tradition, but not very straightforward to answer. As we shall see, an overwhelming proportion of the rural population is still involved in some type of self-employment. However, despite the persistence of petty commodity production, there is a relatively high degree of capital accumulation, when the purpose of production is not solely the satisfaction of needs but the generation of profit, extracted from the labour power of others. In what follows, I first examine the dynamics of rural economic transformation over the past three decades, and then provide a classification of means of accumulation that exist in rural India. The analysis of fieldwork data demonstrates that growing industrialisation in close proximity to these villages has begun to create new modes of accumulation and the emergence of new classes that did not previously exist in rural India. To unpack the current rural economic class structure, I develop a composite analytical instrument that uses labour relations, ownership of the means of productions and modes of reinvestment of surplus. The result is the identification of seven distinct economic classes: (*a*) the *landowning capitalist class*; (*b*) the *new capitalist class*; (*c*) *farm-owning skilled workers*; (*d*) *petty commodity producers (PCPs)*; (*e*) the *farm-owning industrial working class*; and two classes of labour, including (*f*) the *land-owning labouring class* and (*g*) the *landless labouring class*. My primary focus is the examination of diverse dynamics of accumulation in two classes in the middle (classes *c* and *d*). Of particular interest is the class of *farm-owning skilled workers* (which I term the *straddling middle class*), whose non-farm activities are explicitly linked to agriculture. They are conceptualised as middle class because their class position shares selective affinities with both the capitalist and the industrial working classes – yet they cannot be placed in either. Although its members are engaged in skilled employment as supervisors and foremen, they use the income generated from these non-farm activities to expand their farm production and accumulate a surplus in agriculture by hiring labour power and investing in agricultural expansion. Their income generated from skilled work, combined with the availability of cheap agricultural migrant labour, has facilitated diversified forms of accumulation. These class-ambiguous transformations in relations of production are not specific to Rahatwade and Nandur. Although the classifications in this chapter are provided to elucidate socio-economic transformation in these villages, they are also offered as a general framework or analytical device that can be applied to other contexts in rural India.

The chapter is structured as follows: the first section familiarises readers with the ways in which Marx conceptualised the terms 'class' and 'middle class', and how his legatees have dealt with the question of the middle class. The second part provides an overview of the literature on rural class formation following the Green Revolution and, most significantly, after the introduction of economic liberalisation policies. This section also relies on three rounds of macroeconomic surveys: HDPI (1993–94), IHDS-I (2004–05) and IHDS-II (2011–12) to scan the transformation in sources of livelihood over the last 30 years throughout rural India. The final part of the chapter offers an empirical analysis of rural class structure (classes-in-themselves), drawing on two rounds of quantitative household survey data. The quantitative findings are augmented by qualitative interviews relating to economic transformation at the household level over the last 30 years, and the impact of industrialisation on the village economy from the perspective of rural residents.

Karl Marx and Classes

As with other nineteenth-century social thinkers, Marx was concerned with the origins of capitalism and the profound changes sweeping through nineteenth-century Europe and attempted to make sense of the new world that was emerging. In 1847, together with Engels, he was commissioned by the Communist League to write its manifesto, a call to action setting out the conditions for the overthrow of capitalist society. They described their era as the 'epoch of the bourgeoisie', a society becoming increasingly divided into 'two great hostile camps, into two great classes directly facing each other – Bourgeoisie and Proletariat' (Marx and Engels, 2008 [1848]: 34). Marx conceptualised economic organisation as the driving force of history. The economic organisation of society changes in response to technological developments, moving from co-operative or communal living to slave-owning societies, to medieval feudalism dominated by aristocratic landowners and peasants, and finally to the industrial revolution and the birth of factory capitalism. There had always been inequality and class divisions between those who owned property and the means of production and those who did not, but this grew more accentuated under the capitalist system. In 1849, Marx fled to London to escape Prussian spies, and began developing his ideas about the inner workings of industrial capitalism, aiming to expose its true nature and bring about its downfall. His magnum opus, *Das Kapital*, was intended to reveal the economic patterns underpinning the capitalist mode of production, its exploitation of labour, its dynamism and its tendency towards self-destruction.

For Marx, the capitalist mode of production created two core classes – distinguished by relations of production and the exploitation of labour: the owners of the means of production (the *bourgeoisie*, also the exploiters of labour) and the workers (the *proletariat*), defined as 'the class of modern wage labourers who, having no means of production of their own, ... were reduced to selling their labour power in order to live' (Marx and Engels, 2008 [1848]: 33).[1] Marx endeavoured (unsuccessfully) to define the term 'class' on the last page of the incomplete Volume III of *Das Kapital*. He attempted to answer the question

68   Contested Capital

'what constitutes a class?', and before abandoning the task, he began defining the term 'class' as a group of individuals whose sources of revenue were identical (Marx, 1959: 610). On the basis of this definition, he defined three classes in every modern capitalist society: 'wage-labourers' (the owners merely of 'labour–power'); 'capitalists' ('owners of capital'); and 'land-owners' ('receivers of profit and ground-rent'). The sources of income were respectively wages, profits and ground-rents. On the same page of Volume III, a few lines before the manuscript abruptly ended, Marx introduced two additional classes: 'physicians' and 'officials': they constituted two distinct social classes because their respective members received their revenue from sources other than productive capital and manual labour – in each case different (Marx, 1959: 610). However, he did not specify the source of their revenue, nor did he explain why they occupied distinct class locations. It can be suggested that although both professions were in services and unproductive (in Marx's view) in the production process, they were identified as separate classes because the source of income of 'physicians' was private, whereas the 'officials' earned their income from the state.

It is worth noting that, throughout his writing, Marx did not situate occupations such as doctor, lawyer, priest, official or other professions in services in either of the core classes. For Marx, such occupations were unproductive in the production process but necessary for the reproduction of the capitalist system. This brings us to a longstanding criticism of Marx, which relates to his limited class categorisation and his incomplete analytical framework for dealing with the complexity and diversity of class relations in advanced capitalist societies. In particular, the existence of the middle classes has been termed the 'greatest challenge to the political economy of class' in the Marxist tradition (Fine and Saad-Filho, 2004: 169). Empirical evidence of a large middle class in contemporary advanced capitalist societies, where class structures look anything but polarised, has been the primary criticism of Marx and Marxist scholars (Wright, 1989: 3).

I personally find this criticism invalid. Marx did in fact address, although in a scattered and fragmentary manner, the trajectory of the middle class and its historical transformation. He noted that in every civilised society there was a small class of 'petty bourgeoisie', self-employed individuals who owned small-sized productive properties using their own and family labour, unable to survive the competition brought about by the development of modern industry. Marx argued that the middle class, which consists of peasants, small artisans, small traders, shopkeepers and those whose professions were based on honour such as 'the physician, the lawyer, the priest, the poet, the man of science', would not be able to survive the capitalist mode of production as independent economic actors (Marx and Engels, 1969 [1848]: 16). The process of industrialisation resulted in

Marx   69

all forms of labour being performed in factories, destroying the old middle class entirely and transforming the condition of the workers. This led to the creation of two new classes: the big capitalists, or the bourgeoisie, and the proletariat. Marx and Engels stated:

> The lower strata of the middle class – the small tradespeople, shopkeepers, and retired tradesmen generally, the handicraftsmen and peasants – all these sink gradually into the proletariat, partly because their diminutive capital does not suffice for the scale on which Modern Industry is carried on, and is swamped in the competition with the large capitalists, partly because their specialised skill is rendered worthless by new methods of production. Thus the proletariat is recruited from all classes of the population. (Marx and Engels, 2008 [1848]: 44–45)

They continued:

> Thereupon, steam and machinery revolutionised industrial production. The place of manufacture was taken by the giant, modern Industry; the place of the industrial middle class by industrial millionaires, the leaders of the whole industrial armies, the modern bourgeoisie. (Marx and Engels, 2008 [1848]: 35)

Marx offered a more analytical account of the middle class in the first volume of *Das Kapital*, and classified it not in any of the core classes, but as a class which fell between the two. The middle class was described as excluded from control over physical capital within the production process because its members lack the investment necessary to accumulate surplus value. They neither create value nor are they forced to sell manual labour to survive (Marx, 1996 [1887]). They generate their revenue from the services they provide (rather than from physical labour or productive capital) and from the same source (which is neither economic capital nor labour power). Although it is not explicitly mentioned, it can be inferred that their source of revenue is from the skills and education that are particular to their class, or from the ownership of small capital, which is enough to generate their needs but not enough to generate surplus value.

A similar definition is provided in the second volume of *Das Kapital*, where middle classes were described as income earners as opposed to wage earners (Marx, 1978: 50). Marx distinguished between wages and income: the latter is generated from non-manual labour, while the former is generated from manual labour. A similar definition was provided in the first and second volumes of *Das Kapital* for the intelligentsia (which can be interpreted as part of the middle class, because they are not situated in either of the core classes). Marx referred to

70   Contested Capital

government officials, priests, lawyers, soldiers, professors, journalist, writers and doctors as 'the ideological representatives and spokesmen' of the capitalist (Marx, 1969 [1850]: 15), in other words a class working in the interests of the capitalist class (Marx, 1996 [1887]: 297). Marx termed them as such because their role, although unproductive in relation to the process of production, was necessary for capitalism to function (Ollman, 1979: 36). Similarly, in his manuscript on a critical examination of the history of political economy, *Theories of Surplus-Value*, he made references to the role of the middle class in the continuation of capitalism through consumption. For example, in his critique of Ricardo's views on the impact of machinery on the interests of the capitalist and the labouring classes, Marx emphasised the expansion of the middle class:[2]

> What he [Ricardo] forgets to emphasis is the constantly growing number of the middle classes, those who stand between the workman on the one hand and the capitalist and landlord on the other. The middle classes maintain themselves to an ever increasing extent directly out of revenue, they are a burden weighing heavily on the working base and increase the social security and power of the upper ten thousand [the capitalists]. (Marx, 1978 [1861–63]: 746–47)

It is worth noting that Marx's critique of Ricardo for ignoring the growth of the middle class contradicted his earlier account in the *Manifesto*, where he portrayed them as a class that would wane with the development of capitalist system. Despite such contradictions, however, throughout his extensive writings on class, Marx acknowledged the existence of the middle class as unproductive in the production process, whose role was necessary for the reproduction of capitalism (through the services they provided, which would facilitate the functioning of capitalism, and through their consumption needs which perpetuated capitalist production). However, it is still unclear even within this broad depiction how the middle class can be delineated analytically. This question takes us back to Marx's famous page on class, where he conceded that

> the stratification of classes does not appear in its pure form. Middle and intermediate strata even here obliterate lines of demarcation everywhere (although incomparably less in rural districts, than in the cities). (Marx, 1959: 610)

This overview of Marx's conceptualisation of the middle class is necessarily brief, but useful for the examination of what constitutes the middle class within the relations of production in Indian villages. For our purposes, I suggest that Marx broadly deployed two concepts of 'middle class': (*a*) self-employed artisans and PCPs, whom Marx postulated would be transformed into the working class, and (b) the unproductive forces that fall between the two core classes, who generate their revenue from non-manual work, and are necessary for the continuation of capitalism through their services and their consumption needs. I utilise both these concepts in my empirical examination of India's rural middle class. With that in mind, it would be useful to review the ways in which neo-Marxist scholars have conceptualised this class in contemporary societies.

Neo-Marxists and the Problem of the Middle Class

The problem of conceptualising the middle class is sometimes termed the 'embarrassment' of the middle class, and many Marxist scholars have taken up the challenge (Wright, 1985: 19).[3] However, there is considerable disagreement among them about what occupations fall into the middle class category. Wright has identified four broad approaches taken by neo-Marxist scholars to address this conceptual problem (Wright, 1980, 1989). I will outline a summary of these approaches now.

The first and simplest strategy is termed the *simple polarisation* of class structure, and involves placing all the middle classes in the working class category, except for a very small number of top executives and managers, who also own some capital in forms of stocks and are therefore considered to be part of the bourgeoisie. This is because managers, professionals and white-collar employees earn wages from their employer, while top executives own capital in the form of stock. The *simple polarisation* argument relies primarily on the distinction between productive and unproductive labour and the owners and non-owners of capital. Productive labour refers to labour that produce surplus value. The unproductive labour force, including skilled managers and executives, refers to those whose manual labour is not reduced to a commodity form – whose living is supported from the surplus value created, and by assisting the bourgeoisie in appropriating the labour surplus. Within this approach, there are three classes in every capitalist society: the working class; a small class of petty bourgeoisie (owners of small capital who are small self-employed producers); and the capitalist class (Wright, 1980: 327). This approach considers the middle class as an 'ideological illusion' rather than a distinct class, and deals with the problem of the middle class by denying its existence (Wright, 1989: 3).

The second approach to the problem is to view the salary-earning middle class as a *segment* of other classes: a 'new petty bourgeoisie', a segment of the petty bourgeoisie, or a 'new working class'.[4] This approach retains the basic class structure of capitalist societies, while introducing significant internal differentiation within classes. The main proponent of this approach is Poulantzas, who uses the term *new Petty Bourgeoisie* to describe the middle class (Poulantzas, 1975). However, the first and second approaches both remain within the production process and are governed by the concept of ownership and non-ownership of the means of production and enforce a polarised structure of classes. They both deny the existence of a group of activities that may *not* be directly productive in the production process, but are necessary for the process of production and reproduction of labour.

The third approach considers the middle class as a new class in its own right.[5] Barbara and John Ehrenreich have forcefully advocated this approach. They suggest that, in the course of capitalist development, a new class emerged that was distinct from the working class, the capitalist class, and the petty bourgeoisie, which they term 'Professional and Managerial Class' (PMC), 'consisting of those salaried mental workers who do not own the means of production and whose major functions in the social division of labour may be described broadly as the reproduction of capitalist culture and capitalist class relations' (Ehrenreich and Ehrenreich, 1977: 13). This means their existence perpetuates capitalist relations (Wright, 1980). In this view, as a class in its own right, the PMC's interests are clearly differentiated from those of both the capitalist and the working classes. At the same time, however, they depend on the capitalist class for their position in the production system, while they share with the working class antagonism against capitalist domination (because, like the working class, the PMC does not own the means of production and depend on the capitalist class for their survival). They are nevertheless at odds with the working class, both because of their objective role in the continuation of capitalism that results in reproducing the subordination of the working class, and because they are unproductive, whereas the working class consists of productive manual labourers. The PMC is thus caught between the capitalist and the working classes in a complex web of conflicting and complementary class interests (Ehrenreich and Ehrenreich, 1977).

The fourth approach which is the most persuasive and also highly applicable to rural India, conceptualises the middle class as occupying 'contradictory locations within class relations'. This approach, mainly advocated by Erik Olin Wright, departs from the traditional conception of Marxist class structure by altering the term class 'location' and the basic premise of definitions of class. First, it expands the basic definition of class location from an exploitation-centred concept of class (where one group acquires economic gains by restricting access to certain kinds of resources or positions, and benefits from the labour of others), and combines it with the concept of domination (ability to control the activity of others) in class analysis. In this combined approach, the exploiting/dominating group has the ability to 'control the labour of another group to its own advantage' (Wright, 2009: 107). In practice, the concept of contradictory locations within class relations rests almost exclusively on relations of domination and exploitation of labour. For example, the class location of managers is defined as contradictory because they are simultaneously dominators in relation to labourers, but also dominated by capitalists (Wright, 1980: 330). Second, the first three approaches are all based on the premise that there is one-to-one mapping between class locations and classes themselves – in other words, individuals can only exist in one class location, or in simple terms can only belong to one class. Wright rejects this simplistic assumption, suggesting that certain positions can be objectively situated 'in more than one class' or 'straddling between classes' (Wright, 1980: 356). Wright's concept of 'contradictory locations within class relations' is based on the assumption that each class location can be situated in different classes within a class structure.[6] For example, *managers* and *supervisors* occupy a contradictory class location between the working class and the capitalist class. They are excluded from control over physical capital within the production process, because they lack the investment with which they can accumulate surplus value, and in contrast to the working class, they have a certain degree of control over means of production and over the labour of workers. The position of managers and supervisors within the production process is nevertheless heterogeneous. The top managers, supervisors and executives occupy a position which is closer to the capitalist class, while the lower level managers occupy a position closer to the working class.

Similarly, *small employers* occupy a contradictory location between the petty bourgeoisie and the capitalist class. This is because, unlike the capitalist class, they are excluded from direct control over the direction of capital accumulation and control over physical capital: they are themselves directly engaged in the process of production alongside labour, but unlike the petty bourgeoisie they employ some labour power and have a degree of control and domination over labour. Another group that occupies a contradictory location are the *semi-autonomous employees* who occupy a contradictory location between the petty bourgeoisie and the working class. Like the petty bourgeoisie, they have some control over physical capital in the production process, and like the working class they are excluded from control over physical capital and from the labour of others. However, they have some control over their activity within the labour process (Wright, 1980: 329–30).

The explanatory potential of the 'contradictory locations within class relations' provides insight for the analysis of a non-polarised class structure, with classes that belong conceptually neither to the capitalist class nor to the working class. This is particularly useful in rural India where the diversity of income sources

74   Contested Capital

can locate a person or a household in more than one class within a class structure. It has the potential to accommodate diversification in sources of income, when revenues are generated from a diverse range of economic activities. Examples from Rahatwade and Nandur are illustrative of such complications.

Let us examine the class position of 'farm-owning skilled industrial workers' and 'industrial labour contractors': the former group, such as floor supervisors and highly skilled machine operators, sell their labour power to industries (to capital), but are also owners of agricultural land, and by hiring in agricultural labourers they generate surpluses in agricultural production. Are these individuals part of the industrial working class or the agrarian capitalist class? The same question arises when we examine the class position of industrial labour contractors, who supply the labour power of others to factory owners – they do not own the means of production but have control over the labour market and generate surplus value from productive labour. Their relationship to capital and their sources of revenue are not identical to those of capitalists, wage-workers or landowners. Where can we situate them within the relations of production? Similarly, what is the class position of small-holder peasants who are occasionally engaged in farm-work outside their smallholdings, for which they are paid wages?[7] Through detailed empirical investigations in Rahatwade and Nandur, these questions will be addressed later in the chapter. Based on these examples, it becomes evident that although Marxist positions share the common feature of looking at class formation in relation to two related criteria, capital ownership and exploitation of labour, the formation of class has particularities of time and space. The social, political and economic conditions of regions create specificities in forms of production and the process of class formation (Raj, 1973; Zhang, 2015). To adjust a broad theoretical perspective to local specificities, therefore, and to identify class positions, scholars of class use different empirical measures and criteria, and diverse analytical strategies. Before sketching the class structure in rural India, it is useful to briefly review the ways in which rural class formation has been studied hitherto, and how class boundaries have been drawn within the relations of production. The scholarship on the agrarian transformation and class formation through production and merchants' capital is extensive. For the purposes of this chapter, I will primarily focus on class formation in the context of rural non-farm activities.

Class Analysis in Rural India: The Context

In various studies of Uttar Pradesh, Craig Jeffrey traces new forms of class formation in rural India back to transformations in the political economy of India in the mid-1960s when the Indian state shifted the focus of development planning from industrial development to improving agricultural production. This reform in agricultural policy involved moving away from policies intended to keep food prices low, and focused instead on creating price incentives for rural food producers – particularly in northwest India – through the establishment of the Agricultural Prices Commission and the Food Corporation of India in 1965. This resulted in an increase in agricultural production, principally the application of High Yielding Varieties of grains, and fertilisers, pesticides and irrigation improvements, and overall the introduction of new technology to agriculture (Jeffrey, 2010a: 38, 2010b: 7). Jeffrey argues that in many parts of India, particularly the north and northwest, rich farmers (who owned the means of production, holding between 4 and 10 hectares of land in the mid-1960s) benefited from agricultural innovation and Green Revolution technology (Jeffrey, 2010a; Patnaik, 1976). They used subsidised agricultural inputs (such as fertilisers, pesticides, water and electricity) and hired agricultural labourers, intensifying their agricultural practices (Jeffrey, 2008: 519; Lerche, 1999).[8] This expanded their agricultural output, and they used their agricultural dominance in the following three decades to diversify out of agriculture and move into small-scale business and white-collar government employment (Harriss-White, 1996).[9]

Similarly, Varma traces the formation of the rural capitalist class to post-independence policies, suggesting that a numerically small but significant segment of middle-class peasants emerged in the decades following independence. The impact of the Tenancy Legislation Act implemented during the Nehru period, along with several other measures of official policy applied in the rural sector, served to promote the interests of richer peasants. These measures included substantial price subsidies for farm produces, subsidies on water, fertiliser and diesel, better access to credit and the near absence of taxation on agricultural income (Varma, 1998). The Zamindari Abolition Act of 1955, which was implemented in parts of northern India, shifted power from a handful of wealthy upper-caste farmers to middle-level cultivators from the intermediate classes (Rudolph and Rudolph, 1987). These middle-level cultivators owned on average 10 acres or more and benefited the most from the Green Revolution technology introduced in the mid-1960s – they were the first to adopt it as their holdings were large enough to secure credit to pay for the inputs of the new technology. 'The bullock capitalists', defined as small to medium-sized self-employed independent agricultural producers, were the principle beneficiaries of the Zamindari Abolitions, and they emerged as distinctive and powerful determinants of state policy in India (Rudolph and Rudolph, 1987: 50). As a result of these favourable conditions in the mid-1960s, including the nationalisation of banks in 1969, which made capital available to farmers for the first time at a concessionary rate, there was an increase in surplus

76   Contested Capital

in agriculture.[10] Consequently, some farmers moved to more lucrative 'off-farm' activities, such as agricultural and non-agricultural trade and finance, brick production, flour production, sugar cooperatives and transport companies. The expansion of non-farm activities such as silk weaving and petty trading, transport and construction work, and employment in the government or service sector is also evidence of non-agricultural diversification (Harriss-White, 2003).

Similarly, Basile explores the nature of Indian non-farm rural capitalism, often referred to as 'provincial capitalism' or 'regional capitalism'. Basile suggests that rural livelihood diversification developed as a central feature of economic life, as households adapted to social and economic transformations (Basile, 2009: 31; Chari, 2004; Mukhopadhyay, 2009). Moving away from agriculture created new patterns of unequal earnings and new forms of employment (Harriss-White, 2010). However, there also existed lucrative diversification within agriculture – notable examples include dairy and poultry farming (Varma, 1998). Basile identifies two primary paths for class formation for the rural capitalist class in the current literature. First, following Baru's study in Maharashtra, Gujarat, Tamil Nadu and Andhra Pradesh, the formation of the rural capitalist class, or what Baru terms 'regional capitalists', linked to changes in agriculture. He suggests that during the 1970s and 1980s, the vast majority of capitalist farmers and landlords shifted to manufacturing and commerce, thus creating an entrepreneurial class with its roots in agrarian capitalism (Baru, 2000: 214). Similarly, Rutten's study of Gujarat shows that capital accumulation in agriculture was the basis for rural industrialisation: the 'rural capitalist class' emerged as a class of capitalist farmers, who unable to increase their landholdings due to the land ceiling, had to invest their surplus in non-agricultural production (Rutten, 1995: 349). To engage in productive investment, therefore, they sought economic diversification. Basile's second path to rural capitalist class formation is identified by Chari in a study of the industrial cluster of Tiruppur in Tamil Nadu. Chari suggests that the key to class formation is in individual behaviour – rural capitalist class formation is a result both of the profitable contribution of agriculture and of 'cultural resources' – rural capitalists are a class of self-made men who have achieved 'class mobility through their "toil"' (Chari, 2000: 579). Perhaps unconvincingly, accumulation through hard work is suggested as the primary resource that transforms agrarian workers into a class of small-scale industrialists (Chari, 2000: 589).[11] It is not, however, always assumed that all non-farm activities are the result of a surplus in agriculture. Two alternative explanations for the growth of diversification out of agriculture have been suggested, which link the non-farm sector to agriculture. First, Mellor argues from Green Revolution history that technological changes in agriculture result in increases in productivity (which also release the labour force), resulting in an increase in income. This increases farmers' demand for labour-intensive, rurally produced, small-scale consumption goods, which have a wider impact on the economy as local firms respond to the increase in demand. This is the 'prosperity induced model', which Mellor himself termed 'growth linkages' from agriculture (Mellor, 1976, 1995, 1998, cited in Basile, 2009: 39). A contrasting explanation has been provided by Saith, who argues that non-farm activities are the result of the inadequate agricultural income of poor peasants (Saith, 1992). Expansion out of agriculture is a survival strategy for the poor, who are unable to break free from the cycle of low productivity–low income in the agricultural sector, and the low income in agriculture forces them into non-farm economic activities (Jayaraj, 2004; Saith, 1992; Unni, 2000).[12] Diversifying out of agriculture is not the result of surplus or success, but a direct result of poverty and underdevelopment. This is termed the 'distress induced' explanation (Saith, 1992). We can combine both of these explanations. As rural differentiation transforms local economies, inequality is reinforced, and a range of differentiated groups engage with the non-farm economy. The poor take up non-farm activities to survive and because there is little alternative; the increasingly wealthy farmers engage in non-farm activities because they accumulate investible surpluses. Evidence from Rahatwade and Nandur is compatible with both the above explanations. In addition, the development of industries on the fringes of these villages has provided opportunities for non-farm activities (ranging from unskilled to skilled which do not demand migration). We will return to this later in the chapter.

In the context of post-1991 economic liberalisation, many studies suggest that such policies had a severe and negative impact on rural development, particularly in relation to agriculture. This was primarily due to the reduction of state intervention and the decline of government investment in rural infrastructure, especially credit and water supply. Agricultural growth has decelerated since the 1990s, and the share of agricultural investment as a percentage of GDP declined from 5 per cent in 1980–81 to 3.7 per cent in 2006–07, dropping further to 3 per cent in 2010–11 (Ahluwalia, 2011; Planning Commission, 2007–12, 2012–17). Despite an increase in agricultural subsidies, there has been an overall fall in public investment (at both the central and the state level) in agriculture and the rural economy (Ahluwalia, 2011).[13] The decline of state support combined with the opening up of the agricultural sector to international competition has also left Indian farmers vulnerable to the volatility of the international market (Cavalcante, 2009).[14] In examining the rural non-farm sector in the post-liberalisation period, Basile suggests that the growth of capitalism in the Indian countryside has resulted in the emergence of industrial activities and services, changing the production

78 Contested Capital

relationship: agriculture 'is no longer the unique centre of economic life in rural India' (Basile, 2009: 38). Many studies have emphasised the expansion of the rural non-farm sector.[15] In many parts of rural India, as in Rahatwade and Nandur, there have been significant and far-reaching transformations in livelihood patterns since liberalisation. The increase in the post-liberalisation rural non-farm economy can be illustrated by assessing the degree of rural non-farm employment. Table 3.1 and Figure 3.1 show the changes in patterns of livelihood in rural India from 1993 to 2011–12. They reveal that since 1993 there has been a significant decline in the proportion of rural households engaged in cultivation as their primary source of income, from 58.99 per cent in 1993 to 34.1 per cent in 2011–12. Moreover, while engagement in cultivation as the main source of income has declined significantly, the percentage of households that are primarily engaged in non-agricultural activities has increased. Such increases are mainly witnessed in non-agricultural wage work. Analysis of the IHDS-II (2011–12) reveals that 39.32 per cent of rural households generated their income primarily from manual labour, 23.84 per cent from non-agricultural wage labour and 15.48 per cent from agricultural wage labour. Table 3.1 further shows a decline in the population of artisans, an increase in the population of shopkeepers and an increase in the population of salaried employees. In Chapter 1, we discovered that the majority of the top two tiers of the rural middle classes are from this latter section. Salaried employment grew from 1993 to 2004–05, but has fallen slightly since 2005.

Table 3.1   Changes in the main source of household income, by sector (1993–2012)

All-India Rural (per cent)	1993–94 N =35,130	2004–05 N = 26,734	2011–12 N = 27,579
Cultivation	58.99	34.4	34.1
Allied agriculture	N.A.	1.18	1.2
Agricultural wage labour	16.98	20.43	15.48
Non-agricultural wage labour	7.99	17.16	23.84
Artisan-Independent	5.21	4.90	1.33
Petty shop	3.17	3.08	6.9
Organised business	0.69	3.45	0.47
Salaried employment	5.08	9.67	9.14
Profession	0.38	0.67	0.38
Pension/Rent	N.A.	2.24	3.88
Others	1.51	2.82	3.28
Total	100	100	100

Source: HDPI (1993–94); IHDS-I (2004–05); IHDS-II (2011–12).

Figure 3.1   Changes in the main source of household income, by sector (1993–2012)

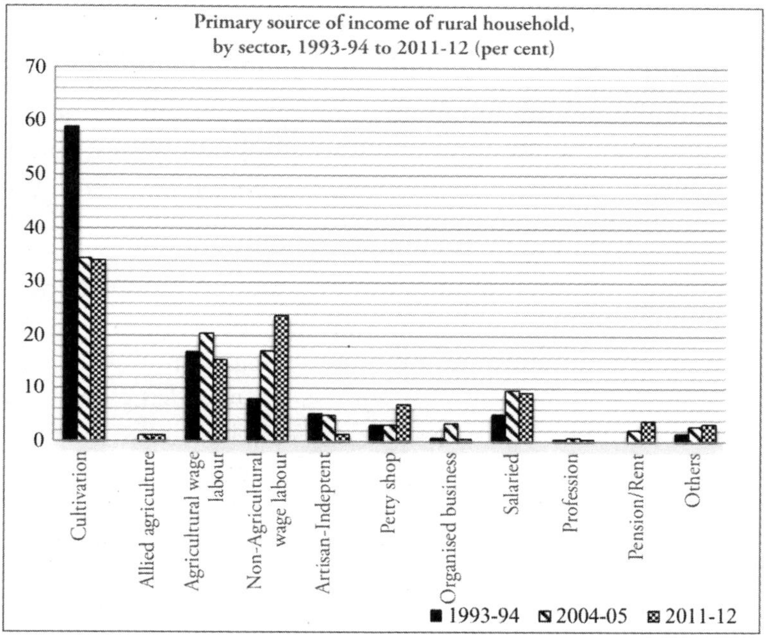

Source: Computed from HDPI (1993–94); IHDS-I (2004–05); IHDS-II (2011–12).

Similar findings have been suggested by Lerche, Shah and Harriss-White (2013) and Pattenden (2016a), although only in relation to the increase in the population of non-agricultural wage labourers. In separate studies, using National Sample Survey (NSS) data, both studies demonstrate that a decline in 'employment in agriculture' has resulted in an increase in the proportion of households whose income is generated from non-agricultural wage labour, to the extent that non-agricultural wage work has become the primary source of income for landless and marginal farmers (Lerche, Shah and Harriss-White, 2013: 342; Pattenden, 2016a: 42). Also, on the basis of NSS data, Pattenden suggests that petty trade, petty production and non-farm employment have not risen fast enough to compensate for the decline in levels of employment in agriculture (Pattenden, 2016a: 42).

Overall, the section above suggests that after the Green Revolution, a set of structural conditions led to the transformation of the rural economy and gave birth to an increase in non-farm activities, which intensified after economic liberalisation in 1991. It is worth noting, however, that not all non-farm activities in Rahatwade and Nandur are the result of either surpluses or deficits in agriculture. As the class analysis in the next section demonstrates, non-farm employment in

80   Contested Capital

the industrial sector has created lucrative sources of income for some households, where the 'earnings from such work are greater than income from agriculture', the work is 'physically less demanding', and 'more prestigious', as narrated by some of my informants. Although rural workforces have increasingly diversified out of agriculture, however, they are still engaged in agricultural production in a myriad of diverse ways including both self-sustaining production and agricultural capitalism (we will return to this later). I will now review the ways in which India's rural classes have been defined within a Marxist perspective, which will guide us towards the examination of economic classes in our sample villages.

Class Categorisation in Rural India

Colatei and Harriss-White have summarised the criteria that have been used to classify agrarian societies. These are primarily based on labour relations, land ownership, income and wealth (Colatei and Harriss-White, 2004: 115–17). One of the primary ways in which rural households have been classified is on the basis of ownership of land as productive capital (Hazell and Ramasamy, 1991; Patnaik, 1976). Patnaik (1976) classifies rural households into three distinct economic classes on the basis of area of land owned: First, landless and near-landless labourers who possess little or no means of production and are primarily or wholly dependent on working for others. Second, landlords, who own sufficient means of production and produce surplus by employing others. The third group consists of those households who possess sufficient means of production to make a living with family labour on their own land. They neither employ the labour of others nor do they sell their labour (Patnaik, 1976). However, classification based on the area of land ownership does not take into consideration the differences in access to irrigation, the degree of land productivity or the value of the land owned (Colatei and Harriss-White, 2004: 115).

Another criterion used to classify agrarian households is the relations of labour in production. Reiterating her earlier classification of households on the basis of land ownership outlined above, Patnaik focuses on the ways in which labour relations result in class differentiation among rural populations (Patnaik, 1976). On the basis of net selling and buying of labour, Patnaik develops a 'labour-exploitation ratio' (E) to examine the 'extent of exploiting or being exploited', taking into account hiring in, hiring out, and the use of family labour. The labour-exploitation ratio (E) is calculated as a ratio of 'net use of outside labour days' to 'family labour days', designed 'as an empirical, and therefore descriptive *approximation* to the analytical concept of economic class' (Patnaik, 1976: A–84).

On the basis of the value of E, Patnaik identifies five distinct economic classes: (*a*) *landlords*, or net buyers of labour power, with a very high labour-exploitation ratio, who do not employ family labour on the farm; (*b*) *rich peasants*, or net buyers of labour power, with a high labour-exploitation ratio, who do employ family labour for major farm activities; (*c*) *middle peasants*, primarily self-employed on their own farms (they might be net exploiters of others' labour, or might be exploited themselves, however marginally, but in both cases, self-employment remains the more important characteristic of Patnaik's middle peasantry); (*d*) *poor peasants*, or net sellers of labour power, either through the direct sale of their labour power or through leasing land and sharecropping – the labour-exploitation ratio of this class is negative, which implies they are being exploited – and (*e*) *full-time labourers*, who do not own or operate any land at all and are entirely dependent on selling their labour power. This class is highly exploited (Patnaik, 1976). Although Patnaik's approach in classifying agrarian households on the basis of labour relations in production is very systematic and highly illustrative of agrarian class differentiations, as noted by Colatei and Harriss-White, classification of households on the basis of labour relations requires a large amount of information and data. This is because many households, in addition to the employment of family labour, are involved in hiring, selling and exchanging labour both in agriculture and outside agriculture (Colatei and Harriss-White, 2004: 116). Furthermore, Patnaik's labour index is formulated on the basis of number of labour days hired in and hired out, and ignores other social relations in the labour market. It is evident from Rahatwade and Nandur that other social relations such as gender and caste interfere in the wages paid to labourers. For example, the average wage for female labour in agriculture is almost half the wage for male labour. Therefore, the labour days index conceals the gendered aspect of exploitation on the labour market. While this weakness is significant and requires further analysis, due to the already complex nature of classification of households, and also because of using the household as the unit of analysis, household dynamics (such as gender) will not be subjected to class analysis in this book.

In a more recent study of classes of labour in rural Karnataka, Pattenden uses labour relations, capital ownership and patterns of reinvestment of surplus to draw a distinction between the 'dominant class', which he suggests is a 'proxy for the capitalist class', and the 'classes of labour' (Pattenden, 2016a: 25).[16] The labour relation is formulated on the basis of net buying and selling of labour power and the ability to produce a surplus. On this basis, Pattenden defines the dominant class as the 'net buyers of labour who tend to produce surplus', including 'those who

82 Contested Capital

produce exclusively through hired labour' and 'those who produce predominantly with hired labour but also work on the land themselves' (Pattenden, 2016a: 25). The classes of labour are defined as 'net sellers of labour power who do not produce a surplus' (Pattenden, 2016a: 25). Pattenden further provides a more detailed classification of households, which allows more internal homogeneity within each class category. He subdivides the dominant class into three sub-categories: 'surplus producers', whose land is cultivated by hired labour, and include households that are more likely to have diversified into non-agricultural forms of accumulation. A second category consists of those households that primarily use hired labour but also use family labour on their own farms; and a third category consists of 'petty capitalists and petty commodity producers' who tend to produce a surplus. Pattenden then introduces an intermediate category, '"pure" petty commodity producers', whose economic activity depends primarily on household labour and 'cannot in itself be seen as capital or labour' (Bernstein, 1977; Pattenden, 2016a: 24–25).[17] This category, 'few in number', includes households that occasionally hire labour but mostly use household labour power for production (Pattenden, 2016a: 24). At the higher level of this class, the producers tend to produce some surplus, which over time can be invested in expanded production. The households at the lower level have to occasionally sell their labour power because their earnings through family labour are insufficient to meet their needs, and are likely to be categorised as a class of labour (Pattenden, 2016a: 25). Pattenden also provides a detailed classification of the labouring class: first, households that primarily earn from their own land but also from wage-labour; second, households that generate more income from wage-labour than they do from their own land; and third, landless households that earn their livelihood only from wage-labour – in both agricultural and non-agricultural activities (Pattenden, 2016a: 23–24).[18]

Categorising Classes in Rahatwade and Nandur

During my first visit to Nandur village in May 2015, as our car drove down a long, narrow *pucca* road branching off the National Highway (NH65) connecting Pune to Solapur, I was struck by the sight of a number of functioning factories on the edge of the sugarcane fields on the outskirts of the village, ranging from automobile manufacturing to food and beverage, dairy and agro-related industries. Nandur was selected as one of the field-sites based on 2011 Census data relating to its population size, literacy rate and caste diversity. The presence of these factories was unexpected. The Census data gave no indication that this remarkable number of factory plants surrounded the village. As we crossed the railway lines and drove through the sugarcane fields, I recall considering the impact these factories would have on farmers and the degree of discontent the factories might have created among village residents. I assumed such extensive levels of industrialisation would create pollution, create competition for limited water resources and generally have a deleterious effect on farming activities. My preconceptions were totally inaccurate and shortlived. Nearly everyone in Nandur perceived the extensive industrial penetration in Nandur as evidence of 'progress' and 'development'. They often spoke of the establishment of the factories as the primary reason behind improvements in their lifestyles, standards of living and incomes. They argued that the industrialisation of the region had a positive overall impact on the village because it provided diversified sources of income, reduced their dependency on income from agriculture and had resulted in an exponential increase in land prices over the last decade. The newly constructed two- and three-storey houses with lavish interiors were material evidence of this newfound prosperity and wealth, in both my perception and that of the village inhabitants. This prosperity, while evident in both villages, was more extensive in Nandur, which is surrounded by more and larger industrial plants just on its border.

The initial impression of these villages contrasted with Marx's historical account of Indian villages as static, unchanging and self-sufficient (Marx, 1853). Marx never visited the subcontinent, and his account of Indian villages was based on colonial reports. He popularised the notion of Indian villages as self-sufficient economic units, described occupations within village society as divisions of labour rather than class positions, which would not change over time, making Indian villages classless societies. However, the decline of the *jajmani* system demonstrates that Marx's idea of Indian villages (if it was ever accurate) was based on assumptions that were not sustained. Although the self-sufficiency of Indian villages was still being debated in the 1960s and 1970s, Indian villages have experienced considerable transformation since the introduction of the Green Revolution in the 1970s, and particularly since the expansion of rural industrialisation after 1991. Political participation (Jaffrelot, 2003), economic diversification, improvements in infrastructure and connections to urban economies are some of the most significant transformations in rural India (Harriss-White, 2015).

Based on evidence gathered during fieldwork, I can say for certain that economic diversification has taken a number of forms in Rahatwade and Nandur, both in relation to the means of generating income and the modes of accumulating surplus. The evidence shows an increasing range of occupations undertaken by family members (both in the agricultural and non-agricultural sectors), and simultaneous participation of family members in multiple economic activities. The

84   Contested Capital

expansion of non-farm activities such as involvement in dairy production, poultry farming, petty trading and petty shop keeping, transport, construction work,[19] employment in various government sectors, and most significantly employment in industrial units (both as skilled employees and unskilled workers), is all evidence of non-farm diversification among rural households.[20] Although livelihood patterns in these villages have undergone major changes, particularly after the arrival of industrial units in the region, capital accumulation and surplus production from non-farm activities are not entirely divorced form agriculture. Fieldwork data suggest that the vast majority of landed households are still engaged in farming, either directly through family labour or indirectly by hiring in agricultural labour. Such a degree of diversification in the sources of livelihood/proliferation of sources of income, combined with a high degree of inequality in the ownership of land (which I will discuss shortly), livestock and other productive assets, has significant implications for class formation.

Land Distribution in Rahatwade and Nandur

In an agricultural economy such as that in Rahatwade and Nandur, where the majority of the population is still involved in cultivation (61.2 per cent of total households in Rahatwade and 45 per cent in Nandur reported agriculture as their primary source of income), agricultural land is the primary identifiable means of production/subsistence, and the highly unequal distribution of land would suggest highly differentiated classes, which are more or less distinct. In Nandur, as will be shown in Figure 3.2, where the land distribution is more unequal than in Rahatwade, class differentiation is more prominent. The 2014–15 distribution of land ownership in each village is presented in Tables 3.2 and 3.3. I have divided the land into two types: irrigated land, which has access to irrigation facilities such as open wells or river water through canals, and is used for cultivation; and dry land, which has no access to irrigation. Total land is the combination of both. The first two columns of Tables 3.2 and 3.3 demonstrate the distribution of irrigated land both in terms of frequency and percentage. The middle two columns demonstrate the distribution of total land. The last two columns show the area of total land that each group owns in real terms and the percentage of the total land surveyed in the village.

In Rahatwade, the average landholding in 2014–15 was 2 acres of irrigated land and 2.6 acres of total land. Twenty households did not own any irrigated land. This included 7 SC households (out of a total of 25 SC households), 11 Maratha households (out of a total of 202 Maratha households), and the only ST and Muslim households in the village. In short, more than half of the households owned less than 2 acres of irrigated land. The top 4 big landowning households, each owning more than 10 acres of total land, owned 9 per cent of the total land surveyed in the village, while the small landholders owning less than 2 acres of total land (141 households, 56.4 per cent of total household) owned together 135 acres or approximately 20 per cent of the total land surveyed in the village. The land distribution was thus highly unequal and the ownership of irrigated land was even more unequal.

Table 3.2 Distribution of land in Rahatwade (2014–15)

Rahatwade (N = 250)	Irrigated land		Total land (Irrigated + Dry)		Distribution of total land	
Area of land (acre)	Freq.	Per cent	Freq.	Per cent	Area (acre)	Per cent of total land
No land	20	8	19	7.6	0	0
Between 0.1 and 1	82	32.8	73	29.2	47.27	7.2
Between 1.1 and 2	59	23.6	51	20.4	88.125	13.5
Between 2.1 and 4	64	25.6	60	24	190.25	29.16
Between 4.1 and 6	19	7.8	29	11.6	152.25	23.3
Between 6.1 and 10	5	2	14	5.6	115.5	17.7
More than 10	1	0.4	4	1.6	59	9
Total	250	100	250	100	652.395	100

Source: Fieldwork data (2015).

Table 3.3 Distribution of land in Nandur (2014–15)

Nandur (N = 240)	Irrigated land		Total land (Irrigated + Dry)		Distribution of total land	
Area of land (acre)	Freq.	Per cent	Freq.	Per cent	Area (acre)	Per cent of total land
No land	80	33.33	75	31.25	0	0
Between 0.1 and 1	34	14.17	32	13.34	25.25	3.5
Between 1.1 and 2	43	17.92	45	18.75	81.75	11.5
Between 2.1 and 4	42	17.92	38	15.84	121	17
Between 4.1 and 6	21	8.75	22	9.16	115	16.2
Between 6.1 and 10	16	6.25	18	7.51	150.5	21.1
More than 10	4	1.67	10	4.16	218	30.6
Total	240	100	240	100	711.5	100

Source: Fieldwork data (2015).

In Nandur, the average landholding in 2014–15 was 2.4 acres of irrigated land and 2.9 acres of total land. However, 75 households (31.25 per cent of total households) did not own any land at all, while 80 households (33.33 per cent) owned no irrigated land. The majority of landless households were SCs and STs. The entire ST population and 80 per cent of SC households were landless. Among the landowning households, 77 households (32.09 per cent) owned less than 2 acres of total land. These 77 households together owned 18.2 per cent of the total land surveyed in the village, while the top 4 big landowning households (those owning holdings of more than 10 acres) owned almost 31 per cent of the total land surveyed in the village.

Figure 3.2 shows the highly unequal nature of land distribution in both villages and the high concentration of land among the few big landowning households, while the majority had access to a disproportionately low share of land. Such an unequal distribution of land implies that Rahatwade and Nandur are highly differentiated economically, but the very complex and multidirectional sources of income both in agriculture and in non-farm economic activities render the classification of rural households based exclusively on land ownership inappropriate. This is because such a classification omits non-agricultural forms of income (Razavi, 1992).[21] To draw a more accurate class structure within the relations of production, one must take into account modes of appropriation of labour.

Figure 3.2 Distribution of land in Rahatwade and Nandur (in acre)

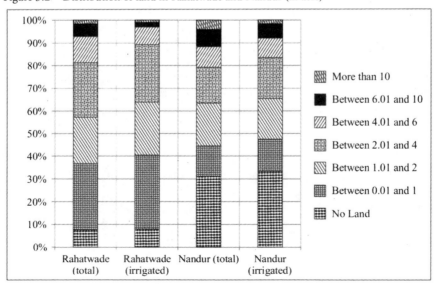

Source: Fieldwork data (2015).

Labour Relations: Formulating the Labour Index

One of the criteria for assessing the extent of the exploitation of labour is the type and the extent of hiring-in outside labour. According to Patnaik, there are two ways for cultivators to use outside labour: *direct* appropriation of labour through the hiring of others' labour, and *indirect* appropriation of others' labour through leasing out land and receiving rent (Patnaik, 1976: A–84). In Rahatwade and Nandur, the use of outside labour is limited to the direct hiring of labour power, as there are no sharecropping arrangements and the renting of agricultural land is almost non-existent (except in a very small number of cases, but these households were identified as labouring households in the sampling stratification). To calculate the net hired labour days, we therefore have two components:

- Agricultural Labour Days Hired-in (ALDH) = total number of labour days hired-in for agricultural production in one year
- Agricultural Labour Days Sold-out (ALDS) = total number of labour days sold for agricultural production in one year

$$NALD = ALDH - ALDS$$

If Net Agricultural Labour Days (NALD), net labour days hired-in agricultural production in one year, is negative and high in terms of absolute value (significantly smaller than zero), then we are dealing with a class of agricultural labourers. This includes landless and near-landless households that depend on selling their manual labour power for agricultural production to meet their livelihood needs. On the contrary, if NALD is positive and high, we are faced with a class of buyers of agricultural labour power (agricultural capitalists). Using only NALD to examine the degree of exploitation of labour in the classification of agrarian households is limited in two significant ways. First, formulating the labour index requires the challenging task of calculating the net number of labour days in non-agricultural activities, usually ad hoc and casual work, as well as in agriculture. This line of inquiry proved particularly challanging during fieldwork, but this limitation does not have a deleterious impact on the analysis of non-labouring classes. As indicated in Chapter 2, households that generated their primary source of income from manual labour in both agricultural and non-agricultural activities were classified as labouring households and eliminated from the potential middle classes. This included agricultural labourers and *helpers* in the industrial sector and other ad hoc manual labourers. Excluding the total labour days hired out for non-agricultural production does not carry any implication, but to examine the

88   Contested Capital

extent of diversification in favour of non-farm production, and whether or not there is appropriation of labour in non-farm production, we take the total labour days hired-in per annum for work in non-agricultural sectors into consideration in addition to the NALD.

Second, it must be acknowledged that using the number of labour days as a measure ignores other social relations of production, most significantly gender. Evidence from fieldwork suggests that 'family engagement in agriculture' is predominantly 'female family engagement in agriculture'. Similarly, the agricultural labour force consists primarily of female labourers. While men usually undertake work in non-farm sectors, women are engaged in family labour, exchange of labour or selling their labour power in agriculture. This is not, however, the same for every household. Among the wealthier classes, women do not usually participate in any agricultural work and agricultural land is entirely operated by hired-in labour. Moreover, the wage of the female labour force varies from between one-third to half the wage of the male labour force for the same task. However, since the household is selected as the unit of analysis, such gendered aspects of labour relations will not have any impact on the construction of a labour index. In short, to classify households by the relations of production, four main criteria are identified: (*a*) the extent of ownership of land and other production units; (*b*) the extent of exploitation of labour, using a net labour index (NALD) in agriculture and the extent of the hiring-in of non-agricultural labour power (the total labour days hired in for work in non-agricultural production); (*c*) whether a household has sold any labour in farm production; and (*d*) the extent of surplus production and modes of accumulation. Other criteria, such as the use of family labour, will be taken into consideration as supplementary factors later in the analysis.[22]

Class Categories, Composition and Characteristics

On the basis of the fieldwork data and the analytical instruments introduced above, seven economic classes were identified. Table 3.4 shows the characteristic of each class in terms of ownership of capital, extent of exploitation of labour, production of surplus and deficit, and the modes of accumulation and investment of surplus.[23] This is followed by a detailed description of each class to enable a better understanding of socio-economic differentiation in these villages, in the context of which the rural middle classes are examined.

Marx 89

Table 3.4 Class structure in villages (capital, labour, surplus and accumulation)

Classes	Capital ownership	Labour relations	Surplus production	Investment and accumulations
Landowning capitalist class Big land owners	Control over physical capital Control over labour power	No selling of labour power Their land is cultivated by hired-in labour Hiring-in of labour outside agriculture No family or exchange labour NALD > 0	Surplus producers by appropriating labour force and controlling capital	Reinvestment in diversified means of production (both in agricultural and non-agricultural sectors) Investment in expensive education for children Purchase of consumer goods
New capitalist class Labour contractors Product contractors Business owners	Surplus producers (control over labour) but minimal capital ownership compared to the first class Medium-sized landholdings	No selling of labour power The land is cultivated by hired in labour No family labour or exchange labour NALD > 0	Accumulation of surplus by appropriating labour force (control over the labour market and wages) Diversified modes of accumulation and surplus production	Reinvestment in non-farm activities such as land rental, non-farm business and units of production Diversified modes of non-farm accumulation (small-size production) Investment in expensive education Purchase of consumer goods
The straddling middle class: Farm-owning skilled workers Industrial skilled workers; supervisors, managers, foremen Government employees	Surplus producers Medium-sized landholders	No selling of labour power No family labour in agriculture (minimal female family labour) The land is cultivated primarily by hired-in labour NALD > 0	Employment in non-farm sectors Surplus producers by appropriating labour force in agricultural production and control over capital in the agricultural sector	Diversified modes of non-farm accumulation (real state, rent, and so on) Reinvestment in education Reinvestment in cars and other consumer durables
Petty commodity producers (PCPs) Petty shopkeepers Farmers	Either small surplus producers or no surplus but no deficit	Land is cultivated by family labour and exchange labour Seasonal hired-in labour Seasonal hired-out labour NALD (mean) = 0	Diversified modes of accumulation in non-farm activities (small-scale production) Use of family labour in non-farm activities	Reinvestment in education Investment in livestock and agricultural improvement

Contd.

90 Contested Capital

Contd.

Classes	Capital ownership	Labour relations	Surplus production	Investment and accumulations
Farm-owning industrial working class	No surplus, no deficit	Produce with family labour and exchange labour Seasonal hired-in and hired-out labour NALD (mean) = 0	Semi-skilled and casual employment in non-farm sectors	None
Landowning labouring class	Deficit producers	Marginal farmers who sell their labour-power more than they work on their own land NALD < 0	Sell labour-power in various sectors	None
Landless labouring class	Deficit	Landless who only sell their labour-power NALD < 0	Sell labour-power in agriculture (seasonal) Sell labour-power in the non-farm sector (casual)	None

Source: Author.

As noted in Chapter 2, 97 non-labouring households in each village were selected as a sample population for a detailed household socio-economic survey. However, analysis of these households based on the criteria outlined above revealed that 6 households in Rahatwade and 17 households in Nandur (identified as non-labouring households in the first round of stratification) were best situated in the two classes of labour. This is because they showed similar characteristics to the classes of labour. They were therefore transferred to the labouring classes for the purposes of the analysis. Tables 3.5 and 3.6 show the distribution of each class among the sample households. The second column in Tables 3.5 and 3.6 shows the number of households in each class. The third column presents the percentage of each class among the non-labouring households, while the last column shows the percentage distribution of each class in the village (the number of households in the sample and the total population have been taken into consideration in the calculation of percentage distributions of each class in the village as a whole).

Table 3.5 Classification of households in Rahatwade

Frequency	Rahatwade N = 97	Per cent of non-labouring households	Per cent of total village
Landowning capitalist class	4	4.4	1.99
New capitalist class	6	6.6	2.98
Farm-owning skilled workers (the straddling middle class)	19	20.9	9.4
PCPs	45	49.4	22.3
Farm-owning industrial working class	17	18.7	8.4
Moved to classes of labour	6	N.A.	N.A.
Classes of labour (137 households in total)	131	N.A.	54.8

Source: Fieldwork data (2015).

Table 3.6 Classification of households in Nandur

Frequency	Nandur N = 97	Per cent of the non-labouring households	Per cent of total village
Landowning capitalist class	9	11.25	4.78
New capitalist class	9	11.25	4.78
Farm-owning skilled workers (the straddling middle class)	19	23.75	10.1
PCPs	34	42.5	18.06
Farm-owning industrial working class	9	11.25	4.78
Moved to classes of labour	17	N.A.	N.A.
Classes of labour (138 households in total)	121	N.A.	57.5

Source: Fieldwork data (2015).

In what follows, we provide a detailed account of the composition and characteristics of each class (see Tables 3.7 and 3.8). Examples and interview extracts are also provided for illustrative purposes. We consider the entire class structure in the two villages, of which the middle classes defined here form a subset.

1. The *landowning capitalist class* contains big landowners whose economic activities consisted mainly of large-scale appropriation of surplus in agriculture. These households were absolute surplus producers, and had very high NALDs. Some in this class had expanded their economic activities into non-agricultural sectors, accumulating surplus in non-agricultural activities such as rents and real estate investments. This class constituted a small population in both villages, wealthy households with large areas of land, high levels of income and high

92 Contested Capital

values of assets and livestock. The households in this class operated more than 10 acres of irrigated land. Four households in Rahatwade and nine in Nandur belonged to this class. On the basis of fieldwork data, shown in Tables 3.7 and 3.8, the average annual household income of this class was INR 620,800 in Nandur and INR 796,000 in Rahatwade in 2014–15. The average value of land owned was INR 91,000,000 in Nandur and INR 82,500,000 in Rahatwade.[24] This class had full access to irrigation throughout the year and was therefore able to operate the land in both *rabi* and *kharif* seasons. Their family members did not perform any manual tasks on their agricultural land and relied entirely on the labour of others. They hired in a large volume of labour all year round. This class was therefore characterised by the accumulation of a large surplus through large-scale appropriation of agricultural labour power, and reinvestment of this agricultural surplus either by developing existing productive assets and expanding their scale of production or by acquiring new forms of productive assets. Its members often tended to adopt diversified modes of accumulation in non-farm activities. These included investment in dairy and poultry farming, workshops, construction, real estate and rental markets in nearby cities, and investment in farm related machinery such as tractor fleets (which could be a source of profit through rental). Accessing data relating to the reinvestment of their surpluses, however, proved very difficult, and the attempt to gather detailed information was unsuccessful. It was clear though that they accumulated surplus in both agricultural and non-agricultural sectors.

In Nandur, the nine households in this class together owned 167 acres or 23.5 per cent of the total land surveyed in the village in 2014–15. They included sugarcane cultivators, who had also diversified out of agriculture, receiving income from other sources such as rent and other agro-business activities such as tractor rental. In Rahatwade, the four households in this class, all Marathas, together owned 57 acres of land, or 9 per cent of the total land surveyed. In Nandur, one household belonged to the Mali, one to the Maratha and seven to the Dhangar caste. They were also heavily indebted, with easy access to credit that came with land collateral.[25]

Vitthal's household is a chief example of this class. Vitthal owned the biggest area of land in Nandur, a total of 50 acres, of which 25 acres were under sugarcane cultivation. This generated him an income of approximately INR 1,000,000 during the agricultural year 2014–15. Having farmed all his land until a decade ago, he was leasing out 25 acres to a factory on a 50-year contract. He told me: 'doing business is trendier than doing farming and is more profitable'.[26] He also had a dairy business, which generated almost INR 120,000 per annum. This relied on their own livestock. Vitthal also owned two houses in the villages, one of which was rented out to a family of migrant workers (at INR 1,500 per month). I asked him why he did not operate the remainder of his land (which was also fully irrigated). 'I can make more and steadier money through renting out the land,' he responded. He hired in 662 agricultural labour days in the agricultural year 2014–15, and one non-agricultural wage labourer throughout the year for livestock and other ad hoc activities. His household did not use family labour in agriculture (except for supervision, which he undertook himself). I asked how he invested his extra income:

> You know, I just invested a huge sum in a *godown* [warehouse] that is currently under construction, which will store raw materials for nearby factories.... I also invest my capital in purchasing lands, and then selling those lands in one or two years. I earn good money in that. I like buying and selling lands. I have also purchased a flat in Uruli Kanchan [a town near Nandur]. I make sure my children receive proper education too.[27]

What differentiated Vitthal and other members of his class from the rest of the village was their successful accumulation of capital, which enabled them to appropriate the surplus value from the labour power of others by systematically hiring in wage labourers, and then investing this surplus in non-agricultural activities. Such diversified accumulation strategies are more prominent in Nandur than in Rahatwade as the water supply is more abundant, and sugarcane harvesting is outsourced to sugar factories, which reduces the requirement for re-investment in agricultural development. There is thus more capital available for reinvestment outside agriculture. In contrast, the land in Rahatwade has little natural irrigation and greater care and financial investment is required to develop agricultural facilities and secure water supplies.

2. The *new capitalist class* constitutes a small population in both villages and is composed of wealthy households (small-scale business owners and industrial labour contractors), characterised by high levels of income and a high value of household assets much above the village average, and positive NALDs. The members of this class do not own the means of production on the same scale as the *landowning capitalist class*, but they accumulate surplus by having control over labour and wages. They usually have medium-sized agricultural landholdings and operate their farms solely by hiring in labour, generating surplus by appropriating this labour power and using it to diversify into non-farm activities such as brokerage, rent, and small-scale workshops and non-agricultural production units

94 Contested Capital

(they usually rent rather than own the production site). These households also hire a small number of non-agricultural labourers in their production units. They are called *new capitalists* because they have become capitalists relatively recently. Although they do not own/ have control over as much capital as the first group, they invest their profits in production and are locked into capitalist accumulation.

Nine households in Nandur and six in Rahatwade were situated in this class. In Rahatwade, five belonged to the Maratha caste and one to the SCs. In Nandur, five households were Malis and four Dhangars. Their average household income for the agricultural year 2014–15 was calculated as INR 1,049,000 in Rahatwade and INR 1,145,800 in Nandur. The average area of irrigated land in this class was 3.7 acres, and the average area of total land owned was 6 acres in Nandur and 4.25 acres in Rahatwade. The family members in this class did not perform any activities in their farm production and their land was cultivated entirely by hired-in labour. As in the case of the first class, this class was also deeply indebted, primarily because of easy access to credit. Their surplus was reinvested in expanding non-agricultural production, purchasing consumer durables (such as cars), and building new residential houses and paying for expensive education for their children. There were some village specificities to this class. In Nandur, in addition to farming, the sources of income for this class were poultry farming, a travel agency, supplying fleets of agricultural machinery such as tractors (generating rent), various workshops (supplying raw materials such as filters and plywood to larger industrial units) and labour contracting. In Rahatwade, this class included an agricultural produce broker, the owner of a goods transport business and a broker of village dairy production.

The local specificities of this class in each of the villages is most clearly demonstrated by the presence of industrial labour contractors in Nandur, who do not exist in Rahatwade. This is due to the presence of industrial factories on the fringes of Nandur. These labour contractors act as gatekeepers to employment in the factories and hold a monopoly over the labour market in the village. They assume sole responsibility (although the process by which they secure their role is far from clear) for recruitment of the labour necessary for the neighbouring factories. They are often told how many workers are needed and the tasks for which they are required. The factory owners pay the wages to the contractors, who take a percentage before paying the workers (the percentage is a closely guarded secret and I was not able to access this information). Although they do not own these factories and are providing services to factory owners, in the process they accumulate a share of the surplus value extracted from the labour force. They invest the surplus in non-farm production activities. Over time, this class of industrial labour contractors are likely to become part of the first class if they generate a large surplus value that can, over time, be invested in purchasing means of production (such as large areas of agricultural land, workshops or other units of production).

The story of Yuvraj and his brother Kishor from Nandur, both in their late 30s and from the Mali caste, is illustrative. Their parents were small-scale sugarcane farmers. These brothers each owned 3 acres of irrigated land, which 'until a few years ago was operated only by family labour, and now, only by hiring in labour', according to Kishor. At the time of fieldwork, Yuvraj's wife was the Deputy (Vice) Sarpanch in Nandur. Yuvraj told me:

> Over the last few years my brother and I have managed to secure contracts from various factories just outside the village, through our connections in the village, to supply them with the necessary labour power. We are responsible for securing factory employment for village residents, with contracts lasting a maximum of six months at a time.[28]

This limited period protected factories from obligations under employment legislation, which required permanent employees (in other words, those employed for a period in excess of six months) to have insurance and other formal rights (this will be discussed in full in Chapter 4).[29] 'We often manage up to 150 labourers on a daily basis. We have also have recently opened a workshop in Nandur to supply raw materials such as plywood to some factories in the region,' Yuvraj told me. He hired four (and sometimes more) workers in his workshop throughout the year. Their class position had changed from medium-sized farmers to new capitalists, or, as Yuvraj described, from 'being poor to being prosperous'. I asked them what had caused such progress: 'It is because of the industrialisation of the region and the increase in the price of land, which is the result of industrialisation,' Yuvraj replied. Following his brother, Kishor stated that the occupations of the people of the village have been transformed since the arrival of industries in Nandur:

> The occupational patterns of village residents have changed. You see, in 2006, I started my own business ... but before 2006, the factories also existed here, and only those who were doing some business with factories would become richer. At that time, sources [of income] and opportunity for generating income outside agriculture were available, but people did not have the education to take advantage of it. People were less educated then. Now education has made people aware of how to do business, gain employment, and earn money from these factories, and hence prosperity has followed.[30]

96   Contested Capital

So, these brothers had benefited from the increase in land prices, and through their privileged position in relation to the local politics of the village (such as being connected to the local Panchayat offices). Like the other members of their class, they had been able to accumulate a surplus in both agricultural and non-agricultural production, which they then used to expand their non-agricultural activities, establishing small-size workshops and the hiring of non-agricultural labourers. The households in this class were not situated in the *landowning capitalist class*, because despite their high levels of income they did not own as much productive capital. There were, however, many similarities between this class and the *landowning capitalist class*: they did not use family labour and were solely purchasers of labour power in agricultural and non-agricultural production. They accumulated and reinvested their surplus in non-farm sectors. Over time, they will join the class of landowning capitalists.

3. *Farm-owning skilled workers* (which I also term the *straddling middle class*) primarily emerged in the 10 years prior to 2014–15 and consisted of households that earned their living primarily from skilled employment. The forms of skilled employment varied, but often included supervisors and managers in factories and a small number of government employees. These households were surplus producers, although at a minimal level. They produced surplus in agricultural production through appropriating the labour of others. They were permanently employed in non-farm sectors (owing to their education, skills and social connections) and used their income from non-farm employment to invest in agricultural production. In agriculture, they relied entirely on the labour of others and, therefore, generated positive NALDs. Its members tended to invest their surplus in real estate and in purchasing profit-making capital (for example, cars and tractors), consumer goods and private education for their children and grandchildren (as a strategy to ensure lucrative employment for them). In Nandur, this class contained 19 households, of which 17 had members working as skilled workers in industrial units, 2 had members engaged in government employment: a school teacher (whose son was also a skilled manager at IBM, an American multinational information technology company, in Pune) and a police officer (in this household, the other working member was a skilled factory worker). In Rahatwade, this class contained 19 households, 4 of which had members working for government sectors (a kindergarten teacher, two municipal bus drivers and a police officer). The other 15 households had members working as skilled factory workers.

On average, this class owned 4 acres of irrigated land, varying between 1 to 7 acres in Rahatwade and 2 to 8 acres in Nandur. The land was cultivated by female family labour and hired-in labour, although the hiring of labour was neither systematic nor large-scale. The average NALD in this class (307 labour days in Rahatwade and 170 labour days in Nandur) was very close to the village average for non-labouring households in the agricultural year 2014–15.[31] These figures were much higher than the average NALD among the PCPs. This class was characterised by an income considerably higher than the non-labouring village average but lower than the first two classes. The average annual household income was INR 692,000 in Nandur and INR 473,000 in Rahatwade in 2014–15. Most of the income in this class was generated from employment in the non-agricultural sector. Members of this class used their income from non-agricultural skilled work to invest in agricultural production. This investment included expanding operational land, improving access to irrigation, hiring-in agricultural labour, purchasing profit-making capital (such as cars and tractors), and investing in non-agricultural forms of capital such as real estate, education and consumer durables (unproductive capital). This class thus had diversified modes of accumulation. It was differentiated from the PCPs and the *farm-owning industrial working class* by the fact that households did not sell any agricultural labour, were not engaged in exchange labour, and family labour was reduced to female labour and was minimal (only for major tasks such as supervision and occasional works and sometimes during harvesting).

This class is termed the *straddling middle class* because in the Marxian framework of classes, its situation was ambiguous and paradoxical – the class position of its members *changed* between that of the working classes and the agricultural capitalists, yet could not accurately be placed in either classes, falling between the two. They were part of the working class because they were exploited as skilled workers in relation to non-agricultural capital – they did not own the means of production and their income was not in the form of shares. They were also simultaneously part of the agricultural capitalist class because they owned the means of production and exploited the labour of others in agricultural production. The expense of hiring-in labour in agricultural production was met from selling their labour power in the industrial sector. The availability of such forms of employment, combined with the abundance of labour power (inward temporary migrant agricultural workers, particularly in Nandur), meant that they had access to cheap labour. They were not part of the labouring class because they neither produced a deficit, and were able to meet their subsistence needs through the use of family labour (if needed), nor were they entirely part of the capitalist class, as they did not systematically hire in labour, and their levels of capital ownership were insufficient for producing a significant surplus for reinvestment. Marxist

98   Contested Capital

scholars have not discussed this possibility with the possible exception of Da Corta and Venkateshwarlu whose gendered analysis of class positions within rural households in Andhra Pradesh revealed instability in class structure (Da Corta and Venkateshwarlu, 1999).

The following example clarifies the economic activities of its members, like that of Kamaledin's family. The household was headed by 50-year-old Kamaledin, who worked with his 27-year-old son in the Fleetguard Filters factory. Kamaledin, a production supervisor, was permanently employed and earned a salary of INR 24,000 per month (in 2016). His son joined the factory in 2013 (although his contract was still temporary) as a skilled machine operator, earning INR 12,000 per month (2016). They also had 2.5 acres of operational land and numerous livestock (which were the responsibility of the women in the family). In addition to skilled industrial employment, they also generated income from small-scale sugarcane farming and livestock. Their farm was operated by hired-in and occasional female family labour (only for supervision). I inquired about the changes in the economic activity of the family over the past decade. While explaining the changes, Kamaledin left the room and returned brandishing a large 'employee of the year' trophy he had received from the factory. This was a symbolic gesture which represented the distance from agricultural work and the reliance on skilled employment. This symbol of prestige and status was accompanied by the following response:

> Let us suppose that there were no factories here: then we would also have to go and work in the [agricultural] fields of other people. These factories have created tools for earning our living. We benefited from them. If people receive monthly payments then they can think about [plan] the future. For example, if I want to purchase a two-wheeler and I am going to receive my salary next month, then I will take a loan from someone this month, pay a down payment and buy a two-wheeler in instalments. How is it in other villages where there are no such opportunities for factory employment? Tomorrow, if we face a shortage of water for cultivation, then our agricultural production is going to suffer, but our household will not suffer, because of the factory income. For now there is enough water for agriculture. We are happy because of our employment in the factory. 101 per cent everything is okay.[32]

I then asked about their small-scale farming operation and who worked the land while they were working in the factories. He replied: 'Labourers, we can afford hiring agricultural labour from our salaries.'[33]

The upper layer of this class, which included factory supervisors and managers, had the possibility to generate a sufficient surplus that over time could be invested in new means of production or expansion of existing production units. Over time, therefore, they have the potential to join the *new capitalist class*. On the contrary the NALD of the lower layer was positive but very low, making them unable to generate a sufficient surplus for reinvestment in production or agricultural expansion. They are vulnerable to fall into the PCPs (if they lose their skilled employment in the industrial sector) or into the industrial working class (particularly if their agricultural production fail over a sustained period). In Rahatwade, all the households in this class belonged to the Maratha caste. In Nandur, 12 households were Malis, 6 were Dhangars and 1 was an SC household.

4. *Petty commodity producers (PCPs)* include households that rely primarily on family labour, in agriculture and in non-farm activities. They also hire in, hire out and exchange labour, although the average net difference between the selling and buying of labour is usually zero. They produce little or no surplus (both in the forms of labour and produce). The majority of the population of non-labouring households in both villages are PCPs. There is a vast literature on petty commodity production in rural India, as production that is not seen as capital (Harriss-White, 2016). PCPs are defined as households that produce and reproduce themselves through family labour. They are neither net buyers nor sellers of labour power. However, PCPs often rely on complex labour relations, and their labour practices in relation to purchasing or hiring are flexible (Pattenden, 2016a: 25). In Rahatwade and Nandur, the average size of landholding in this class is close to 4 acres of total land and 3 acres of irrigated land. Members of this class generate their living primarily from farming, livestock (dairy production), petty shops and other independent non-agricultural activities such as plumbing, transport and other ad hoc independent activities, which gives them a certain degree of autonomy (Adnan, 1985), distinguishing them from the classes of labour. This class is characterised by low income (lower than the village average and other non-labouring classes) and low NALD. The average annual household income in this class was INR 231,400 in Rahatwade and INR 233,900 in Nandur over the agricultural year 2014–15.

There were 45 households in Rahatwade in this class: 2 Dhangars, 41 Marathas, 1 SC and 1 from OBCs. In Nandur, there were 34 households in this class: 16 Dhangars, 15 OBCs, 2 Muslims (1 from the Mulani caste) and 1 SC. In Nandur, 9 of these households generated their living exclusively from agriculture and did not have any secondary source of income; 11 households generated their income primarily from agriculture with livestock as their secondary source of income;

2 relied solely on petty shop keeping; and in 6 households, agriculture was the secondary source of income, while the major proportion of their income was from a range of sources such as small shops, livestock (dairy production), small family-run business units and other independent activities such as plumbing, electrical repair services and transport.

The remaining 6 households were engaged in agriculture (as the main source of income) and other non-agricultural activities as secondary sources of livelihood, often in the form of casual semi-skilled factory employment. In Rahatwade, only 3 out of the 45 households earned their livings exclusively from agriculture; 12 households generated their income from livestock and agriculture, and the remainder of households were engaged in petty-shop keeping, transport and other independent non-agricultural activities such as plumbing and electronic repair work. Some members of this class were also engaged in miscellaneous off-farm work, for example, in agricultural market yards or as industry-related casual workers.

The agricultural production of this class depended primarily on family and exchange labour, although some in this class occasionally needed to hire-in or hire-out labour power depending on crop intensity or weather conditions in a given agricultural season. Anecdotal evidence, particularly from Rahatwade (where cropping depends primarily on weather conditions during the *kharif* season), suggests that the members of this class sometimes subsidised their living by selling their labour power in agriculture. Perhaps this is the reason why only 3 households in this class generated their living solely from agricultural production.

The salient feature of PCPs is their flexibility in the hiring-in or hiring-out agricultural labour. Overall, their average NALD tends to be zero or marginal in absolute terms, distinguishing them from the classes of labour. In Rahatwade, the average NALD for this class was 77 labour days in the agricultural year 2014–15, and fluctuated between –160 and 635 labour days. In Nandur, the average NALD stood at 85 labour days in agricultural year 2014–15, and ranged from 0 to 440 labour days. In Nandur, the NALD for this class was always positive, which reflects the differences that exist between the two villages in relation to irrigation and the availability of non-farm work in Nandur.

As with any other class, this class is not homogenous. Its upper layer consists of upper middle peasants, who occasionally exploit the labour of others (they have positive NALDs). Their land is cultivated by family labour and hired-in labour and they are surplus producers. They tend to have diversified modes of non-farm accumulation (small-scale production). The most significant difference between the upper layers of this class and the previous two classes is their reliance on family labour. At the lower layer, family labour is combined with the hired wage labour. Their livelihood does not, however, primarily depend on the wages they receive. Although this class also sell labour power within and outside agricultural production, it is not necessarily considered as a labouring class, because the income from wage labour can subsidise the cost of production associated with their capital (land, shops, livestock, water resources, tractors, cars and tempos) to ensure continuity of reproduction.[34] Over time, however, they are more likely to move towards the classes of labour, or the industrial working class, and not the capitalist class, because their earnings are not sufficient for reinvesting in and expanding their capital. The availability of non-agricultural work in industrial sites also attracts the younger generation of work-seekers, who prefer such employment to self-employed farming and petty production. The following example is illustrative of the economic activities of this class.

Rajo's family (a Dhangar family) owned 2 acres of irrigated land. They earned their living by cultivating sugarcane and engaging in livestock production. They had a small house in the main part of the village (Gāvāta) and were able to make a modest living from their farming and livestock activities. However, Rajo, who was 20 when I visited their home, was not content with their living conditions and was seeking to gain employment in one of the nearby factories. After finishing his 10th standard, he completed a Diploma in Mechanical Engineering in order to pursue his 'dream of working in a factory'. He told me: 'I wish to secure a position as a machine operator in one of the factories in the region, to be able to earn 10,000 to 15,000 rupees per month as fast as possible.' He further explained that he preferred working in factories so that he could meet his desired living standard, which was not possible through farming and livestock activities alone.[35]

There were many similar examples of households in this class who engaged in non-farm employment. Depending on the nature of their employment, however (skilled or unskilled; permanent or casual), individuals could move either up or down the class hierarchy. In contrast to those who had only casual work, those in this class who had managed to secure skilled employment on a permanent basis were more likely to move up the class hierarchy because they had the ability to invest in family capital and own productive assets that could generate more income. Overall, this class is similar to one of the groups that Marx included in the middle class (the PCPs and artisans) as explained at the beginning of this chapter, and it is therefore considered to constitute one fraction of the rural middle classes.

102 Contested Capital

5. *The farm-owning industrial working class* consisted of households whose economic activities were centred on agriculture and casual employment in the industrial sector. They used family labour and exchange labour, and occasionally hired in and hired out (female members) in agriculture, but they earned their livelihood primarily from casual employment in non-farm sectors (this included semi-skilled to skilled machine operation). These households were not surplus producers, and generally produced little or no deficit. The NALD was usually zero, but tended to fluctuate below and above zero (in a minimal way). This class was very similar to PCPs, except for its industrial working members, because its members owned enough operational land to generate their livelihoods. However, the younger members of this class were mainly engaged in industrial work, and their income from such work tended to be greater than the income the household generated from agriculture and livestock, and that is why they were situated in a different class, from PCPs. This class was also differentiated from the two classes of labour (explained later) because its members owned enough agricultural land and livestock to enable them to meet their subsistence needs, and because, unlike the labouring classes, their average NALD was positive, however modestly. The occupations of members of this class included primarily skilled machine operating, although they also included factory storage supervision, quality control, packaging and other semi-skilled services. In this class, the average area of land owned was almost 3 acres of total land and 2.5 acres of irrigated land. This class was characterised by a low income, lower than the village average for non-labouring households. The average annual household income was INR 307,000 in Nandur and INR 192,000 in Rahatwade, in the agricultural year 2014–15. The households in this class had a lower level of indebtedness than other non-labouring classes, perhaps because they did not have access to credit because of their relatively small landholdings and modest capital ownership. Their income from industrial work was used to subsidise their agricultural production. This class in fact was the result of the transformation of a segment of PCPs into the industrial working class – because of their level of engagement in industrial work. The class position of its members is best defined as industrial working class because their primary source of income was generated from casual employment in industrial sector.

The main differences between this class and the class of *farm-owning skilled workers* were (*a*) the degree of their direct engagement in agriculture and (*b*) the nature of their employment in non-farm activities and skills required for their employment in the non-farm sector. Furthermore, unlike the *straddling middle class*, its members were not surplus producers in agriculture and thus were unable to invest in agricultural expansion. This class has the tendency to be transformed completely into the labouring class over time, specifically when their income from farming is no longer sufficient to meet their subsistence needs and if they lose their casual employment in the industrial sectors.

Overall, 17 households in Rahatwade (13 Marathas, 2 Dhangars, 1 from OBCs and 1 SC household) and 9 in Nandur (3 Dhangars and 6 Mali households) belonged to this class. The Maratha household in Rahatwade, headed by Baburao, is typical of this class. Baburao worked as a skilled machine operator in a factory in Kundhanpur, the village adjacent to Rahatwade. He earned INR 10,000 per month in 2015 and worked in a factory for six months of the year, before switching to another factory for a further six months, where he received the same income. During the 2014–15 agricultural year, his household earned INR 50,000 from rice and onion cultivation. He owned 3.5 acres of irrigated land and half an acre of dry land. The land was operated by family labour, and sometimes exchange and hired-in labour. Baburao's wife occasionally worked as an agricultural labourer (for approximately 20 days per annum), but they also hired in labour in agriculture and this gave them a positive NALD, marginally above zero. The total annual household income was INR 176,000 for the agricultural year 2014–15. This household would have fallen into the labouring class had Baburao not had any income from agricultural production. Similarly, they could not be placed in the class of *farm-owning skilled workers* for three reasons: first, because Baburao's employment was casual and his income was therefore insecure; second, he worked as a machine operator and did not have the required qualifications to secure skilled employment as a supervisor or manager; and third, in contrast to the class of *farm-owning skilled workers*, his wife occasionally worked as agricultural wage-labourer.[36] Overall, the trajectory of this class is similar to what Marx had suggested regarding the transformation of PCPs to factory workers.

The Two Labouring Classes

The two labouring classes were briefly discussed in Chapter 2. They are the group of households that did not qualify as potentially middle class and thus did not participate in the second round of the household survey (and therefore I do not have detailed information on them). Overall, these households included those which depended primarily on selling their physical labour power for daily survival. They were distinguished from other classes based on the difference in the net selling and buying of labour, the ownership of land and other productive assets, and whether or not the household produced a surplus or deficit (Athreya et al., 1987; Patnaik, 1976; Pattenden, 2016a: 23). They usually owned little or no

104 Contested Capital

land and were unable to produce any surplus. Their members ran on deficits and systematically sold their labour power. I have further categorised these households into the following classes:

6. *Land-owning labouring class* which consisted of marginal farmers who owned some land, usually a small area between 0.05 and 2 acres. They generated more income from selling their labour power than from working on their own land. They were deficit producers, with negative NALDs.

7. *Landless labouring class* which consisted of households who possessed no land at all and only generated income from selling their labour-power in both agricultural and non-farm sectors. They ran on deficit, with negative NALDs, often high in terms of absolute value.

Tables 3.7 and 3.8 summarise the characteristics of the identified classes in relation to land ownership, net agricultural labour days, value of assets and livestock (in terms of actual means), with respect to every variable.[37] It is worth noting that a substantial proportion of households in both villages belonged to the labouring classes and therefore no such data were available for them.[38]

The seven class categories were all present in Nandur, but only five of them (classes 3 to 7) had a significant presence in Rahatwade, where the population of households categorised in the first two classes was minimal. The reason for this was the presence and proximity of industrial sites in Nandur and the direct influence of the Gram Panchayat committee board of Nandur in the recruitment process for these factories (this will be explained in detail in Chapter 4). Overall, the rural middle classes, which are the primary focus of this chapter, were situated between the capitalist class (including *the new capitalist class*) and the classes of labour and the *farm-owning industrial working class*. They consisted of the *farm-owning skilled workers* (the *straddling middle class*) and PCPs. The upper layer of the rural middle class contained the *farm-owning skilled workers*, because this class had some similarity to the capitalist class in terms of the appropriation and exploitation of labour power in agricultural activities, positive NALDs and (when compared to the PCPs) the households in this class owned larger irrigated land. In its lower strata, the rural middle class contained PCPs. These two classes, in simple terms, fell between the two core classes and could not be situated either in the capitalist classes or in the classes of labour. They were both compatible with Marx's two definitions of the middle class explained at the beginning of the chapter.

Table 3.7 Classes in Rahatwade: composition and characteristics

Classes		Landowning capitalist class	New capitalist class	Farm-owning skilled workers (SMC)	PCPs	Farm-owning industrial working class	Village average (non-labouring)
Frequency (N = 91)		4	6	19	45	17	91
Average landholdings (acre)	Irrigated land	10.75 (8 to 15)	3.75 (0.5 to 7)	3.4 (1 to 7)	2.9 (0.25 to 5)	2.5 (0 to 5)	3.3 (0 to 15)
	Total land	14.25 (10 to 21)	6 (2 to 8.5)	4.7 (1 to 8)	4.1 (0.25 to 12)	2.8 (0.1 to 6)	4.5 (0.1 to 21)
Total land (median)		13	6.5	4.5	3.5	3	4
Average total land value (INR)		82,500,000	26,600,000	19,400,000	14,900,000	11,500,000	18,900,000
Average other asset value (houses, productive units, shops)		6,450,000	2,980,000	1,263,000	589,000	673,500	1,161,000
Average value of livestock (INR)		348,900	756,000	62,000	100,800	53,900	138,100
Total land owned by this class		57	36.5	89	186	49.1	417.6
Average NALD		540	235	307	77	−8	2
Average annual net agricultural wage paid (INR)		96,250	43,600	45,700	12,600	−1920	22,500
Average Agricultural labour days sold		0	0	0	12	26	11
Average annual net non-agricultural labour hired-in (days)		0	182	0	8	0	16
Average debt (INR)		1,390,000	687,500	87,000	77,400	52,000	194,000
Average household annual income (INR)		796,000	1,049,000	473,000	231,400	192,000	353,300
Sources of income		Farming, rent, livestock	Farming, livestock, brokerage, own business	Skilled work, government jobs, farming	Farming, livestock, petty shops, independent work	Semi-skilled industrial work, machine operations, farming, livestock	N.A.

Source: Fieldwork data (2015).

Table 3.8   Classes in Nandur: composition and characteristics

Classes		Landowning capitalist class	New capitalist class	Farm-owning skilled workers (SMC)	PCPs	Farm-owning industrial working class	Village average (non-labouring)
Frequency (N = 80)		9	9	19	34	9	80
Average landholdings (acre)	Irrigated land	11.5 (9 to 25)	3.7 (1.5 to 6)	4.3 (2 to 8)	3.15 (0 to 8)	2.5 (1.5 to 4)	4.4 (0 to 25)
	Total land	18.5 (10 to 50)	4.25 (2 to 8.5)	4.8 (2 to 11)	3.7 (0 to 12)	3 (1.5 to 6)	5.6 (0 to 50)
Total land (median)		15	3.25	4.5	2.5	3	4
Average total land value (INR)		91,000,000	20,800,000	20,600,000	14,400,000	12,000,000	24,800,000
Average other asset value (houses, productive units, shops)		1,655,000	1,905,500	1,531,600	667,600	1,000,000	1,160,630
Average value of livestock (INR)		76,994	160,800	18,200	80,000	35,000	69,000
Total land owned by this class		167	38.25	93.75	125.625	27	451.625
Average NALD		344	338	170	85	97	165
Average annual net agricultural wage paid (INR)		122,800	89,500	35,400	14,900	17,400	40,610
Average agricultural labour days sold		0	0	0	6 (0 to 80)	5.5 (0 to 30)	3.3 (0 to 80)
Average annual net non-agricultural labour hired in		188	635	0	15	0	99
Average debt (INR)		975,000	971,700	347,700	286,400	515,000	470,195
Average household annual income (INR)		620,800	1,145,800	692,000	233,900	307,000	497,000
Sources of income		Farming, rent from land, livestock	Business owners, labour contractors, farming	Skilled workers, government jobs, farming	Farming, livestock, petty shop, rent, independent work	Farming-machine operators (casual and semi-skilled work)	N.A.

Source: Fieldwork data (2015).

This analysis relating to the nature and composition of the seven classes in these villages, particularly the rural middle classes, demonstrates that, over the last decade, non-agricultural economic activity has been a significant feature of transformation. The most salient aspect of this transformation was the shift towards employment in the industrial sector. These activities, however, were highly gendered, and it was primarily the male population of these villages who had benefited from this socio-economic transformation.[39] Women continued to carry the overwhelming burden of agricultural work. Overall, there were two primary reasons for these transformations. First, the spread of industrialisation and the establishment of factories had evidently allowed access to new forms of relatively lucrative employment. These new forms of employment had been combined with the widespread and increasing availability of vocational educational qualifications, which did not require a university degree and which allowed individuals to acquire the skills needed for certain roles in factories (this will be discussed in detail in Chapter 4). Second, other parts of Maharashtra, particularly the Marathwada region in eastern Maharashtra, suffered from a water scarcity that inhibited the type of development and economic growth seen in Nandur and Rahatwade. This forced the inhabitants of water-scarce villages to seek employment elsewhere, including in Rahatwade and (particularly) in Nandur. The availability of cheap labour because of seasonal in-migration allowed cultivators to hire these labourers for performing agricultural activities on relatively cheap and informal terms, while the majority of permanent inhabitants of the villages worked in industrial sites. Industrial work was more lucrative than agricultural labour, although (with the exception of highly skilled employees with permanent contracts) it was insecure and casual, lasting for a period of maximum six months per contract.

This categorisation of classes, however, and the assertion that the class structure and dynamics of the villages have changed over time, presents a methodological problem. How, one might ask, can we argue that the villages have transformed over time without a similar dataset from the past relating to employment, landholding, income, labour relations and other variables included in the household survey questionnaire? Such a historical data set is unavailable, but this potential pitfall is overcome in a number of ways. First, the literature on rural India does not indicate that a class of skilled workers existed in the past, and the extensive literature review provides strong evidence that the widespread significance of rural industrial skilled workers is a recent phenomenon. Second, it is logical to assume that socio-economic classes, inextricably linked to the industrial units recently established on the peripheries of both villages, did not exist before the entrance

108   Contested Capital

of those factories. Third, and perhaps most significantly, there is overwhelming evidence collected during interviews with residents to support the argument that the establishing of the factories has had a transformative and far-reaching impact on these villages, and no doubt across some parts of rural India more generally. The following extract summarises the ways in which residents perceive the transformations relating to class and prosperity:

> Almost 20 years have passed since the first company [factory] was built outside Nandur. Some [factories] came in more recently; some were founded in the last eight years, and the latest ones were built only two years ago. Currently, there are a total of 16 factories here [in Nandur], 14 of them are functioning; two have closed down recently. When these industries reached our village, they brought with them various sources of income. The Gram Panchayat office receives in total 4,000,000 rupees per annum from these 14 factories, some of which is invested in the water supply of the village, the filter water supply, making cement concrete roads, proper intact closed drainage lines and streetlights. Such developments have taken place with the money gained from these factories. From every house, one or two sons are [working] in these industrial units – every family has at least one child working in these industries, and earning between 10,000 to 20,000 rupees per month. Hence, Nandur village is developed.... Apart from farming there are many sources of income now.... Our standard of living is developed. All this has happened because of the arrival of factories.[40]

This extract is representative of many other accounts telling a similar story of factories bringing 'development', 'progress' and socio-economic 'mobility'. Some participants also provided a comparative perspective to further exemplify the nature and form of rural transformation and the contrasting trajectories of different rural regions. For instance, Ramchandra, the former *sarpanch* of Nandur, compared Nandur with Khed Shivapur, 'some 40 to 60 km away' (close to where Rahatwade is located):

> Because of its mountainous location, agricultural production is minimal, and there are no chances for agricultural expansion ... no development. Enterprising residents are forced to start restaurants on the side of roads, selling Vada pav [vegetarian fast food native to Maharashtra] from the stall ... or start tea stalls. That is all they have as a source of income outside agriculture .... In Nandur, there is work available in factories, and because of that they [residents of other villages] migrate to Nandur.[41]

More subtle differences between Rahatwade and Nandur were also evident. While transformation had occurred in both villages, it had been more extensive and rapid in Nandur because of its proximity to factories. There were a number of factories within less than 5 kilometres of Rahatwade located on the outskirts of the neighbouring village of Kundhanpur. These factories were not connected to Rahatwade in relation to labour and access to other resources, so access to employment in factories was more difficult for residents of the village (this will be discussed in Chapter 4). The second difference between the two villages relates to irrigation access. While the majority of land in Nandur was irrigated, mainly by canals flowing from the Mula River, Rahatwade was a dry land village with a greater proportion of unproductive land and its agriculture was therefore less profitable, and the surplus was mainly reinvested in securing water for agriculture and other agricultural facilities. In contrast, in Nandur, the surplus was reinvested in non-farm activities and education (the latter enabling access to skilled employment in the industrial sectors). These differences had implications for class structure and income. In Nandur, land distribution was more polarised, income levels were on average higher, and the class divisions were more clearly evident. This is significant because it augments the argument that industrial work and employment out of agriculture have been the driving forces behind middle-class formation and class differentiations in these villages.

The Rural Middle Classes: Classes In-themselves or For-themselves?

In this chapter, the rural middle classes have been examined as 'classes-in-themselves', categories of people that have a common relationship to the means of production, and not as 'classes-for-themselves', groups of people who organise themselves in active pursuit of their mutual interest (Byres, 1981; Gupta and Sharan, 2004). In simple terms, the chapter did not explore whether the rural middle classes shared mutual class interests or had similar political behaviours. The reason for this is twofold: first, and primarily, as highlighted earlier, the rural middle classes were dynamic and unstable categories and there was considerable circulation/straddling of individuals between the different class fractions. For example, a person who was a skilled factory worker could also be a capitalist farmer; and PCPs could often be engaged in semi-skilled or skilled factory work. Similarly, the class position of individuals could change within a short period of time. For example, a person who was a cultivator one year could be transformed into a factory worker the next year (either a skilled, semi-skilled or even unskilled worker) due to unfavourable weather condition or failed crops. Such instability seemed to impede the development of class interest among the rural middle classes.

110   Contested Capital

Second, anecdotal evidence in both villages and interviews with members of middle-class households in Nandur (where a population of inward migrant skilled workers existed) suggests (in an extreme summary) that the class interest of skilled industrial workers, and the industrial working class appeared to come into existence, when faced by the perceived threats posed by migrant skilled industrial workers (who shared the same or similar class location), and who were commonly understood to be 'more hardworking and serious, and also happy with a lower salary'.[42] However, such interest was not acted upon (unless in subtle ways).[43] I have not examined the collective interest/action of the middle classes (or lack of it), as such topic was beyond the enquiry of my research.

To conclude, the analysis of the dynamics of rural industrialisation and class-ambiguous transformations in sources of livelihood provided us with a classification of the emerging class structure within the relations of production in these villages. The most salient feature of this structure was classes that were located between the capitalists and the classes of labour; in particular, the industrial skilled workers whose class position rested on the acquisition of a certain level of education and training, and as we shall see in Chapter 4, social connections. This class challenges the Marxist structure of classes because they do not fit into any of the conventional class categories. Although its members sold their labour power to the owners of factories, the income from these economic activities enabled them to create a surplus in agriculture by buying agricultural labour and taking family members out of farming. They were in fact both skilled industrial working class and agrarian capitalists, but could not be positioned in either: they were situated in the middle. These middle classes are not necessarily unproductive (as Marx and many Marxist scholars have portrayed them); they take part in the production process, either indirectly through management and supervision or directly through operating automated production machinery.

The seven-class categorisation identified in this chapter is significant because not only does it retain the Marxist structure in relation to ownership of the means of production and labour relations but also reflects flexibility within this structure. It also mirrors regional specificities such as the diversity of livelihoods and forms of accumulation that exist in rural India. These economic transformations and the emergence of rural middle classes are unlikely to be specific to Rahatwade and Nandur, and there are undoubtedly considerable regional variations. However, the identification of new class structures is an initial stage for understanding contemporary transformation and agrarian change, and represents the first step in a new political economy of rural India.

Notes

1. Marx conceptualised labourers as physical labourers.

2. Ricardo argued that the introduction of machinery into the production process would keep the cost of production low, resulting in the reduction of the price of the commodity produced, and thus benefiting both the capitalist and the workers. The capitalist would make the same or more profit, even after the reduction in the price of commodity, because the cost of production had equally been reduced. The class of labourers also benefited from the use of machinery, because with the decrease in the cost of the product they had the means to buy more commodities out of the same wages. One of Marx's critiques of this argument was that Ricardo did not take the expansion of the middle class into consideration, which resulted in an increase in the demand for the produced commodities, thus keeping product prices high due to the high demand. See Marx (1978 [1861–63]: 737– 41).

3. With the expansion of the middle class in post-industrial societies, and more recently in developing economies, many Marxist scholars have paid considerable attention to this group, which falls between the two core classes. They are often referred to as the *petty bourgeoisie*; *managerial classes; segment of other classes*; a *new petty bourgeoisie*; *new working class*; or the *professional and managerial class* (PMC). See Wright (1985).

4. The term 'new', as in 'new petty bourgeoisie', is to distinguish this class from the traditional middle class and the petty bourgeoisie, including artisans, independent shopkeepers, small peasants and the professions based on honour and status. See Wright (1980: 327).

5. See, for example, Ehrenreich and Ehrenreich (1977), Gouldner (1979), Konárd and Szelenyi (1979) and Wright (1980, 1989).

6. Another strategy for analysing such contradictory locations has emerged in the literature, referred to as the *functional* account, developed by Garchedi, who defines class position in relation to three dimensions: *ownership, expropriation* and *functional* elements. See Garchedi (1977).

7. As noted by Bertell Ollman, Marx sometimes placed the small-holding peasant in the proletarian class. For example, he stated '[t]he owning peasant does not belong to the proletariat, and there where he does belong to it by his position, he does not believe that he belongs to it' (see Ollman 1979: 34). However, Marx also referred to peasants as a distinct class 'whose distinctive qualities are aptly summed up in the phrase, a "class of barbarians"' (see Marx 1959, Vol. III: 567).

8. Also see Rutten (1995).

9. Also see Breman (1993), Jeffrey (1997, 2010a), Jeffrey and Jeffrey (1997) and Rutten (1995).

10. Also see Mellor (1995).

11. Similarly, in a study of coastal Andhra Pradesh, Upadhya demonstrates that the making of the rural capitalist class necessitates ideological changes and cultural transformation. She notes that reorientation of cultural values and social restructuring are both required to ensure a common lifestyle and social

112   Contested Capital

values, and to adapt similar political orientations and attitudes. Therefore, the formation of a rural capitalist class necessitates both capital accumulation as a result of economic diversification and social and cultural identity. See Upadhya (1997: 47–80).

12. See Basile (2009: 39).

13. Harriss-White suggests that as a result of reduction in public investment after 1991, many rich farmers in India found their access to state subsidies threatened (Harriss-White, 2003). As a consequence of these threats to the availability of government subsidies and a reduction in the supply of government jobs, this class of rich famers in many parts of India expressed their anxiety by engaging in formal politics in an attempt to maintain their claim on state resources, subsequently becoming a highly visible political bloc. See Harriss-White (1999) and Jeffrey (2010a, 2010b).

14. When rich farmers became involved in agrarian movements in the late 1980s and early 1990s, their primary aim, suggests Jeffrey, was to protect agricultural subsidies (see Jeffrey 2010b: 8). The two most prominent examples of such movements were Shetkari Sanghatana in Maharashtra (1980s) and Bharatiya Kisan Union (BKU) in Punjab and Uttar Pradesh (see Dhanagare 1995; Lindberg 1995). The Shetkari Sanghatana movement was formed by cash-crop cultivators who agitated against the state to maintain higher prices for their produce and access to state subsidies. Dhanagare suggests the movement consisted of rich farmers and better-off peasants with substantial land-holdings. These were the rural classes who benefited from higher prices for agricultural products (for example, wheat, sugarcane, cotton and tobacco) and formed a powerful political group as the main drivers of the farmers' movements (see Dhanagare 1995: 73). Similarly, Nadkarni argues that the farmers' movement in Punjab (BKU) was dominated by rich capitalist farmers who were the principal beneficiaries of the Green Revolution (see Nadkarni 1987). Charan Singh, the first Jat Prime Minister of India, is perhaps the most prominent example of a member of this class who became, in Varma's words, 'the most eloquent spokesman for this agrarian bourgeoisie' (see Varma 1989: 99; Byres 1988).

15. See, for example, Basile (2009), Breman (1996), Ghosal (2002), Harriss-White (2003, 2010, 2015, 2016), Unni (2000), Islam (1987) and Saith (1992, 2001).

16. The term 'classes of labour' was developed by Henry Bernstein and later developed for India by Jens Lerche (see Bernstein 2006). The classes of labour are defined through income and autonomy (bondage, casual/regular contracts and self-employment) (see Lerche 2010; Harriss-White and Heyer 2010: 64–85).

17. See Gibbon and Neocosmos (1985).

18. Overall, there is a vast body of literature on transformation of rural economy and class formation in India (see Athreya et al. 1987; Patnaik 1976, 1987; Pattenden 2016a). For example, Athreya et al. (1987), focusing on the reproduction of the farming households in Tamil Nadu, used a locally sensitive minimum consumption level of grains to form the basis for 'surplus criteria' of

rural class differentiations. They categorised households according to their level of income in relation to the minimum grain deficit. Similarly, Patnaik (1976, 1987) used labour 'exploitation ratio' to classify rural households. However, they do not examine class formations in rural India through the framework of the middle class, which in turn results in not addressing the issue of a growing middle class in rural India, nor do they identify the phenomenon of rural industrial skilled workers.

19. Similar findings have been provided by Harriss-White. See Harriss-White (2003).

20. The complete list of non-farm sources of income in Rahatwade and Nandur are shown in Appendix A1.

21. See Colatei and Harriss-White (2004).

22. A vast literature exists on merchants' capital, commercial capital, the relations of exchange that secure control over surplus, and the mercantile and moneylending classes in rural India; for example, see Harriss-White (2008). However, such classes were not found in Rahatwade and Nandur and are therefore not examined in the analysis of class in these villages.

23. In his analysis of classes in rural Karnataka, Pattenden (2016a) has drawn a similar table, and Table 3.4 is inspired by Pattenden's categorisation of classes, to demonstrate the characteristic of each class in Rahatwade and Nandur. See Pattenden (2016a: 24).

24. In Rahatwade, during my fieldwork, the average price for operational land varied between 40 and 50 lakhs (INR 4,000,000 to 5,000,000) for 1 acre. In Nandur, the average price for 1 acre of operational land was from 40 to 60 lakhs (INR 4,000,000 to 6,000,000).

25. See also Colatei and Harriss-White (2004: 129).

26. Vitthal J. Gh., personal interview, 30 May 2016, Nandur.

27. Vitthal J. Gh., personal interview, 30 May 2016, Nandur.

28. Yuvraj B. B., personal interview, 29 May 2016, Nandur.

29. The types of industrial employment in Rahatwade and Nandur and the role of contractors are discussed in Chapter 4.

30. Kishor B. B., personal interview, 29 May 2016, Nandur.

31. The smaller NALD among this class in Nandur, compared to Rahatwade, is due to outsourcing of sugarcane harvesting to sugar factories – this results in lower number of hired-in labour since no labour power is hired in by these households during harvesting.

32. Kamaledin Sh., personal interview, 26 June 2016, Nandur.

33. Kamaledin Sh., personal interview, 26 June 2016, Nandur.

34. Pattenden (2016a) has found similar evidence in relation to the PCPs in rural Karnataka.

35. Rajo B. T., personal interview, 30 May 2016, Nandur.

36. Baburao Sh. Ch., personal interview, 23 June 2016, Rahatwade.

37. In this study, the household is taken as a unit of analysis. The categories apply

114 Contested Capital

to the main source of household income, which is defined as the occupation that generates the biggest proportion of the total annual household income. The initial intention was to estimate the wealth of households in relation to both assets and households goods, using an item-by-item listing and valuation of all assets of the household (excluding gold and ornaments, which are extremely sensitive topics). But such an approach to evaluation proved to be very unreliable. This is because of the difference between the estimated current market value of the goods and the value at which they were purchased. It was difficult to estimate the value of goods at the current market price. While it was based on self-reporting, it was clearly explained to respondents that the valuation had to be based on current market value and not the purchase price. However, in terms of household's goods, it is extremely difficult to tell the market value of the goods if they were purchased few years ago or received as gifts. This method of collecting estimates of household wealth was, therefore, abandoned. As such, estimations of wealth were limited to the value of possessed properties, such as land, houses and any other properties such as shops and workshops.

38. To crosscheck the validity of land prices given by the respondents, the prices of 1 *guntha* of land (40 *guntha*s equal 1 acre) in the various locations of both villages were checked with the members of Gram Panchayat office and my local guide in each village.

39. Similar findings have been offered by Jonathan Parry, whose fieldwork has focussed on the rapid industrialisation in a previously backward rural area of Bhilali in Chhattisgarh. Parry's findings suggest that industrial workers are almost exclusively male. See Parry (2009: 184).

40. Ramchandra Gh., personal interview, 26 June 2016, Nandur.

41. Ramchandra Gh., personal interview, 26 June 2016, Nandur.

42. Laximan Kh. Gh., personal interview, 28 June 2016, Nandur.

43. In a fascinating account of industrialisation in a previously backward rural area of Bhilali in Chhattisgarh, Jonathan Parry argues the existence of the industrial workers, which he calls the 'working class', challenges the Marxist structure of classes (for-themselves). Parry illustrates the class conflict not only defines the relationship between the capitalist, and the working class, whose labour is reduced to a commodity form, but also characterises the relationship between various segment of the working class. He argues that such conflict among the working classes is due to the structural division that the state has created through its labour legislations, dividing the workers into formal and informal sector workers (including flexible contract workers). Parry goes on demonstrating the working class is further divided into two camps of 'locals' and 'outsiders'. While the outsiders are further divided by regional identities, the locals, who are more 'likely to do the least remunerative, and most arduous and insecure jobs', are divided by caste and religion. Such fractions among the working class not only prevent class unity but also create conflicts between various segments of the working class. See Parry (2009: 175–202).

4

Weber
Marketable Capital, Status and the Rural Middle Classes

> In the village, many people think they belong to the middle class. They feel that whoever has a car, whoever can afford to educate his children to a good level in a good high school or in a well-reputed college, he [*sic*] belongs to the middle class. And those who cannot afford to send their children to study in a good college in cities are at the lowest level (class); such is the feeling of others.
>
> —Rambhau Gh., personal interview (2016)

This chapter shifts the analysis of the rural middle class from Marx's notions of classes defined on the basis relations of production to a Weberian perspective, examining the formation of the rural middle class through market relations, occupational mobility, education, skill differentials and caste. We have so far seen that the process of industrialisation in Rahatwade and Nandur has resulted in the formation of new forms of livelihood and have established conditions for the development of the middle class. In what follows, I aim to explore the ways in which the boundaries of the rural middle class are shaped by shifts in the direction of employment aspirations. I reveal how the acquisition and distribution of various forms of capital – defined by Weber as including education, skill credentials and social networks – have enabled segments of the rural population to take advantage of industrialisation, gaining access to the middle-class labour market.

The first section provides an account of the ways in which Max Weber defined the term 'class' in his project of theorising social stratification, and outlines Weber's categorisation of classes – the *property classes*, *commercial classes* and *social classes* – which are less well-known than other aspects of Weber's theoretical work. The second section outlines the ways in which Weber defined the middle

116   Contested Capital

class, followed by a brief overview of how the Indian middle class is situated within the Weberian framework. The third part provides a brief account of Weber's conception of the caste system and its economic impact. In the fourth section, the literature on caste-class relations in India is reviewed. Following a brief overview of the socio-economic context in Rahatwade and Nandur, the fifth section introduces the occupational class structures within the Weberian framework and identifies the rural middle classes using empirical data. The sixth section offers a descriptive account, spliced with case studies, of the ways in which rural households gain entry to the middle-class labour market. The chapter moves on to examine caste and class relations, with empirical examples of the impact of caste on income distribution, occupational mobility and access to socio-economic resources using fieldwork data. The final section examines the caste composition of the rural middle classes. The chapter primarily relies on two rounds of quantitative household survey data collected during fieldwork, augmented by qualitative interviews relating to education, employment aspirations and socio-economic transformation at the household level over the last 10 years. Three rounds of macroeconomic surveys, HDPI (1993–94), IHDS-I (2004–05) and IHDS-II (2011–12), are also used to examine the salience of caste in accessing opportunities and resources throughout rural India.

Max Weber and Conceptions of Class

The Weber-inspired analysis of the rural middle class in India is based on his fragmented analysis of classes in his incomplete magnum opus, *Economy and Society*, written in Weber's final years and published in 1922 after his death. Born in 1864 in Prussia, Weber spent his life analysing dramatic changes sweeping through nineteenth century society, including the emergence of vast factories and the formation of new managerial elites replacing the old aristocracy in the industrial revolution. He developed a three-dimensional theory whereby stratification is formed by the interplay between class (economic position), status ('effective claim to social esteem in terms of positive or negative privileges') and power ('the probability that one actor within a social relationship will be in a position to carry out his own will despite resistance') (Weber, 1978: 53, 305).[1] Like Marx, Weber recognised the importance of class as the primary form of stratification in modern societies. However, in contrast to the Marxian historical materialism, which focused fundamentally on the ownership of the means of production as a basis for class differentiation, Weber developed a more complex and multidimensional concept of class. He identified: 'Class situation is ... ultimately market situation. The effect of net possession *per se* ... is only a forerunner of real "class" formation' (Weber, 1978: 928). In his view, the possession and non-possession of property is the basic category of all 'class situations', but in contrast to Marx, Weber saw that differences in property ownership were not the only factors determining class. He defined class as 'all persons in the same class situation' (Weber, 1978: 302):

> The typical probability of (1) procuring goods (2) gaining a position in life and (3) finding inner satisfactions, a probability which derives from the relative control over goods and skills and from their income-producing uses within a given economic order. (Weber, 1978: 302)

In simple terms, a given class consists of individuals who share the same or a similar level of control over, and access to, marketable resources (not necessarily productive property) from which income can be generated income (Weber, 1978: 302; Weber, 1991). For Weber, the 'class situation' was primarily determined by the 'market situation': *life chances* were distributed by the market, and that distribution was determined by the resources that individuals bring to the market, such as social networks, skills and education (Breen, 2005: 32). In short, the concept of life chances is understood as an individual's opportunity to access resources and to have particular life outcomes available to them: 'the chances an individual has for sharing in the socially created economic or cultural "goods" that typically exist in any given society' (Giddens, 1973: 130–31). In Weber's view, different classes existed in every market situation, including, but not limited to, their location in the property market, the labour market and the commodity market – 'the various controls over consumer goods, means of production, assets, resources and skills each constitute a particular class situation' (Weber, 1978: 302).[2] However, he further narrowed the definition: class situations are fundamentally differentiated 'according to the kind of property that is usable for returns' and 'according to the kind of services that can be offered in the market' (Weber, 1978: 927–28). To simplify this, Weber identified two primary markets within which classes are identified: the property market and the labour market. For Weber, every other class situation is a consequence of one's situation in one of these two primary markets.

Weber's Three Types of Class

In *Economy and Society*, Weber conceptualised primarily three types of class:

1. *Property classes*, distinguished mainly in terms of possession and non-possession of income-generating properties. Here, class is a kind of social

118   Contested Capital

distribution including both extremes. Weber further analysed the property classes on the basis of 'privilege'. The members of *positively privileged property classes* are those individuals who own highly profitable property. They typically include *rentiers*, who receive income from property such as land, mines, ships and factories; slave owners, who earn income from the physical labour of others; and creditors (Weber, 1978: 303). They are characterised by their 'exclusive acquisition of high-priced consumer goods', monopolisation of accumulation of wealth (which is more than their consumption needs), the ability to re/invest in capital out of saving and surplus production, and their monopolisation of expensive education (Weber, 1978: 303). On the other hand, the *negatively privileged property classes* typically consist of individuals who do not own any income generating property. They include 'the unfree', 'the declassed (the *proletarii* of Antiquity)' and 'debtors' (Weber, 1978: 303). They can only rely on irregular wage-work and manual labour to generate income (Weber, 1978: 303). Weber's categorisation of classes on the basis of ownership and non-ownership of property brings him closer to Marx in his conceptualisation of class,[3] but unlike Marx, property (and lack of it), although the basic category of all class situations, is not the only cause of class variations. This is elaborated in the next section.

2. *Commercial* (or *acquisition*) *classes* are primarily defined in the labour market in modern societies. They are distinguished on the basis of differences in the degree of 'marketability of goods and services' that individuals control in the market, and possession of income generating non-property capital such as education, skills and social networks (Weber, 1978: 302). Similar to propertied classes, the commercial or acquisition classes may be positively or negatively privileged. The *positively privileged* are those individuals whose marketable skills and education enable them to receive significant income, and who are characterised by their access to monopolised qualifications and skills. They control 'entrepreneurial management for the sake of its members and their business interests' and safeguard such interests through their influence on political organisations (Weber, 1978: 304). They consist of 'industrial and agricultural entrepreneurs' and 'merchants', 'shipowners', 'bankers and financiers', professionals with 'privileged education (such as lawyers, physicians, artists)' or 'workers with monopolistic qualifications and skills', either gained naturally or 'acquired through drill or training' (Weber, 1978: 304). The *negatively privileged* are characterised by lack of access to privileged education and skill credentials. They are forced to sell their manual labour to generate income. They include labourers whose

education and skills are not privileged or unique in the labour market (Weber, 1978).

3. *Social classes* are classes within which 'individual and generational mobility is easy and typical' (Weber, 1978: 302). They include the working class in 'automated' work places, whose work depends on the acquisition of skills and training (their skills training has freed them from manual labour, and facilitated upward mobility). The *social classes* also include 'the propertyless intelligentsia and specialists (technicians, various kinds of white-collar employees, civil servants – possibly with considerable social differences depending on the cost of their training)', 'the petty bourgeoisie' and 'the classes privileged through property and education' (Weber, 1978: 305). Weber's definition of the social classes is brief: they did not appear in his writings on social actions (Cox, 1950). As indicated earlier, social classes are the consequences of the class situation in the property and/or the labour market; therefore, the social classes consist of individuals whose class situation becomes privileged either through their property, education, social network or through their status/caste, which allows socio-economic mobility and aspirations (Crompton and Gubby, 1977: 8). Breen expands on Weber's definition of social class as a class that is not formed simply 'on the basis of the workings of the market', but based on factors outside the market, such as social relationships that intervene to facilitate social mobility (Breen, 2005: 42).

Weber criticised Marx for his unsuccessful attempt at dealing with class formation based on education and skill differentials. For him, particularly in the era of the industrial revolution, 'the increasing importance of semi-skilled workers, who can be trained on the job in a relatively short time, over the apprenticed and sometimes also the unskilled workers' was crucial for class variations (Weber, 1978: 305). 'Semi-skilled qualification too can often become monopolistic', suggested Weber (Weber, 1978: 305). This point is illustrative of the importance of education and skill training in the class situation of propertyless individuals, and is particularly relevant to class formation in rural India in the current phase of rural industrialisation. However, as noted by Cox, Weber's theory of classes is non-dynamic and highly abstract, being determined essentially in the context of the market, making it very difficult to apply to empirical realities (Cox, 1950). Similarly, Parkin notes that Weber's association of classes with market situations becomes problematic when one attempts to identify the boundaries between classes – where one class ends and the other class begins (Parkin, 2002: 93). Within the Weberian categorisation of classes also, the class situation of an individual

120   Contested Capital

can differ depending on the type of market within which the class definition is framed. For example, a propertyless individual, negatively privileged in the property market, can be positively privileged in the labour market through the acquisition of marketable education or social networks. Weber's absolute separation between the property market and the labour market, which appears to respond to Marx's focus only on the ownership of productive property, is highly abstract and makes the boundaries of classes very slippery and problematic to identify, and thus highly complex for empirical applications. There seem in fact to be only two definite class situations in the Weberian analysis: one in which an individual has access to both profitable property and highly marketable education and skills, and another in which an individual is deprived of both, whose manual labour takes the form of a commodity and is the only source of income. This simplification brings Weber's class analysis much closer to Marx's.

Weber's Middle Classes

Like that of Marx, Weber's analysis of the 'middle class' is fragmented and brief. In his categorisation of classes in *Economy and Society*, he defined the 'middle classes' (*Mittelstandsklassen*) as those situated between the negatively and positively privileged classes in two dimensions: the property classes and the commercial classes. They include groups who make their living 'from their property or their acquired skills' (Weber, 1978: 303). The middle class then consists of those situated in the middle of the distribution of income, credentials and property ownership (Wacquant, 1991). It includes independent peasants, 'self-employed-farmers and craftsmen', officials both in public and private employment (workers with formal credentials), skilled workers who earn their living from their acquired skills and training, and proletarians who have acquired some 'exceptional qualifications' (Weber, 1978: 304). Although its members are negatively privileged in terms of (productive) property ownership, they are situated in the middle class because of their skill differentials. Weber's conceptualisation of the middle class appears to have much in common with social classes. In short, Weber located the middle class between 'dominant entrepreneurial and propertied groups' and those completely unskilled and propertyless individuals whose only asset is their manual labour power (Weber, 1964: 425).

In the All-India context, to the best of my knowledge, the only Weberian analysis of the middle class to date is that of Fernandes and Heller, in a study of 'new middle class' (urban) politics in contemporary India (although they do not explicitly state that their analysis is situated within the Weberian framework). Fernandes and Heller broadly define the Indian middle class as the class 'whose economic opportunities are not derived primarily from property (the bourgeoisie)', but are rather derived from resources such as 'organizational authority' or the possession of 'scarce occupational skills', and these opportunities do not primarily rely on property ownership (Fernandes and Heller, 2006: 500). Its members earn wages which are 'specific to their class position' – this 'contrasts with the working class whose labour is reduced to commodity form' and who do not have access to the salary or skills of the middle classes. They have the ability to reproduce these skills by 'securing institutional sanction (legal recognition of credentials and administered returns to scare skills) or otherwise hoarding the skill through social networks and gatekeeping' (Fernandes and Heller, 2006: 500). Fernandes and Heller then categorise the middle classes into three overlapping 'strata'. In the first tier are the advanced professionals occupying positions of authority, whom they term 'the dominant fraction', and whose economic interests are similar to those of the bourgeoisie; in the second tier are the 'petty bourgeoisie' or small business owners and rich farmers, who enjoy some economic independence and aspire to join the dominant fraction; and in the most numerous third tier are the salaried workers who have gained educational capital but neither translated this into material gain, nor do they occupy positions of authority. This tier includes clerical staff, office workers, teachers and nurses (Fernandes and Heller, 2006: 500).

Weber in Empirical Studies of Middle Classes

Despite the criticism of Weber earlier in this chapter, his conceptualisation of classes, and in particular *the commercial classes*, defined on the basis of marketable skills, education and social networks, can be a useful framework or analytical device to examine the formation of the rural middle class in the current phase of industrialisation. As stated in Chapter 3, the process of industrialisation has resulted in the emergence of new occupations that are contingent on the acquisition of formal education and skills training. In the face of industrialisation, therefore, besides the ownership of productive assets, educational qualifications and other forms of non-property income generating capital (such as social networks) all take on a particular significance to enhance one's privilege in the labour market. As also noted by Giddens, among individuals with no property, those who obtain marketable skills and education are in a different class situation from those without

122   Contested Capital

property who have no marketable assets other than their unskilled manual labour power (Giddens, 1981: 43). This makes the Weberian analysis of class very relevant. Evidence from the fieldwork suggests that a central feature of rural middle-class formation over the last decade has been the increasing number of skilled workers and skilled machine operators whose parents were solely engaged in farming activities. The empirical part of this chapter thus draws on Weber's conception of class formation on the basis of acquisition of marketable capital as a heuristic device to examine the rural class formation. As the chapter will demonstrate, however, individual privileges in the labour market in India intersect with social inequalities relating to caste to which we now turn.

Weber on Status Groups and Caste

Status is the second dimension of Weber's theory of stratification.[4] Weber defined 'status groups' as communities or 'plurality of persons who, within a larger group, successfully claim a) a special social esteem, and possibly also b) status monopolies' (Weber, 1978: 306). Weber drew a distinction between classes and status groups:

> 'Classes' are groups of people who … have the same economic position. Ownership and non-ownership of material goods, or possession of definite skills constitutes a class situation. 'Status', however, is a quality of social honor or a lack of it, and is in the main conditioned as well as expressed through a specific style of life. (Weber, 1958: 39)

It is particularly stated that the status group is 'most unlike the commercial class': commercial classes are formed as a function of the market and 'in a market-oriented economy', whereas status groups are formed in traditional societies 'through monopolistic liturgies', or in feudal and patrimonial fashion (Weber, 1978: 306–07). Therefore, 'depending on the prevailing mode of stratification, we shall speak of a "status society" or a "class society"' (Weber, 1978: 306).

Caste as a Closed Status Group

Weber wrote a great deal about castes as status groups, based primarily on the colonial reports and the colonial censuses of Indian cities and villages.[5] In his major writing on India, *The Religion of India*, originally published in 1916, he referred to the caste system as a status hierarchy or a 'social rank' founded on religious and ideological grounds – asserting that the religious beliefs of Hindu society on the basis of the Varna system had resulted in the segregation of society and the formation of different status groups or castes (Weber, 1958: 30–39). The caste structure brings about social ranking, with Brahmins occupying the highest place, and this 'brings about a social subordination and an acknowledgement of "more honor" in favor of the privileged caste' (Weber, 1978: 934). It is further emphasised by Weber: 'A caste is doubtless a closed status group. All the obligations and barriers that membership in a status group entails also exist in a caste, in which they are intensified to the utmost degree' (Weber, 1958: 39–40). However, Weber predicted that in an era of economic advancement and a transition from a traditional Hindu society to a modern society, the caste system would lose its religious and ideological grounds resulting in the disappearance of caste relations. Referring to the economic transition of Calcutta in the early part of the twentieth century, he noted:

> Today [written in 1916] the Hindu caste order is profoundly shaken. Especially in the district of Calcutta, old Europe's major gateway to India, many norms have practically lost their force. The railroads, the taverns, the changing occupational stratification, the concentration of labor through imported industry, colleges, etc., have all contributed their part. The 'commuters to London', that is, those who studied in Europe and maintained voluntary social intercourse with Europeans, were outcasts up to the last generation; but more and more this pattern is disappearing. And it has been impossible to introduce caste coaches on the railroads.... All caste relations have been shaken, and the stratum of intellectuals bred by the English are here, as elsewhere, bearers of a specific nationalism. They will greatly strengthen this slow and irresistible process. For the time being, however, the caste structure still stands quite firmly. (Weber, 1958: 30)

Weber's distinction between the religious/ideological and the socio-economic significance of the caste system is particularly interesting. The latter had obvious implications for the economy, and hence for class formations. Enquiring about the economic impact of the caste system, Weber began by invoking traditional forms of 'Indian' capitalism and their relation to the caste system. He drew on some comparisons with urban Western capitalism and based his views on a deductive method of research 'inferences', as he put it, to 'phrase a few generalizations' (Weber, 1958: 111). Referring to a component of the division of labour, namely the 'artisan in the Indian village', Weber agrees with Marx that the 'stability' of Asiatic societies was secured by a 'fixed payment in kind', and 'not upon production for the market' (Weber, 1958: 111). He further explains this 'stability'

124   Contested Capital

by taking into consideration other forms of labour, such as 'the merchant' and the 'urban artisan' in India, and by drawing comparisons with similar Western forms of labour, where urban labour worked for the market, and was economically dependent upon merchant guilds. In India, he distinguished, on the one hand, the urban labour run 'mercantilistically' by princes and, on the other hand, the predominant 'village labor' (as India was mostly a country of villages). Hence, its 'stability' was due not only to the urban/village labour distinction but also to the 'caste order', he argued (Weber, 1958: 111). However, 'one must not think of this [caste] effect too directly' – that the caste system should not be seen as something too rigid in relation to the economy (Weber, 1958: 111). On the contrary, Weber seemed to infer that the 'law of caste' (referring to Budhayana's *Sacred Books of The East*, 1, 5, 9, 1) had an elastic aspect to it, as it contained a prescription according to which all domestic servants must have their hands cleaned in their respective occupation. For Weber, this was a concession similar to work done by 'wage workers' or 'itinerant workers' not belonging to households. In this law, he argued, there seemed to be no hindrance in the way of the use of different castes in a workshop. With the advancement of industrialisation in India, which results in the 'necessities of the concentration of labour in workshops', the rigidity of caste in the division of labour would become flexible, he argued (Weber, 1958: 111). Drawing on the 1911 colonial Census, Weber illustrated the elasticity of caste by pointing towards the occupational mobility of lower-caste groups in modern industries in Calcutta, where some modern skilled labour was recruited from peasants and from the fisher caste (Weber, 1958: 111–15). The only hindrance Weber saw as regards the caste system and economy was in the 'spirit', not in the letter, of the law.

Weber's view of the caste system is nuanced. Although it was not easy, employing labour from different castes in modern factories was possible. Weber concluded that even so, the caste system (regulated by 'ritual law') prevented capitalism from originating in India, or at any rate not capitalism as understood in the West (what Weber called 'the Occident'). If any form of capitalism, or 'accumulation of wealth', was to thrive in India, Weber saw it taking place especially in the lower castes, which had little ethical and ritual legalistic regulation (Weber, 1958: 111). Even so, he did not see anything in either of these two forms of labour (regulated and less-regulated) that indicated that they had reached a stage of modern capitalism.

It is notable that Weber's writing on the economic impact of the caste system is limited to the early period of industrialisation, when the demands for labour made the occupational mobility of caste groups inevitable. It is not clear whether he assumed a decline in the monopolisation by Brahmins, of education and access to wealth, or whether caste groups in principle would have equal opportunities to access socio-economic resources in a new era of industrialisation. In simple terms, it is not clear whether caste played any role in economic condition or class membership. Moreover, Weber's writing in relation to the flexibility of caste only pertained to the mobilisation of labour and so, in omitting the caste stratification of other dimensions of Weberian class, it cannot be considered conclusive. His views on the caste order were also not empirically grounded. By contrast, in what follows, we will enquire through empirical research into the economic role of caste on rural middle-class formation. We now turn to review the literature on the economic impact of caste, in particular caste and class relations (identified in economic terms).

The Caste–Class Debate in Contemporary India

Caste is deeply embedded in Indian society and has been understood as the central organising principle determining opportunities, discrimination and patterns of inequality. It has been the subject of sustained historical and sociological analysis, particularly in studies of rural areas.[6] Dumont's seminal work on caste, *Homo Hierarchicus*, published in 1966, conceptualised the caste system as one of different ethnic groups constantly in competition for resources. In emphasising the religious and ideological over the material formation of caste, he argued that the opposition pure–impure is the foundation of the caste system, which appears consistent and rational to those who experience it. However, the religious view of caste has been seen as problematic by a number of scholars, who consider caste as a fundamentally social relation, a particular form of status ranked community/ethnic community that is common across religions in South Asia. In *Beyond Caste*, a path-breaking historical survey of caste, Sumit Guha considers religious ideology as only one strand in the structure of the caste system. Guha, shifting the focus from the ritual religious perspective, proposes a historical political-economic view of the evolution of caste, and presents it as a 'politicized form of ethnic ranking shaped by the constant exercise of socio-economic power' at the level of the village cluster (Guha, 2013: 2). He suggests, while being status-ranked and hierarchical, caste is nonetheless constantly reconfigured by state power (used as an efficient tool of governance), and increasingly by forces of market competition and capital. In other words, it is fluid and historically constituted. For example, focussing on the historical analysis of *balutā* in western Maharashtra, he argues that 'baluta was not a primitive institution, but rather one that was created by the state out

126   Contested Capital

of competition between specialists in a commercializing but still well-knit rural society' (Guha, 2013: 83). It was a 'secular' system in the sense that the exchange itself was not based on any religious traditions, but was formed by market forces. Overall, Guha's argument is close to Weber's idea of status ranking or caste as a particular form of status-ranked corporate ethnic community, with the idea of ranking and hierarchy being central to his argument. Although this corporate ethnic group is often maintained by political power, the more important point is that it tends to be historically fluid.

Current scholarship on caste includes many competing narratives about whether caste differentiation translates into social and economic inequalities and class membership. Fuller argues that while class distinction is culturally constructed in all capitalist societies, in India the language and practice of caste provides the most potent and pervasive structure of inequality. Caste continues to shape people's ideology which prevents the formation of class consciousness (Fuller, 1996). However, more recent scholars have suggested that caste is becoming a less salient feature of Indian social life. In the context of post-independence history, Jayaram writes:

> The combination of caste and class status is no more a sociological axiom – the decline of the *Jajmani system* and the commercialisation of agriculture, the implementation of land reforms, the release from bondage of serfs, and the consequent changes in agrarian relations; and the rise of land-owning 'upper-Shudra' caste groups, have all profoundly altered the economic bargaining of the caste system. (Jayaram, 1996: 62)

Differentiation within a particular caste means that all castes in India have become diverse in terms of class, regardless of their rank in the social hierarchy, and all castes have members in different class positions. Caste and class intersect, and the formation of new classes across established boundaries of the caste hierarchy creates 'new alliances and antagonism' (Mukherjee, 1999: 1761). Through a historical examination of the making of the middle class in India, Sheth observes that, with the creation of the middle class and notions of a specific self-identity, individuals within the middle class display interests and lifestyles based on consumption patterns that converge with other members of their class and not with individuals from their own caste (Sheth, 1999a: 2508). Jaffrelot and van der Veer, however, suggest that class and caste, the 'status group par excellence', must be analysed together because they interact very closely in Indian social life (Jaffrelot and van der Veer, 2008: 17). Similarly, emphasising the significance of the interplay between caste and class, Harriss highlights that caste 'entails an ideology that explains and legitimates the material differences of class and power relations', and therefore, caste and class cannot be separated in the analysis of Indian society (Harriss, 2012: 2).

In a more detailed empirical study on the relationship between caste, class and power in the south Indian village of Sripuram in the 1960s, Béteille similarly suggests that the class system and caste structure overlap to a considerable extent, but that class cuts across caste at a number of points. For example, access to education, government jobs and land is no longer the monopoly of the upper castes. This is mainly the result of a social system that has acquired a much more complex and dynamic character, which creates a tendency for cleavage between caste and class. The class system thus seems in part to have detached itself from the caste structure (Béteille, 1996). Béteille nevertheless recognises that caste still determines the physical structure of the village, because caste (or a group of castes) constitutes a community in space, whereas this is rarely, if ever, true of class. However, as discussed in full in Chapter 2, the findings from Nandur suggest that economic status and class determine the physical structure of part of the village, while in Rahatwade the village is structured on the basis of caste.

Sheth also examines the relationship between caste and middle-class membership through the labour market. Based on a survey conducted by the Centre for the Study of Developing Societies in 1996, he demonstrates there has been a significant transformation in the caste composition of the middle classes, where lower-caste individuals have gained entry to the middle class, a transition primarily made possible by affirmative action (Sheth, 1999a; 1999b). Caste nevertheless continues to play a salient role in generating socio-economic differentiation within the middle class.

> [U]pper caste individuals entering the middle class have at their disposal the resources that were attached to the status of their caste in the traditional hierarchy. Similarly, for lower caste members, lacking in traditional status resources, their entry into the middle class is facilitated by modern legal provisions like affirmative action to which they are entitled by virtue of their low traditional status. (Sheth, 1999a: 2509)

Through examining the relationship between caste and occupation, a number of studies suggest that there has been a significant decline in the persistence of caste inequalities in the labour market in post-independence India, and that in the past few decades the linkage between caste and occupation has weakened. Some point out that the decline of the *jajmani* system resulted in 'market-based

128   Contested Capital

pricing for services rendered' (Commander, 1983; Desai and Dubey, 2012: 3). Sharma argues that the rise of new occupations that require education and training has resulted in the entry of large numbers of people from different castes gaining educational qualifications and securing 'modern' professions (Sharma, 1999; cited in Desai and Dubey, 2012). Béteille offers similar findings, that the politics of affirmative action have further strengthened the power of lower castes by enabling them to benefit from reservations in accessing higher education and government employment (Béteille, 1992). By drawing on extensive fieldwork in a small town of Arni in northern Tamil Nadu, however, Harriss-White shows that caste still influences access to non-farm employment (Harriss-White, 2003). My research in Maharashtra offers similar findings. Srinivasan, based on fieldwork in Arni, also shows that caste-based occupations persist and caste acts as a profound and significant 'stratifier of the local business economy' (Srinivasan, 2016: 77).[7] For rural Uttar Pradesh, Jeffrey has presented similar findings in relation to the active role of caste in the non-farm labour market in India (Jeffrey, 2001).[8]

Before exploring the relationship between caste and the middle class in Rahatwade and Nandur, we first provide a comprehensive account of the formation of the middle class in these villages. Here, an account of the socio-economic transformations that have occurred in these villages with the spreading waves of industrialisation is provided. This context helps us think beyond relations of production and productive capital as the basis of class formation. We then move on with our analysis by identifying the rural middle classes, revealing how the acquisition and distribution of various forms of capital such as education, skill credentials and social networks have enabled segments of rural residents to take advantage of industrialisation, thus gaining a foothold in the middle-class labour market.

Rahatwade and Nandur: The Socio-economic Context

During my fieldwork, I observed various repetitive scenes that revealed the very diverse socio-economic characteristics of the sample villages. These scenes included farmers returning home from their agricultural fields and female agricultural labourers moving in groups towards a payment point, usually where a man paid them their daily wages and allowed them to take some of the leftover agricultural produce. In Rahatwade, numerous middle-aged and older men often gathered in the courtyard of the main village *mandir* in the evenings, usually dressed in farmers' clothing, to engage in 'local gossip' and 'political discussions'. In Nandur, a group of up to 10–15 middle-aged men met regularly in the *mandir* courtyard in Gāvāta to play cards and gamble until late at night. Neither these men nor their children engaged substantially in agricultural work, except for the supervision of agricultural labourers and the undertaking of significant activities on their farms (such as managing water pipes).[9] Their children worked in nearby factories and had relatively high incomes, which were used to hire in agricultural labourers, as discussed in Chapter 3. The most interesting scenes were those of small numbers of young men gathering at various points every evening. These scenes of young men in both villages (but mainly in Nandur), dressed in office clothes (black trousers, white shirt and black formal shoes) often sitting on parked motorbikes playing with smartphones, revealed a transition in the class structure of these villages and provided me with anecdotal or *prima facie* evidence of the rural middle class (both in terms of consumption and employment patterns). These young men signalled an increase in the spending power of village residents due to an increase in their earnings. Although similar scenes were also evident in Rahatwade, they were less frequent and conspicuous, primarily because of differences between the two villages in income and living standards (discussed in Chapter 3). Comparing these young men with the older generation, including their fathers, also revealed the degree of social mobility in contemporary Indian villages. These young men, primarily employed in industrial sites either as skilled workers (supervisors or managers) or skilled machine operators, are prime examples of the emerging rural middle classes. They have managed to move beyond reliance on income from agriculture (which depends primarily on ownership and size of agricultural land, and availability of water) and gain access to the middle-class labour market, enabling them to adopt new patterns of consumption. Access to such forms of employment is due primarily to the existence of factories in close proximity to these villages, but it is also contingent on what is commonly known in these villages to be some of the most marketable assets: education, skill credentials and local networking.

The expansion of industrial units close to the village was frequently understood to have resulted in increases in income, changes in consumption patterns, and the formation of a middle class in these villages. Despite complaints about the low price of agricultural products and the government's failure to introduce agricultural market support prices, along with the unreliable nature of agricultural income, an overwhelming majority of respondents (from the non-labouring households) emphasised the increase in their living standards that had taken place over the past 10 years – they indicated that the economic condition and standard of living of their households had improved (Table 4.1).

130   Contested Capital

Table 4.1   Changes in the economic condition of non-labouring households over the last 10 years (2015)

Changes in economic condition	Rahatwade (N = 97)		Nandur (N = 97)	
	Freq.	Per cent	Freq.	Per cent
Improved	88	90.72	86	88.66
Worsened	1	1.03	7	7.22
Remained the same	8	8.25	4	4.12
Total	97	100	97	100

Source: Fieldwork data (2015).

Reasons for this improvement were expressed later during in-depth interviews. It was mostly stated that such improvement had been due to the availability of factory 'jobs'; they had been 'lifted out of poverty', had gained 'access to higher incomes', were 'able to purchase consumer goods' and 'build pucca houses', and overall their standard of living had 'developed'. This was because agriculture was no longer the only source of income. Industrialisation had benefited the small- and middle-sized landowning households, because they could not produce adequate income through just agriculture. Surrdin's family is one such example. Surrdin was from the Mulani caste, residing in the Gávāta in Nandur. He was employed at Fleetguard Filters factory as a skilled machine operator, earning INR 12,000 per month in 2015. He and his family were previously engaged only in sugarcane farming on a 2-acre land, which in 2014–15 generated approximately INR 100,000. His statement below is representative of how the economic impact of industrialisation was understood by many:

> Since the arrival of companies [factories] people have become wealthy. These factories have had a positive impact on our lives. The economic condition of village people has become better. If you go around the village you will not see badly built houses that are just roofed by sugarcane leaves. Many in the village now have good cement houses. Because our village is located close to factories, people get jobs.... Even if by chance there is no farming, they earn through their salary and fill their stomachs. Earlier, there were no such opportunities for work.[10]

Such statements were very common among those that had already benefited from industrialisation and those that aspired to join the new labour market. Many other families talked about increases in their income. Some said that prior to the appearance of factories close to the village, their households were poor and depended solely on agriculture and agricultural-related activates, including ad hoc agricultural wage labour. Such reliance on income from farming left the insecure and did not allow them to have a 'developed' standard of living, and the size of their holdings did not allow them to generate a surplus. Some highlighted that the recent access to industrial 'jobs' had 'lifted them from being poor to being middle class', which the majority of the respondents defined as 'households with a monthly income between 10,000 and 15,000 rupees'. The following extract from my conversation with Ajay, a 35-year-old man from the Mali caste in Nandur, is representative of the ways in which many have experienced the economic transformation in their village:

> Generally speaking, before the companies [factories] came to our village, our houses were made of corrugated tin sheets, and the roofs were made either of sugarcane grass or the remains of sugarcane, or tin sheets, or just anything we could get our hands on. But after a few factories were built close by, changes started occurring in the village. For example, the educated boys of our village who joined the companies at the start, and those who secured permanent contracts, have very good salaries now; they built their own bungalows, they bought good cars, and such improvements continues to happen in their lives. These factories are thus very important for creating employment in the village. I can say for certain that our village progressed at the fastest speed. We can witness this progress now. Just look around you [referring to the newly constructed houses].[11]

References to changes in the style of housing were frequently used to illustrate the improvement in the standard of living of those who had gained access to industrial 'jobs' (see Figures 4.1–4.4.). At first glance, indeed, the emergence of the rural middle class manifested itself in the building of new houses. In Nandur, there was an unprecedented wave of new houses under construction (as indicated by respondents, and also clearly evident). These new houses sometimes consisted of two storeys, and all had a similar style and interior. These newly constructed houses were generally large and made of cement and concrete blocks, and were often floored with ceramic tiles. Some of the central features of these houses were the separation of the kitchen from the rest of the house, an indoor toilet, balconies and, most importantly, piped water inside the house (see Figure 4.3).

Figure 4.1 gives an idea of the transformation in the style of houses in Nandur from a 'typical' house to a house of 'modern' construction. The mud house depicted in Figure 4.1 had been a home to Sujay's family of the Mali caste in Nandur for the last few generations. At the time of the fieldwork, the mud house

132   Contested Capital

accommodated six people: 32-year-old Sujay (the head of the household), his wife, his parents and his two children. 'Until five years ago, the only sources of household income were a 2-acre sugarcane farm and ad hoc agricultural labour. Over the past five years, however, I have managed to secure casual/ rotational employment as a skilled machine operator in the Fleetguard Filters factory,' Sujay tells me. He continues: 'Since these factories were built around our village, land prices in Nandur started to increase; this encouraged me to sell 1 acre of my land' (at the time of the interview he only owned 1 acre, on which he cultivated sugarcane). Sujay sold the land partially because he had to pay back the loan he had taken for a college course, which gave him a diploma in mechanical engineering, and an opportunity to work in a factory as a skilled machine operator through a labour contractor in Nandur. This meant that his family was no longer solely dependent on agriculture. He used the remainder of the cash to pay for building a new house. While I was given a tour of his new house, he did not hesitate to tell me: 'Selling the land might have been a mistake, because like many industrial workers I do not have the benefit of job security due to the casual nature of my employment.'

The newly constructed house, orange in colour, behind the mud house in Figure 4.1 is carpeted with ceramic tiles and equipped with a separate bedroom, a living room, a separate kitchen and an indoor toilet. At the time of interview, the family still resided in the mud house, waiting for the 'good luck of Diwali season' to move into the new house. The new house was only used by his small children to watch television on a flat-screen TV hung on the living room wall. Such transformations in housing style were evident in many parts of the village, particularly in the Borate Basti in Nandur (Figure 4.2). The visibility of the changing style of housing suggested the increased spending power of the rural residents, and was evidence of the emergence of the rural middle class.

The economic significance and role of industries in the changing class structure in Rahatwade and Nandur was beyond dispute; it very clearly manifested itself in the changing consumption behaviour of segments of rural households, which was primarily the result of their entry into the new labour market. In general, there had been shifts in occupational patterns among segments of rural residents. For example, younger generations from farming families have moved into skilled and semi-skilled non-farm employment. Such generational shifts, as indicated at the beginning of the chapter, are consistent with Weberian class theory when generational class mobility is gained through marketable capital. In what follows, we will provide classifications of occupations in Rahatwade and Nandur through a Weberian perspective.

Figure 4.1 Transformation in the housing style of the rural middle class in Nandur

Source: Author.

Figure 4.2 Residence of a middle-class family in Nandur

Source: Author.

Note: The typical style of new construction: the house is equipped with a separate kitchen and a private indoor toilet, and has access to piped water from the water tank on the rooftop. It is carpeted with ceramic tiles and has a private gated yard. Such features are common in middle-class houses.

Figure 4.3 Typical old style of housing: residence of a farmer in Rahatwade

Source: Author.

Note: The majority of households whose main source of income is farming reside in such buildings. They are characterised by corrugated metal roofing, no toilet and no kitchen inside the house. The floors are mainly made of dung.

Figure 4.4 Typical style of housing of the majority of Dalit agricultural labourers

Source: Author.

Note: These corrugated iron houses, which shelter most landless SC families, are situated on Gram Panchayat land. Many of these SC households are from outside and have recently settled in Nandur, seeking employment as agricultural labourers or as unskilled labourers (helpers) in factories.

Household Classifications and Middle Classes in Rahatwade and Nandur

In Chapter 2, we used the primary source of household income to identify the labouring households. These households, *negatively privileged* in both property and the labour markets, were eliminated from the analysis of the middle classes. To categorise occupational classes among the remaining households from a Weberian position, it is possible to apply a schema formed by relations in both the property market (differentiation on the basis of income generating property) and the labour market, which distinguishes between manual and non-manual work and is further differentiated by types of employment and the degree of education and skills required (Goldthorpe, 1997).[12] John Goldthorpe developed seven occupational classes within a Weberian framework where occupation was mainly differentiated on the basis of income and the degree of economic security, employment status, and degree of authority in the workplace. These occupational classes included high-grade managers and professionals; routine non-manual employees (including higher and lower grade non-manual employees); the self-employed, small employers and proprietors (including farmers); supervisors of manual workers and technicians; skilled manual workers; and non-skilled manual workers (Goldthorpe, 1997; Crompton, 1993: 58–59; Chan and Goldthorpe, 2007: 513). Goldthorpe's schema was not confined to the middle class, but is a useful guide in categorising occupational classes in Rahatwade and Nandur, within which the rural middle class is situated.

Guided by Goldthorpe's approach, it is possible to take into consideration both the theoretical foundations of the Weberian approach and the empirical reality of diverse occupational patterns in the sample villages to categorise occupational classes. Most non-labouring households were engaged in different occupations (both in agricultural and non-agricultural activities). On the basis of fieldwork data, only 5 non-labouring households in Rahatwade and only 19 in Nandur had no one in any occupation outside agriculture and thus lived off agriculture alone. Among the non-labouring households, 47 in Rahatwade and 35 in Nandur had a minimum of one member working in the industrial sites. Given the diversity of economic activities within each household, I used the primary source of household income to allocate occupational class positions to households that combined various occupations and multiple sources of income.

On such a basis, the non-labouring households fit into nine occupational categories: (*a*) farmers, who earned their income primarily from agricultural activities (this class was further divided into two sub-categories based on area of

136 Contested Capital

land owned: farmers owning more than 10 acres of land, and farmers owning less than 10 acres of land); (*b*) PCPs, including petty shop keepers and those earning their living from livestock; (*c*) skilled workers, including managers, supervisors and foremen (some of whom had a university degree and had mostly secured permanent employment contract); (*d*) government employees, including primary school teachers, police and army officers (there were only retired ones) and other low-ranked government employees (the government employees were categorised in one group because they all shared the same features of permanent employment – they enjoyed job security and retirement benefits); (*e*) entrepreneurs or the owners of workshops and other business units; (*f*) rentiers, who earned their living from leasing out their land, agricultural equipment or other property; (*g*) skilled industrial machine operators working on automated machines, who had acquired technical diplomas in private institutes and whose employment was characterised as 'casual' and 'rotational'; (*h*) independent workers, including plumbers, electricians and drivers; and (*i*) semi-skilled factory 'helpers', who acquired quick training on the job and were engaged in various manual activities in industrial units, such as packing and handling, and worked on short-term contracts.

The category of farmers owning more than 10 acres of agricultural land, and rentiers were distinguished because of their 'positive privileges' in the property market. The category of entrepreneurs was distinguished because of their 'positive privileges' in the labour market. This group did not necessarily own the production-site on which they established their non-farm economic activities. The remaining occupations in each category shared a broadly similar employment status, required education and skills, with a degree of manual work involved. The Weberian occupational classification in Rahatwade and Nandur is shown in Table 4.2.

I suggest that the Weberian middle classes are broadly situated between big landowning farmers, entrepreneurs and rentiers on the one hand, and the landless and near-to-landless unskilled wage labourers and semi-skilled manual industrial workers on the other. The former group owned profitable property and invested their surplus in expensive education for their children (the positively privileged propertied and commercial classes); they were characterised by ownership of large operational holdings and other productive property such as manufacturing workshops and other production units. Their economic activities mainly involved the large-scale appropriation of surplus in the form of agricultural labour and produce. The latter group neither owned profitable property nor any marketable educational qualification. Their only marketable capital was their manual labour power (the negatively privileged propertied and commercial classes). The rural middle class thus consisted of self-employed farmers (owning less than 10 acres of agricultural land), PCPs, independent workers, government employees, skilled industrial employees including supervisors and managers (whose occupations required formal education and skills, which tended to be exceptional in the village), and industrial machine operators (who required special training and skill credentials, and whose physical labour was not reduced to commodity forms).[13] Evidence from the fieldwork suggests that, over the last decade, a central feature of middle-class formation in Rahatwade and Nandur was the increasing number of industrial skilled workers and skilled machine operators.

Table 4.2   Occupational classification of households in Rahatwade and Nandur

Income sources	Rahatwade (N = 97)		Nandur (N = 97)	
	Freq.	Population	Freq.	Population
Cultivation (10 acres or more)	1	10	6	39
Cultivation (less than 10 acres of agricultural land)	22	131	44	278
Entrepreneurs	8	62	10	46
Petty shop and livestock	9	57	5	22
Skilled work	8	57	15	110
Government jobs	4	32	2	14
Rent	2	12	2	10
Skilled machine operators	11	54	9	61
Independent	16	129	2	10
Semi-skilled manual industrial worker (helpers)	16	118	2	15
Total	97	662	97	605

Source: Fieldwork data (2015).

Household Classifications, Household Income and Employment Types

Tables 4.3 and 4.4 show the distribution of household income in the agricultural year 2014–15 among different occupational classes in Rahatwade and Nandur, respectively. The mean and median total household incomes (generated from all sources) in each occupational category are shown in the fourth and fifth columns.[14] The last column shows the average per capita income. We can see important differences between the occupational categories/classes based on total annual household income. For example, if we look at the distribution of income among the middle classes identified above, we see that income was highest among households that earned the larger proportion of their income from skilled work.

138   Contested Capital

Table 4.3   Distribution of annual household income among different occupational categories in Rahatwade

Income sources (N = 97)	Freq.	Total income Mean (INR)	Median (INR)	Mean Per capita (INR)
Cultivation (less than 10 acres of agricultural land)	22	190,800	150,000	32,173
Cultivation (10 acres or more)	1	344,000	344,000	34,400
Petty shop and livestock	9	169,222	125,000	27,776
Skilled work	8	634,000	643,000	91,500
Government jobs	4	466,500	513,000	64,910
Entrepreneurs	8	1,251,000	955,000	150,565
Rent	2	279,000	279,000	52,875
Skilled machine operators	11	214,000	160,000	46,352
Independent	16	274,125	244,000	37,359
Semi-skilled manual industrial worker (helpers)	16	184,200	175,000	27,911
Total	97	343,400	220,000	49,980

Source: Fieldwork data (2015).

Table 4.4   Distribution of annual household income among different occupational categories in Nandur

Income sources (N = 97)	Freq.	Total income Mean (INR)	Median (INR)	Mean Per capita (INR)
Farming (less than 10 acres of agricultural land)	44	282,000	233,500	46,162
Cultivation (10 acres or more)	6	639,200	575,000	117,886
Petty shop and livestock	5	124,900	135,000	31,200
Skilled work	15	725,300	668,000	121,969
Government jobs	2	607,000	607,000	86,500
Entrepreneurs (including the labour contractors)	10	997,400	680,900	231,990
Rent	2	595,000	595,000	119,000
Skilled machine operators	9	255,800	252,000	43,682
Independent	2	266,500	266,500	54,833
Semi-skilled manual industrial worker (helpers)	2	212,500	212,500	30,750
Total	97	447,100	305,000	82,672

Source: Fieldwork data (2015).

The skilled worker category was limited to a few positions, including supervisors, managers and foremen. Their monthly income in 2015 varied from INR 12,000 to 25,000, depending on the nature of their employment. Those who had secured permanent contracts received higher salaries of between INR 20,000 and 25,000 per month. In Nandur, 19 households had at least one member working as a skilled worker in one of the industrial sites on the periphery of the village, and 15 of them earned the greater proportion of their annual household income from skilled work. In Rahatwade, 19 households had members working as skilled workers, and 8 of them earned the greater proportion of their annual household income from skilled work.[15]

These skilled workers were not necessarily big landowners. For example, of the 15 households in Nandur whose primary source of income was skilled employment, 10 owned less than 4 acres of land, 4 owned between 4 and 5 acres, and 1 owned 8 acres. In Rahatwade, out of 8 households in this category, 4 owned less than 4 acres, 2 owned 5 acres, 1 owned 6 acres and 1 owned 7 acres of agricultural land. Through acquiring marketable education and local connections, however, they had gained access to industrial jobs. The category of skilled industrial machine operator is self-explanatory. Machine operators earned between INR 6,000 to 12,000 per month in 2015 and were engaged in casual and rotational employment. In Rahatwade, 15 households had at least one member working as a skilled machine operator, out of which 11 earned the largest proportion of their income from industries. In Nandur, 31 households had at least one member working as a machine operator, out of which 9 earned the largest proportion of their income from industries. Among the category of skilled machine operators the average holding of agricultural land was 2.4 acres in Rahatwade and 2.2 acres in Nandur.

As indicated in Tables 4.3 and 4.4, there is a sharp distinction in income between different segments of industrial workers due to differences in the employment status and type of education required and the degree of manual labour involved. While supervisors and managers usually had university degrees (bachelor's and master's degrees in registered colleges and universities), machine operators had diplomas in technical subjects from informal private institutes. The majority of skilled workers were successful in obtaining permanent employment contracts, whereas employment as a machine operator was characterised by insecure casual contracts. The importance of high educational qualifications in obtaining permanent employment was highlighted by the former *sarpanch* of Nandur:

> Factories often do not offer permanent contracts. Only those who are well qualified have a chance of becoming permanent in their workplace. Relationships and networks do not always secure contracts; whether you have good relations or not, you really need to have good education qualifications. If a man becomes an engineer or is well qualified, then only he is likely to be offered a permanent contract, but not always, sometimes only, otherwise he too remains a casual employee.[16]

140   Contested Capital

Although there were some permanent contract holders among supervisors and managers, casual/rotational employment was typical among industrial workers, particularly among machine operators. Despite being known as a lucrative source of income (and more desirable than agricultural activities), therefore, the casual nature of industrial employment in these factories did not guarantee a fixed or permanent income for middle-class households (and, as discussed in Chapter 3, they still generated income from agriculture). The following interview extract with Vijay is illustrative of frustration of casual industrial workers:

> Many middle-class families earn their income from the casual contracted jobs in factories. They receive 6,000 to 12,000 rupees per month, with which they have to run their houses and meet their family expenses. Whatever requirements they have, and the basic necessities in life, should be fulfilled from that amount. These young men will keep on working in casual employment while their youth goes away. They will grow old without any savings or securities, because they do not have any benefits and pensions from their work place. Also they cannot save any money from the income they receive, which could be beneficial in their old age. That is why they have no financial securities. It is my opinion that those boys who work in the company roughly until the age of 25 or 30 should be given a permanent contract and a fixed salary, and their work place should keep aside some fixed amount for them for their retirement, so in future they do not face any difficulties, or in old age they do not face any hurdles in their lives.[17]

The overall analysis of the middle classes in these villages reveals a certain characteristic of this class: an individual employed in an industrial site might not secure the same employment in the subsequent six-month period and could consequently lose the class position (the membership of the middle class) which is contingent on his/her employment. It is worth noting that a propertyless individual who is positively privileged in the labour market through possession of a high-quality education may not be able to retain his/her class situation in the labour market in the case of a decline in the demand for factory workers. Despite the possession of skills and education, therefore, the Weberian 'class situation' of the majority of industrial workers remains unstable, a possibility Weber omitted to discuss.

The Paradoxical Role of Labour Contractors as Hubs in Social Networks

A further difference between other skilled employees and skilled machine operators is their reliance on labour contractors. The recruitment process for casual employment for machine operators and semi-skilled workers ('helpers') in these factories takes place through various labour contractors, who have secured a contract with these factories to recruit their required labour force. Parry presents similar findings in a study of industrialisation in rural Chhattisgarh. He shows that most private-sector factories, similar to those on the periphery of Rahatwade and Nandur, only recruit industrial workers through labour contractors, who then act as 'the notional employer' of the workers they recruit (Parry, 2013).[18] These labour contractors routinely hire temporary staff for a period of six months or less, followed by a six-month break, during which time the workers can accept another temporary job in a different factory through the same labour contractor or remain unemployed for half a year until they rejoin the same factory: 'The company pays contractors, and then they remove their commission and then pay the salaries of the workers,' Vijay, a machine operator in Nandur, told me.[19]

> Only those who are powerful in our village become industrial labour contractors. People like us who have no power do not have such possibilities. In Nandur, there are several contractors, all well connected to the Gram Panchayat office. The Gram Panchayat members hold all the power; they bully the factory managers, pressurising them, or demanding that the factories give them the contracts for recruitment. The owners of factories are afraid of the local Gram Panchayat because they fear if they do not give in to such demands they may face barriers in production process. So to avoid any local troubles, they meet the demand of the Gram Panchayat committee and give the contracts to fixed X, Y, and Z persons chosen by the Gram Panchayat members. So what the factory manager does is to select two, three or four people suggested by the Gram Panchayat committee to act as labour contractors, so that their production can be operated smoothly. That is how some people become labour contractors; and then they take the local and nearby boys to be hired in factories.[20]

When I enquired about whether the residents who seek employment were able to approach the factories directly, I was told that factories did not directly hire labourers and often made a variety of excuses, such as 'we have taken required number of workers and we no longer have any vacancies'. Overall, 'it is not possible to secure employment directly from factories'.[21]

I was told there were five labour contractors in Nandur, four of whom I identified. There were none in Rahatwade. In the early stages of the fieldwork, when I was collecting data related to the ways in which people gain access to industrial employment, I thought that the absence of labour contractors in Rahatwade was positive for village residents because their pay would not have to go through the hands of middlemen. I soon realised, however, that despite their

142   Contested Capital

negative role, the presence of local labour contractors had some advantages for local industrial workers because it facilitated access to employment through local connections and kinship. In contrast, if village residents had to negotiate with contractors from another village where they had no local or kinship ties, they had limited bargaining power. In Rahatwade, those who sought employment in local factories had to approach contractors in the neighbouring village of Kundhanpur. This is because the factories were located in Kundhanpur and not connected to Rahatwade in terms of water and electricity supply and overall local support. Perhaps, this is one of the reasons why there were fewer industrial workers in Rahatwade. A respondent in Rahatwade explained to me the crucial role of labour contractors in facilitating employment for the rural workforce:

> See, today's scenario or the position of the poor people is that, even after taking commission, the labour contractor is still giving access to industrial jobs to our boys, without which our boys will remain unemployed, then our gas stoves do not burn in our houses.[22]

Overall, the presence of labour contractors was disadvantageous in relation to their dominant economic role in the labour market, and through the exploitation of labour due to their taking commissions (also the process of recruitment might be mediated through kinship and caste).[23] On the other hand, gaining access to industrial employment appeared to be impossible without them – they are as gatekeepers to industrial works. This made the role of labour contractors paradoxical: despite their disadvantageous economic role, they acted as local social network hubs (in Weberian terms) for the village working population seeking industrial employment.

Education and Skills

The empirical evidence from Rahatwade and Nandur suggests that education is commonly understood to be a gateway to well-paid 'jobs' not associated with the uncertainty and hard work of agriculture, enabling upward class mobility. In Weberian terms, apart from the possession of productive property and wealth, 'life chances' become largely dependent on skills, education and qualifications that enhance income-earning capacities (Weber, 1978). Individuals from different castes and economic backgrounds attempt a range of strategies to acquire credentials, skills, education and knowledge necessary for entry into the new economy of the labour market.

Chapter 3 showed that the surplus-producing classes (the capitalist class, new capitalist class and the middle classes) reinvested part of their surplus in their children's education (primarily in English-medium schooling) to ensure lucrative occupations. The majority of respondents referred to education as a 'gateway' to market opportunities, enabling access to well-paying, secure 'jobs'. The richer families, whose aim was to give their children a university education, often sent their children to private boarding schools in Pune, particularly from the 10th to 12th standards, where the children stayed in hostels. This was to ensure that the children received a 'proper quality education' which would 'increase chances of admission to well-reputed universities/colleges'.[24] The brief story of 19-year old Pallavi captures the educational aspirations of wealthier middle-class families. Her father was a production supervisor in one of the factories outside Nandur, and also owned a sugarcane farm (8 acres). At the time of the fieldwork, Pallavi was boarding in a private college in Pune, completing her 12th standard in an English-medium private school and majoring in sciences. Her tuition fee was INR 100,000 a year and her family spent an additional INR 120,000 on her maintenance in Pune. She expressed her desire to gain a Master's degree, 'becoming an engineer and then moving on to do a PhD degree to increase chances for a lucrative city employment'.[25] This example highlights the importance of private English-medium education among the members of the middle class for upward economic mobility. Obtaining a university education, however, was not preferred by all families and their young members, because it offers no guarantees for white-collar employment either in the public or in the private sector, or even for permanent skilled industrial employment. Rapid access to earnings after a vocational and technical training is therefore more desirable. Many individuals I interviewed expressed their preference for informal private institutes that offer vocational training, which allows them to obtain English-medium technical education in 'engineering' as a strategy for upward economic mobility. Such 'fast-track' education (as it is called in these villages) enabled them to gain employment in factories, and have higher incomes than in agriculture.

The example of 20-year-old Rajo offers an insight into the strategic education patterns of young men (and some young women) seeking to gain access to middle-class occupations. Rajo came from a farming family in Nandur that earned its income primarily from a 2-acre sugarcane farm. Rajo and his family, including his parents, younger sister and grandparents (six members in total), lived in a small room. The room had a stove in the corner for cooking; in the other corner, a small area separated by a small wall made from barrels and a curtain, where they washed. They all slept in the same room. Rajo's father completed his 10th standard and his mother her 7th standard. His grandparents were illiterate. Rajo studied in at

144 Contested Capital

Nandur's public school, but continued his education in secondary school in the neighbouring village of Sahajpur. After completing the 10th standard, he went on to pursue further education at a private college in Uruli Kanchan (a small town outside Nandur). He enrolled in a two-year diploma course in Mechanical Engineering (which, according to Rajo, was undertaken 'compulsorily in English'), hoping to become a skilled machine operator, preferably in one of the factories near Nandur. Rajo's sister was also enrolled on a diploma course in Computer Engineering at a private college in Uruli Kanchan. I asked Rajo why he chose this educational path instead of completing secondary school and then pursuing a formal university degree. He answered:

> Because this way I can earn 10,000 to 15,000 rupees per month as fast as possible. Had I continued onto my12th standard, and then to a university degree, that would have taken four to six years. That is a long time! So, I can always do a university degree in the future if I decide to, later on in life. My family now requires money. In our village there are new houses, new bikes, new cars, but my family is not in a good condition, so that is why I want to have a job in a factory, and for that I needed a technical diploma. I want to buy my own bungalow, a car, and be able to take my family for a tour [holiday trip]. They will be happy and life will be enjoyable.[26]

Rajo's story also highlights some important aspects of aspirations and attempts to break through the boundaries of the middle class: first, a change in the level and type of education for younger family members aiming at securing jobs and higher incomes; and second, seeking industrial jobs, at least in part, to gain access to consumer goods. Many individuals in the village aspired to own consumer goods associated with the middle class, a phenomenon van Wessel describes as 'needing in order to become or remain a social equal with others' (van Wessel, 2004: 97).[27] Rajo's narrative relating to his ambition and educational pattern was similar to that of other young men who had joined the middle class or aspired to do so. The expansion of industries in these villages had influenced the educational preferences of young men and women. Many left formal education after completing the 10th standard (matriculation) and enrolled in private technical colleges to embark on 'fast-track' courses that ensured employment in factories. These pathways had become very popular and had captured the imagination of young men and some women as a route to a decent income outside agriculture. In both Rahatwade and Nandur, more than half of the non-labouring households had members undertaking (or having undertaken) such technical education courses. The demand for this type of education was accompanied by a corresponding growth in the number of private institutes offering technical education in rural areas. Advertisements for informal and private educational institutions offering diploma courses mainly in Mechanical Engineering, Civil Engineering, Computer Engineering, and E&TC (Electronics and Telecommunications) were widespread in Rahatwade and Nandur. These findings are similar to those of Leela Fernandes examining the urban middle class in India. Fernandes showed how individuals from the aspirant middle class, who did not have access to substantial financial capital to pay for marketable degrees such as an MBA, enrolled in institutions that granted certificates or diplomas in computer training courses, English language classes, and various areas of management and 'public speaking training' to 'gain a foothold' in the new middle-class labour market (Fernandes, 2006: 94). Such practices were particularly popular among new college graduates who had not joined the labour market, and those already in employment who sought to increase their marketable skills and enhance their chances of promotion and higher income (Fernandes, 2006). From the discussion above, we can conclude that education, skill credentials and social networks constitute a specific kind of labour market privilege in rural India in the newest phase of industrialisation, enabling individuals to move from agriculture and agriculture-related activities to higher paying employment, and thus to cross the middle-class boundaries.[28] This is in accordance with Weber's concept of the life chances that individuals bring to the market.[29] To sum up, the combination of industrialisation and the mushrooming of new educational institutes in rural areas have enabled a segment of the rural population to enter the middle-class labour. However, this trajectory is less common among the lower castes: the majority of SC and all ST households in these villages earned their living primarily from unskilled wage labour, both in the agricultural and the non-agricultural sectors. This indicates that there exist caste cleavages in the formation of the rural middle class. We now turn to explore how the two dimensions of Weber's theory of stratification (caste and class, and in particular the middle class) are interlinked.

Caste in Rahatwade and Nandur

The castes of Rahatwade and Nandur were described in Chapter 2. As demonstrated in that chapter, the physical structure of these villages continue to be cleaved by caste, which also indicated sharp social divisions.[30] Anecdotal evidence from these villages suggests, however, that some areas of social life, such as access to education, had become relatively unaffected by caste. Caste endogamy was nevertheless still commonly practised in both villages. Participants

146   Contested Capital

repeatedly stated that the practice of arranged marriage within castes continued to be followed, and that marriage outside one's caste was unthinkable.[31] There had been a number of cases in which relationships had developed between young people from different castes, and such cases were strongly opposed by the whole village. In some cases the couple eloped; one eloping couple from Rahatwade was eventually tracked down and punished by having their genitals electrocuted. It was not clear from the story whether they survived. While caste stratification continued to be omnipresent in marriages, surnames, and in the physical structure of these villages, the extent to which caste informed the structural boundaries of socio-economic stratification (class) in Rahatwade and Nandur, and in contemporary rural India more generally, is a context-specific question requiring careful empirical investigation. In what follows, I first examine whether the process of industrialisation and the diffusion of new occupations had resulted in the dissociation of caste from occupation, or whether caste still affected access to non-farm occupations in Rahatwade and Nandur and in rural All-India. The results then frame the second exploration, examining the role caste played in accessing socio-economic resources that determined middle-class membership. This exercise was carried out by examining the impact of caste on income, access to education, social networking and access to consumer goods.

Caste and Occupations

During my fieldwork, I was often told that, regardless of what caste an individual belonged to, it was possible to perform a variety of economic activities that were not part of traditional caste occupations (termed the *bara balutedar* system in Maharashtra).[32] Respondents frequently stated that the servant-cum-caste system of the *bara balutedar* had completely vanished in the two decades prior to 2014–15, partly because of access to education and opportunities for factory employment, and also because of employment outside the village. The former *sarpanch* of Nandur explained in an extended interview that the occupation system of *bara balutedar* is no longer practised:

> Even if an individual decides to carry on with the profession of their ancestors, it is completely his/her choice, and even in such a case such activities will be on the basis of cash payment, rather than exchange of services. Migration to cities and the availability of industrial work, combined with the possibility of acquiring education, have encouraged people to move away from the occupations of their parents. Nowadays, regardless of their caste, people are free to choose their occupation.[33]

This point was illustrated by an example: 'Back in the day, if someone's animal was dead, it was the responsibility and job of Dalits to remove the body of the dead animal. Nowadays, the owner of the animal, regardless of caste, is responsible for taking it away.'[34] Such statements are not conclusive, however, and should be treated with caution because I did not cross-check their validity with the members of the lower castes (primarily because majority of SC and ST households being identified as manual labouring households were excluded from in-depth qualitative interviews). Similarly, many respondents (albeit excluding the SCs and STs) stated that educational opportunities had enabled people to acquire skills outside their traditional caste-related economic activities, particularly because of the availability of new occupations there were contingent on one's education, and that the 'arrival of industries in the village had helped this'.[35] Occupations thus appeared to have become disassociated from caste. However, findings of the fieldwork indicated a broad congruence between the caste hierarchy and the occupational structure, particularly when we look at the village as a whole and not just at the middle classes.

In Chapter 2, I made a basic socio-economic division on the basis of the primary source of household income in both villages. The households were divided into two broad categories: those that relied primarily on selling their physical labour power to earn a living, and the rest of the village. Looking at the caste composition of this broad socio-economic division makes the caste inequality immediately evident. Tables 4.5 and 4.6 demonstrate the caste affiliations of these two categories. The second column in each table shows the number of households in each caste group. The third column shows the number of households in each caste group identified as labouring households. The fourth column shows the percentage of labouring households within each caste group.

Table 4.5   Caste affiliations among the labouring households in Rahatwade

Rahatwade (N = 250)	Total	Freq.	Per cent of the caste group
OBCs	4	2	50
SCs	25	24	96
STs	1	1	100
Marathas	202	100	49.5
Dhangars	17	12	70.6
Muslims	1	1	100
Total	250	140	56

Source: Fieldwork data (2015).

148   Contested Capital

Table 4.6   Caste affiliation among labouring households in Nandur

Nandur (N = 240)	Total	Freq.	Per cent of the caste group
OBCs	90	45	50
SCs	34	30	88.2
STs	4	3	75
DTs & NT-B	12	12	100
Marathas	8	6	75
Dhangars	86	33	38.4
Muslims	6	5	83.3
Total	240	134	55.8

Source: Fieldwork data (2015).

In Rahatwade, out of a total of 25 SC households, only 1 qualified as a non-labouring household. The only ST household in Rahatwade was identified as a manual labouring household.[36] In Nandur, out of 34 SC households, only 4 were identified as non-labouring. The household head in 1 of them was a primary school teacher, educated and employed through reservations. His son, who spoke fluent English during the interview, had acquired an MBA (his fees were reduced through caste reservations) and was employed at IBM in Pune. The second non-labouring SC household ran a small-scale dairy production business and was also involved in sugarcane farming. Out of the 16 STs and other tribal households (excluding Dhangars) in Nandur, 15 were identified as manual labouring. Only 1 ST household was identified as a non-labouring household. Indeed, the majority of SC and ST households in both villages were agricultural labourers.

The exclusion of SCs and STs from non-labouring households, and consequently as potential middle-class households, is highly significant, because it reveals a very important caste cleavage relating to the rural middle classes. Overall, despite the diffusion of new occupations, there are no signs of dissociation between caste and occupation when we look at the occupations of lower castes. To draw a more generally valid conclusion about the relations between caste and the labour market, we can use rural evidence collected at the All-India level. The analysis of the IHDS-II database (2011–12) relating to caste and the primary source of income among rural households is summarised in Table 4.7 (the analysis is confined to the caste classifications of Brahmins, Forward Castes, OBCs, SCs and STs). Table 4.7 shows the existence of caste disparities in the labour market throughout rural India. Approximately 60 per cent of rural India's SCs earn their living primarily from manual labour (26.94 per cent earn their living primarily from agricultural wage labour and 33.22 per cent from non-agricultural wage labour), which is significantly higher than in the case of other caste groups in rural India. Only 7.8 per cent of SC households in rural India have salaried employment as their primary source of income, which is significantly lower than the percentage of the upper and middle caste population engaged in salaried employment. If we consider SCs access to reservations in government jobs, the difference becomes even more significant. A similar trend is also evident among the STs. The distribution of the main source of household income among different caste groups in urban India is shown in Appendix A2. Comparing the result of caste disparities in the labour market in rural India with that of urban India reveals greater caste inequality in labour markets in rural India, which also indicates that SCs and STs in urban areas have easier access to reservations.[37]

Table 4.7 Occupational distribution among caste groups in rural All-India (2011–12)

Main source of household income	Brahmins	Forward Castes	OBCs	SCs	STs	Total
Sample size	1,135	5,548	11,103	6,298	3,129	27,205
Cultivation	45.53	41.98	37.25	18.28	39.39	34.08
Allied agriculture	0.91	1.08	1.51	0.85	1.04	1.19
Agri. wage labour	2.22	9.38	13.03	26.94	15.87	15.61
Non-agri. wage labour	9.46	15.64	22.58	33.22	25.97	23.73
Artisan/independent	0.82	1.21	1.85	0.92	0.62	1.33
Petty shop	7.27	8	8.33	5.13	3.51	6.92
Organised business	0.69	0.85	0.56	0.14	0.048	0.46
Salaried	17.33	11.41	7.89	7.8	9.31	9.06
Profession	1.84	0.41	0.33	0.33	0.05	0.38
Pension/rent, etc.	8.75	5.82	3.38	3.28	2.43	3.92
Others	5.17	4.21	3.31	3.1	1.75	3.33
Total	100	100	100	100	100	100

Source: Computed from the IHDS-II.

To examine the persistence of caste inequality in the labour market in rural India over the past 30 years, I have used three rounds of macro data at the All-India level: HDPI (1993–94), IHDS-I (2004–05) and IHDS-II (2011–12). The analysis shows there has been a marginal decline in the relationship between caste and occupation (see Appendix A3).

Caste and Socio-economic Indicators in Rahatwade and Nandur

Tables 4.8 and 4.9 show the distribution of various socio-economic indicators embedded in Weber's theory of classes (and indicators of middle-class membership)

150   Contested Capital

among different caste groups in Rahatwade and Nandur. These markers include the extent of land ownership; ownership of durable consumer goods (relating to the propertied classes); the highest level of male adult education; the existence of social networks; access to social media (relating to Weber's commercial classes); house type (*pucca* or *kutcha*); access to a toilet; and the availability of a kitchen in the house (related to the degree of privilege in Weber's categorisation of classes). The last row in each table also shows self-identification as members of the middle class (in contrast to being a member of 'the poor').

Tables 4.8 and 4.9 show major caste inequality in the ownership of land. SCs and STs had the highest proportion of landless households and the lowest average area of total landholdings and of cultivated land – in Rahatwade 28 per cent of the SCs, and the only ST household, did not own any land. In Nandur 79.4 per cent of SC households, and none of the STs owned any land. Examining the highest level of mean male adult education in different caste groups shows that it was lowest among the SCs and STs. Caste disparities were also evident in access to other socio-economic resources; for example, the majority of SCs and STs had fewer doctors, teachers, university professors, politicians, police officers, office managers, lawyers and bank employees in their social circles, while Marathas and Dhangars scored better in terms of the size and sophistication of their social networks. There was a further major difference in the self-identification of households as middle classes: the majority of SCs and STs did not self-identify as middle class but as members of the poor class.

The most significant indication of caste inequality, however, remained land ownership. Considering the emergence of local industrialisation and the availability of employment outside agriculture, land may appear no longer to be the principle source of livelihood. An increase in the number of non-agricultural wage workers in the rural population (this finding was presented in Chapter 3; see Figure 3.1) illustrated a decrease in dependency on land for survival among the rural population. However, the field evidence suggests that despite the availability of other sources of livelihood, land ownership remained the most important marker of class membership. The lack of access to land not only deprived households of agricultural income but also made it near impossible to invest in education, which was also the means of securing access to skilled and semi-skilled employment in industrial units. This was because among the less well-off families who did not produce any surplus and did not have enough savings, many were forced to take out crop loans or other private credit (using the land as security) to pay for private education. Loan facilities offered by co-operative banks were not available to those

Table 4.8 Descriptive statistics for socio-economic variables among different caste groups in Rahatwade

Rahatwade (N = 250) Dependent variables	OBCs	SCs	STs	Marathas	Dhangars	Muslims	Total
Household frequency	4	25	1	202	17	1	250
Total population	42	129	4	1,284	138	7	1,604
Owns any land	4 (100%)	18 (72%)	0	192 (95%)	17 (100%)	0	231 (92.4%)
Average total holdings (acre)	3.125	0.78	0	2.88	2.20	0	2.82
Average area under cultivation (acre)	1.87	0.57	0	2.28	1.94	0	2.06
Highest level of male adult education	9.7	9.6	9	11	9.2	9	10
Ownership of consumer goods (owns any motorcycle, car, colour TV, air cooler, mobile, smartphone, computer and refrigerator)	3	2.5	2	3.6	3.3	4	3.4
House type (pucca roof and pucca wall)	1 (25%)	1 (4%)	1 (100%)	51 (25.25%)	9 (52.94%)	0	63 (25.2%)
Access to toilet (mean: freq. and percentage)	2 (50%)	23 (92%)	1 (100%)	158 (78%)	11 (64.7%)	1 (100%)	196 (78.4%)
Availability of kitchen (mean: freq. and percentage)	1 (25%)	9 (36%)	0	119 (59%)	7 (41.2%)	1 (100%)	137 (54.8%)
Social network index (knows any doctors, teachers, university professor, politician, police officer, office manager, lawyer and bank employee)	0.5	0.64	1	1.3	1.8	0	1.2
Social media: anyone in the household uses Facebook or Twitter (mean: freq. and percentage)	1 (25%)	7 (28%)	0	82 (40.6%)	6 (35.3%)	1 (100%)	97 (38.8%)
Considers themselves as a middle-class household	3 (75%)	12 (48%)	0	151 (74.7%)	10 (58.8%)	1 (100%)	177 (70.8%)

Source: Fieldwork data (2015).

Table 4.9 Descriptive statistics for socio-economic variables among different caste groups in Nandur

Nandur (N = 240) Dependent variables	OBCs	SCs	STs and others	Marathas	Dhangars	Muslims	Total
Household frequency	90	34	16	8	86	6	240
Total population	501	178	80	31	482	29	1,301
Owns any land	73 (81.1%)	7 (20.6%)	0	2 (25%)	74 (86%)	4 (66.7%)	160 (66.7%)
Average total holdings (acre)	2.43	0.68	0	1.5	5.2	0.58	2.94
Average area under cultivation (acre)	2.1	0.44	0	1.5	4	0.58	2.36
Highest level of male adult education	10.5	8.5	5.9	8.6	8.7	9	9.2
Ownership of consumer goods (owns any motorcycle, car, colour TV, air cooler, mobile, smartphone, computer and refrigerator)	4.4	3.4	3.4	3.2	4.4	3.5	4.1
House type (*pucca* roof and *pucca* wall)	77 (85%)	23 (67.6%)	12 (75%)	6 (75%)	75 (87.2%)	4 (66.7%)	198 (82.5%)
Access to toilet (mean: freq. and percentage)	81 (90%)	23 (67.6%)	12 (75%)	5 (62.5%)	78 (90.7%)	4 (66.7%)	203 (84.6%)
Availability of kitchen (mean: freq. and percentage)	60 (66.7%)	16 (47.1%)	6 (37.5%)	4 (50%)	51 (59.3%)	3 (50%)	140 (58.3%)
Social network index (knows any doctors, teachers, university professor, politician, police officer, office manager, lawyer and bank employee)	2.1	1.3	0.9	2.5	2.1	1	1.9
Social media: anyone in the household uses Facebook or Twitter (mean: freq. and percentage)	49 (54.4%)	14 (41.2%)	4 (25%)	2 (25%)	45 (52.3%)	1 (16.7)	115 (47.9%)
Considers themselves as a middle-class household	62 (68.9%)	13 (38.2%)	3 (18.7%)	5 (62.5%)	52 (60.5%)	4 (66.7%)	139 (57.9%)

Source: Fieldwork data (2015).

who possessed little or no land, making it near impossible for landless households to invest in their children's education. This increased the likelihood that the next generation would remain wage labourers and suffer the same level of poverty.[38]

Similarly, Tables 4.8 and 4.9 show that the highest level of adult education, in combination with land ownership and the differences in the social network index, could be responsible for access to the middle-class labour markets. In which case, unless caste was mediated through reservations, lower-caste households were likely to remain wage labourers. Caste therefore continued to play a significant role in the formation of the middle class.

Significant class variations exist within the single Maratha caste, as indicated in Chapter 2, which can be examined in Rahatwade, where the majority of households belonged to the Maratha caste. Out of a total 202 Maratha households, 100 households were identified as manual labouring households, earning their income primarily from agricultural or non-agricultural wage labour (see Table 4.5). Class variation among the Marathas of Rahatwade was also evident from the distribution of their land, shown in Table 4.10. The top four landowning Marathas together owned as much as 10 per cent of the total land owned by all Maratha households in the village, while the bottom 50 per cent of Maratha households together owned less than 20 per cent.

Table 4.10 Distribution of land ownership (irrigated and dry combined) among Marathas in Rahatwade

Total land (N = 202)	Freq.	Per cent	Total land owned (acre)	Percentage of total land owned by all Marathas
No land	10	4.95	0	0
Between 0.1 and 2 acres	97	48.06	114.145	19.6
Between 2.1 and 4 acres	54	26.75	172.25	29.56
Between 4.1 and 6 acres	23	11.4	122	20.9
Between 6.1 and 10 acres	14	6.94	115.5	19.82
Above 10.1 acres	4	1.99	59	10.12
Total	202	100	582.895	100

Source: Fieldwork data (2015).

A similar indicator of class division among Marathas becomes evident through their income distribution.[39] The second round of household survey in Rahatwade included 88 non-labouring Maratha households. Given the high number of Marathas in the survey, it is possible to examine the income differences between

154 Contested Capital

Marathas in Rahatwade. If we divide the population of the Maratha households and look at the annual per capita income of different quintiles, we see clear class variations. Table 4.11 shows this. We can see that the richest Maratha quintile had as much as 45.5 per cent of the total income of the Marathas with a mean annual per capita income of INR 121,200. The poorest income quintile had a mean annual per capita income of INR 16,350, and had as little as just under 6 per cent of the total income of non-labouring Maratha households in Rahatwade.

Table 4.11   Income distribution among the non-labouring Maratha households in Rahatwade

Total non-labouring households (N = 88)	Freq.	Annual per capita income range (INR)	Mean annual per capita income (INR)	Total (INR)	Percentage of total per capita income of non-labouring Marathas
Poorest 20%	17	23,850 and below	16,350	278,022	6.15%
Second 20%	18	Between 23,850 and 32,940	28,100	505,971	11.2%
Third 20%	18	Between 32,940 and 42,830	37,540	675,842	14.94%
Fourth 20%	18	Between 42,830 and 70,400	55,750	1,003,495	22.2%
Richest 20%	17	Above 70,400	121,200	2,060,452	45.5%
Total	88	N.A.	51,406	4,523,800	100%

Source: Fieldwork data (2015).

Similarly, in a study of Marathas' attempt to access reservation quotas, Jaffrelot and Kalaiyarasan (2017) examined income and class differentiation among the Marathas caste overall. Drawing on the IHDS-II (2011–12), they showed that the richest Maratha quintile had as much as 48 per cent of the total income of the Marathas with a mean per capita income of INR 86,750. On the other hand, the poorest income quintile earned 10 times less (INR 7,198) and the adjacent quintile only earned INR 16,285. This means that 40 per cent of the poorest Marathas obtained less than 13 per cent of the total income of all Marathas. Their analysis demonstrated that the bottom 40 per cent of the Maratha income group lagged behind the richest Dalit quintile (with a mean per capita income of INR 63,030), and that the per capita annual income of Dalits (INR 28,897) exceeded the mean per capita income of the three lowest Maratha quintiles (the bottom 60 per cent of income groups) (Jaffrelot and Kalaiyarasan, 2017). On the basis of our data from Rahatwade and findings provided by Jaffrelot and Kalaiyarasan, we can thus conclude that Marathas are differentiated in class terms.

Similar income disparities are evident when we look at the income distribution of different caste groups in rural India as a whole. To provide a better illustration of the differences in income within and between different caste groups, we use the Lorenz curves based on data from IHDS-II (2011–12), which are shown in Figure 4.5.[40] This figure shows the distribution of per capita income deciles amongst different caste groups in rural India. It illustrates the variations in household per capita income both within the same caste groups, and between different caste groups. This further strengthens the argument that there is a difference in income distribution both *between* and *within* different castes. According to the graph, the income disparities within castes are the highest among the Forward Castes. The income distributions of the poorest 90 per cent of the population in the three backward caste groups (SCs, STs and OBCs) are almost identical and they only differ significantly among the richest 10 per cent of their population. Similarly, the income distributions of the poorest 90 per cent of the population among members of the Forward Castes and Brahmins are similar and only differ among the richest 10 per cent.

Figure 4.5 Lorenz curve for household income distribution between and within different caste groups in rural India (2011–12)

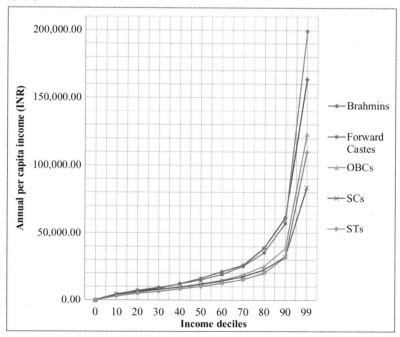

Source: Computed from the IHDS-II.

156   Contested Capital

Despite the income differentiation within caste groups, Brahmins and Forward Castes overall have a higher income compared to other castes in rural India, while SCs and STs are at the bottom of the aggregate income distribution. However, the major income difference between caste groups is sharper for the top 50 per cent of the population. A detailed analysis of (*a*) the differences in income distribution among different castes in rural and urban India, (*b*) the relationship between caste and income in rural India and (*c*) the impact of caste on accessing socio-economic resources in rural and urban India is provided in full in Appendices A4 and A5.

Caste Composition of the Rural Middle Class

In Rahatwade and Nandur, all STs and the majority of SCs earned their living primarily from manual wage labour, and were thus excluded from the 'middle class' classification. On the basis of the fieldwork data, therefore, it is possible to argue that our identified rural middle classes did not include STs and SCs, except for a negligible number of SC households that had benefited from access to reservations. However, due to the low population sizes in these villages, we are not able to generalise this finding. The question of generalisability can be addressed using the IHDS-II to assess the caste composition of middle classes (identified in Chapter 1) throughout rural India. Table 4.12 shows the class composition of each caste group in rural India.[41] We can see majority of SCs and STs were manual workers (60.78 per cent of SCs and 42.62 per cent of STs throughout rural India). This is much higher than the average percentage of the total population in the labouring classes. Furthermore, almost 40 per cent of Brahmins and 31.12 per cent of Forward Castes belonged to the three categories of the rural middle classes, while this is only 7.5 and 9.6 per cent among the SCs and STs respectively. This is evidence of caste disparities in class formation in India, with the middle and the upper class consisting primarily of the upper castes.[42] Its upper and middle caste character is thus one of the defining characteristics of the middle class, particularly in rural India.

To sum up, in this chapter I shifted the conceptualisation of class from 'relations of production' to 'life chances' and occupational mobility through possession of non-propertied capital such as education and skill differentials, social networks and caste privileges. I sought to provide a preliminary guide to the varied ways in which members of aspirant rural households seek upward social mobility, to gain access to the middle-class labour market. We have seen that the emergence

Table 4.12   Caste composition of classes in rural India – percentage (2011–12)

Classes	Freq.	Brahmins	Forward Castes	OBCs	SCs	STs	Total
Manual labouring households	10,238	11.89	25.7	36.34	60.78	42.62	40.07
Lowest class	5,211	16.9	18	23.81	15.94	32.39	21.3
Second lowest class	5,830	30.19	24.64	23.18	15.65	15.12	21.03
Lower middle class	3,583	25.02	18.34	11.01	5.28	6.35	11.01
Comfortable middle class	1,777	13.84	10.51	4.76	1.99	2.66	5.34
Upper middle class	370	2.04	2.27	0.8	0.32	0.62	1.03
Upper class	73	0.13	0.53	0.083	0.038	0.23	0.2
Rural All-India	27,082	100	100	100	100	100	100

Source: Computed from the IHDS-II.

of factories in outskirt of these villages, together with mushrooming of informal educational institutes has created a condition for many rural inhabitants (mainly young men) to acquire 'fast-track' technical qualification, as a form of marketable capital, to break cross the middle-class boundaries. The increasing importance of skilled industrial workers is therefore central to the formation of the rural middle class in these villages, and possibly in many parts of rural India. In short, rural middle-class formation is informed by shifts in the direction of employment aspirations, and in this context, education and social connections are central drivers of class formation. However, two main observations stand out. First, as the empirical evidence suggested, the income, occupation and status of the large segment of the rural middle class are inherently precarious and very much contingent on industrial development planning, employment regulations and local relations – the latter often mediated through kinship, caste and gender. Second, it is important to recognise the caste cleavages in the rural middle class, which is primarily constituted of the upper and middle castes. The SCs and STs are mainly excluded from its membership and such restrictions are mainly due to absence of local connections, and inability to pay high tuition fee cost which results in unequal access to educational institutions. Therefore, we can say for certain that caste acts as a gatekeeper to middle-class frontiers. This illuminates the usefulness of a Weberian class-status analysis in the current phase of industrialisation in rural India. Furthermore, Weber gives us a productive tool to expand on the purely ownership-based definition of class, while retaining the structural complexity in relation to the ownership of both productive capital, and other forms of marketable

158   Contested Capital

capital that are drivers of class formation. What other forms of capital can create class boundaries? It is with this question in mind that we now turn to Bourdieu.

Notes

1. This chapter is *only* concerned with the formation of the rural middle classes and the relationship between classes and status (caste in the context of India). Therefore, the dimensions of Weber's sociology that are most meaningful in relation to our analyses are class and status. Weber's third dimension of stratification (power distribution) will not be addressed in this book.
2. However, for Weber, these classes are very fluid and dynamic and can interchange or overlap. The only class situation that remains rigid is that of 'completely unskilled and propertyless persons ... dependent on irregular employment'. See Weber (1978: 302).
3. The similarities between Weber and Marx in the categorisation of property classes can be illustrated in rural India, where the *positively privileged property classes* include big landowners, capitalist farmers and business owners (classes one and two were identified in Chapter 3: the *landowning capitalist class* and the *new capitalist class*), who are characterised by the ownership of large operational land and other productive properties such as business units and production workshops. Their economic activities mainly constitute large-scale appropriation of surplus in the form of agricultural labour and produce. The *negatively privileged property classes* include the landless and near-landless labourers, whose primary source of income is limited to their manual labour power, both in agricultural and non-agricultural sectors (two classes of labour were identified in the previous chapter: the *land-owning labouring class* and the *landless labouring class*).
4. Weber's conception of status also includes lifestyle and consumption practices. In this chapter, I only focus on the caste system as a closed status group, and its economic role.
5. It is notable that Weber drew a distinction between caste and ethnicity. Weber stated: '[A] status segregation grown into a caste differs in its structure from a mere ethnic segregation: the caste structure transforms the horizontal and unconnected coexistences of ethnically segregated groups into a vertical social system of super- and subordination.... Ethnic coexistence, based on mutual repulsion and disdain, allows each ethnic community to consider its own honor as the highest one'. See Weber (1978: 934).
6. See, for example, Ambedkar (1936), Béteille (1996), Deshpande and Palshikar (2008), Fuller (1996), Harriss (2012), Colatei and Harriss-White (2004); Jaffrelot (2003, 2005, 2007), Jayaram (1996) and Srinivasan (2016).

7. Similarly, Aseem Prakash has examined the relationship between caste and economics opportunities in India through histories of 90 Dalit entrepreneurs in six states to show the persistence of caste discrimination in the market. See Prakash (2015).

8. The impact of caste is not, however, limited to its impact on objective markers of the middle class such as income, employment and education. Many studies suggest that, even for those who attain middle-class status, caste still plays a crucial role in their subjective identity, often creating an ambiguous self-identity among members of the lower-caste middle class. For instance, Sheth argues that the new emerging middle class in India have a specific self-identity that diverges from individuals of the same caste, and converges with those from the same class. Members of the middle class gradually become more distant from the specific rituals associated with their caste group (see Sheth 1999a: 2509). Similarly, based on a field study among the urban middle classes in Hyderabad, Säävälä shows that the social position of urban middle class families, who have managed to secure economic status but who belong to a low-caste background, remains contradictory. This is because 'at face value they share their way of life with middle-class families of higher-caste background. Many, especially those of ex-Untouchable identity, nevertheless feel a need, which is at time desperate, to hide their social background and to avoid being exposed and recognised through their *jaati*' (see Säävälä (2001: 294). Similar finding is offered by Patil based on research on Mahar middle-class identity. Patil observes that middle class Dalits suffer from the same status anxiety, because they can neither associate themselves with the higher-caste middle class, due to feelings of inferiority, nor do they have any association with poor Dalits, who do not share their economic status (see Patil 2000).

9. It is worth noting that in Nandur, the harvesting of sugarcane is often outsourced to sugar factories. In relations to other crops, engagement in faming activities particularly takes place at the time of harvesting in both villages.

10. Surrdin K. Sh., personal interview, 30 June 2016, Nandur.

11. Ajay A. B., personal interview, 17 May 2016, Nandur.

12. Erik Olin Wright also differentiates between employees by taking into consideration the skills and authority involved in the job. Based on the degree of required skills at the workplace, Wright distinguishes between skilled supervisors, non-skilled supervisors and skilled workers (see Wright 1997: 19–26). For similar discussion outside the Indian context, but in the context of South African middle class, see Seekings and Nattrass (2005).

13. Supervisors and managers also have a degree of authority and control over machine operators and other labourers, but not full authority like factory owners and main shareholders.

160 Contested Capital

14. Due to the diversity of economic activity in rural households, estimating the annual household income was a challenging task. To calculate the approximate annual income of each household income from the following sources was estimated separately and then combined: agriculture (based on the agricultural year 2014–15); livestock produce; agricultural wage labour; long-term and causal wage labour in agriculture and allied activities; non-agricultural casual activities; salaried employment in private sectors; salaried employment in the public sector and government employment; business and trade activities; brokerage; remittances; pensions; rent; interest; artisanal work and other sources. The income from agriculture was calculated on the basis of a prior listing of cultivated crops during the previous agricultural year (2014–15). To calculate income from agriculture, information on each crop was gathered separately. The net income from agriculture was calculated as the accumulation of gross income from all crops, minus the costs incurred in the production process. To avoid the issue of over- and under-reporting of agricultural incomes, information on the average quantity of a given crop produced on 1 acre of land and their selling prices was acquired from Gram Panchayat offices. This enabled me to have my own estimated calculation of the agricultural income and cost of production, and also facilitated a dialogue about agricultural produce with the respondents during the data collection. The cost in crop production refers broadly to irrigation costs (water and electricity charges), purchase of seeds, fertilisers, manure, and pesticides, cost of hiring tractors and bullocks, transport, brokerage and cost of labour. Income from animal resources was difficult to estimate. For livestock products, which were usually limited to milk, the average annual productivity of cows and buffalos was estimated. The cost of livestock maintenance (such as feeding and fodder, labour, veterinary charges, and so on) was deducted from gross income. For wage labour (non-agricultural) the estimation was based on detailed information on each activity that members of households engaged over the last one year, the approximate number of days they were involved in those activities and the daily wages. In cases of casual employment in agriculture, detailed information was collected separately on each individual engaged in such activities. Detailed information of the number of days, types of work and the daily wage was collected. To calculate the net income from agricultural labour, the wage paid for hiring agricultural labourers was deducted from the combined income from agricultural labour from all family members. Of course, many families were engaged in the exchange of labour without exchanging money. These labour days were not considered in accounting the income from agricultural labour. Income earned by each working member of the family was calculated separately, and then combined.

15. Here, and throughout the book, the household is taken as a unit of analysis. The categories apply to the main source of household income, which is defined

as the occupation that generates the biggest proportion of the total annual household income.

16. Rambhau Gh., personal interview, 10 July 2016, Nandur.

17. Vijay A. B., personal interview, 15 May 2016, Nandur.

18. The process of recruitment might be mediated through kinship and caste. Parry presents similar findings in a study of industrialisation in rural Chhattisgarh. See Parry (2009, 2013).

19. Vijay A. B., personal interview, 15 May 2016, Nandur.

20. Vijay A. B., personal interview, 15 May 2016, Nandur.

21. Vijay A. B., personal interview, 15 May 2016, Nandur. My attempts to interview factory owners in Nandur were unsuccessful, and such statement cannot therefore be confirmed.

22. Dattatray V. T., personal interview, 13 June 2016, Rahatwade.

23. A vast body of literature exists on labour contractors in India, which is outside the focus of this chapter, and also for reasons of space is not fully discussed here. See, for example, Guérin, et al. (2009), Lerche, (2012), Pattenden (2011) and Parry (2009).

24. Sayaji K., personal interview, 22 May 2016, Nandur.

25. Pallavi S. K. and Sayaji K., personal interview, 22 May 2016, Nandur.

26. Rajo B. T., personal interview, 30 May 2016, Nandur.

27. In examining the consumption patterns of the urban middle class in Baroda, van Wessel argues that consumption is the primary way through which people claim to have middle-class status. The middle classes 'seek self-expression through goods' by displaying consumer choices considered appropriate for the middle class. See van Wessel (2004).

28. In examining occupational patterns in Rahatwade and Nandur, a few observations are salient. First, shifts in employment patterns have not necessarily resulted in the transformation of a household's gendered division of labour. The findings suggest that middle-class occupations are primarily performed by men, while the majority of rural women (except in a small number of households) are primarily engaged in agricultural work, either on the household's farming land or as casual agricultural labourers, alongside the household domestic work. Gender-related inequalities in the labour market were briefly discussed in Chapter 3. Since the household, and not individuals, is the unit of analysis here, differentiations within the households are not addressed in details.

29. In Rahatwade and Nandur, educational credentials act as social capital, which may generate high income and skilled employment outside agriculture. This is in part because there are opportunities for skilled employment outside agriculture in close proximity to these villages, as well as significant restrictions on supply of highly educated people. The restrictions are mainly due to high tuition fee cost which results in unequal access to educational

162 Contested Capital

institutions. Therefore, education acts as a social capital and a driver of class formation. It can be argued, were the industries located far away from these villages, resulting in a lower availability of skilled employment, then the role of intermediaries might be more significant, and the relation between educational status and socio-economic position might become weaker. However, the reverse argument can also be made: if supply of work is mediated through contractors, then education (as well as social networks) may indeed act as determining factors in accessing employment, since the contractors may be more selective. Furthermore, the oversupply of education would also lower its value, since the latter depends to a significant extent to its scarcity. In *Homo Academicus*, an ethnological and sociological analysis of France's academic world, Bourdieu describes how the expansion of higher education in the late twentieth century created an oversupply of assistant lecturers whose upward mobility was consequently challenged. This resulted in devaluation of degrees, which did not give students access to expected jobs. For discussion regarding the aspirations and opportunities and oversupply of education, see Bourdieu (1988 [1984]) and Wright (2009).

30. This geographical distinction could be the continuation of the historical patterns of settlement and may not necessarily reflect contemporary caste cleavages.

31. One effective strategy, to discuss caste endogamy, was to discuss the newly released Marathi film, *Sairat,* at the time of fieldwork, which was widely watched on smartphones through 3G network connections in both villages. *Sairat* depicts the love story of Archi, an upper-caste girl, and Parshya, a lower-caste boy, in a village in Maharashtra, who elope because of resistance to their love from their families. In the final scene of the film, the couple are brutally murdered by the girl's family, including her brother. During various discussions about *Sairat*, participants repeatedly stated that it is unthinkable to allow people to marry outside their caste.

32. The *bara balutedar* system is a division of labour among 12 caste groups based on the caste system in villages in Maharashtra. The caste groups involved in the *bara balutedar* system were: (*a*) Gurav (temple servants); (*b*) Chambhar (cobblers, shoemakers); (*c*) Sonar (goldsmith); (*d*) Nhawi (barbers); (*e*) Koli (water carriers); (*f*) Kumbhar (potters); (*g*) Sutar (carpenters); (*h*) Mahar (people who removed the skin of dead animals); (*i*) Parit or Dhobi (washers); (*j*) Chougula, Naik and Mang (watch people); (*k*) Lohar (blacksmiths); (*l*) and Dhor (makers of ornaments for cattle). In some villages, Shimpi (tailors) were also part of the *bara balutedar* system. However, some of them have either disappeared or are in the process of disappearing from the village economy in both Rahatwade and Nandur. If required, such services are brought into the village from outside and are compensated with cash: Dattatray V. T., personal

interview, 11 September 2016, Rahatwade; Ramchandra B. Gh., personal interview, 4 September 2016, Nandur.

33. Ramchandra B. Gh., personal discussion, 4 September 2016, Nandur.

34. Ramchandra B. Gh., personal discussion, 4 September 2016, Nandur. However, it is notable that Ramchandra's statement is not conclusive and should be treated with caution, because it is not clear whether the upper-caste individuals personally undertake the removal of their dead animals or they hire others to remove the animals in exchange for cash.

35. Dattatray V. T., personal discussion, 11 September 2016, Rahatwade.

36. A harrowing story involves the family, who initially had identified themselves as middle class at the beginning of my fieldwork but later changed their position and self-identified as *poor* in the second round of household survey conducted a few months later. During the course of the fieldwork, the daughter-in-law of the family set herself on fire (for reasons that have remained unknown to me), following which the son (her husband) was arrested and sentenced to a number of years in prison. Prior to this incident, he was a supervisor in a factory, but now that their circumstances have changed: the sources of income are from agriculture and casual agricultural wage labour.

37. To examine the persistence of caste inequality in the labour market in rural India over the past 30 years, I used three rounds of macro data at the All-India level: HDPI (1993–94), IHDS-I (2004–05) and IHDS-II (2011–12). The analysis shows there has been a marginal decline in the relationship between caste and occupations in rural India. See Appendix A3.

38. A number of households have sold a segment of their land to invest in the education of their children, enrolling them in English-medium private schools and colleges, usually in nearby towns. Such capital conversion highlights the significance of moving away from an ownership-based definition of the middle class as used in Chapter 3, but also indicates the importance of the ownership of land, which makes such capital conversion possible.

39. It is not possible to conduct a conclusive exercise for other caste groups among the non-labouring households in Rahatwade and Nandur, because their number is not statistically significant.

40. The Lorenz curves are strong tools to demonstrate inequality in income distribution as well as comparing incomes in different sub-populations.

41. The caste composition of urban middle classes is shown in Appendix A6.

42. The caste composition of different classes in rural Maharashtra is shown in Appendix A7. Similar to findings from All-rural India, there are caste disparities in class formation in rural Maharashtra, with the middle and the upper class consisting primarily of the upper castes.

5

Bourdieu
Cultural Capital, Self-perception and the Middle-class Identity in Rural India

The question that middle-class families have to ask themselves is, what separates them from those below them? There are many differences between the middle class and the poor. For one thing, nobody likes to be associated with poor people – the poor remain quite isolated socially; their income is low and unstable; they do not possess properties; they have to do manual work; and their life style is less than modest. I believe, my household belongs to the middle class category, *middle middle class*. We have a fixed monthly income which allows us to cope with our daily needs and plan for our future requirements. We are able to meet our financial necessities without needing to borrow money from others or perform manual tasks; we are free from financial dependency. That is why we belong to the middle class. We are self-reliant, and therefore, surely, we belong to the middle class. That is what I feel anyway, since we are not dependent on others.

—Nitesh L. Ch., personal interview (2016)

This chapter departs from the materialist-economic approach to class analysis and examines the formation of India's rural middle class from a perspective influenced by Pierre Bourdieu's approach to social classes. Bourdieu was concerned with symbolic representations, in the realms of culture, art, literature, science and language. However, it must be noted at the outset that although Bourdieu is a major theorist of class, his account of social classes is applied here differently to the way in which Marx and Weber's accounts were applied in Chapters 3 and 4. The fundamental difference arises from the fact that Bourdieu is critical of abstract conceptualisations, and his analyses of class are primarily drawn from empirical investigations and in relation to social practices. Bourdieu's approach is used in our analysis as a heuristic device, and not as a prescriptive definition of class membership. The chapter is arranged in four sections: the first examines

Bourdieu's sociology and his approach to the study of social classes. The second section reviews existing scholarship on the urban middle class in India that is based on Bourdieu's approach to social classes. The third section suggests productive ways in which this sociology of class can be applied to the rural Indian context, prompted by a discussion of interior design and 'living rooms' in Rahatwade and Nandur. The fourth section presents the central findings. Overall, this chapter is an attempt – the first of its kind in rural India – to examine the ways in which the term 'middle class' is understood by the people themselves, and to analyse its symbolic and cultural markers in early twenty-first century Indian villages.

The arguments of this chapter are developed from a set of in-depth qualitative interviews with members (above the age of 18) of 84 households in both villages. The population sampling method for in-depth interviews was fundamentally different from that of Chapters 3 and 4: it relied on the self-identification of middle classes, and within this sample were participants from a wide range of socio-economic backgrounds. This decision was influenced by numerous limitations in identifying and understanding markers of class, such as not speaking the local language, and also by Bourdieu's opposition to boundary drawing. During the pilot study, many respondents stated that they perceived themselves as 'lower middle class', 'upper middle class' or most commonly as 'middle middle class'. These responses informed the creation of five categories of classes: *poor, lower middle class, middle middle class, upper middle class* and *rich*.[1] A representative number of households from each of the five identified classes were then selected for in-depth interview.

The interviews were semi-structured and based on a set of pre-designed questions, aimed at capturing class aspirations and cultural markers of the middle class, and understanding the ways in which people distinguished themselves from members of classes below and above them. They primarily addressed the following issues: the meaning of the term 'middle class' and middle-class membership; the class structure of the respective villages and differences in terms of expenditure, education and lifestyle; the importance of English language education; and ambitions for the future of their children. However, the conversations were not limited to the above and respondents were encouraged to talk freely about other relevant issues. I have also used quantitative household survey data collected from 490 households to examine the consumption patterns of different classes. In addition, my understanding of the villages was deepened through general observations and informal discussions. That the extensive survey data and interviews were not only concerned with Bourdieu is one reason why this chapter does not provide the same analytical depth as found in Bourdieu's magnum opus,

166   Contested Capital

Distinction. My status as an outsider and my lack of familiarity with the nuanced cultural markers of class and status in rural India, also limited the depth of this approach.

Bourdieu and Social Classes

Between 1958 and 1995, Bourdieu published over 30 books and 340 articles, an opus that culminated in the development of a new school of French sociology comparable to that established a century earlier by one of his primary influencers, Émile Durkheim. It is impossible to provide a comprehensive overview of Bourdieu's sociology; here, I will primarily draw on his work on social classes, classes in *Distinction*.[2] Originally published in 1979, and based on an extensive survey of French society undertaken throughout the 1960s and 1970s, *Distinction* provides a model of the relationship between economic and social conditions of existence and lifestyle. Introducing to the sociological lexicon terms such as 'habitus', Bourdieu brought new meaning to the long studied concept of capital. He examined culture as a scientific object, and sought in the structure of social classes 'the basis of the systems of classification which structure perception of the social world and designate the objects of aesthetic enjoyment' (Bourdieu, 1984: xvi). Bourdieu suggested there exists an 'economy of cultural goods, but it has a specific logic' (Bourdieu, 1984: 1). The role of sociology as a discipline was to 'establish the conditions in which the consumers of cultural goods, and their taste for them, are produced, and at the same time to describe ... the social conditions of the constitution of the mode of appropriation that is considered legitimate' (Bourdieu, 1984: 1). There is nothing objective about decorating your living room in a certain way, or choosing to wear certain styles of clothing: such choices are imbued with social meaning. Drawing on the scientific observation of his population, Bourdieu argued that cultural practices (in his examples drawn from France: reading, opera, concerts and museum visits) are the product of upbringing and education. A 'socially recognised hierarchy of the arts, and within each of them, of genres, schools or periods, corresponds to a social hierarchy of the consumers. This predisposes tastes to function as markers of "class"' (Bourdieu, 1984: 1–2; 1990).

Bourdieu wrote of his concern that *Distinction* might strike the reader as 'very French', and by virtue of its empirical case study, could have been read as an ethnography of France. He also recognised the specific historical conditions that pertained in France in the 1960s and 1970s and created a French tradition which developed over different historical periods, of an aristocratic model of 'court society' which was personified by what he termed a Parisian upper middle class or high society (*haute bourgeoisie*) which combined 'all the titles of economic and cultural nobility' and had no counterpart elsewhere (Bourdieu, 1984: xi). However, his ambition was greater than elucidating the complexity of social classes in the French context, and he suggested that the empirical evidence from France presented a 'particular case of the possible'. He did not renounce the ambition of drawing out universal propositions (Bourdieu, 1984: xi). Thus, he stated:

> The model [...] seems to me to be valid beyond the particular French case and, no doubt, for every stratified society, even if the system of distinctive features which express or reveal economic and social differences (themselves variable in scale and structure) varies considerably from one period, and one society, to another. (Bourdieu, 1984: xi–xii)

Notably absent from *Distinction* is any mention of the social class systems of non-western societies, and how comparisons might be drawn with very different societies or historical periods. Bourdieu invites readers to search in other societies for equivalents of the empirical phenomena in France – equivalents in song, cinema, dress, interior decoration, sport and cooking. In rural India and elsewhere around the world (particularly in rural contexts), the equivalents may not necessarily be found in opera or museums, but studies of interior decoration, dress, cooking, song, sport and other markers that may be more relevant in that context to class as culture. The aim in this chapter is to identify such class markers in rural India.

It is useful to outline two major elements in Bourdieu's approach to social classes that need to be distinguished, as previously suggested by Weininger. First, Bourdieu rejected the abstract demarcation of one class from another and the drawing of class boundaries, as in Marx and Weber. The *a priori* drawing of boundaries risked viewing classes as pre-existing entities and subject to a substantialist logic (Emirbayer, 1997; Weininger, 2005a, 2005b). In the 1960s and 1970s, debates over lines of division separating classes, notably the proletariat from the middle class, were prominent. For Bourdieu, boundaries had to be understood in relation to social practices rather than abstract conjecture. The following extract from his keynote address to the Dean's Symposium on 'Gender, Age, Ethnicity and Class' at The University of Chicago, wonderfully sums up Bourdieu's discomfort with boundary drawing (translated from the French by Loïc Wacquant):

> The boundaries between theoretical classes which scientific investigation allows us to construct on the basis of a plurality of criteria are similar … to the boundaries of a cloud or a forest. These boundaries can thus be conceived of as lines or as imaginary planes, such that the density (of the trees or of

168 Contested Capital

the water vapour) is higher on the one side and lower on the other, or above a certain value on the one side and below it on the other – in fact, a more appropriate image would be that of a flame whose edges are in constant movement, oscillating around a line or surface. (Bourdieu, 1987)

The second major element in Bourdieu's approach to social class derives from his endeavour to critique Weber's conception of class and status (that of lifestyle), which he sees as distinguishing between the material and the symbolic. According to Bourdieu, these should not be viewed as different forms of stratification. The style of life is the manifestation of social class differences. As a consequence, analysing social classes should not be reduced to analysing material relations, but should include a simultaneous analysis of symbolic relations. There are three central analytical concepts in Bourdieu's approach: capital, habitus and field, each of which is now addressed in turn.

For Bourdieu, multiple species of capital exist, and the two most relevant are economic and cultural capital. The former is defined as what is 'immediately and directly convertible to money' (Bourdieu, 1986: 241). Cultural capital refers to a range of resources and includes general cultural awareness, aesthetic preference, educational credentials, knowledge of the educational apparatus and linguistic ability (Swartz, 1997: 75). Later writings suggested that cultural capital is more accurately termed informational capital, emphasising the knowledge that one requires to navigate, or recognise the significance of, certain forms of such capital, particularly in relation to the educational system (Bourdieu, 1986: 243; Bourdieu and Wacquant, 1992: 160). Of particular significance for our purposes, considering the salience of educational attainment and its importance in rural India, is that the notion of cultural capital was used to explain differing levels of academic achievement of children from similar social backgrounds. Bourdieu explained these differences, not with reference to notions of intelligence which were popular at the time, but by the type and extent of cultural capital. He suggested it exists in three states: (*a*) In an embodied state, referring to the assembly of cultivated behaviours and dispositions which are 'internalized by the individual through socialization and that constitute schemes of appreciation and understanding' (Swartz, 1997: 76–77). This socialisation has two primary sites, the family and the school. (*b*) In an objectified form (books, artwork, and so on) which requires specialised cultural knowledge to understand. (*c*) In an institutionalised form, primarily referring to educational qualifications and their significance in the allocation of social credentials.

The second and most influential analytical concept in Bourdieu's approach to social class, and indeed of his sociology in general, is the concept of *habitus*. At the core of this is the notion of the regulation of individual action. It addresses the question of how people act without being subject to a conventional force or without their actions being the result of obedience to certain rules. In simplified terms, habitus does not allow the notion that action is mechanical or the result of conscious decision-making (Bourdieu and Wacquant, 1992: 121). This dispositional understanding suggests that in 'normal' or 'everyday' circumstances, human behaviour is 'pre-reflexive' and is not the product of conscious reflection of rules, nor of consideration of results, risks or rewards (Weininger, 2005a: 131). This understanding of human action cannot simply be reduced to habit in the common understanding of the term – behaviour that is compulsive, repetitive and not reflective or thoughtful. Instead, over and above habit, embodied dispositions are composed of the ways in which individuals perceive and understand their social world, including, but not limited to, tastes, perceptions, mannerisms, deportment, speech and attitudes. Bourdieu suggested that an individual's combination and volume of capital, corresponding to a specific set of life conditions, or 'class conditions', corresponds with his/her location in social space (Weininger, 2005a: 132). 'Class conditions' imprint these embodied dispositions, or habitus, on the individual. In this way, habitus is inextricably linked to the cultural markers of class, and provides a route to understanding the relationship between aspects of behaviour that tend to be associated with social class (but which are difficult to grasp analytically or sociologically) and material conditions of existence. The notion of habitus links structure with human behaviour. This is one of the primary reasons why Bourdieu's sociology has been widely used in the study of class.

The third analytical concept is *field*, a spatial metaphor that is central to Bourdieu's sociology and his approach to social classes. This conceptualises the world as being divided into distinct 'fields', denoting arenas of production, goods, services and knowledge. If we think of a society as a room, the room is divided into several fields that each operate with their own rules of access. Examples of field include education, religion and art, while rules of access relate to performance, dogma and faith, and specialised knowledge, respectively. Agents possess types of capital that are appropriate to each field – skills, knowledge or talents. One of the purposes of the concept of field is to undermine an understanding of the nature of social space in terms of structuralism, where agency is subject to structural relations. 'Field' evokes a dynamic relationship where individuals are in competition with each other (Bourdieu and Wacquant, 1992: 94–115).

These three analytical concepts continue to have a profound impact on the study of class, and are useful in understanding class in rural India. The notion of social and cultural capital is most clearly demonstrated in the field of education,

170   Contested Capital

which is discussed in detail later. Habitus clearly indicates class-related differences in taste, expression and behaviour. Perhaps the most important feature of the middle class in rural India is the explicit statement made by self-identified members of the middle class, who, as we found, not only describe themselves as 'middle class' but also distance themselves from the poor, from dependency and from any form of manual labour. Such statements are related to the notion of habitus, although it lacks its subtlety and nuance. This is due to the context of a rural middle class emerging in a rapidly transforming village, where tastes are perhaps still inchoate and explicit boundaries (material/economic) might be more important and obvious. The notion of field, again in some general sense, relates to education and employment (competition for jobs) and also, as Craig Jeffrey suggests, to politics (Jeffrey, 2010b). These three central concepts have also been used in studies of the middle class in urban India, and it is to these that we now turn.

Bourdieu in the Indian Middle-Class Literature

Many studies of the middle class in urban India have been heavily influenced by Bourdieu's *Distinction*. Despite the centrality of the concept of class to Bourdieu's writing, and in particular to *Distinction*, Weininger notes that understandings of Bourdieu's concepts of class in secondary literature remain poor, and he suggests numerous reasons for this: that Bourdieu's concepts and understandings do not rely on a single canonical figure such as Marx and Weber; Bourdieu was opposed to the separation of theory and practice which makes his arguments and methods difficult to follow; and he did not rely on rational action theory (Weininger, 2005b).

Christiane Brosius' recent study of India's middle class (urban), which was influenced by Bourdieu, examines new forms of consumption, urban leisure and wealth among the urban middle classes in Delhi. Based on interviews conducted between 1997 and 2007 with members of what she called the 'arrived urban middle classes', Brosius examines the lifestyle of this new social group, the upwardly middle class, in the context of economic liberalisation. Her account is based essentially on a study of representations. She clearly states that she does not examine the middle class as 'an entity' or 'essence', but rather traces 'middle class dynamic and complexity in and through its practices of distinction and regimes of pleasure' (Brosius, 2010: 14). Following economic liberalisation and increasing urbanisation, Brosius describes a social class that negotiates new opportunities and a national discourse which no longer places India at the margins of development,

Bourdieu 171

where it was before 1991. Particularly notable among her participants was the notion of belonging to a 'world-class' (Brosius, 2010: 15). However, Brosius's study is problematic for a number of reasons, not least because of its interpretation of Bourdieu. In a simplification of Bourdieu's *Distinction*, Brosius writes:

> To ensure that the borders towards culturally and socially 'lower' groups can be drawn efficiently, and the position pointing towards upper classes strengthened, distinction is required. According to Pierre Bourdieu, distinction is an important element that shapes habitus, capital and cultural production. The properties of habitus are practice and dispositions. They render social practice and perceptions meaningful. The focus is on the particular kinds of activities by which a field of social positions and relations can be explored, for instance, as regards weddings. (Brosius, 2010: 15)

For Bourdieu, distinction was not something that is required, to the extent that it can be said to be a 'thing' at all, nor does it shape habitus, capital and cultural production. Furthermore, the analytical richness of habitus is not explained by suggesting that its properties are 'practice and dispositions', nor do the properties of habitus (again, to the extent that it has properties at all) 'render social practice and perceptions meaningful'. Rather, habitus is a concept that seeks to explain the ways in which individuals act compliantly, without being subjected to various forms of coercion or force, and not as a result of risks/rewards or trade-offs. The main criticism of Brosius' account is that it does not extend analysis beyond sanitised representations of urban India. It neither engages with the complexity and messiness of everyday life nor recognises the full significance of symbolic practices. Beyond her broad notion of global connectivity, there is little in her account that resonates with the middle classes in rural India.

Craig Jeffrey provides a more developed account of the middle class in Meerut, Uttar Pradesh. Following liberalisation, Jeffrey suggests that middle-class accumulation strategies coalesced around a number of points: developing links to the urban upper middle class; aspiring to expensive English-medium education for children and establishing cultural distinctiveness through the purchase of 'urban' consumer goods (Jeffrey, 2010b: 10; Jeffrey, Jeffrey, and Jeffery, 2005).[3] While the purchase of consumer goods is highly significant, there is little evidence to suggest these purchases are an attempt to imitate urban lifestyles however. Jeffrey also suggests that numerous features of the middle class – the formation of civic institutions, the adoption of global symbols claiming middle-class lifestyles, and the formation of Hindu nationalist organisations offering cultural distinction based on religious nationalism – signify a shift towards symbolic

172   Contested Capital

political engagement, away from competitive electoral politics.[4] It is the rise of these symbolic forms of political engagement and the various new forms of association and consumption, which, Jeffrey argues, 'demand a new theory of class formation ... [that] places central emphasis on social and cultural dimensions of power and attends to the spatial representation of dominance' (Jeffrey, 2010b: 10). Jeffrey considers that the significance of the social and cultural expression of power, symbolic representation and consumption make Bourdieu's work on class particularly relevant to the Indian context. In *Timepass* (2010a), an ethnography of the student politics and youth activism in which young middle-class men participate in response to 'waiting' (persistent underemployment), Jeffrey uses Bourdieu's concepts of capital: institutionalised cultural capital (educational qualifications), objectified cultural capital (consumer goods) and embodied cultural capital (such as the ability to present oneself as distinguished). Between 1960 and 2005, all three forms of cultural capital were significant in the attempts by Jats to improve their status and position in local society. In a very literal sense, Bourdieu's notion of 'field' was also instructive in understanding how people compete for power in northwestern Uttar Pradesh, with men literally describing politics as a game within a field (Jeffrey, 2010a).

Similarly, drawing on fieldwork in Mumbai, Leela Fernandes provides an analytical account of the post-liberalisation middle class through a Bourdieuian perspective. Fernandes draws an important contrast between the rise of the middle class in Indian and western industrialising contexts, noting that in India, transformations in identity and practices of distinction are linked to shifts in global power relations and mediation between notions of 'Indianness' and representations of westernisation or globalisation in the symbolic politics of advertising images. Another important feature of Fernandes' work is her recognition of the different historical trajectories of social group formation both in post-colonial and in European societies, with the paradigmatic French case presented by Bourdieu. In the post-colonial context, the rise of an Indian middle class is accompanied by notions of westernisation, globalisation and discourses of India's relationship with these processes. These processes of interaction and differentiation unfold through complex social processes and are a distinctive part of the creation of the identity of the new middle class. Fernandes cites examples from television media, such as talk shows targeting middle-class audiences addressing 'new' issues relating to gender, consumerism and changing youth attitudes and the proliferation of American shows and their Indian equivalents, and interprets the interchanging and hybrid use of English and Hindi as significant in the creation of a middle-class identity, creating an

'English speaking public sphere that is associated with the rising new middle class' (Fernandes, 2006: 69). In Bourdieuian terms, the ability to speak English is not just a form of cultural capital but also a marker of middle-class status, which can be transformed into both economic and social capital. English language proficiency not only 'marks an individual with the distinction of class culture' but also enables access to skilled jobs in 'the new economy', and places them in the middle class in socio-economic terms (Fernandes, 2006: 69). There is also the interesting phenomenon identified by Fernandes and others of 'personality courses' aimed at inculcating behaviours. One example she provides is of a private institution established in 1935, running courses on hotel catering, marketing and dressmaking. They recently established a course on 'Personality Development and Communication Skills' which focuses on manners, deportment, style and taste (Fernandes, 2006: 222).[5] Fernandes uses Bourdieu to argue that a range of diverse practices establish boundaries of social groups, forms of behaviour akin to Bourdieu's 'classificatory practices' used to convert different forms of capital and preserve social status (Fernandes, 2006). In doing so, she examines the multiple ways in which this new middle class deploys capital in 'fields' (although it is unclear whether these are Bourdieuian): the media and public sphere, the labour market, urban neighbourhoods and democratic politics (Fernandes, 2006).

There are features of the urban middle classes identified by Brosius, Jeffrey and Fernandes which resonate with middle-class membership in rural India. The notion of belonging to a 'world class', which was significant in Brosius' account, was evident in a modified form in Rahatwade and Nandur. Those who self-identified as middle class expressed vague notions of the importance of global connectivity, and of being successful beyond the village. Moreover, two of Jeffrey's three features of the middle class in Meerut – aspiring to English-medium education and the purchase of 'urban' consumer goods – are relevant to rural India. Indeed, the former was particularly significant and is discussed in detail later. Fernandes' work on consumption is also insightful and augments an understanding of the social meaning of consumerism in rural India. The inculcation of distinction, evidenced by the existence of colleges offering personal development courses, was not identified in my field-sites. However, there was evidence of advertisements for vocational courses such as computer engineering, mechanical and electronic engineering, and English language classes in both villages. These courses, although they may not have directly inculcated cultural capital, were perceived as necessary for entry to non-farm employment (which carried some prestige), enhancing an individual's ability to access consumer goods and a better lifestyle.

174   Contested Capital

In keeping with differences in his conception of social class, I draw on Bourdieu here in a different way from the ways in which I drew on Marx and Weber. Unlike Marxist and Weberian concepts of class, the Bourdieuian approach to social class cannot be explicated by proceeding from a set of guidelines or definitions. As Weininger points out, 'such an elaboration must, first and foremost, take as its point of departure a concrete exercise in class analysis' (Weininger, 2005a: 121). Bourdieu's *Distinction* provides an empirically rich and detailed framework, which is used as an exploratory device to guide analysis of the cultural expressions of aspiration, distinction from those below, self-perception in relation to class, and a whole set of prescriptions relating to middle-class status in rural India.

Table 5.1 shows the extent of middle-class identification among households in Rahatwade and Nandur.[6] Out of the 97 non-manual labouring households surveyed in each village, 90 in Rahatwade and 93 in Nandur were identified by their members as middle class. Perhaps surprisingly, only a very small number of participants (2 households in Rahatwade and only 1 in Nandur) did not understand the term 'middle class'.

Table 5.1   Is your household a middle-class household?

Middle-class household?	*Rahatwade (N = 97)*		*Nandur (N = 97)*	
	Freq.	*Per cent*	*Freq.*	*Per cent*
Do not know what middle class is	2	2	1	1
No	5	5.2	3	3.1
Yes	90	92.8	93	95.9
Total	97	100	97	100

Source: Fieldwork data (2015).

Table 5.2 displays the self-identified class distributions of households in these villages. These class distributions are used as a point of reference for the quantitative analysis that is presented in the remainder of the chapter. Indeed, the awareness of internal class divisions and their self-proclaimed distinction from both 'poor' and 'rich' classes was a very characteristic feature of the self-identified rural middle classes. The differences between Nandur and Rahatwade visible in Table 5.2, such as the greater percentage of *middle middle class* in Nandur, were more than incidental, and related to the relative prosperity of Nandur, due to the presence of factories on the fringes of the village. This is explored further in this chapter. Out of the 90 households in Rahatwade and 93 households in Nandur that self-identified as middle class, a total of 84 households (40 from Rahatwade and 44 from Nandur) were selected for in-depth interviews.

Table 5.2 Self-identified class distributions of households

Self-identified classes	Rahatwade (N = 97)		Nandur (N = 97)	
	Freq.	Per cent	Freq.	Per cent
Poor	7	7.2	3	3
Lower middle class	30	31	22	22.7
Middle middle class	57	58.8	65	67
Upper middle class	3	3	6	6.2
Rich	0	0	1	1
Total	97	100	97	100

Source: Fieldwork data (2015).

Findings: Images and Experiences of Middle-class-ness

The analysis of fieldwork data resulted in three central findings. First, members of the self-identified rural middle class expressed their class differentiation by stating that their middle-class status was derived from being 'in the middle'. In fact most significant for defining the middle-class-ness was a reference to a class that was very visible and could be used as a complete counterpart, 'the poor class' – in a way the members of the middle class needed a social opposite to confirm their own class position. This was mainly articulated by outlining the privileges which differentiated them from the poor: property ownership and economic self-reliance, both of which were unquestionably important class markers. Most importantly, the self-identified middle classes used accounts that reflected their distance from manual labour, something that was only associated with the poor. However, such distinction went beyond a given set of material conditions, and was extended to daily routines and life style. Claims to be able to live a 'normal' life, 'unlike the poor', were also significant. For those who perceived themselves as middle class, it was about not being at the bottom, not struggling and not depending on others for a livelihood. This language of differentiation was a central feature in self-perceptions of middle-class status.

Second, members of this self-identified rural middle class demonstrated a specific type of ambition and aspiration for their children. This was most clearly expressed in the desire that their children should receive a private English-medium education and should be proficient in the use of English. Indeed, many enrolled their children in English-medium schools in nearby towns. This English proficiency was not only perceived as an economic asset for the future, which enabled better access to non-farm employment, but also as prestigious and

176　Contested Capital

related to notions of global connectivity. Furthermore, members of these self-identified rural middle classes expressed very strong opposition to their children's involvement in agriculture, which were associated with the poverty, manual work, and uncertainty of the past.

Third, there was strong anecdotal evidence that there was a 'social life of things' in rural India, and this was most clearly evident in the living rooms of residents of Rahatwade and Nandur (Appadurai, 1986). We can trace different patterns of taste and consumption among different self-identified classes. There had been a rapid and significant transformation in both villages over the past 10 years which had made residents more prosperous. This prosperity was characterised by new forms of employment, new building styles and the widespread purchase of a range of consumer goods – from motorbikes to fridges, flat-screen TVs and smartphones. However, this prosperity had not been experienced by all sections of the villages, and there remained a desperately poor underclass living in corrugated iron houses on the edge of both villages. In what follows, I provide a detailed account of these features of the rural middle classes. Examples and interview extracts are provided for illustrative purposes.

Self-identification: Distinction from the 'Poor' and the 'Rich'

Self-identification as middle class was expressed in different ways. When describing themselves as belonging to the middle class, respondents usually used the English term, although a few also used the Marathi word *madhyamavarga*. In general, to emphasise their class positions as being in the middle, they often distinguished themselves from the 'poor' by explicitly describing the ways in which their lives contrasted with the poor. For example, some said that unlike the poor (*garīb*) they had a 'normal' (the English word was used) life and would use evidence such as self-sufficiency, family size, property ownership, access to 'jobs' (referring to non-farm and factory employment), the ability to afford good diets, having access to medical services, giving importance to one's appearance and presentation (such as wearing 'ironed' clothes), the ability to afford decent schools for their children and English-medium education. Unlike members of the *lower middle class* and the *middle middle classes*, who articulated their middle-class membership in comparison to the poor, members of the *upper middle class* continuously compared themselves to the rich. Respondents often stated that they were also different from the 'rich' (śrīmanta), and used evidence relating to income and affordability of education in metro cities and abroad. Often, they referred to 'rich' people 'being able to send their children abroad for education', or to 'an expensive private school

Bourdieu 177

in the city', or their ability to afford to 'educate their children to postgraduate level', or as those 'who do not have to worry about money and enjoy an income far in excess of their basic requirements'. The following interview extract with Ajay, a 28-year-old factory machine operator from the Gurav caste in Nandur, which was prompted by a question – 'is your family a middle-class family, and why?' – is illustrative. Ajay identified various ways of distinguishing his family from the poor. For him, being middle class was fundamentally about not being poor.[7]

> A middle-class family is small in size, usually with two kids. Those who have television, bikes, cars, etc., fall in the middle class – these are the people whose living condition is common or ordinary... Those families that do not have a house to live in, and struggle to feed themselves come under the poor class. Middle class people can at least afford good housing and food for the whole family, without depending on others.[8]

I heard a similar narrative from Kamaledin, the head of a Muslim family living in Nandur, and his 27-year-old son, Surrdin. Kamaledin was the village head for a period of two years, and they lived in an old-style house (but renovated), with plastered brick walls and a recently laid polished ceramic tiled floor (to which they eagerly drew my attention). Their living room was decorated with a display cabinet, flat-screen TV, two air coolers and a large bed used for seating. In addition to their factory *jobs*, they also undertook farming activities (through hired-in agricultural labour) and owned a number of cows. Kamaledin stated:

> Middle class refers to those people who can live a good life with the income they have. In a middle-class family if one family member falls sick they can afford good medical treatments. They surely can afford spending money for medical care of a sick family member, whereas poor people have to mortgage their land or borrow money for medical expenses. Middle-class people can spend easily 10,000 to 20,000 rupees for hospital and medical expenses. We belong to the middle class.[9]

Kamaledin's account reveals the way in which he differentiated his lifestyle and security, expressed in the form of access to medical care, which he understood to be a basic need. Emphasising his middle-class membership, he stressed the importance of self-sufficiency in differentiating his family from a poor family, who 'have no farming land' and 'who have no security in life' – 'poor people have to get up very early in the morning, finish all their household work and go to others' farms and do manual agricultural labour, something that middle-class individuals do not need to do'. His son then states 'we are from the upper middle class' because:

> ... Everything is ok for us with our level of income. We have a bit of outside knowledge too. Hence we are not in *the middle middle class*, but in *the upper middle class*. [This] means when we go to a hotel or a restaurant in a city, we have the knowledge of what to order from the menu, having such knowledge is necessary if you want to be part of the upper middle class. When we request for a menu card then, we have the familiarity of what to order and how much to order.[10]

Surrdin's account is particularly interesting because it relates to the 'outside world' and evokes a Bourdieuian concept of distinction – his family have the 'knowledge' (a form of cultural capital) 'to order from the menu' of a hotel or a restaurant, which distinguishes his family from the ordinary 'middle middle class'. This is indeed relevant to the notion of cultural capital, or more accurately informational capital – the knowledge one requires to navigate, or recognise the significance of, certain forms of such capital. Furthermore, Surrdin indicated that they were not in the rich class, or 'class one', as he put it, either, because 'rich people have lots of money, savings and large lands – perhaps 50 to 60 acres of farming land, four-wheelers [cars] and air conditioners in their houses'.[11]

To provide a better picture of local notions of middle-class-ness, let me offer more examples: Santosh, the head of a Maratha family in Rahatwade, argued that they were middle class by referring to his level of annual income, INR 288,000 in 2015. His income was from a variety of sources including farming, car rental and rental income from a bakery in Pune. He told me that being 'a middle-class man' meant being 'a normal everyday man, who is neither rich nor poor'. He explained further: 'The middle class usually run small businesses, have company [factory] jobs or are farmers, which is often combined with informal work, and have an income of between 10,000 and 15,000 rupees per month'.[12]

Suresh, another self-identified middle class, and a supervisor in a factory responded to my questions about what middle class meant and whether he was from a middle-class family: 'I have heard the term middle class in television serials. It refers to people like us and how we are (referring to his family). I am a middle-class citizen.'[13] As with almost every other respondent, he stated that the middle class also required a certain level of income, between INR 15,000 to 20,000 per month. Also of significance was the way in which he distinguished his family from the poor to emphasise their middle-class status: 'poor people have to do manual labour, but middle-class people do not have to', adding that the middle class 'have some grains of their own, hence less expenditure on food, and they have property and can save money. In contrast poor people do not have their own grains and no property and have to spend all the money they earn on food and housing, having nothing left for education'.[14] The implication was that poor people did not even have food of their own – their most basic needs (food) could only be met by working for others as manual wage labourers.

When asked about the meaning of middle class, Nitesh, a 32-year-old low-ranked 'policeman' from a Maratha family in Rahatwade, said 'being middle class means having a regular, reliable income which enables one to continuously meet one's most basic requirements. The middle class do not need to take small loans to meet their basic needs, as the poor class often do in the village'. He described the 'poor class' as the 'manual labouring class' or 'farmers without alternative sources of income, who have no fixed income', relying on the uncertainty of agricultural markets: 'when they [farmers] have their yield, if it is sold in the market, only then they get money in their hands'.[15] This implies that their lives were uncertain because they had an irregular income, and did not have any capital for investment. He also stated that his family were middle class, because they could meet all their daily needs without taking loans: 'we are self-sufficient, hence, surely, we are from middle class, that is what we feel. In short we are not dependent on anyone'.[16]

Another interviewee, Yuvraj, a labour contractor in Nandur, suggested that middle-class status was determined by having a regular monthly income of around INR 10,000 to 15,000, enough to meet the basic requirements of one's household and the private education of the next generation. He disclosed his income as INR 3,250,000 per annum (in 2016), although my own calculation suggested it was closer to INR 5,000,000. Yuvraj also stressed the importance of self-sufficiency for middle-class households: 'a poor family need to put in lots of physical hard work to earn [their] bread, but for middle-class families, business goes on, on the phone only', meaning that a middle-class individual did not need to undertake any manual labour. Working 'on the phone only' implied a certain ease and comfort in the way income was generated. He specified that 'both the middle class and poor people have to work, but the middle class have *jobs* in factories, the poor undertake agricultural labour in fields'.[17] Yuvraj also elaborated on this self-sufficiency of the middle class by suggesting – perhaps more metaphorically than literally – that a poor family would often go to another household and ask 'do you have some old shirt of yours? Do you have your old trousers?' He added:

> If someone gives him his old shoes he (a poor person) would use that. If someone gives him his bed, he would use that. He will use others worn clothes, given to him, or else he will have to live in his own old clothes only.[18]

For Yuvraj, the poor were not self-sufficient, the middle classes were. Similarly, Tanaji, a lady in her 30s, from a Maratha family in Rahatwade, identified her family as middle class, a term she recalled first hearing while working in a nursery

180   Contested Capital

school before her marriage. She described the middle class as those who had an income of INR 10,000 to 15,000 per month, and maintained 'everyday regular living and meet the daily needs and are also able to save'. Tanaji understood the difference between the poor and the middle class in relation to the position of women:

> You will not believe, but a woman in a poor family has to work 365 days a year just to be able to eat. Unless they work in the farm as labourers then they cannot afford to eat. There are usually alcoholic husbands in poor families. You cannot call them middle class; you can only call them poor.[19]

Prior to getting married, Tanaji used to work in the McDonald's in Hadapsar (a suburban area on the outskirts of Pune), and before that in a nursery school, and she had hoped to continue working after marriage because it gave her some degree of independence, but she was forced to quit her job after her marriage. She also indicated that among the middle classes, there were more restrictions on married women, something that was not the case in rich or poor families, even if the latter were restricted by their extreme poverty. My other female interviewee, Rupali from the Mali caste (whose husband owned the biggest grocery store in Nandur), listed her family as middle class because:

> Everything is in order in our household; hence we are a middle-class family. All necessities, requirements of everyone in our house are met. Our living standard is good ... we have everything, whatever we require ... we have ... now we have cars, we have a bungalow, what else do we want? [Our] children are receiving good education.[20]

Many others offered the same narrative, and perhaps a sentence by one of my village guides, Baburao, sums it up: 'Middle-class people are those common people who earn enough for their daily requirements, without depending on others.'[21] These interview extracts with self-identified middle classes demonstrate that the primary way to define the middle class was to distinguish it from the poor and the manual labouring classes, and through the notion of self-sufficiency. This definition was often accompanied by a reference to having a monthly income of at least INR 10,000 to 15,000. However, it is notable that the reference to income was not necessarily about the economic aspect of income; rather, it was about the perception of 'being able' to generate income, and about self-sufficiency and prestige.[22] How do we relate this very direct self-categorisation to the Bourdieuian concept of distinction? To recapitulate, Bourdieu's concept of distinction refers to judgments of taste: the different aesthetic choices people make are all distinctions and are the basis for social judgment. It refers more clearly to the strategies of social pretension than to clearly demarcated self-identification. There undoubtedly do exist various judgements of taste and behaviour that create boundaries between different social classes in rural India, and some of these are discussed in the later sections. However, these judgements are preceded by a different and parsimonious form of distinguishing that involves distancing one's family from desperately poor manual labourers. Such simple forms of distinguishing remind us that Bourdieu's concept was based on a comprehensive ethnography of 1960s French bourgeois society. Despite attempts at universality and an invitation to readers to seek equivalents in different contexts, it is difficult to reconcile this form of simple distinction/distinguishing with a Bourdieuian understanding. Rural India in the early decades of the twenty-first century presents a contrasting sociological landscape and historical specificity to that of 1960s France. The rapid transformation in post-liberalisation rural India (particularly in this case in the 10 years preceding 2014–15) created a highly unequal society, including the creation of relatively prosperous families living alongside communities of agricultural wage-labourers, who were often Dalits, living on the edge of villages in corrugated iron shacks with mud floors.

Ambitions and Aspirations

The second feature of rural middle classes is the existence of a specific type of ambition and aspiration, which I will explore through examples here. This was most clearly articulated in the desire that their children should obtain a private English-medium education and should be proficient in the use of English. This has been recognised in the urban context (Fernandes, 2006; Jeffrey, 2010b; Ganguly-Scrase and Scrase, 2009). English proficiency is not only perceived as an economic asset for the future, which enables better access to non-farm employment, but also as 'prestigious' and is related to notions of 'inclusiveness' and 'global connectivity'. Furthermore, members of the self-identified rural middle classes expressed very strong opposition to their children's involvement in farming activities, which were associated with the poverty, manual work and economic insecurities. English-medium education was referred as 'compulsory' if one wished for a non-farm occupation.

Knowledge of the English language, referred to as a 'global language' by many respondents, acted as a bridge that connected them to the world beyond India. This was mainly expressed in numerous references to me, who as a foreign researcher had 'travelled halfway across the world to conduct research in Maharashtra'. Some

182 Contested Capital

informants also commented on my English language proficiency and stated that they would like their children to be able to travel the world like me. When asked about the importance of English, Laximan, a skilled machine operator from a Dhangar family in Nandur, and the father of two young boys, answered: 'Look at you, you are here [in India] because you know English, we want our children to be able to do the same, and travel the world without any problem. Without the knowledge of English they will not be able to do that.'[23] Later in the interview, when I turned to talk to my research assistant, Laximan interrupted: 'See how you are speaking well in English, I like my children to speak good English too.'[24] Similarly, Yuvraj (described earlier) who self-identified as *upper middle class* stated, 'Now in the world market, English is only the most important and most used language in all the fields, one remains very restricted without knowing the English language.'[25] He further articulated his point: 'The *poor* can only have Zilla Parishad schools [public Marathi medium education] and this leaves them with no way out.'[26] That is, public education leaves them without access to the social capital (in Bourdieu's sense), which can enable them to find a way out of poverty. Yuvraj sends his children to a private school in Uruli Kanchan 'because the level of education they receive at Zilla Parishad schools is inadequate, and the medium of education is not English over here'.[27]

Pandhurang, a Maratha farmer in Rahatwade, spoke of his view of the importance of English language education for his grandchildren, and expressed his regret at not having had the chance to enrol his children (who are now in their 30s) in English-medium schools:

> People who have a better financial situation and know the importance of education, enrol their children in the English-medium school in Khed Shivapour [a town near Rahatwade]. There is no English-medium school in the village. If I had a chance I would have enrolled my children at the English school. English is important, if you want to go anywhere in the world you need to know English and without it you will not be able to do that.[28]

His account too highlighted the importance of speaking English, which went beyond securing access to non-farm employment. Many respondents spoke of the embarrassment they felt when their poor knowledge of English was exposed. For example, Yuvraj (described earlier) spoke of the awkwardness he experienced in situations when, as a labour contractor, he was unable to communicate with employees: 'When I visit various factories and an employee speaks to me in English, I am not able to respond and that makes me feel very uncomfortable.'[29] Similarly, Tanaji (described earlier), mother of a small boy, expressed her regrets

Bourdieu 183

about not learning English and recalled anxiety and embarrassment because of her poor knowledge of English and said that she hoped to prevent her child from having similar experiences:

> Nowadays when people talk they keep bringing in a word or two in English and if someone speaks something in English and I do not understand that word then I feel anxious and embarrassed, and I feel very small. That is why I feel learning English is very necessary. Therefore I have enrolled my child at the English-medium nursery school.[30]

Many other participants said that they had a similar sense of shame and regret in relation to their poor knowledge of English. Not only was English recognised as an important global language but also as an essential element of cultural capital. Although my interlocutors did not discuss cultural capital explicitly, or conceptualise the importance of English in abstract terms, their embarrassment caused by not speaking English demonstrated that it had significant symbolic value. English language proficiency conferred prestige on the speaker, and was the language of status and privilege in both villages – and most likely across all of rural India. Indeed, the importance of 'English-medium education' was revealed by the strategies some relatively less wealthy households employed to secure funding for educating their children in English. Discussions with my village guide, Datta, who was in his 30s, a farmer and a very active person in the village, revealed that many families sought to 'secure crop loans or agricultural development loans, but in fact spent the money on private school fees'.

Of significance also was a desire that the children should not take up farming activities in the future. The stated reasons for this (although it also related to differentiation from the poor) were two-fold: first, farming was associated with uncertainty and suffering; second, they emphasised the physical work involved in agriculture. Most families who owned agricultural land emphasised the fact that they employed farm-labourers to undertake work and did not permit their children to work on the land. I continuously learnt that agriculture was associated with 'isolation from the outside world' because it required 'living in the village'. English-medium education was obviously seen as an essential asset in attempts to secure employment outside agriculture. Non-farm skilled employment, particularly in factories, was associated with some form of 'prestige' and 'success', in contrast to farming, as I was repeatedly told. The following interview extract exemplifies the ways in which the importance of English education is articulated. When I asked about the significance of education, Tanaji stated that it was not only education that was important, but the English-medium education:

184   Contested Capital

> Now everyone gives a very high importance to English education. Now even in most jobs all the interviews are conducted in English. Even if English is not needed at the workplace, if for example an employee is unable to speak or understand English, then he would surely suffer the consequences: he would lack something in the environment of the job and he fails to understand what other people are saying around him. He would be at a disadvantage position just because of not knowing English, despite how hard working he might be. He will be isolated and unable to create a social network.[31]

Although neither she nor her husband had been to an English-medium school, they were adamant that their children should attend one. For her husband, imagining his children working in agriculture was 'impossible': 'No, no, there is nothing at all in agriculture, there is no profit in agriculture.... They should be educated in English so they can find a good job outside.'[32] As highlighted again and again, English education was seen as an essential component that conferred a tangible social advantage, was respected, and was a resource that would enable access to professional employment in cities. It can be suggested that English language education is a strategy for accessing lucrative employment outside agriculture and therefore acts as economic capital. However, as Swartz notes, in modern societies, cultural capital in the form of education and skill credentials (English language in the case of rural India) acts as a source of income. In such a case, it is not possible to make a distinction between the two types of capital (Swartz, 1997: 74).[33] For these self-identified middle-class families, ability to speak English was to be accessed at any cost, whether this be travelling two hours per day to and from school, spending the majority of household income on education, or using agricultural loans to pay children's school fees. English-medium education was the most salient type of social capital, which in Bourdieuian terminology enabled individuals to compete in the most important of 'fields' – the workplace.

Presentation and Consumption

In a review essay on the study of consumption in anthropology, Daniel Miller suggests that interest in consumption (culminating in what he terms an 'anthropology of consumption') dates to the publication of Bourdieu's *Distinction* and Douglas and Isherwood's *The World of Goods* (Miller, 1995: 266; Bourdieu, 1984; Douglas and Isherwood, 1979). There now exists a voluminous literature on the anthropology of consumption, which is fundamentally concerned with interpreting consumption practices and the 'social lives' of goods (Appadurai, 1986, 1996). Social and economic inequalities are the foundations of consumer societies, and access to financial resources determines an individual's ability to purchase certain products – the markers of class described in this chapter generally require an income and lifestyle in which subsistence and basic needs are not the only concerns. Despite this material reality, it is too simplistic and reductionist to suggest that middle-class families purchased sofa sets, flat-screen TVs or spent on English-medium schooling simply because they had sufficient income. The decision to purchase these goods and services was imbued with social meaning. We must always interrogate the reasons why certain patterns of consumption emerge. As Bourdieu states in his introduction to *Distinction*, 'there is an economy of cultural goods, but it has a specific logic', and the role of sociology as a discipline is to 'establish the conditions in which the consumers of cultural goods, and their taste for them, are produced, and at the same time to describe ... the social conditions of the constitution of the mode of appropriation that is considered legitimate' (Bourdieu, 1984: 1).

Interpreting class and consumption as mutually constitutive, Liechty suggests that middle-class culture is uniquely embedded in the 'social trajectory of things' and, although middle-class consumption practices vary across different global contexts, 'consumption... [is] their primary mode of cultural production, middle-class practice is inescapably consumer practice' (Liechty, 2003: 31). The goods people buy and services they enlist (such as private schooling) not only display privilege but are also obvious 'markers' because of the way in which they include and exclude others.[34]

Identifying markers of status in rural India was a difficult task, and one that was far from complete by the end of my field research. Although I had lived in India for several years, the nuanced markers of status remained difficult for me to identify, particularly in the rural context. Despite these limitations, the domestic built environment of participants provided a *prima facie* and highly visible marker of status. Over the course of my fieldwork, my research assistants and I sat in 490 different rural houses. This allowed us to identify and discuss the built environments and interiors of our participants' homes. The living room was the most significant room for both the researcher and participant (because we conducted the majority of interviews in the living room). The living room was also significant for participants because they hosted visitors and friends there. This room was usually the first entered on stepping into the house. For me, the living room was also the place in which I literally and figuratively stepped into the lives of participants. The living room provided a range of signs that revealed

186   Contested Capital

the class position of the household. Without knowing their income, expenditure and consumption, their children's education, or any other information about the household, I cursorily analysed its living room before starting any interview.

A description of three very different living rooms is provided here. The first (Figure 5.1) is of the living room, the only room of a family of landless agricultural labourers. The photograph is only of the exterior of the shack. On entering the house, which had corrugated iron walls and roof, supported by wooden poles, one encountered an unpolished mud-floor and a large cast-iron bed with a thin mattress. On the bed was a middle-aged man, who did not participate in the discussion, which was primarily with the female breadwinner, who sat with her two daughters on the floor. There was one blanket that she used as a carpet for us to sit on, and a mud-made cooker in the corner, surrounded by a few scattered pots and pans. The fact that this was a desperately poor Dalit family of agricultural labourers was reflected clearly in their domestic environment. There was no sign of superfluous consumption – no sofa set, motorcycle, mobile phone or television – just somewhere to cook and shelter from the elements. Similarly, impoverished built environments depicted in Figures 5.2 and 5.3 were typical of agricultural labourers in the villages. Most of these families had annual incomes of less than INR 50,000 in 2014–15.

Figure 5.4 depicts the living room (and the only room of the house) of Rajo's family, who belonged to the Dhangar caste in Nandur. The main participant was Rajo, who was discussed earlier. During the interviews, Rajo discussed his ambition to work abroad and sought advice about 'working in England and Dubai'. In identifying his class position, he claimed to belong to the *lower middle class*. The first noticeable feature was the tiled flooring, bricked and plastered walls and a washing corner. There was a mattress laid out for sitting on, a television, a fridge and an electric fan. There had been some attempt to decorate the interior of the room. On the back wall, there were two decorative pictures (of Shivaji Maharaj and a religious icon), and a picture of two white children with the caption 'We are a perfect match' written in English above their heads. This living room, the built environment with its decoration and consumer goods, was typical of families who self-identified as the *lower middle class*.

Figure 5.5 depicts the living room of Anil's family, who owned a grocery shop, and were identified as middle class in both Marxist and Weberian definitions and self-identified as the *middle middle class*. The family belonged to the Mali caste, and had an annual income of INR 410,000 (INR 360,000 from their grocery shop and INR 50,000 from agriculture) in 2014–15. Before the entrance to the living room, there was a swing bamboo chair on a balcony overlooking the village

Figure 5.1 Residence of a Dalit agricultural labouring family in Nandur

Source: Author.

Figure 5.2 Residence of a Dalit agricultural labouring family in Nandur

Source: Author.

Figure 5.3 Residence of a Dalit agricultural labouring family in Rahatwade

Source: Author.

Figure 5.4 Living room of a self-identified *lower-middle-class* family in Nandur

Source: Author.

(the shop was below the house, the living room on the first floor). Anil's living room was perhaps one of the most elaborate in the village and had a number of striking features, among which was an extravagant marble floor, polished and spotless. The rear wall was decorated with sky-blue and gold leaf wallpaper, and there was a hanging 32-inch flat-screen TV. The cabinet below the TV set against the decorated back wall displayed photographs of their two sons, educational achievement trophies, speakers, house-plants and a back-up light. On the shelf below the photographs were sets of crystal cups. There was a leather sofa set covered in blankets, and there were spotlights fitted into a two-layered ceiling. Similarly impressive living rooms are depicted in Figures 5.6, 5.7, 5.8 and 5.9. These are typical of the living rooms of those who identify as *middle middle class* and *upper middle class*.

These living rooms were my starting point for an analysis of the cultural markers of class in rural India. The built environments presented a very obvious form of distinction, which did not require a deep knowledge of the society. They showed me that there was indeed an economy of cultural goods with a specific logic and they revealed the relevance of a Bourdieuian analysis of the rural middle class. The contrasting living rooms are obviously the result of families being able

Figure 5.5   Living room of a self-identified *middle-middle-class* family in Nandur

Source: Author.

Figure 5.6 Living room of a self-identified *middle-middle-class* family in Nandur

Source: Author.

Figure 5.7 Living room of a self-identified *middle-middle-class* family in Nandur

Source: Author.

Figure 5.8 Living room of a self-identified *middle-middle-class* family in Rahatwade

Source: Author.

Figure 5.9 Living room of a self-identified *upper-middle-class* family in Rahatwade

Source: Author.

to afford to purchase, for example, a television or a sofa set, but their decision to purchase such goods and present them in a particular way is imbued with social meaning.

It was difficult to compare existing forms and levels of consumption with those of the past because there was no historical data. However, participants provided insight into changes over the last decade. The notion of 'change' and 'development' was significant for them. Many members of the middle class spoke of 'positive' transformations over the previous 10 years. Arjun (discussed earlier), for example, spoke of how people now mixed their language with English; the fact that it was now 'compulsory to have a smart phone'; and that there had been a lot of 'changes in clothing'.

But of course, not everyone had experienced such improvement in their standard of living – Arjun estimated that '80 per cent of the village have experienced such positive changes in the last decade', and that these were 'the middle-class families, because they run profitable agriculture and have access to jobs in factories'.[36] Similarly, Nitesh (described earlier) provided insight into the changes in the village and connected his family's entry to the middle class with 'non-farm, non-manual employment'. He gave a vivid account of his family being 'very poor' when he was a child when they 'used to work only for subsistence':

> Ten years ago in my family no one worked outside agriculture. Every day we were earning our bread, and we only had enough to feed ourselves, nothing above our daily needs. Then I got a [skilled] job, and slowly slowly our living situation became better and we started progressing. It all started five years ago. We are now a middle-class family. Yes, middle class means all of these: television, fridge, cooker, smart phone, etc. It is not necessary that all needs of a middle-class family be fulfilled at once, the progress happens slowly slowly. Even in a high-class family few things are not available.... It is important how much your income is and how much you can satisfy your needs. I have a definite [fixed] income. But what about farmers? They do not have any definite income. For example an onion cultivator should immediately find a buyer; second, his income depends on the market price; and finally, what is the final sum that comes into his hands – that is very important. There is no certainty in what he can earn, and all depends on the nature, and depends on the market. That is why farmers do not fall in the middle-class category.[37]

Further, there had also been significant changes, as discussed in Chapter 4, in the housing of residents, 'from *kutcha* houses to proper *pucca* houses today'. Yuvraj also examined the changes in the village over the previous 10 years.

> Our village has changed a lot in terms of standard of living. First, until few years ago there were only tin shades or just mud houses in the village, but as you see now most of houses all are R.C.C. [reinforced cement concrete] built.... There has been a lot of difference in the education of people too. Ten years back all used to go to Zilla Parishad schools for education, now we go to Uruli Kanchan for English-medium education, in schools where all facilities are available. Also 10 years ago people wore only pyjamas and *dhoti*s, the Indian dress, now pants, trousers, t-shirts, shirts are used. There have been changes in the appearance of ladies too: they have started wearing dresses instead of saris. Until very recently they never wore dresses [laughs out loudly], now they are wearing them.[38]

He continued:

> Also, the rich class wear more gold etc.... Also they will go to hotels a lot to eat. They buy their clothes in big malls in cities only. We will buy our clothes in Uruli Kanchan.[39]

A similar narrative was given by Jaibai (the daughter-in-law of a Maratha household in Rahatwade) about village development over the recent years and progress in their living standards, describing how 'all the houses in the village did not use to be tiled or stone floored'. 'Our house was not like this', she told me, pointing to her polished stone living room flooring. She also commented on the increasing number of vehicles in the previous few years – and 'the changes happened', she thought, 'because of education, information, and contacts ... when people started travelling outside ... hence people started gaining knowledge of how to live'.[40] A parallel account was given by Laximan (described earlier), who explained that significant changes in the living standards of some residents had happened over the previous 10 years, primarily because of the establishment of factories:

> So economically we can say everything has become good.... Lots of changes have taken place. Smart mobile phones are now very common in the village;

194   Contested Capital

people have started earning more income, because the companies [factories] are established outside our village. Many people have started to live in an up-to-date condition. People started purchasing good vehicles, good cars, two-wheelers and four-wheelers. They just started buying blindly.[41]

The positive impact of industrialisation on the living standards of village inhabitants was also articulated by my other interviewee, for example Sitesh: 'People are now living up to date, and are well groomed and well dressed. They now go to Pune to buy goods, some to malls, some to branded shops like Dmart.'[42] Dutta, my village guide in Rahatwade, provided an overall view of the change in life style and new patterns of consumptions in the village, which according to him had been emerging in the previous 10 years. He stated:

Economically the village has undergone a major change in the last 10 years ... private vehicle ownership has increased. First there were hardly any two-wheelers in the village, now there are 60 to 70 two-wheelers and some four-wheelers in the village.... As factories have been established in the neighbouring village, the income of people has increased. They have provided jobs, which pay for television, for vehicles, etc. Regarding education, people have become more educated than before. Education has become very important. There is more inclination towards English education, rather than Marathi education. Ten years ago this was not the case. Lifestyle of people has become better, previously people used to own less clothes or low quality clothes, but now even every two or three months they can go and purchase new dresses, new clothes, because of this their standard of living has become better.[43]

These changes were also evident in quantitative surveys. We do not have data relating to consumption patterns from the past, so Tables 5.3 and 5.4 must be seen as evidence of the presence of goods that were either not present or present in very small numbers in the villages in the past. As mentioned during interviews, vehicles and domestic appliances were significant.

Tables 5.3 and 5.4 show widespread ownership of both motorbikes and cars in both villages. However, the most striking feature of the data is the difference between the two villages. In Nandur, the majority of households owned a motorcycle, which was not the case in Rahatwade, and the proportion of the total population that owned cars was smaller in Rahatwade. The sample of non-labouring households in both villages was then broken down according to self-identified classes. If we disregard the 'upper middle' and 'rich' classes in both villages, we can see that car and motorbike ownership in Nandur was higher across all categories than it was in Rahatwade.

Bourdieu 195

Table 5.3 Vehicle ownership among Rahatwade's self-identified classes

Rahatwade	Motorbikes		Cars	
	Freq.	*Per cent*	*Freq.*	*Per cent*
Total village (*N* = 250)	154	61.6	22	8.8
Total manual labouring (*N*= 131)	56	42.7	2	1.5
Total non-labouring (*N* = 119)	98	82.35	20	16.81
Total sample (*N* = 97)	78	80.4	14	14.42
Poor (*N* = 7)	2	28.6	0	0
Lower middle class (*N* = 30)	22	73.3	2	6.7
Middle middle class (*N* = 57)	51	89.5	11	19.3
Upper middle class (*N* = 3)	3	100	1	33.3
Rich (*N* = 0)	N.A.	N.A.	N.A.	N.A.

Source: Fieldwork data (2015).

Table 5.4 Vehicle ownership among Nandur's self-identified classes

Nandur	Motorbikes		Cars	
	Freq.	*Per cent*	*Freq.*	*Per cent*
Total village (*N* = 240)	205	85.4	39	16.25
Total manual labouring (*N* = 123)	93	75.61	6	4.9
Total non-labouring (*N* = 117)	112	95.73	33	28.21
Total sample (*N* = 97)	95	98	27	27.8
Poor (*N* = 3)	3	100	0	0
Lower middle class (*N* = 22)	21	91.3	3	13.6
Middle middle class (*N* = 65)	64	98.5	20	30.8
Upper middle class (*N* = 6)	6	100	3	50
Rich (*N* = 1)	1	100	1	100

Source: Fieldwork data (2015).

Tables 5.5 and 5.6 show a similar situation with respect to domestic appliances. In both villages, the possession of refrigerators and colour televisions was widespread, particularly among all categories of the middle class. Air coolers were more popular in Nandur than in Rahatwade. The data relating to possession of water purifiers is particularly interesting. Clean water was closely associated with progress and 'development', and the desire to 'purify' water with a new sensitivity and awareness of hygiene/disease, highlighted during interviews. In Nandur, 38.7 per cent of the total sample households owned a water purifier. In Rahatwade, the proportion was only 2 per cent.

196   Contested Capital

Table 5.5   Possession of domestic appliances among Rahatwade's classes

Rahatwade	Refrigerator		Colour TV		Air cooler		Water purifier	
	Freq.	Per cent	Freq.	Per cent	Freq.	Per cent	Freq.	Per cent
Total village (N = 250)	108	43.2	222	88.8	7	2.8	N.A.	N.A.
Total manual labouring (N = 113)	37	28.2	109	83.2	0	0	N.A.	N.A.
Total non-labouring (N = 119)	71	59.7	113	95	7	5.88	N.A.	N.A.
Total sample (N = 97)	53	54.6	90	92.8	5	5.1	2	2
Poor (N = 7)	1	14.3	5	71.4	0	0	0	0
Lower middle class (N = 30)	10	33.3	27	90	0	0	0	0
Middle middle class (N = 57)	39	68.4	55	96.4	4	7	1	1.75
Upper middle class (N = 3)	3	100	3	100	1	33.3	1	33.3
Rich (N = 0)	N.A.	N.A.	N.A.	N.A.	N.A.	N.A.	N.A.	N.A.

Source: Fieldwork data (2015).

Table 5.6   Possession of domestic appliances among Nandur's classes

Nandur	Refrigerator		Colour TV		Air cooler		Water purifier	
	Freq.	Per cent	Freq.	Per cent	Freq.	Per cent	Freq.	Per cent
Total village (N = 240)	122	50.8	227	94.6	23	9.6	N.A.	N.A.
Total manual labouring (N = 123)	86	29.3	113	91.9	4	3.25	N.A.	N.A.
Total non-labouring (N = 117)	38	73.5	114	97.4	19	16.2	N.A.	N.A.
Total sample (N = 97)	78	80.4	92	94.9	10	10.3	37	38.1
Poor (N = 3)	1	33.3	3	100	0	0	1	33.3
Lower middle class (N = 22)	17	78.3	18	81.8	1	4.5	6	27.2
Middle middle class (N = 65)	53	81.5	64	98.5	5	7.7	26	40
Upper middle class (N = 6)	6	100	6	100	3	50	3	50
Rich (N = 1)	1	100	1	100	1	100	1	100

Source: Fieldwork data (2015).

Similarly, Tables 5.7 and 5.8 reveal the widespread use of smartphones among the three categories of the middle class in both villages, but limited use of computers, tablets and laptops. Again, we see higher rates of possession in Nandur than in Rahatwade. In Nandur, 48.3 per cent of the total population and 68.4 per cent of the non-labouring population owned a smartphone; in Rahatwade, the proportions were respectively 36 and 55.5 per cent.

Bourdieu 197

Table 5.7 Possession of communications devices among Rahatwade's classes

Rahatwade	Smartphone		Computers, laptops, tablets	
	Freq.	*Per cent*	*Freq.*	*Per cent*
Total village (*N* = 250)	90	36	15	6
Total manual labouring (*N* = 113)	24	18.3	0	0
Total non-labouring (*N* = 119)	66	55.5	15	12.6
Total sample (*N* = 97)	57	58.8	12	12.4
Poor (*N* = 7)	1	14.3	0	0
Lower middle class (*N* = 30)	17	56.7	3	10
Middle middle class (*N* = 57)	37	64.9	8	14
Upper middle class (*N* = 3)	2	66.7	1	33.3
Rich (*N* = 0)	N.A.		N.A.	
Total	57	58.8	12	12.4

Source: Fieldwork data (2015).

Table 5.8 Possession of communications devices among Nandur's classes

Nandur	Smartphone		Computers, laptops, tablets	
	Freq.	*Per cent*	*Freq.*	*Per cent*
Total village (*N* = 240)	116	48.3	31	10.4
Total manual labouring (*N* = 123)	36	29.3	5	4.1
Total non-labouring (*N* = 117)	80	68.4	26	22.2
Total sample (*N* = 97)	63	65	25	25.8
Poor (*N* = 3)	1	33	0	0
Lower middle class (*N* = 22)	8	36.3	1	4.3
Middle middle class (*N* = 65)	49	75.4	24	37
Upper middle class (*N* = 6)	4	66.6	0	0
Rich (*N* = 1)	1	100	0	0

Source: Fieldwork data (2015).

The use of social media (such as Facebook) is shown in Tables 5.9 and 5.10. The widespread use of social media among the self-identified middle classes, particularly among *middle-middle-class* households across both villages was a surprising finding to emerge from the data.

198   Contested Capital

Table 5.9   Social media use in Rahatwade

Rahatwade (N = 97)	Freq.	Per cent
Total village (N = 250)	91	36.4
Total manual labouring (N = 113)	32	24.4
Total non-labouring (N = 119)	59	49.6
Total sample (N = 97)	46	48.4
Poor (N = 7)	0	0
Lower middle class (N = 30)	13	43.3
Middle middle class (N = 57)	30	52.6
Upper middle class (N = 3)	3	100
Rich (N = 0)	N.A.	N.A.

Source: Fieldwork data (2015).

Table 5.10   Social media use in Nandur

Nandur (N = 97)	Freq.	Per cent
Total village (N = 240)	107	44.6
Total manual labouring (N = 123)	33	23.8
Total non-labouring (N = 117)	74	63.25
Total sample (N = 97)	60	61.8
Poor (N = 3)	1	33.3
Lower middle class (N = 22)	9	40.9
Middle middle class (N = 65)	48	73.8
Upper middle class (N = 6)	2	33.3
Rich (N = 1)	0	0
Total	60	61.8

Source: Fieldwork data (2015).

The possession of sofa sets among different self-identified classes is shown in Table 5.11 and 5.12. As discussed earlier in the section, the presence of a sofa set in the living rooms of respondents was a significant, albeit anecdotal, finding.

The in-depth interviews with self-identified middle-class families, together with Tables 5.3 to 5.12 demonstrating the access to, and possession of, consumer goods, revealed significant change and 'progress' in both villages. Recognising that these changes (in income, education, consumption and lifestyle) have occurred in some parts of rural India is a significant finding on its own. However, although it could be thought that these changes in consumption and life style had happened because of an increase in income and purchasing power, some of the interviews also reveal a deeper social meaning in some of these changes. Of course, there

Table 5.11   Possession of sofa set among Rahatwade's classes

Rahatwade (N = 97)	Freq.	Per cent
Poor (N = 7)	0	0
Lower middle class (N = 30)	12	40
Middle middle class (N = 57)	33	57.9
Upper middle class (N = 3)	1	33.3
Rich (N = 0)	N.A.	N.A.
Total	46	47.4

Source: Fieldwork data (2015).

Table 5.12   Possession of sofa set among Nandur's classes

Nandur (N = 97)	Freq.	Per cent
Poor (N = 3)	2	66
Lower middle class (N = 22)	12	54.5
Middle middle class (N = 65)	41	63
Upper middle class (N = 6)	5	83.3
Rich (N = 1)	1	100
Total	61	62.88

Source: Fieldwork data (2015).

were many other ways in which the status of the middle class was demonstrated, most notably by way of their representation of hospitality and attempts to display a certain style of treating their guests; their leisure activities; engagement in civic society; food habits and travelling; to name a few, but it is not possible to provide a comprehensive account of each here. Overall, the fieldwork evidence and narratives highlight that there had been a transformation in the cultures of consumption over the 10 years preceding 2014–15, which was characterised by new building styles, the purchase of cars and motorbikes and the presence of other consumer goods. The assertion that the culture of consumption had changed over time presents a methodological problem. How can we make an argument about transformation without a similar data set from the past, also relating to consumption patterns? Such a historical data set is unavailable, and this potential methodological pitfall is overcome in a number of ways. First, the literature on rural India does not indicate that a self-identified rural middle class existed in the past. Second, it is logical to assume that new consumption patterns of the rural middle class, which were inextricably linked by the respondents to the development of industries on the outskirts of both villages, did not exist before the arrival of industrial units, and therefore was a recent phenomenon. Third, and perhaps most significantly,

200   Contested Capital

there is overwhelming evidence collected during interviews which indicates that a decade prior to fieldwork such consumption patterns did not exist. Furthermore, the building of new houses was evidence enough of the transformation of living styles. Domestic goods such as fridges and televisions were widely owned and could be found in almost all middle-class houses – but were very rare 10 years prior to fieldwork (as indicated repeatedly by the respondents). This prosperity, however, had not reached all residents of the village, and as the cursory comparison of living rooms demonstrated, there was still a desperately poor underclass living in corrugated iron shacks in both villages. It was clear that the ownership of certain consumer goods and the contrasting interior styles were about more than just a rapid increase in purchasing power – these patterns of consumption were imbued with social meaning and attempts to display middle-class status.

It should be noted this chapter should not be understood as an attempt to locate a 'Bourdieuian middle class' because such a notion is antithetical to Bourdieu's approach. Rather, it should be viewed as an attempt – the first of its kind in rural India – to examine the ways the term 'middle class' is understood and defined, and to explore its symbolic and cultural markers in rural India. I have aimed in this chapter to suggest productive ways in which the sociology of Bourdieu and his approach to social class can be applied to Indian villages, prompted partly by a discussion of the interior design of 'living rooms' in Rahatwade and Nandur. Although it was difficult to grasp analytically the meaning behind certain forms of consumption, the chapter revealed that there was indeed an economy of cultural goods that was specific to middle classes.

Notes

1. The categories of the five identified classes did not derive from existing literature. Rather, they were developed by combining the outcome of pilot interviews and discussion with village people based on a very practical question: 'How many classes or socio-economic categories are in the village?'
2. For a comprehensive discussion on Bourdieu's contribution, see Swartz (1997).
3. Rutten (1995) and Upadhya (1988) show something similar.
4. Similar arguments, not in a Bourdieuian framework, are made by Fernandes (2006), Fernandes and Heller (2006), Hansen (1996) and Harriss (2006).
5. Gooptu makes similar observation in a study of young workers in retails sector in shopping malls in urban Kolkata. Young workers seek various strategies for self-development to be compatible for what they perceive to be expected from them in the workplace. See Gooptu (2009: 45–54).

6. It is notable that during interviews, the term 'middle class' was often used in English.

7. The narratives that are included in this chapter are drawn from in-depth interviews and some participant observations. I have included as much as much interviews as the space allows me, although some of the statements may sound repetitive, this repetition in the participants' narrations demonstrates a pattern of expression that is not only unique to some individuals but rather confirms the arguments of this chapter. Together with my research assistant, we were participant observers in variety of settings including, but not limited to, the place of residence, children activities, and so on.

8. Ajay G., personal interview, 3 July 2016, Nandur.

9. Kamaledin K. Sh., personal interview, 30 June 2016, Nandur.

10. Surrdin K. Sh., personal interview, 30 June 2016, Nandur.

11. Surrdin K. Sh., personal interview, 30 June 2016, Nandur.

12. Santosh B. Ch., personal interview, 12 June 2016, Rahatwade; Santosh's oldest son has finished his high school education, and after obtaining a technical diploma, currently works as a skilled machine operator in a factory outside Rahatwade. The second son is in 10th standard in a private school.

13. Suresh P. Ch., personal interview, 25 June 2016, Rahatwade.

14. Suresh P. Ch., personal interview, 25 June 2016, Rahatwade.

15. Nitesh L. Ch., personal interview, 9 May 2016, Rahatwade.

16. Nitesh L. Ch., personal interview, 9 May 2016, Rahatwade.

17. Yuvraj B. B., personal interview, 29 May 2016, Nandur.

18. Yuvraj B. B., personal interview, 29 May 2016, Nandur.

19. Tanaji Ch., personal interview, 19 June 2016, Rahatwade.

20. Rupali A. B., personal interview, 29 May 2016, Nandur.

21. Baburao Sh. Ch., personal interview, 15 June 2016, Rahatwade.

22. It is notable that while describing the meaning of middle-class-ness, the respondents did not refer to their caste affiliations and parental educational level as markers of middle-class status.

23. Laximan Kh. Gh., personal interview, 28 June 2016, Nandur.

24. Laximan Kh. Gh., personal interview, 28 June 2016, Nandur.

25. Yuvraj B. B., personal interview, 29 May 2016, Nandur.

26. Yuvraj B. B., personal interview, 29 May 2016, Nandur.

27. Yuvraj B. B., personal interview, 29 May 2016, Nandur.

28. Phandhurang M. Ch., personal interview, 24 June 2016, Rahatwade; Arjun P. Ch., personal interview, 24 June 2016, Rahatwade. The household's annual income in agricultural year of 2014–15 was INR 450,000 (INR 150,000 from agriculture, INR 120,000 from one son's employment in an agricultural market yard in Pune and another son earning an annual income of INR 180,000 as a supervisor at the construction site).

202   Contested Capital

29. Yuvraj B. B., personal interview, 29 May 2016, Nandur.
30. Tanaji Ch., personal interview, 19 June 2016, Rahatwade.
31. Tanaji, Ch., personal interview, 19 June 2016, Rahatwade.
32. Laximan, Kh. Gh., personal interview, 28 June 2016, Nandur.
33. Swartz (1997: 76–77) states,

> Expanded higher education has created massive credential markets that are today decisive in reproducing the social class structure. Since educational credentials increasingly have become necessary for gaining access to desirable positions in the job market, it becomes essential for parents to invest in a good education for their children so they can reap the 'profit' on the job market. This process of investment involves the conversion of economic capital into cultural capital, which is a strategy more readily available to the affluent.

34. Many scholars have recognised, mass media is central to this process in urban India (Brosius, 2010) and Nepal (Liechty, 2003). For example, Liechty argues that mass-media consumption should be situated alongside other forms of consumption (see Liechty 2003). See also Brosius (2010). Acknowledging that media is also a scientific fact in a Bourdieuian analysis (that mass media and the multitude of ways in which it informs the subjectivities of rural residents is undoubtedly significant), in this chapter due to limitation of space, we are not covering the role of media in analyses of the rural middle classes.
35. Arjun P. Ch., personal interview, 24 June 2016, Rahatwade.
36. Nitesh L. Ch., personal interview, 9 May 2016, Rahatwade.
37. Nitesh L. Ch., personal interview, 9 May 2016, Rahatwade.
38. Yuvraj B. B., personal interview, 29 May 2016, Nandur.
39. Yuvraj B. B., personal interview, 29 May 2016, Nandur.
40. Jaibai Sh. Ch., personal interview, 21 May 2016, Rahatwade.
41. Laximan Kh. Gh., personal interview, 28 June 2016, Nandur.
42. Shitesh K., personal interview, 10 April 2016, Nandur.
43. Dattatray V. T., personal interview, 13 June 2016, Rahatwade.

Conclusion
Understanding the Rural Middle Classes

The 'middle class' has become one of the key categories of economic analysis and developmental forecasting for all observers of India – whether from government, academia, policymaking, business or media. All this discussion suffers, however, from one major oversight: it assumes that the middle class is a uniquely urban category. Studies dedicated to understanding the middle class, in India and globally, almost entirely overlook its rural presence. As this book has demonstrated, however, more than a third of India's middle class is rural, and 17 per cent of rural households belong to the middle class. My purpose has been to bring this vast and dynamic population into view, and to fully confront the neglected questions surrounding India's rural middle class.

However, probing the development of the rural middle class required an exploration of the ways in which the middle class is defined theoretically, and the application of theoretical insights to generate empirical understandings. Given that there is no single overarching theory, critical pluralism came to be the order of the day. Three analytical lenses have helped me examine in considerable detail the making of the Indian rural middle classes – those of Marx, Weber and Bourdieu. This plural approach elucidates the dynamics of middle class formation in the wake of the introduction of economic liberalisation, and contributes to a holistic understanding of the economic characteristics, social composition, cultural practices, aspirations, everyday worlds and social identifications of the rural middle classes.

While urban India is being liberalised, rural liberalisation has been an uneven process in both economic and social terms. For some decades, agriculture has no longer been the primary focus of life in rural India. Diversification is now a central feature of rural economy and society, as households have undergone social and economic transformations, and in so doing have developed a new sense of class identity and aspirations. In the villages I have studied, and probably in many other parts of rural India, industrialisation has produced new social relations of

204　Conclusion

production, accumulation strategies and labour relations. For the rural youths it has facilitated entry into the skilled labour market, a process they have accelerated with intensive pursuit of education and training, fast-tracked through the informal economy of technical credentials. The resulting rural middle class has created distinctive lifestyles, aspirations and consumption patterns. In what follows I will condense the findings of this book.

Constructing the Rural Middle Classes in Maharashtra: Theory and Practice

The Marxist framework enabled us to see how the many attempts to identify agrarian classes all provide an incomplete analysis of class formation in the contemporary phase of rural industrialisation. In applying Marx's analytical categories of ownership of the means of production and capital–labour production relations, I developed a composite analytical instrument that used rural households' net selling and buying of labour power, their ownership of land and other productive assets, and modes of accumulation of surplus. With this, I classified the emerging class structure in the villages as a whole. Seven discrete economic class categories were identified, including two groups comprising the rural middle classes: *farm-owning skilled workers* and *petty commodity producers* located between the capitalist class and the classes of labour. Of particular significance was the class of *farm-owning skilled workers* (what I term the *straddling middle class*), which has not been identified elsewhere, whose non-farm economic activities are nonetheless linked to agriculture. They were conceptualised as middle class because their class position has features of both the agricultural capitalist class and the working class – yet they cannot be situated in either. Although members of this class are engaged in skilled employment – as supervisors, managers and foremen – they use this income to expand agricultural production and accumulate surplus by hiring in agricultural labourers. Their class position 'in-itself' oscillates between, and straddles, the working class and the class of capitalist farmers. These forms of 'awkwardness' in class relations make the case for moving beyond the rigidities of polar classes. They call for more flexibility in the analysis of class-in-itself, so as to incorporate the oscillation of households between different class positions.

The Marxian rural middle class constitutes approximately 32 per cent of the total village population in Rahatwade (22 per cent petty commodity producers, and 9.5 per cent the straddling middle class). In Nandur they make up 28 per cent of the population (18 per cent pretty commodity producers and 10 per cent the straddling middle class). In both villages most people belong to the classes of labour (almost 55 and 58 per cent of households in Rahatwade and Nandur respectively).

The Marxist perspective revealed that class formation was taking place rapidly in a process that was fluid and unstable. The rural middle classes are characterised by a great range of occupations, by complexity and paradox in terms of their relations of production, labour relations and instability in terms of class locations. The seven-class typology that emerged retains the Marxist structure, but it also provides the flexibility to reflect local specificities such as the diversity of livelihoods and of developing forms of accumulation. It further incorporates the rapid transformation of class structure in the current phase of India's rural industrialisation, when households can simultaneously belong to a range of classes-in-themselves.

Meanwhile, the Weberian analysis of the rural middle classes demonstrated that the growing industrialisation on the peripheries of these villages has resulted in the formation of new occupational opportunities, which require new types of education and training. These are fast-tracked in the informal economy of technical education and credentials. They have created the conditions for the development of the rural middle class. Indeed Weber criticised Marx for his unsuccessful attempt to deal with class formation based on education and skill differentials. For Weber, particularly in the era of industrial development, skilled and semi-skilled workers, who could be trained on the job in a relatively short period of time, were increasingly important in production and manufacturing, but also significant for class variations. These competences are particularly relevant to class formation in the current phase of rural industrialisation in India. In the villages I have studied, for example, we saw that aspiring rural households often sought upward social mobility through private 'engineering' courses, to gain access to the middle-class skilled-labour market.

Our Weberian analysis also identified nine economic classes, which retain structural complexity in relation to the ownership of productive property and other marketable capital, which is central to Weber's concept of class formation. It also takes into consideration the economic and social specificities of rural India. The middle classes are here identified as households whose primary source of income was generated from skills and education plus assets. They consist of farmers owning less than 10 acres of land, skilled workers, government employees, independent workers, and skilled industrial machine operators (together constituting approximately 34 and 39 per cent of the total number of households in Rahatwade and Nandur respectively). Central to the formation of the rural middle classes here is the increasing importance of skilled workers and

206   Conclusion

skilled machine operators (exactly what a Marxist analysis would term a skilled working class).

As found in the Marxist analysis, but for different reasons, the Weberian 'class situation' of the majority of industrial workers remains unstable. A property-less individual who is positively privileged in the labour market, because of his high quality education, may not be able to retain his class position if demand for skilled employment declines, a possibility that Weber himself and Weberian scholars after him have mostly omitted from their analyses. Indeed, there seem to be only two definite class positions in a Weberian analysis: one in which an individual has access to both profitable property and highly marketable education and skills, and one in which an individual is deprived of both, when manual labour takes the form of a commodity and is the only source of income. In this way, Weber's categorisation of two classes on the basis of ownership and non-ownership of property brings him closer to Marx. Similarities between Weber and Marx are well illustrated in rural India, where our Weberian *positively privileged propertied classes* overlap with our Marxian *landowning capitalist class* and the *new capitalist class*, whose economic activities mainly constitute large-scale appropriation of surplus from agricultural labour through production, exchange and marketing. Similarly, our identified Weberian *negatively privileged propertied classes* overlap with our Marxian classes of labour, whose primary source of income is derived from their manual labour power, both in agricultural and non-agricultural sectors.

Thirdly, the concepts of social and cultural capital of Bourdieu were applied to rural India and adapted to regional specificities. Bourdieu himself invited his readers to find the equivalents of social distinctions and habitus in other global contexts. I found that the most important features of this class according to the statements made by its members emphasised the middle-class membership, social distance from manual work, and from dependency. Almost no one outside the labouring classes whom I interviewed defined themselves as 'poor'. On the contrary they were adamant that their lives had a decent material quality, equal or above the village average. Claims to self-sufficiency, being middle class and not poor, and not being wage labourers are the central feature of middle-class-ness in these villages. These self-identified rural middle classes demonstrated a specific type of ambition and aspirations for their children. These were most clearly expressed in the desire for private English-medium education, proficiency in the use of the English language, and employment outside agriculture. Most significantly, proficiency in English was not only perceived as an economic asset for the future, enabling better access to non-farm employment, it was also perceived as a prestigious distinction in itself and related to ideas and practices of global connectivity. The Bourdieuian approach also required an unravelling of the economy of cultural goods – it demonstrated that there has been a rapid and significant transformation in the patterns of consumption in both villages, characterised by new housing construction styles, interior designs and the widespread purchasing of a range of consumers goods, previously perceived to be unnecessary to rural households.

These distinctions are related to the Bourdieuian concept of 'habitus'. As rural middle classes emerge in rapidly transforming villages, where tastes are still unstable, explicit boundaries (material and economic) are more important and obvious markers of class. Bourdieu's approach informed my research as a heuristic device, and not as a prescriptive definition of class identity. Outside France and other western societies, his approach can be developed further as a model to study class in general and the middle classes in particular.

It is notable that in both villages, the middle class is developing in such a way that households' entry to the middle class is achieved through male youths, with the help of acquired informal educational credentials and ascribed caste. Shifts in employment patterns have not necessarily resulted in the transformation of a household's gender division of labour: middle-class occupations are primarily performed by men, while the majority of rural women (except in a small number of households) are engaged in agricultural work, either on the household's land or as casual agricultural labourers, alongside their household domestic work (neither Marx nor Weber, nor Bourdieu, placed much emphasis on gender). The findings further suggest striking caste stratifications within rural middle classes. They are primarily constituted by upper and middle castes. Scheduled Castes and Scheduled Tribes are mainly excluded.

Comparing and Contrasting the Three Theories: A Brief Note on Contested Capital

The three theories of class that frame this book examine the rural middle class from different perspectives. In bringing together the empirical findings from each, we are reminded once again of the conceptual complexity of the term 'class' which results from the various types of capital that can inform class boundaries in each theory. Bourdieu's approach, for example, was derived from his endeavour to critique Weber's conception of class and status (that of lifestyle), which for him made an erroneous distinction between two forms of capital: material and symbolic. According to Bourdieu these should not be viewed as different forms of capital. Social class differences are manifested in lifestyles. As a consequence,

208   Conclusion

social class analysis should not be confined to material relations, but should encompass a simultaneous analysis of symbolic relations. Similarly, Bourdieu's main criticism of Marx is that he failed to take into account the increasing impact and influence of fields of symbolic production, which produced their own social capacities to exploit. The economic sphere, which Marx had assumed to be the primary, determining, field, was for Bourdieu no longer predominant. In Bourdieu's conception of social reality, power is decentralised and enacted across varied social fields, rather than concentrated in economic relations. For Bourdieu, all spheres of activity, not just the economic, determine particular bodily practices that constitute the habitus within a particular social field (Burawoy, 2012: 31–46). For Bourdieu, cultural capital is identified as the means of distinction in coexisting social fields, which intersect to produce dominating regulatory dispositions, perceptions and appreciations that are together congealed in the concept of 'habitus'. It is habitus which disciplines and regulates social behaviour, and is the major factor in the reproduction of social relations. For a Marxist, the first problem with Bourdieu's concept of social capital is, the perversion of the notion of capital in the manner in which Bourdieu understands it in relation to privilege and distinction – capital in any form should be a means for accumulation rather than mere distinction. Personal endowments, which are identified as social capital by Bourdieu, reflect the habitus of privilege and social aspirations; these privileges might permit easy access to resources, but unless they function as a means of surplus accumulation, these forms of social capital cannot be considered 'capital' in the Marxist sense (Harvey, 2015). Similarly, for Weber social capital (or what are called 'life chances' in Weberian terminology) is only considered 'capital' if it improves one's market situation by enhancing access to resources, and control over the labour of others, which enables particular life outcomes or styles of living.

For Bourdieu, the coexistence of social fields changes the base-superstructure hierarchical model into a plane of coexisting social fields that impact and influence one another. In such a planar model, there is no scope for exploitation or domination, as each social field produces its own habitus, which provides the governing regulatory principle for social reproduction. Moreover, while habitus focuses on the individual and his/her adoption of, or interpellation into, particular social roles, Marx was more interested in the collective class conflict, in which individual bodies are understood as having been disciplined for the sake of exploitation and surplus accumulation (Harvey, 2015).

Despite these theoretical differences, at the empirical level the various types of capital each theorist imagined overlap significantly. Many elements of each of the three theoretical approaches to rural middle-class-ness interact with the others. Let us look at education for example, and in particular English-medium education. For all the self-identified middle-class families I interviewed, an English-medium education was the most important resource or capital that could guarantee the future success of their children. It was to be accessed at any cost. English education was seen as essential to securing non-farm, non-labouring careers that confer a tangible social advantage. English-medium education acts as economic capital, which resonates with the Weberian concept of 'life chances' that an individual brings to the labour market. Education was also the most salient type of Bourdieu's social capital, which enables individuals to compete in the most important of 'fields' – the workplace. It was also perceived as cultural capital and related to notions of global information. However, my field evidence suggests that only landholding families could afford to educate their children in English-medium schools, which means they had to be owners of capital in the Marxian sense. In such cases it is not possible to draw distinctions between the three theorists, or to identify what type of capital we are dealing with, as they are very much intertwined. This in turn makes each theory operationally relevant.

Furthermore, the respondents' stories as they defined what the term 'middle class' meant to them during in-depth interviews, made unwitting reference to all three theories of class. First, middle classes are not wage labourers; they possess enough land to be able to maintain their economic independence without having to sell their manual labour power – these resonate with Marx's conception of class and highlight their productive capital. Second, the self-identified middle classes also argued that middle-class-ness is about acquiring non-farm skilled employment (which depends on certain levels of education, skill credentials and social network). This description of middle-class-ness is consistent with Weber's definition of commercial classes, as well as his concept of 'life chances', and features both economic and social capital. Lastly, the ways in which the self-identified rural middle classes distinguish themselves from the poor and the classes below them, through consumption and life-style resonates with Bourdieu's concepts of 'distinction', and underlines the concept of cultural capital. Overall, we can trace all three theories of class in the ways in which the rural people themselves define and understand the middle class, underscoring the operational relevance of each theory.

The Rural Middle Classes

The expansion and transformation of Asian economies is producing class structures, roles and identities that could not easily be predicted from other times

Conclusion

and places. The industrialisation of the countryside, in particular, generates new, rural middle classes which straddle the worlds of agriculture and industry in complex ways. Their class position is improvised on the basis of numerous influences and opportunities, and is in constant evolution. Enormous though the total population is, meanwhile, it remains invisible to most scholars and policymakers. Without detailed empirical research, we can make very few confident statements about the present condition and future aspiration of these hundreds of millions of people.

The formation of India's rural middle classes rests on a set of economic, social and cultural processes that have begun to unfold in our Maharashtrian field conditions as the peripheries of some villages have witnessed industrialisation in the wake of economic liberalisation. As economic activities in Indian villages are moving toward industrialisation and the development of modern services, theories of class and of social and economic stratification are crucial for understanding the underlying causes of systematic class inequalities, agrarian transformations and rural economy and society. The rural middle classes see their economic concerns, social and political interests, and claims on the state as distinct from those of the urban middle classes. Furthermore, their economic aspirations will translate into demands for industrial and agricultural policies quite different from those expected by rural elites or the rural poor. The rural middle classes will therefore come to shape processes of state planning, forms of wealth redistribution, and rural development. While there are undoubtedly considerable regional variations, these transformations are unlikely to be specific to the villages I have studied. The work is at an early stage: for the identification of the rural middle classes represents the first step in a new political economy of India.

Appendices

Appendix A1   Non-farm Occupations in Rahatwade and Nandur

Table A1.1   Non-farm occupations in Rahatwade

Broker of agricultural produce	Assistant in fertiliser laboratory	Cargo business (carrier transport)
Milk collection and delivery	Hospital guard	Assistant to a builder (supervisor)
Supervisor in agricultural market committee in Pune (government employee)	Pune municipal bus conductor (government employee)	Skilled workers (supervisors, managers, foreman) in factories
Rent (land, car, house, tractor)	Salesman (in a four-wheeler showroom)	Clark in the cooperative bank
Computer operator in Gram Panchayat office	Clerk in agricultural college	Skilled machine operator in factories
Mathadi servant (head-loader)	Electricians, plumbers, painters	Semi-skilled machine operators in factories
Hamal (carrier) and truck loaders in vegetable market	Driver (bus, tempo, rickshaw, school bus, cab and tractor)	School bus driver (government employment)
Casual *hamal* (carrier) in factories	Contractors (agricultural produce)	LKG (kindergarten) servant
Street lecturer and street music artist	Accountant in a factory	Delivery boy in a post office
Teacher	Owner of a hotel	Transport business
Krushi sevak	Collector in a bank	Surveyor (land measuring)
Retired army officer	Building supervisor	Watchman in a factory
Broker of milk	Shop assistant	Barber
Shopkeeper	Milk seller	Ice cream maker
Politician	Beautician	*Paan* stall keeper
Low-ranked police officer	Trader in the vegetable market	Rickshaw driver

Source: Fieldwork data (2015).

212 Appendices

Table A1.2 Non-farm occupations in Nandur

Grain miller	Drivers (tractors, trucks, bus, rickshaw, cab)	Labour supervision in private factories
Bus driver (government employee)	Labour contractor – providing labour to companies	Skilled workers (executives, supervisors, managers, foremen) in private factories
Vehicles repairing	Machine operator in private factories	Transport business
Barber	Quality checker in in private factories	Real estate agent
Electricians, plumbers, painters	Storage keeper in in private factories	Small-scale alcohol producer
Transport (owner of a travel agency)	Owner of a plywood workshop	Poultry farming
Dairy brokerage	Shopkeeper	Milk business
Secretary in a cooperative society	Tractor contractor	Builder (construction work)
Teacher (government school)	Junior executive officer in private factories	Horse grass supplier
Clark in a sugar factory	Owner of a workshop	Bank worker
Contractor (supplier of row materials to factories)	Providing tractors for agricultural works	Broker of livestock
Rent (form home, car rental, tractors, land)	Filter supplier to a private company	Factory watchman
Asset acquisition analyst at IBM	Gram Panchayat servant (water management)	Working in the mess (tiffin making)
Milk seller	Security guard	Packer and dispatcher
Teacher (government employee)	Agricultural labour contractor	*Hamal* (carrier) and truck loaders in factories
Storage keeper	Housekeeper	Kindergarten teacher
Laundry shop keeper	Soap maker	Sweeper
Politician	*Paan* stall keeper	Wet soil provider

Source: Fieldwork data (2015).

Appendix A2 Caste and Occupations: The Urban Middle-Class Labour Market

The analysis of the IHDS-II (2011–12) in relation to caste membership and primary source of household income among urban households is shown in Table A2.1. The analysis shows continuation of caste disparity in the labour market in urban India. The table illustrates that the highest proportion of lower caste groups (SCs and STs) primarily earn their living from wage labour (both in agriculture and non-agricultural sectors). For example, more than half the SC population (53.92 per cent) are primarily engaged in wage labour (21.38 per cent in agriculture and 32.54 per cent in non-agricultural wage labour). Among ST households, in total 31.47 per cent earn their living primarily from wage labour (3.27 per cent in agriculture and 28.2 per cent in non-agricultural wage labour), while among upper caste groups (Brahmins and Forward Castes) only a small segment earn their living from wage labour. Table A2.1 also shows that among upper caste groups, the highest proportion, 52.59 per cent of Brahmins and 41.57 per cent of Forward Castes, are engaged in salaried employment, while only 15.83 per cent of the SCs and 43.22 per cent of the STs earn their living primarily from salaried employment. The percentage of salaried employment among STs in urban India is much higher than rural India, which indicates that STs in urban areas have easier access to government reservations. Overall, caste continues to play a significant role in the labour market in urban India.

Table A2.1 Distribution of main source of income among different caste groups in urban India (2011–12)

Main source of household income	Brahmins	Forward Castes	OBCs	SCs	STs	Total
Sample size	1,057	4,114	5,950	8,941	514	14,278
Cultivation	2.13	2.68	3.13	13.94	3.54	2.67
Allied agriculture	0.13	0.32	1.22	0.69	Neg.	0.41
Agri. wage labour	0.08	0.86	9.57	21.38	3.27	2.44
Non-agri. wage labour	4.98	13.52	24.1	32.54	28.2	22.53
Artisan/independent	1.98	2.19	2.21	1.33	2.51	2.57
Petty shop	16.95	22.46	12.22	6.75	9.33	18.7
Organised business	2.71	4.3	1.22	0.3	1.42	2.7
Salaried employment	52.59	41.57	14.94	15.83	43.22	36.54
Profession	2.94	1.02	0.43	0.34	0.53	0.85
Pension/rent, etc.	12.71	9	4.34	3.8	5.99	7.31
Others	2.79	2.08	3.62	3.11	2	3.27

Source: Computed from the IHDS-II.

214   Appendices

Appendix A3   Caste and Occupations in Rural India since 1991

In addition to examination of occupational distribution among different caste groups in rural India in 2011–12, which was presented in Chapter 4, here we use another two rounds of data at All-India level to examine the persistence of caste inequality in the labour market over the last 30 years. Tables A3.1 and A3.2 present the occupational distribution among different caste groups in rural India in 1993–1994 and 2004–2005, respectively. Figure A3.1 illustrates the distribution of occupations among different caste groups in rural India from 1993 to 2012. Data from 1993 to 1994 (Table A3.1) does not disaggregate among the Brahmins, Forward Castes and OBCs, and therefore, only occupational distribution among SCs and STs and overall rural India is included in the graph. The graph demonstrates caste inequality in occupations has changed over time. For example, there has been an increase in the percentage of the SCs and STs engaged in salaried employment. In 1993–94, only 4.68 per cent of SC and 3.65 per cent of ST households in rural India primarily earned their income from salaried employment. In 2004–05, their percentage increased to 8.42 and 8.76 and in 2011–12 to 7.8 and 9.31, respectively. In sum, there has been a marginal decline in the relationship between caste and occupation in rural India, when we examine the occupational pattern of SCs and STs in rural India.

Table A3.1   Distribution of main source of income among different caste groups in rural India (1993–94)

Main source of household income	Others	SCs	STs	Total
Sample size	21,067	7,943	4,220	33,230
Cultivation	65.2	41.18	61.52	58.99
Agri. wage labour	11.23	31.16	19	16.98
Non-agri. wage labour	5.93	13.37	8.13	7.99
Artisan/independent	5.54	5.04	3.86	5.21
Petty shop	3.83	2.18	1.75	3.17
Organised business	0.83	0.4	0.55	0.69
Salaried employment	5.52	4.68	3.65	5.08
Profession	0.41	0.3	0.38	0.38
Others	1.52	1.69	1.16	1.51

Source: Computed from the HDPI.

Appendices 215

Table A3.2 Distribution of main source of income among different caste groups in rural India (2004–05)

Main source of household income	Brahmins	Forward Castes	OBCs	SCs	STs	Total
Sample size	1,092	3,876	9,592	5,952	2,936	23,448
Cultivation	45.48	50.71	39.92	16.19	41.01	35.52
Allied agriculture	0.47	1.49	1.28	0.97	0.41	1.09
Agri. wage labour	2.39	10.51	17.23	35.54	23.41	21.32
Non-agri. wage labour	4.74	7.65	13.86	26.07	18.63	16.45
Artisan/independent	3.42	2.47	7.61	3.32	1.44	4.82
Petty shop	4.38	3.01	3.3	1.62	2.63	2.77
Organised business	3.96	4.13	3.24	2.84	1.05	3.04
Salaried	21.94	13.23	8.17	8.42	8.76	9.64
Profession	2.68	0.27	0.83	0.38	0.25	0.64
Pension/rent, etc.	7.04	3.81	2	1.56	1.23	2.27
Others	3.51	2.72	2.57	2.38	1.19	2.43
Total	100	100	100	100	100	100

Source: Computed from the IHDS-I.

Figure A3.1 Graph illustrating the persistence of caste inequalities in occupational patterns in rural India (1993–94 to 2011–12)

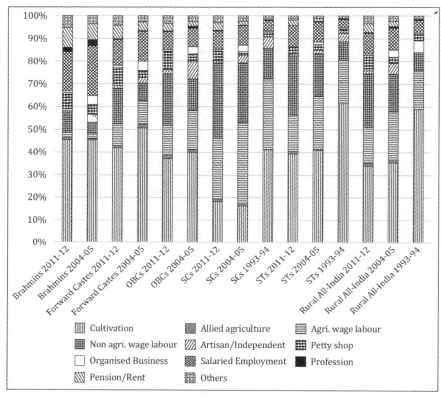

Source: HDPI (1993–94); IHDS-I (2004–05); IHDS-II (2011–12).

Appendix A4 Caste and Income Distribution

In the following section, I use data from the IHDS-II to provide information on the average annual household income among different caste groups in 2011–12 (Tables A4.1 and A4.2). Comparing the mean annual income of the different caste groups, the tables show a significant difference between the average annual household incomes across different caste groups. In both rural and urban India, Brahmins and Forward Castes have the highest average annual income and SCs and STs the lowest. However, the high value of standard deviation, represented in the last column of both the tables indicates that annual household incomes are significantly higher than the mean values, suggesting a large variation of household income *within* the caste groups. Such a high level of standard deviation suggests a low level of confidence in any statistical conclusion (in this case, the relationship between caste membership and household income).

Table A4.1 Distribution of annual household income by caste category in rural India (2011–12)

Caste group (N = 27,130)	Freq.	Mean (INR)	Median (INR)	Std. Dev.
Brahmins	1,121	117,287	69,900	176,036.1
Forward/General Castes	5,441	122,394	64,960	206,422.8
Other Backward Castes	10,907	84,628	52,450	137,479.1
Scheduled Castes	6,242	72,468	49,500	202,604.1
Scheduled Tribes	3,099	63,250	41,200	81,608.23
Others	320	151,205	83,000	183,851
Total	27,130	88,380	52,670	168,190.2

Source: Computed from the IHDS-II.

Table A4.2 Distribution of annual household income by caste category in urban India (2011–12)

Caste group (N = 14,484)	Freq.	Mean (INR)	Median (INR)	Std. Dev.
Brahmins	1,055	235,360	168,000	234,492.9
Forward/General Castes	4,112	207,922	130,000	331,120.4
Other Backward Castes	5,931	148,834	99,000	181,999.2
Scheduled Castes	2,642	140,064	99,000	140,646.8
Scheduled Tribes	514	183,724	111,275	192,792.4
Others	230	148,239	94,200	204,399.1
Total	14,484	170,352	109,300	233,760.3

Source: Computed from the IHDS-II.

The following two histograms (Figures A4.1 and A4.2) show the distribution of annual household income in rural and urban India, respectively. It is evident that the distributions are highly skewed and heavy-tailed, suggesting that there are few data points (annual household income) with extremely large values on the right side of the distribution. In simple terms, this means that the annual household incomes are very likely to be highly heterogeneous. This type of distribution is referred to as the Pareto distribution. Such a highly skewed distribution of income will create issues when we compare the statistics of the income distributions between different castes. The average and other statistical features of fat-tailed distributions are not well defined and this is easily observed in Tables A4.1 and A4.2 – the standard deviations calculated for the income within each caste is far greater than the mean value, leading to a large error in the calculated mean.

To resolve this issue, we must transform the income variable logarithmically and work with the logarithm of annual household income from this point on. The logarithmic transformation will turn the skewed distributions with extremely

Figure A4.1   Annual household income distributions in rural India (2011–12)

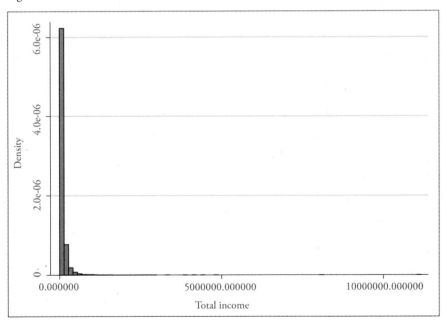

Source: Computed from IHDS-II.

Figure A4.2   Annual household income distributions in urban India (2011–12)

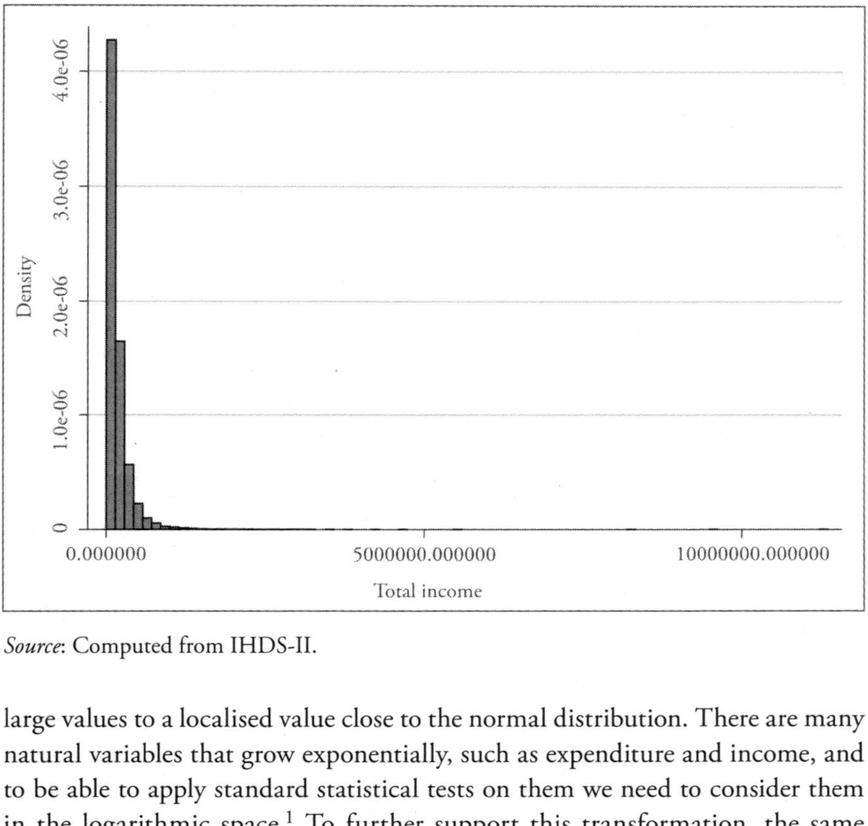

Source: Computed from IHDS-II.

large values to a localised value close to the normal distribution. There are many natural variables that grow exponentially, such as expenditure and income, and to be able to apply standard statistical tests on them we need to consider them in the logarithmic space.[1] To further support this transformation, the same distributions for the log-transformed income are illustrated in the following two histograms. The log-normal distribution of annual household income in rural and urban India have been illustrated in Figures A4.3 and A4.4, respectively. The log-transformed income is normally distributed for both sub-populations (rural and urban), suggesting that the underlying distribution for the annual household income is a log-normal distribution. The log-normal distribution follows the following formula, where m is the mean of the log-transformed variable and s^2 is the variance of it:

$$P(\log(\text{income}) = x) \sim \exp((x\text{-m})^2/s^2)$$

---

[1] To see examples of Pareto's income distribution, log income and linear income distributions see Clementi and Gallegati (2005), Nadarajah (2005) and Ermini and Hendry (1995).

220 Appendices

Figure A4.3 Annual household income distributions on logarithmic scaled axes in rural India (2011–12)

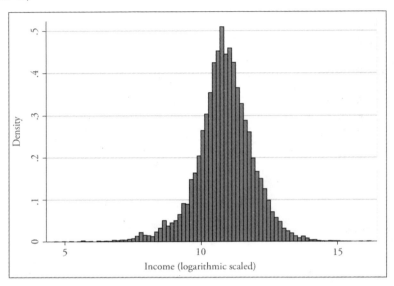

Source: Computed from IHDS-II.

Figure A4.4 Annual household income distributions on logarithmic scaled axes in urban India (2011–12)

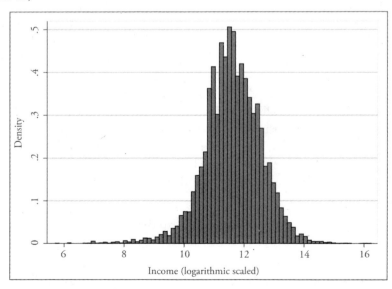

Source: Computed from IHDS-II.

Tables A4.3 and A4.4 below provide information on the average annual household income in logarithmic scale among different caste groups in rural and urban India, respectively. When we examine the difference between mean annual household incomes among different caste groups in the logarithmic scale, we notice that in urban India, the difference in the mean annual income of the different caste groups is not significant. However, in rural India, there are differences in income distribution among different castes; Brahmins and Forward Castes have the highest mean annual household income and SCs and STs the lowest. The relationship/correlation between caste and income is much stronger in rural than urban India.

Table A4.3 Distribution of annual household income by caste groups in rural India (2011–12)

Caste group N = 27,130	Freq.	Mean	Median	Std. Dev.
Brahmins	1,121	11.14006	11.16053	1.075672
Forward/General Castes	5,441	11.10622	11.08981	1.117896
Other Backward Castes	10,907	10.8399	10.87142	1.030667
Scheduled Castes	6,242	10.7756	10.81366	0.9112572
Scheduled Tribes	3,099	10.59446	10.62765	0.9700932
Others	320	11.32826	11.3266	1.148318
Total	27,130	10.86415	10.87616	1.02969

Source: Computed from the IHDS-II.

Table A4.4 Distribution of annual household income by caste groups in urban India (2011–12)

Caste group N = 14,484	Freq.	Mean	Median	Std. Dev.
Brahmins	1,055	11.99169	12.03172	0.9144549
Forward/General Castes	4,112	11.79161	11.79056	0.9621357
Other Backward Castes	5,931	11.49549	11.51293	0.9478057
Scheduled Castes	2,642	11.5149	11.50288	0.8378017
Scheduled Tribes	514	11.65542	11.61976	1.012996
Others	230	11.46214	11.46897	0.9581144
Total	14,484	11.61817	11.60824	0.9466289

Source: Computed from the IHDS-II.

222   Appendices

In the next step, we examine the degree of difference between the distributions of income in rural India among different caste groups using an ANOVA (Analysis of Variance) test on the log-transformed income. ANOVA is a generalised form of a t-test, which compares several (more than two) sub-populations to test whether the mean of a variable is significantly different between the sub-population.[2] However, the implicit assumption in t-test and ANOVA is that the underlying distribution of the variable in each sub-population is close to a normal distribution. But, as discussed above, the income does not follow a normal distribution, and an ANOVA test is only reliable on log-transformed values of income.

To examine whether there are any statistically significant differences between the average annual household incomes among different caste groups in rural India (or in simple terms, to determine if caste membership has a significant effect on annual household income), a one-way ANOVA is conducted. The Stata output for the analysis of variance is shown in Table A4.5.

Table A4.5   One-way ANOVA in rural India

Source	SS	df	MS	F	Prob > F
Between groups	957.416107	4	239.354027	227.15	0.0000
Within groups	28,160.2883	26,725	1.05370583		
Total	29,117.7044	26,729	1.08936752		
Bartlett's test for equal variances: chi2(4) = 241.3036 Prob>chi2 = 0.000					

Source: Computed from the IHDS-II.

The analysis, illustrated in Table A4.5, shows the significance level ($P = 0.000$), is below 0.05, indicating there is a statistically significance difference between mean annual household incomes of the different caste groups in rural India. Although caste disparities proved to be significant in income distribution in rural India, there is a vast difference within the caste groups as well, indicated by large values of standard deviation, as discussed earlier.

Regression Analyses: Caste/Income Relations

The above analyses suggested that in rural India SCs and STs have lower annual household income compared to Brahmins and Forward Castes, which

---

[2] For an overview of usage of ANOVA and other statistical methods in social sciences, see Hilton (2005).

Appendices 223

is suggestive of intersection between caste and income in rural India. To test the hypothesis that caste and income intersect, the following sections present results from multivariate analyses to examine the impact of caste on income in rural India. First, in what follows, we present results from multivariate analyses, to examine the impact of caste (independent variable) on income (dependent variable) in rural India on the basis of IHDS-II. The analyses focus on regressing the mean of the distribution of the income. However, in case of a dependent variable (annual household income), which is skewed, the income is used in the logarithmic scale. The caste variable is defined as a categorical variable in the regression analysis. The p-value, which is calculated based on the t-value, can be used to identify which independent variable is relevant in the model. If the p-value is smaller than 0.05 for an independent variable, that variable is contributing to the model significantly. The F value and corresponding p-value show the level of significance of the whole model and the R-Squared determines how much of the variation in the dependent variable can be explained by the selected independent variables.

To begin with, we only consider the caste parameter as an independent variable. The results are shown in Table A4.6. According to the table the caste impact is a significant factor in explaining the income ($p < 0.001$). However, the overall model only explains 0.0206 variations in the income (R-squared = 0.0206).

Table A4.6 Linear regressions: relationship between income in logarithmic scale and caste (categorical)

Number of strata	=	1	Number of observations	=	26,730
Number of PSUs	=	27	Population size	=	167,841,748
			Design df	=	26
			F (1, 26)	=	263.65
			Prob > F	=	0.0000
			R-squared	=	0.0206

Income (Log)	Coef.	Linearised Std. Err.	t	$P > t$	[95% Conf.	Interval]
Caste	0.1477	0.0091978	16.24	0.000	0.1290217	0.1664233
Constant	11.3307	0.0221771	510.92	0.000	11.28511	11.37628

Source: Computed from the IHDS-II.

224 Appendices

Next, we run a regression to see the relationship between income and other socio-economic resources (on the basis of availability in the dataset) that can generate income in the market; we consider a set of variables including caste (categorical variable), highest level of adult education, total household assets, education of head's father/husband, area of land owned or under cultivation, and social network index, to run the regression model.[3] These variables, as indicated in Chapter 4, are related to Weber's theory of classes, and are hypothesised to contribute to one's capacity in generating income.

As shown in Table A4.7, using caste, defined as a dummy variable, we see that overall caste factor is not significant ($p = 0.168 > 0.05$). When we use caste as a categorical variable (instead of defining a dummy variable), the caste factors for OBCs and STs are not significant ($p = 0.672 > 0.05$ and $p = 0.537 > 0.05$). However, the p-values for Forward Castes and SCs are less than 0.05 for an independent variable, and therefore these variables (when we consider only Forward Castes and SCs) are significant. A model based on the above variables can explain 0.2913 of the variation in the income, which is more significant than the model solely based on caste. Nevertheless, the whole model is significant ($p = 0.0000 < 0.05$). Including the caste variable in the linear regression model along with the other independent parameters tells us again that overall caste has a negligible predictive power on income. This is due to the large variations of income within castes that we discussed above (evident from the large standard deviation compared to coefficient).

Finally, to cross check the above result, we will remove the caste variable from the list of independent variables, and run a third regression model based only on the remaining socio-economic parameters (highest level of adult education, total household assets, education of head's father/husband, area of land owned or under cultivation, and social network index) to test whether the model produce exactly the same goodness of the fit. The result of regression analysis, presented in Table A4.8, is almost identical to the result of the above regression that included caste in the model (Table A4.7). This further confirms that the caste in itself has no exploratory power. The differences we observe between castes are rooted in the socio-economic variations within and between castes (this will be explained in Appendix A5).

---

[3] Social network index is calculated on the basis of social acquaintance with members of the following professions (either among relatives, friends, caste/community or outside community/caste). The professions for which data is available are: doctors; health workers; teachers; government officers; other government employees; elected politicians; political party officials; police inspectors; and military personnel.

Appendices 225

Table A4.7 Linear regressions: relationship between income (dependent variable) and caste, highest level of adult education, education of head of the household, area of land owned and social network

Number of strata	=	1	Number of observation	=	26,529
Number of PSUs	=	27	Population size	=	166,490,738
			Design df	=	26
			$F_{(9, 18)}$	=	3,029.99
			Prob > F	=	0.0000
			R-squared	=	0.2913

Income (Log)	Coef.	Linearized Std. Err.	t	P > t	[95% Conf.	Interval]
Highest level of adult education	0.022132	0.0024045	9.20	0.000	0.017189	0.027074
Total household assets	0.075286	0.0016846	44.69	0.000	0.071823	0.078748
Education head's father/husband	−0.009313	0.0020049	−4.65	0.000	−0.013434	−0.005192
Area of land owned or under cultivation	0.015898	0.0043958	3.62	0.001	0.006862	0.024934
Social network index	0.286716	0.0419228	6.84	0.000	0.200542	0.372889
Caste (Dum)	−0.008221	0.0057963	−1.42	0.168	−0.020136	0.003693
Caste						
Forward Castes	0.072274	0.0334514	2.16	0.040	0.003513	0.141034
OBCs	−0.011939	0.0279052	−0.43	0.672	−0.069299	0.045420
SCs	0.092274	0.0335099	2.75	0.011	0.023393	0.161154
STs	0.002449	0.0391199	0.63	0.537	−0.055920	0.104903
Constant	9.691461	0.0391192	247.74	0.000	9.611050	9.771871

Source: Computed from the IHDS-II.

226 Appendices

Table A4.8 Linear regressions: relationship between income (dependent variable) and highest level of adult education, education of head of the household, area of land owned and social network (to compare the reliability of the two models, this model excludes caste)

Number of strata	=	1	Number of observation	=	26,529
Number of PSUs	=	27	Population size	=	166,490,738
			Design *df*	=	26
			F (5, 22)	=	2,161.87
			Prob > F	=	0.0000
			R-squared	=	0.2894

Income (Log)	Coef.	Linearised Std. Err.	t	P > t	[95% Conf.	Interval]
Highest level of adult education	0.02191	0.002371	9.24	0.000	0.017040	0.026791
Total household assets	0.07512	0.001841	40.8	0.000	0.071341	0.078911
Education head's father/husband	−0.00979	0.001869	−5.24	0.000	−0.013642	−0.005957
Area of land owned or under cultivation	0.01553	0.004284	3.63	0.001	0.006726	0 .024342
Social network index	0.28991	0.045400	6.39	0.000	0.196584	0.383229
Constant	9.72895	0.016468	590.76	0.000	9.695105	9.762809

Source: Computed from the IHDS-II.

Appendix A5   Caste and Socio-economic Indicators in Rural and Urban India

In what follows, using IHDS-II, we show statistically significant caste disparities in each marker of middle-class status in rural and urban India, with SCs and STs at the bottom, OBCs in the middle, while the other Forward Castes and Brahmins on the top of distribution of socio-economic resources. The analyses suggest that the caste divide continues to play a significant role in social mobility, and is therefore also a significant determinant of middle-class membership. Caste still impacts individuals' access to the income generating capital and directly affects class cleavages. Tables A5.1 and A5.2 provide information on per capita consumption expenditure (mean), average household expenditure on education, average total number of household assets, social networks, and highest level of adult education by caste groups in rural and urban India, respectively.[4] The first row of each table provides information on household caste. Of the total 27,213 sample households in the IHDS-II in rural areas, 4.17 per cent (1,135 households) were Brahmins; 18.27 per cent (5,548 households) belonged to the Forward Castes (except Brahmins); 42.26 per cent (11,103 households) to OBCs; 24.3 per cent (6,298 households) to SCs; and 11 per cent (3,129 households) to STs.

As evident in Table A5.1, there are statistically significant caste disparities in land ownership, highest level of education in adults (aged 21 and above), total number of household assets, and consumption expenditure across rural India. When compared to the Brahmins and the Forward Castes, SCs and STs are less likely to own any land, have smaller average landholdings and have higher proportions of illiterates in the households. In rural India, SCs and then STs have the highest proportion of landless households (52.82 per cent of the SCs and 38.37 per cent of STs in rural India do not own any land). They also have the lowest average area of land owned and cultivated. Similarly, examining the highest level of adult education (mean) among different caste groups in rural India shows the average highest level of adult education is the lowest among SC and ST households, followed by OBCs: the average highest level of education in adults among Brahmins is 10 years, for Forward Castes is 8 years, while among the SCs and STs the average highest level of adult education is 5 years.

---

[4] The weighting for being acquainted with anyone in the following professions is 1/9, with all sub-components adding up to a maximum of 1 and a minimum of 0: doctors; health workers; teachers; government officers; other government employees; elected politicians; political party officials; police inspectors; and military personnel.

228 Appendices

Table A5.1 Descriptive statistics for socio-economic variables among different caste groups in rural India (2011–12)

Caste groups		Brahmins	Forward Castes	OBCs	SCs	STs	Total
Sample size		1,135	5,548	11,103	6,298	3,129	27,213
Per cent		4.17	18.27	42.26	24.3	11	100
Total population		5,573	27,592	54,966	30,371	14,909	133,411
Mean number of persons in a household		4.9	5	4.9	4.8	4.7	4.9
Dependent variables							
Percentage of household who own or cultivate no land		22.67	32.69	35.52	52.82	38.37	39.04
Average holding (acre)		2.46	2.45	1.78	0.65	1.46	1.63
Highest level of adult education		10	8	6	5	5	6.8
Proportion of illiterate adult (per cent)		5.64	17.2	24.52	31.27	33.67	25.04
Per capita consumption expenditure (mean)		26,335	26,126	22,045	17,577	15,785	21,195
Annual college, school fee (mean)		4,331	4,048	2,728	1,482	1,232	2,815
Average number of total household assets (minimum 0 and maximum 33)		15	14.2	12.5	10.8	9.2	12.1
Social networks (know anyone working in school, medical field, government)		0.33	0.29	0.22	0.18	0.21	0.23
Self-perception of economic status	Poor	33.18	43.36	4.87	66.98	63.87	45.44
	Middle class	60.86	49.48	47.28	30.94	33.53	48.83
	Comfortable	5.96	7.16	4.01	2.08	0.26	5.73
	Total	100	100	100	100	100	100

Source: Computed from the IHDS-II.

Therefore, the results (presented in Table A5.1) suggest that caste membership plays a significant role in access to both productive and marketable resources, particularly education and social networks. Furthermore, when compared to the upper caste group, SCs and STs have lower per capita consumption expenditure and have a lower proportion of total expenditure on education. The annual per capita consumption expenditure in rural India is highest among the Brahmins

(INR 26,335), followed by the Forward Castes (INR 26,126). The annual per capita consumption expenditure among the lower caste is significantly lower. The rural ST households have the lowest annual per capita consumption expenditure (INR 15,785), followed by the SCs (INR 17,577), which are also significantly lower than the average annual per capita consumption expenditure in overall rural India (INR 21,195). Similarly, average annual expenditure on education is highest among the Brahmins and Forward Castes, when compared to other caste groups.

Similarly, Table A5.2 provides information on socio-economic indicators by caste groups in urban India. From a total of 14,285 sample households, 1,057 households were Brahmins; 28.1 per cent (4,117 households) belonged to the Forward Castes (except Brahmins); 43.84 per cent (5,953 households) to OBCs; 18.4 per cent (2,643 households) to SCs; and 2.88 per cent (515 households) to STs. Table A5.2 shows that Brahmins and Forward Castes have on average the highest level of annual per capita consumption expenditure, INR 47,946 and 39,186, respectively. They also the highest level of adult education, own more consumer goods and are more likely to own land.

Both Tables A5.1 and A5.2 show statistically significant caste disparities in each marker of the middle class with SCs and STs at the bottom, and Brahmins and Forward Castes at the top. Desai and Dubey offer similar findings on the basis of analysis of the IHDS-I, conducted in 2004–05 (Desai and Dubey, 2012). Comparing both tables (caste disparities in rural and urban India), we see caste disparity is more prominent in rural areas. Particularly, the comparison reveals that SCs and STs in rural India have the lowest per capita consumption expenditure and a lower level of adult education, when compared to urban India. To sum up, when compared to Forward Castes and Brahmins, SCs and STs have lower average annual household income; they are less likely to own land; have fewer years of education; have lower household consumption expenditure; a smaller number of social connections; and spend a lower proportion of their expenditure on education. In short, access to marketable resources, particularly education, skills and social connections, remains closely associated with caste.

Therefore, although the result of regression analyses conducted in Appendix A4 showed no direct relation between caste and income distribution (Table A4.6), the second and third regressions analyses (Tables A4.7 and A4.8) showed that there is a correlation between income and highest level of adult education, and between income and social network and income and assets. Combining the result of the regression analyses with results presented in Tables A5.1 and A5.2, we can conclude that caste membership affects access to social networks and education; therefore, caste indirectly affects the distribution of income. Furthermore, as indicated earlier, there is a strong correlation between caste and occupation pattern

230 Appendices

but not between caste and income. This suggests that lower castes earn their living primarily from wage labour, as opposed to salaried employment (which requires education and skill credentials). However, it is also notable that caste groups are also very much differentiated internally and there is variations in terms of access to socio-economic resources, as variations in income within each caste groups, and therefore caste are differentiated in terms of class. However, when we look at the rural India as a whole, despite the variations, overall there are significant caste disparities in accessing socio-economic resources.

Table A5.2 Descriptive statistics for socio-economic variables among different caste groups in urban India (2011–12)

Caste groups		Brahmins	Forward Castes	OBCs	SCs	STs	Total
Sample size		1,057	4,117	5,953	2,643	515	14,285
Per cent		6.79	28.1	43.84	18.4	2.88	100
Total population		4,680	19,270	28,963	12,766	2,471	68,150
Mean number of persons in a household		4.4	4.7	4.9	4.8	4.8	4.8
Dependent variables							
Percentage of household who own or cultivate no land		87.6	90.1	89.8	93.85	85.4	90.6
Highest level of adult education		13.2	11.5	9.8	9.2	9.8	10.4
Proportion of illiterate adult (per cent)		1.5	4.4	9.1	10.6	12	7.6
Per capita consumption expenditure (mean)		47,946	39,186	32,242	28,014	33,921	34,530
Annual college, school fee (mean)		10,300	8,970	7,300	4,900	7,060	7,500
Average number of total household assets (minimum 0 and maximum 33)		22.5	21.13	19.26	17.84	18.11	19.71
Social networks (know anyone working in school, medical field, government)		0.39	0.37	0.27	0.27	0.38	0.31
Self-perception of economic status	Poor	15.6	22	31.27	41	36.65	29.5
	Middle class	70.6	65.5	61.19	54.52	52.82	61.6
	Comfortable	14.34	12.5	7.54	4.48	10.54	8.9
	Total	100	100	100	100	100	100

Source: Computed from the IHDS-II.

Appendix A6 Caste Composition of Urban Middle Classes in India

In Chapter 1, using IHDS-II (2011–12) and on the basis of primary source of household income, households were categorised in different classes, including three categories of middle class. Here, we will examine the caste compositions of different identified classes in urban India. Table A6.1 presents the class composition of each caste group in urban India. According to the table, among the SCs and STs in urban India the majority of households belong to the labouring households (36.36 per cent of SCs and 31.84 per cent of STs throughout urban India), which is much higher than the average percentage of the total population in the labouring classes in urban India. Furthermore, almost 56.5 per cent of Brahmins and 40.17 per cent of Forward Castes belong to the top two categories of the middle class, while only 19 per cent of the SCs and 28.9 per cent of ST households in urban India belong to the top two categories of the middle class. This is indicative of the caste disparities in class membership in urban India, with the middle and the upper classes being consisting primarily of upper castes. Therefore, the upper caste character is one of the defining characteristics of the urban middle classes. However, comparing the result of caste compositions of middle classes in urban India with the result from rural India (presented in Table 4.12) shows greater caste disparities among rural classes.

Table A6.1 Caste compositions of identified classes in urban India (2011–12)

Classes	Freq.	Brahmins	Forward Castes	OBCs	SCs	STs	Total
Labouring households	3,506	5.12	14.51	30.02	36.36	31.84	25.37
Lowest class	599	2.25	2.5	4.6	5.41	4.09	4
Second lowest class	2,593	10.29	15.56	20.52	18.99	12.8	17.93
Lower middle class	3,121	21.02	23.55	20.93	19.56	18.06	21.26
Comfortable middle class	3,187	38.86	29.09	18.26	15.24	20.84	22.13
Upper middle class	1,106	17.7	11.08	4.62	3.76	8.14	7.24
Upper class	322	4.75	3.72	1.05	0.68	4.23	2.07
All	14,434	100	100	100	100	100	100

Source: Computed from the IHDS-II.

232   Appendices

Appendix A7   Caste Composition of the Rural Middle Classes in Maharashtra

Table A7.1 offers the class composition of each caste group in rural Maharashtra. Evident in the table, the majority of households among the SCs and STs belong to the labouring households (60.62 per cent of SC and 52.79 per cent of ST households). This is much higher than the average percentage of the average population in the labouring classes in rural Maharashtra. Furthermore, almost 55 per cent of Brahmins and 44 per cent of Forward Castes in rural Maharashtra belong to the three categories of the rural middle classes, while only almost 8 per cent of SCs and 11.72 per cent of STs in all rural Maharashtra belong to the three categories of the middle classes. This is illustrative of caste disparities in class membership in rural Maharashtra, with the middle and the upper classes consisting primarily of the upper castes, which is consistent with findings on caste disparities in class formation in rural All-India, illustrated in Chapter 4. It is notable that due to a low population (Frequency) of Brahmin households in rural Maharashtra in the survey, the absence of Brahmin households in the top two classes is not statistically conclusive.

Table A7.1   Caste compositions of identified classes in rural Maharashtra – percentage (2011–12)

Classes	Freq.	Brahmins	Forward Castes	OBCs	SCs	STs	Total
Manual labouring households	718	8.15	13.77	27.84	60.62	52.79	32.91
Lowest class	215	3.64	8.56	10.43	9	18.17	10.59
Second lowest class	582	33.2	32.63	33.53	22.09	17.32	29.03
Lower middle class	447	25.38	29.76	18.33	7.57	8.01	18.32
Comfortable middle class	163	29.63	11.04	7.8	0.62	3.15	6.97
Upper middle class	39	N.A.	3.23	1.92	0.1	0.56	1.82
Upper class	12	N.A.	1.02	0.15	Neg.	Neg.	0.37
Rural All-India	2,176	100	100	100	100	100	100

Source: Computed from the IHDS-II.

Appendices   233

Appendix A8   Household Survey Questionnaire 1

Village Name	1 = Rahatwade 2 = Nandur
Case ID	
Household name	
Interviewer name	
Supervisor name	
Number of visits to complete the questionnaire	
Completion status	0 = Incomplete 1 = Complete

Visits	Interview date	Interview time		Place of Interview
		Start	Finish	
First visit				
Second visit				
Third visit				

S. No.	i. Household General Information		
1	Household ID		
2	A.	Name/s of the household head/s	
	B.	Name of respondent	
	C.	Relation of respondent to household head	
3	Caste of the household head		
4	Which caste category does the household head/s belong to?		1 = Brahmin 2 = OBCs 3 = SCs 4 = STs 5 = Others If other, specify:
5	Religion of the household head?		1 = Hindu 2 = Muslim 3 = Christian 4 = Sikh 5 = Buddhist 6 = Jain 7 = Tribal 8 = Others If other, specify:

234   Appendices

6	Number of people living in the household	
7	Number of adults (18 and above)	
8	Number of people below the age of 18	

9   Specify the age and gender of people in the household below the age of 18:

S. No.	Male or female	Age	Relation to household head
A	1 = Male 2 = Female		
B	1 = Male 2 = Female		
C	1 = Male 2 = Female		
D	1 = Male 2 = Female		
E	1 = Male 2 = Female		
F	1 = Male 2 = Female		
G	1 = Male 2 = Female		

	ii. Occupation and Income	
10	What is the primary source of household income?	
11	Who in the family does this job? (Relation/s to household head)	
12	IF AGRICULTURE: Is it cultivation on your own land, is it agricultural labour working on someone else's field, or both?	1 = Own land 2 = Someone else's land 3 = Both (own land + someone else's land)
13	IF OWN or BOTH: What crops do you cultivate?	
14	Is the work mentioned in question 10, main work (more than 6 months per year), or casual work (less than 6 months per year)?	1 = Main work 2 = Casual work
15	Can you please estimate the annual income of the household from all sources in the previous year (2014)? (including income from all sources, rent, pension, scholarships, gift, other government benefits, etc.)	1 = Less than INR 20,000 2 = Between INR 20,000 and 50,000 3 = Between INR 50,000 and 1,00,000 4 = Between INR 1,00,000 and 1,50,000 5 = Above INR 1,50,000 6 = Do not know or do not want to tell

	iii. Ownership of Assets		
16	Do you own the house you live in? (IF YES, GO TO QUESTION 19)	0 = No 1 = Yes	
17	IF RENTED: Do you pay cash for rent? (IF YES, GO TO QUESTION 19)	0 = No 1 = Yes	
18	IF NO CASH PAYMENT: How do you pay rent?		
19	Does this household own any shop/ factory/ workshop? (IF NO, GO TO QUESTION 22)	0 = No	1 = Yes
20	How many shop/s, factory/ies, workshop/s does this household own? Type?	__ __	
21	Where is this shop/workshop/factory?	1 = Same village 2 = Different village 3 = Urban area IF URBAN: specify where	
22	Does this household own any agricultural land? (IF NO, GO TO QUESTION 27)	0 = No	1 = Yes
23	What is the overall area of the cultivated land owned?	__ __ __ . __ Acres	
24	What area of your own cultivated land is irrigated?	__ __ __ . __ Acres	
25	What is the main source of irrigation? (ONLY TICK ONE OPTION; If it is rain water, select 6 and then specify it as rain water)	1 = Tube well 2 = Other well 3 = Government 4 = Private canal 5 = Tank 6 = Other If other, specify:	
26	How many months of the year is the cultivated land irrigated?	__ __ Months	
27	Does this household own any non-cultivated land? (IF NO, GO TO QUESTION 32)	0 = No	1 = Yes
28	What type of land is it? Please specify (example: pastoral, grazing, dry land, un-used land, land under construction, etc.)		
29	What is the area of non-cultivated land owned?	__ __ __ . __ Acres	

236 Appendices

30	Where is this non-cultivated located?	1 = Same village 2 = Different village 3 = Urban area IF URBAN: specify where?
31	Have you given this non-cultivated on rent?	0 = No 1 = Yes

32. Does this household own any of the following?

	0 = No 1 = Yes
Motorcycle	
Car	
Generator set	
Colour TV	
Air cooler	
Water boiler	
Mobile	
Smartphone	
Computer	
Video games	
Refrigerator	
Tractor	
Lorries	
Water well	
Pumping set/motor	

iv. Lending and Borrowing Money		
33	Does anyone in this household lend money?	0 = No 1 = Yes
34	Does this household borrow any money?	0 = No 1 = Yes
35	Do you lend more then you borrow?	0 = No 1 = Yes

Appendices   237

v. Education

36   Number of literate members of the household (above the age of 7)
(Literate person is defined as a person aged 7 years and above whom can both read and write with understanding in any language. It is not necessary for a person to have received any formal education or passed any minimum educational standard for being treated as literate.)

Male	
Female	

37   Highest level of education of people aged 21 and above in the household?

Adults	Highest level of education	Medium of education	Public or Private	Location of school	Relation to household head
Male		1 = English 2 = Semi-English 3 = Marathi 4 = Hindi 5 = Other	1 = Public 2 = Private		
Female		1 = English 2 = Semi-English 3 = Marathi 4 = Hindi 5 = Other	1 = Public 2 = Private		

38   Please give information about children's/ sons'/ daughters' education in the table (only include persons age 5 and above)

Child		M1	M2	F1	F2
Age					
Relation to household head					
Primary School	Attended?	0 = No 1 = Yes	0 = No 1 = Yes	0 = No 1 = Yes	0 = No 1 = Yes
	No. of years completed?				
	Type	1 = Public 2 = Private	1 = Public 2 = Private	1 = Public 2 = Private	1 = Public 2 = Private
	Medium	1 = English 2 = Semi-English 3 = Marathi 4 = Hindi 5 = Other	1 = English 2 = Semi-English 3 = Marathi 4 = Hindi 5 = Other	1 = English 2 = Semi-English 3 = Marathi 4 = Hindi 5 = Other	1 = English 2 = Semi-English 3 = Marathi 4 = Hindi 5 = Other

Secondary and higher secondary school – including 11 and 12	Attended?	0 = No 1 = Yes	0 = No 1 = Yes	0 = No 1 = Yes	0 = No 1 = Yes
	No. of years completed?				
	Type	1 = Public 2 = Private	1 = Public 2 = Private	1 = Public 2 = Private	1 = Public 2 = Private
	Medium	1 = English 2 = Semi-English 3 = Marathi 4 = Hindi 5 = Other	1 = English 2 = Semi-English 3 = Marathi 4 = Hindi 5 = Other	1 = English 2 = Semi-English 3 = Marathi 4 = Hindi 5 = Other	1 = English 2 = Semi-English 3 = Marathi 4 = Hindi 5 = Other
College (graduate and above)	Attended?	0 = No 1 = Yes	0 = No 1 = Yes	0 = No 1 = Yes	0 = No 1 = Yes
	No. of years completed?				
	Type	1 = Public 2 = Private	1 = Public 2 = Private	1 = Public 2 = Private	1 = Public 2 = Private
	Medium	1 = English 2 = Semi-English 3 = Marathi 4 = Hindi 5 = Other	1 = English 2 = Semi-English 3 = Marathi 4 = Hindi 5 = Other	1 = English 2 = Semi-English 3 = Marathi 4 = Hindi 5 = Other	1 = English 2 = Semi-English 3 = Marathi 4 = Hindi 5 = Other
	Degree type	1 = Bachelor 2 = Master 3 = PhD 4 = Other	1 = Bachelor 2 = Master 3 = PhD 4 = Other	1 = Bachelor 2 = Master 3 = PhD 4 = Other	1 = Bachelor 2 = Master 3 = PhD 4 = Other
	Completion status (put highest)	1 = Completed 2 = On-going 3 = Drop out	1 = Completed 2 = On-going 3 = Drop out	1 = Completed 2 = On-going 3 = Drop out	1 = Completed 2 = On-going 3 = Drop out

vi. Social network			
39	Among relative or friends, are there any of the following people?		
A. Scientist		0 = No　　　　　1 = Yes	
		☐ Relative ☐ Friend	
B. Doctors		0 = No　　　　　1 = Yes	
		☐ Relative ☐ Friend	

C. Nurse	0 = No	1 = Yes
	☐ Relative ☐ Friend	
D. Teachers	0 = No	1 = Yes
	☐ Relative ☐ Friend	
E. University lecturer	0 = No	1 = Yes
	☐ Relative ☐ Friend	
F. Engineer	0 = No	1 = Yes
	☐ Relative ☐ Friend	
G. Lawyer	0 = No	1 = Yes
	☐ Relative ☐ Friend	
H. Artist	0 = No	1 = Yes
	☐ Relative ☐ Friend	
I. Social worker	0 = No	1 = Yes
	☐ Relative ☐ Friend	
J. Call centre worker	0 = No	1 = Yes
	☐ Relative ☐ Friend	
K. Office manager	0 = No	1 = Yes
	☐ Relative ☐ Friend	
L. Politician	0 = No	1 = Yes
	☐ Relative ☐ Friend	
M. Police officer	0 = No	1 = Yes
	☐ Relative ☐ Friend	
N. Bank employee	0 = No	1 = Yes
	☐ Relative ☐ Friend	

240 Appendices

O. Money lenders	0 = No	1 = Yes
	☐ Relative ☐ Friend	
P. Lorry driver	0 = No	1 = Yes
	☐ Relative ☐ Friend	
Q. Agricultural labourer	0 = No	1 = Yes
	☐ Relative ☐ Friend	
R. Cleaner	0 = No	1 = Yes
	☐ Relative ☐ Friend	
S. Shop assistant	0 = No	1 = Yes
	☐ Relative ☐ Friend	
T. Electrician, plumber or carpenter	0 = No	1 = Yes
	☐ Relative ☐ Friend	

viii. Cultural activities		
40. Does anyone in the household take part in any of the following cultural activities:		
A. Take part in religious festivals?	0 = No	1 = Yes
	How often?	
	Which festivals?	
B. Visiting temples?	0 = No	1 = Yes
	How often?	
C. Managing temples?	0 = No	1 = Yes
	How often?	
D. Go to cinema	0 = No	1 = Yes
	How often?	
E. Go to live music	0 = No	1 = Yes
	How often?	
F. Listen to English music	0 = No	1 = Yes
G. Listen to Hindi music	0 = No	1 = Yes
H. Listen to Marathi music	0 = No	1 = Yes

I. Play video games	0 = No	1 = Yes
J. Watch sports	0 = No	1 = Yes
K. Go to the gym or any other fitness clubs	0 = No	1 = Yes
L. Use Facebook/Twitter	0 = No	1 = Yes
M. Go to museums	0 = No	1 = Yes
	How often?	
N. Go to historical sites	0 = No	1 = Yes
	How often?	
O. Do arts or crafts	0 = No	1 = Yes
P. Read books (excluding course books) Religious books; novels; political books; history; other educational books	0 = No	1 = Yes
	What kind of books?	
Q. Read newspaper	0 = No	1 = Yes
R. Surf internet	0 = No	1 = Yes
S. Go to restaurants to eat	0 = No	1 = Yes
	How often?	
T. Travel on holiday	0 = No	1 = Yes
	How often?	
	Where?	
	Purpose of traveling: ☐ Pleasure ☐ Pilgrimage ☐ Both	
U. Go to bars	0 = No	1 = Yes
	How often?	
V. Go to cafes	0 = No	1 = Yes
	How often?	
W. Attend live sports events	0 = No	1 = Yes
	How often?	
X. Take part in political meetings	0 = No	1 = Yes
	Specify which meetings?	
Y. Take part in educational activities? For example: taking language courses (specify); taking other personal development classes; ITI classes, IT classes, cooking classes, etc.	0 = No	1 = Yes
	Specify which classes?	

242 Appendices

ix. Social media		
41	Does anyone in the household have access to Internet? (IF NO, GO TO QUESTION 44)	0 = No 1 = Yes
42	Do they use social media channels such as Facebook and Twitter, or emails?	0 = No 1 = Yes
43	Specify who in the family (relation to household head) uses social media?	

x. House type		
44	Roof	1 = No roof 2 = Thatch/palm leaf/grass 3 = Mud 4 = Plastic 5 = Palm/bamboo 6 = Timber 7 = Unpainted brick 8 = Metal/Tin 9 = Wood 10 = Asbestos sheets 11 = Cement/concrete 12 = Tiles 13 = Slate 14 = Burnt brick (painted) 15 = Other Specify: __ __
45	Wall	1 = No walls 2 = Mud 3 = Grass/reeds/thatch 4 = Stone with mud 5 = Unpainted brick 6 = Raw wood/reused wood 7 = Cement/concrete 8 = Burnt bricks (painted) 9 = Cement blocks 10 = Metal/asbestos sheets 11 = Other Specify: __ __

46	Floor	1= Mud/clay/earth
		2 = Sand
		3 = Dung
		4 = Raw wood plans
		5 = Palm/bamboo
		6 = Brick
		7 = Stone
		8 = Vinyl or asphalt
		9 = Ceramic tiles
		10 = Cement
		11 = Carpet
		12 = Polished stone/marble/granite
		13 = Other
		Specify: __ __
47	Number of rooms in the house	
48	Does the house have a separate kitchen?	0 = No 1 = Yes
49	Private toilet?	0 = No 1 = Yes
50	Toilet type?	
51	Type of shower/bath?	

xi. Self-perception and the middle class		
52	Have you heard of the term 'middle class' before? - (IF NO, GO TO QUESTIONS 56 and 59)	0 = No 1 = Yes
53	What does middle class mean? (Descriptive answer)	
54	Do you consider your family as a middle-class family? (IF NO, GO TO QUESTION 56)	0 = No 1 = Yes
55	Why do you consider yourself as middle class? (SELECT ALL THAT APPLY)	☐ Because of our income level ☐ Because of our occupation ☐ Because of our land ownership ☐ Because of our assets ownership ☐ Because of our education ☐ Because of our social circle ☐ Because of our life style ☐ Others (specify) Descriptive answer: __ __

56	Between the richest family and the poorest family in this village where do you sinuate yourself? Rank between 0 and 10 (0 if you think you are the poorest in the village and 10 if you think you are the richest in the village).	
57a	And what percentage of this village you think is middle class?	Percentage:
57b	Which other family in the village do you consider as middle class?	Name a family _____ □ Don't know or don't want to tell
58	Why do you think they are middle class? (SELECT ALL THAT APPLY)	□ Because of their income level □ Because of their occupation □ Because of their land ownership □ Because of their assets ownership □ Because of their education □ Because of their social circle □ Because of their life style □ Others (specify) Descriptive answer: __ __
59	Where do you dispose your waste (garbage)?	

Appendices   245

Appendix A9 Household Socio-economic Survey Questionnaire 2

Village Name	1 = Rahatwade 2 = Nandur
Case ID	
Household name	
Respondent's name	
First interviewer's name	
Second interviewer's name	
Number of visits to complete the questionnaire	
Completion status	0 = Incomplete 1 = Complete

Visits	Interview date	Interview time		Place of interview
		Start	Finish	
First visit				
Second visit				
Third visit				

i. Household general information		
1	Household ID	
2	Relation of respondent to household head	1 = Head 2 = Wife or husband 3 = Son or daughter 4 = Son-in-law or daughter-in-law 5 = Grandchild 6 = Parent 7 = Parent-in-law 8 = Brother or sister 9 = Brother–in-law or sister-in-law 10 = Niece/nephew 11 = Other relative 12 = Adopted/foster/step child 13 = Domestic servant 14 = Other not related, specify: __ __
3	Caste of the household head	
4	Which caste category does the household head belong to?	1 = Brahmin 2 = OBCs 3 = SCs 4 = STs 5 = Maratha 6 = N.T. (Nomadic Tribes) 7 = Others, specify: __ __

246   Appendices

5	Religion of the household head?	1 = Hindu 2 = Muslim 3 = Christian 4 = Sikh 5 = Buddhist 6 = Jain 7 = Tribal 8 = Others
6	How many years ago did this household first come to this village? IF 98, GO TO QUESTION 9.	__ __ Years (Write 98 if they are native from the village, or if they have been living in the village for more than 98 years ago)
7	From where did the family come?	1 = Same state, same district 2 = Same state, another district 3 = Another state 4 = Another country (include Pakistan or Bangladesh even if before partition)
8	From where did the family come?	1 = Village 2 = Town/city
9	Number of people living in the household	
10	Are there any other family members who do not live in the house? IF NO, GO TO QUESTION 13.	0 = No 1 = Yes
11	Where do they live?	1 = Another village 2 = Town 3 = Metro city like Pune, Mumbai, Delhi, etc. 4 = Abroad
12	Why do they live outside the household?	1 = Education 2 = Jobs 3 = Others, specify: __ __

ii. Education					
13	Education of household members between the ages of 5 and 25				
Member	1	2	3	4	5
Age					
Sex	1 = M 2 = F	1 = M 2 = F	1 = M 2 = F	1 = M 2 = F	1 = M 2 = F
Relation to household head					

Primary school (up to 5th grade)	Attended?	0 = No 1 = Yes	0 = No 1 = Yes	0 = No 1 = Yes	0 = No 1 = Yes	0 = No 1 = Yes
	Completion status	1 = Completed 2 = On-going 3 = Drop out	1 = Completed 2 = On-going 3 = Drop out	1 = Completed 2 = On-going 3 = Drop out	1 = Completed 2 = On-going 3 = Drop out	1 = Completed 2 = On-going 3 = Drop out
	No. of years completed					
	Type	1 = Public 2 = Private	1 = Public 2 = Private	1 = Public 2 = Private	1 = Public 2 = Private	1 = Public 2 = Private
	Medium	1 = English 2 = Semi-English 3 = Marathi 4 = Hindi 5 = Other	1 = English 2 = Semi-English 3 = Marathi 4 = Hindi 5 = Other	1 = English 2 = Semi-English 3 = Marathi 4 = Hindi 5 = Other	1 = English 2 = Semi-English 3 = Marathi 4 = Hindi 5 = Other	1 = English 2 = Semi-English 3 = Marathi 4 = Hindi 5 = Other
Secondary and higher secondary school (including 11 and 12)	Attended?	0 = No 1 = Yes	0 = No 1 = Yes	0 = No 1 = Yes	0 = No 1 = Yes	0 = No 1 = Yes
	Completion status	1 = Completed 2 = On-going 3 = Drop out	1 = Completed 2 = On-going 3 = Drop out	1 = Completed 2 = On-going 3 = Drop out	1 = Completed 2 = On-going 3 = Drop out	1 = Completed 2 = On-going 3 = Drop out
	No. of years completed					
	Type	1 = Public 2 = Private	1 = Public 2 = Private	1 = Public 2 = Private	1 = Public 2 = Private	1 = Public 2 = Private
	Medium	1 = English 2 = Semi-English 3 = Marathi 4 = Hindi 5 = Other	1 = English 2 = Semi-English 3 = Marathi 4 = Hindi 5 = Other	1 = English 2 = Semi-English 3 = Marathi 4 = Hindi 5 = Other	1 = English 2 = Semi-English 3 = Marathi 4 = Hindi 5 = Other	1 = English 2 = Semi-English 3 = Marathi 4 = Hindi 5 = Other

248 Appendices

College (graduate and above)	Attended?	0 = No 1 = Yes	0 = No 1 = Yes	0 = No 1 = Yes	0 = No 1 = Yes	0 = No 1 = Yes
	Completion status	1 = Completed 2 = On-going 3 = Drop out	1 = Completed 2 = On-going 3 = Drop out	1 = Completed 2 = On-going 3 = Drop out	1 = Completed 2 = On-going 3 = Drop out	1 = Completed 2 = On-going 3 = Drop out
	Type	1 = Public 2 = Private	1 = Public 2 = Private	1 = Public 2 = Private	1 = Public 2 = Private	1 = Public 2 = Private
	Medium	1 = English 2 = Semi-English 3 = Marathi 4 = Hindi 5 = Other	1 = English 2 = Semi-English 3 = Marathi 4 = Hindi 5 = Other	1 = English 2 = Semi-English 3 = Marathi 4 = Hindi 5 = Other	1 = English 2 = Semi-English 3 = Marathi 4 = Hindi 5 = Other	1 = English 2 = Semi-English 3 = Marathi 4 = Hindi 5 = Other
	Degree type	1 = Bachelor 2 = Master 3 = PhD 4 = Diploma Specify:	1 = Bachelor 2 = Master 3 = PhD 4 = Diploma Specify:	1 = Bachelor 2 = Master 3 = PhD 4 = Diploma Specify:	1 = Bachelor 2 = Master 3 = PhD 4 = Diploma Specify:	1 = Bachelor 2 = Master 3 = PhD 4 = Diploma Specify:
	If drop out: No. of years completed?					
Subject (college)						
Location						
Annual fees, if currently enrolled at private school						
If drop out at any stage, OR did not attend college, what was the reason for dropping out? (Insert code- – see next page)						

Why did [Name] drop-out of school, or did not attend college/university?

1 = Failed
2 = School was far/Inaccessible
3 = Poor quality/Lack of facilities
4 = Financial problems
5 = Health problems
6 = Not interested in school
7 = Household work/Child care

8 = Work for pay
9 = Gender/Puberty
10 = Lack of separate school/College for girls
11 = Marriage
12 = Parents/husband didn't allow studying further
13 = Getting teased/Bullied at school
14 = Others

iii. Income, sources of income, and occupation				
14 Please provide information about the working members in the household.				
Working members	1	2	3	4
Relation to the HHH				
Primary occupation				
Type Main: If the member has worked more than 6 months in the last 12 months Casual: If the person has worker less than 6 months during the last 12 months	1 = Main 2 = Casual	1 = Main 2 = Casual	1 = Main 2 = Casual	1 = Main 2 = Casual
Place of work	1 = Same village 2 = Different village 3 = Town 4 = Metro city 5 = Abroad	1 = Same village 2 = Different village 3 = Town 4 = Metro city 5 = Abroad	1 = Same village 2 = Different village 3 = Town 4 = Metro city 5 = Abroad	1 = Same village 2 = Different village 3 = Town 4 = Metro city 5 = Abroad
Approximate income from this work in the last 12 months.				
Secondary occupation				
Type	1 = Main 2 = Casual	1 = Main 2 = Casual	1 = Main 2 = Casual	1 = Main 2 = Casual
Place of work	1 = Same village 2 = Different village 3 = Town 4 = Metro city 5 = Abroad	1 = Same village 2 = Different village 3 = Town 4 = Metro city 5 = Abroad	1 = Same village 2 = Different village 3 = Town 4 = Metro city 5 = Abroad	1 = Same village 2 = Different village 3 = Town 4 = Metro city 5 = Abroad
Approximate income from this work in the last 12 months.				
Third occupation				
Type	1 = Main 2 = Casual	1 = Main 2 = Casual	1 = Main 2 = Casual	1 = Main 2 = Casual

250 Appendices

Place of work (choose a code from above)	1 = Same village 2 = Different village 3 = Town 4 = Metro city 5 = Abroad	1 = Same village 2 = Different village 3 = Town 4 = Metro city 5 = Abroad	1 = Same village 2 = Different village 3 = Town 4 = Metro ity 5 = Abroad	1 = Same village 2 = Different village 3 = Town 4 = Metro city 5 = Abroad
Approximate income from this work in the last 12 months.				
14W1	WORKSHEET: Calculate total income earned by all members during the last 12 months)			INR __ __
14W2	WORKSHEET: What is the main source of household income?			Code: __ __

15	Can you please estimate the annual income of the household from all sources in the previous year (2014–15)? (Include income from all sources such as rent, pension, scholarships, gift, other government benefits, etc.)	1 = Less than INR 20,000 2 = Between INR 20,000 and 50,000 3 = Between INR 50,000 and 1,00,000 4 = Between INR 1,00,000 and 1,50,000 5 = Between INR 1,50,000 and 2,50,000 6 = Above INR 2,50,000 7 = Don't know or don't want to tell or cannot be estimated

Land ownership: Agricultural land		
16	Does this household own any agricultural land? IF NO, GO TO QUESTION 18.	0 = No 1 = Yes

17	Please give information about the agricultural land owned.	
	Agricultural Land	*Area (Acres)*
A	Total agricultural land owned	
B	Total area irrigated by all sources except for rain	
C	What is the main source of irrigation?	1 = Tube well 2 = Other well 3 = Government sources 4 = River/canal 5 = Tank/pond/*nala* 6 = Other, specify: __ __
D	If you were to sell the total agricultural land you own, approximately how much would you receive for it?	INR __ __ __ per Guntha OR INR __ __ __ per Acre
17W	WORKSHEET: Calculate total value of agricultural land owned.	INR __ __

Appendices 251

		Non-agricultural land		
18	Does this household own any non-cultivated land? IF NO, GO TO QUESTION 22.	0 = No		1 = Yes
19	What is the area of non-cultivated land owned?		__ __ __. __ Acres __ __ __. __ Gunthas	
20	What type of land is it? Please specify.	1 = Grazing, pastoral 2 = Dry land, unused 3 = Under construction, building plot 4 = Other, specify: __ __		
21	If you were to sell your non-cultivated land, approximately how much would you receive for it?	INR __ __ __ __ per Guntha OR INR __ __ __ __ per Acre		
21W	WORKSHEET: Calculate total value of land owned.	INR __ __		
22	Does the household lease/rent out any land? IF NO, GO TO QUESTION 29.	0 = No		1 = Yes
23	In the last 12 months did you receive cash/kind for this land or did you divide the crop between you and the tenant?	0 = None 1 = Cash 2 = Share crop/or other product 3 = Both 1 and 2		
24	IF CASH OR BOTH: How much did you receive in INR equivalent during last 12 months for this land?	INR __ __		
25	IF CROP/OTHER PRODUCT OR BOTH: What proportion of crops did you receive?	__ __ Per cent		
26	About how much was the value of the crop you received in the last 12 months?	INR __ __		
27	Did you supply inputs/cultivation cost to the tenants?	0 = No		1 = Yes
28	IF YES: what was the cash value of your inputs/ cultivation cost you provided to the tenant in the last 12 months?	INR __ __		
28W	WORKSHEET: Total value received from the rented land: 24 + 26 − 28 = __ __	INR __ __		

29	Do you lease/rent in any land? IF NO, GO TO QUESTION 36.	0 = No	1 = Yes

252 Appendices

30	In the last 12 months did you pay cash/kind for this land or did you divide the crop between you and the tenant?	0 = None 1 = Cash 2 = Share crop 3 = Both 1 and 2
31	IF CASH OR BOTH: How much did you pay in the last 12 months for this land?	INR __ __
32	IF CROP OR BOTH: What proportion of crops did you give to the landlord?	__ __ Per cent
33	About how much was that worth last year?	INR __ __
34	Did the landlord supply inputs/cultivation cost to you?	0 = No 1 = Yes
35	IF YES: what was the cash value of the inputs/cultivation cost you received during the last 12 months?	INR __ __
35W	WORKSHEET: Total value paid for the rented land: 31 + 33 − 35 = __ __	INR __ __

v. Animals/livestock

36	Does this household own any livestock such as cows, buffalos, goats or chickens? IF NO, GO TO QUESTION 40.	0 = No 1 = Yes

37	Give details about any livestock owned by the household			
S. No.	Type	0 = No 1 = Yes	How many	Value of them (INR)
A	Sheep			__ __ __ × __ __ = __ __ __
B	Goat			__ __ __ × __ __ = __ __ __
C	Milch buffalo			__ __ __ × __ __ = __ __ __
D	Milk cow			__ __ __ × __ __ = __ __ __
E	Draft animals (bullock, buffalo)			__ __ __ × __ __ = __ __ __
F	Poultry, chicken, duck			__ __ __ × __ __ = __ __ __
G	Other (specify)			
37W	WORKSHEET: Estimate the value of livestock	INR __ __		

Appendices 253

38	Estimate annual total expenditure on livestock.	Value of purchased feed & fodder __ __ Value of home produced feed & fodder __ __ Veterinary Services __ __ Hired labour for grazing/care __ __ Other costs (ropes, chain, transport, etc.) __ __ Total expenditure INR __ __ __ Per year		

39		Give details of livestock products and receipts approximately:				
	Item	Output	Sale of product	What is the market value of the product per kg/l? (INR)	WORKSHEET	
		Quantity (kg/l) per (day/week/ month/year)	Quantity (kg/l) per (day/week/ month/year)		Total value of sold product last year?	
A	Milk and milk product	__ __ litre/ per __ __	__ __ litre/per __ __			
B	Meat	__ __ kg/ per __ __	__ __ kg/ per __ __			
C	Poultry, eggs					
D	Leather, wool, etc.					

39W	WORKSHEET: Calculate the total value of sold product in the last 12 months.	INR __ __

How many months last year did your cows produce milk? __ __ Months
How many months last year did your buffaloes produce milk? __ __ Months
How many months last year did your goats produce milk? __ __ Months
Any additional comment about livestock?

vi. Household assets

40 Do you own any of the following items?

S. No.	Item	0 = No 1 = Yes	How many	S. No.	Item	0 = No 1 = Yes	How many
1	Bicycle			27	Refrigerator		
2	Motorcycle			28	Washing machine		
3	Car			29	Microwave		
4	Generator set			30	Pressure cooker		
5	B/W TV			31	LPG gas		
6	Colour TV			32	Clock/watch		
7	Cable/dish TV			33	Mixer/grinder		
8	Radio			34	Water purifier		

254 Appendices

9	Cassette player			35	Speakers			
10	Air cooler			36	Bed			
11	Electric fan			37	Cupboard			
12	Air conditioner			38	Iron			
13	Heater			39	Sewing machine			
14	Water boiler			40	Bank account			
15	Chair/table			41	Credit card			
16	Sofa set			42	Tractor			
17	Cot			43	Lorry/tempo			
18	Telephone			44	Cart			
19	Simple mobile			45	Plough			
20	Smartphone			46	Thresher			
21	Computer			47	Water well			
22	Laptop			48	Bore hole			
23	Tablet			49	Electric pump			
.24	Camera			50	Hand/power sprayer			
25	Video player			51	Seed drill			
26	Video games			52	Others			

vii. Other assets			
41	Do you own the house you are currently living in? IF NO, GO TO QUESTION 43.	0 = No	1 = Yes
42	If you were to sell this house today, how much would you receive for it approximately?	INR __ __	
43	If you do not own this house, how much rent do you pay monthly?	INR __ __ __ __ Per month (0 if they pay no rent)	
44	Do you own any other house other than the house you currently live in? IF NO, GO TO QUESTION 48.	0 = No	1 = Yes
45	If you were to sell this today, how much would you receive for it approximately?	INR __ __	
46	Have you given this on rent? IF NO GO TO QUESTION 48.	0 = No	1 = Yes
47	How much rent do you receive for it monthly?	INR __ __ __ __ Per month	

Appendices   255

48	Do you own any shop/factory/workshop, or restaurant or cafe, etc.? IF NO, GO TO QUESTION 54.	0 = No 1 = Yes
49	Specify the type? Is it a factory, workshop, restaurant, etc.?	
50	Where is/are it/they located?	1 = Same village 2 = Different village 3 = Urban area
51	If you were to sell this today, how much would you receive for it approximately?	INR __ __
52	Have you given any of them on rent? IF NO, GO TO QUESTION 54.	0 = No 1 = Yes
53	IF YES: How much rent do you receive monthly?	INR __ __ __ __ Per month

viii. Crops		
54	Did you cultivate any crops in 2014–15? IF NO, GO TO QUESTION 57.	0 = No 1 = Yes

55	Please give information about crops you cultivated in 2014–15				Worksheet
S. No.	Crop names	Output per year	Quantity sold	Price per unit	Price sold
55W	Worksheet: Calculate total value sold				INR __ __

56	What was the approximate cost of the following in one year (2014–15)?	Cost (INR)
A	Seeds	
B	Fertiliser	
C	Pesticides	

Appendices

D	Manure		
E	Water		
F	Others		
42W	Worksheet: Calculate total cost.		INR __ __

ix. A. Hiring agricultural labour

57	Did you hire any labourers to work on your agricultural land (own or rented) during the year 2014–15? IF NO GO TO QUESTION 59.	0 = No 1 = Yes

58 Please provide information about the agricultural labour hired in during 2014–2015.

Crop list	Labour	Number of people hired	Number of days in the last year	Wage per day	WORKSHEET Total labour days	WORKSHEET Total wage paid in 12 months
	Male					
	Female					
	Male					
	Female					
	Male					
	Female					
	Male					
	Female					
	Male					
	Female					
WORKSHEET: Calculate the total days and wage paid in 2014–15.				__ __ days		INR __ __

ix. B. Hiring non-agricultural labour

59	Did you hire anyone as non-agricultural labourers during the year 2014–15 (This includes labour hired for household maintenance, servants, and labour working for business)? IF NO, GO TO QUESTION 61.	0 = No 1 = Yes

Appendices   257

60. Please provide information about the non-agricultural labour hired during 2014–15.						
Type of work	Labour	Number of people hired	Number of days in the last year	Wage per day	WORKSHEET Total labour days	WORKSHEET Total wage paid in 12 months
	Male					
	Female					
	Male					
	Female					
	Male					
	Female					
	Male					
	Female					
60W. WORKSHEET: Calculate the total days and wage paid in 2014–15.				__ __ days	INR __ __	

ix. C. Working as agricultural labourers for wages		
61	Did any of the family member work for wages as agricultural labourers on someone else's land during the year 2014–15? IF NO, GO TO QUESTION 63.	0 = No 1 = Yes

62	Please provide information about family members who has worked as agricultural labourers in 2014–15.				
S. No.	Gender 1 = Male 2 = Female	Age		Approximate number of days in the last 12 months	Wage (INR) per day/week
62W	WORKSHEET: Calculate the total number of labour days and wage		__ __ days		INR __ __

258   Appendices

ix. D. Working as non-agricultural labourers for wages		
63	Did any of the family members work as non-agricultural labourers in 2014–15? (This includes work in *mandi*s and mills – post-harvest agricultural activates, or in workshops, shops, factories, etc.) IF NO, GO TO QUESTION 65.	0 = No 1 = Yes

64	Please provide information about the household members who worked as non-agricultural labours in 2014–2015.				
S. No.	Gender 1 = Male 2 = Female	Age	Type of work	Approximate number of days in the last 12 months	Wage per day (INR)
64W	WORKSHEET: Calculate the total number of labour days and wage			_ _ days	INR _ _

x. Sanitation		
65	What is the main source of drinking water?	1 = Gram Panchayat water 2 = Bore well 3 = Bottle water from shops 4 = Others
66	What do you mainly use for cooking?	1 = LPG 2 = Biogas 3 = Electricity 4 = Kerosene 5 = Coal 6 = Firewood 7 = Cow dung 8 = Crop residue 9 = Charcoal
67	What do you think is the first thing that the Gram Panchayat office should do to keep the village clean?	

Appendices 259

xi. Household consumption expenditure					
68	Please tell me how much of these items have been consumed in your household in the past 30 days.				
S. No.	Item	Total quantity used (kg/l)	Over the past 30 days what was the average market price of one kg/l of the item?	WORKSHEET: Calculate total Value (INR)	
				Home grown (INR)	Purchased (INR)
	Rice				
	Wheat/Flour				
	Sugar				
	Kerosene				
	Maize				
	Pulses & pulse product				
	Eggs				
	Milk				
	Milk product				
	Mutton				
	Chicken				
	Fish				
	Vegetables				
	Fruits				
	Sweeteners				
	Cooking oil				
	Dry fruits and nuts				
68A	WORKSHEET: Total			_ _ INR	_ _ INR
68B	WORKSHEET: Total per month (INR)			_ _ INR	

69	Over the past 30 days, what was the total value of the following items that the household consumed?		
S. No.	Item	Total value	W? M? D?
	Salt and spices	INR	
	Tea and Coffee	INR	
	Fruit juices	INR	

260 Appendices

	Drinking water (bottle water)	INR	
	Processed foods (such as biscuits, cake, pickles, sauce, etc.)	INR	
	Pan & tobacco & other intoxicants	INR	
	Alcohol	INR	
	Eating out	INR	
	Entertainment (cinema, theatre, live music, etc.)	INR	
	Household fuel (LPG, firewood, cow dung – exclude kerosene)	INR	
	Mobile bill	INR	
	TV cable bill	INR	
	Electricity bill	INR	
	Internet bill including mobile internet	INR	
	Water bill (excluding drinking water)	INR	
	Cosmetic/toilet articles (including toothpaste, hair oil, shaving blades, etc.)	INR	
	Soap, detergent/washing powder	INR	
	Agarbati, HH insecticide, etc.	INR	
	Household items (electric bulb, tube light, glassware, bucket, etc.)	INR	
	Transportation (railway, bus, hired taxi, rickshaw, air fares, porter charges, auto, school bus/van, etc.)	INR	
	Diesel, petrol, CNG, maintenance (owned vehicle)	INR	
	House loan instalment	INR	
	Other loan instalments	INR	
	Other rent (appliances, cooler, AC, etc., and agricultural equipment)	INR	
	Consumer taxes (includes house tax)	INR	
	Services (barber, laundry, etc.)	INR	
	Domestic servants/sweepers	INR	
	Medical expenses (outpatient services)	INR	
	Newspapers, magazines	INR	
	Others not mentioned here	INR	
B	WORKSHEET: Total	INR	

Appendices 261

70	For the following expenses/purchases, about how much did you spend in the past 365 days?	
	Medical in-patient (hospitalisation of any family members)	INR
	School fees (private school)	INR
	College fees	INR
	Private tuition fees	INR
	Language classes fees	INR
	Other personal development classes, computer classes, diploma courses, etc.	INR
	School books & other educational articles, library charges, stationery	INR
	Clothing	INR
	Clothes for occasions	INR
	Footwear and shoes	INR
	Bedding	INR
	Personal goods, clock, watch, PC, telephone, mobile	INR
	Therapeutic appliances, eye-glass, hearing aids, etc.	INR
	Furniture and fixtures, bed, suitcase, carpet, paintings	INR
	Goods for recreation, TV, radio, tape, recorder, musical instruments	INR
	Crockery & household appliances	INR
	Vacation, travelling for pilgrimage	INR
	Transport equipment (car, bike, motor bikes, and repairing parts)	INR
	Insurance premiums	INR
	Social functions (birthday parties, wedding, other celebrations)	INR
	Sport clubs, gyms and other fitness classes	INR
	Festivals expenses, religious function, gifts	INR
	Repair and maintenance in the house	INR
C	WORKSHEET: Total	INR __ __

70 W.1. WORKSHEET:
Calculate total annual expenditure: (A × 12) + (B × 12) + C = INR __ __

262 Appendices

70	W.2. WORKSHEET: Total monthly consumption expenditure	INR __ __

	xii. Saving and debt		
71	Has the household taken any loan in the last 5 years? IF NO, GO TO QUESTION 75.	0 = No	1 = Yes
72	How many loans do you currently have?		
73	What is the total amount of debt?	INR __ __	

74	Please provide information about the last loan taken	
A	Which year was the last loan taken?	
B	Purpose — why did you take this loan?	1 = Buy/improve a house 2 = Buy land 3 = Buy livestock 4 = Buy or improve agricultural equipment 5 = Business 6 = Buy household goods 7 = Buy Car 8 = Buy two wheelers 9 = Pay for education 10 = Medical Expenses 11 = Marriage 12 = to pay off and old loan 13 = To buy crops 14 = to buy tractors 15 = Others Specify: __ __
C	Whom did you take this loan from?	1 = Bank 2 = Money lenders 3 = Cooperatives 4 = Relative or friend 5 = Self-help group 6 = Others Specify: __ __
D	Amount of loan (INR)	INR __ __
E	Rate of interest (%) per month/per year	
F	Type of security	
G	Outstanding	INR __ __

75	Has the household given any loan, including to relatives and friends? IF NO, GO TO QUESTION 78.	0 = No 1 = Yes
76	How many loans and to whom?	

77	What is the total amount of current credits?	INR __ __

	xiii. Membership of civil society organisations	
78	Is anyone in the household a member of any groups or organisations? IF NO, GO TO QUESTION 83.	0 = No 1 = Yes
79	Who/relation to the household head?	
80	IF YES: Please name the organisations and groups [Name] a member of.	
81	What is [Name]'s status/ role in this group or organisation?	
82	Why has [Name] become a member of this organisation/group?	

	xiv. Food	
83	Is this family vegetarian or non-vegetarian?	1 = Vegetarian 2 = Non-vegetarian 3 = Mix
84	Where would be your preferred place (if you had a choice) to buy household food items from?	1 = Locally grown produce 2 = Organised retail shops such as Dorabjee's, Reliance Fresh, Nature's Baskets, etc. 3 = Unorganised retail shopping or supermarkets 4 = Open markets 5 = Others Specify __ __
85	While purchasing food items/groceries or preparing food, what is your main/most important consideration?	1 = Cost only 2 = Health only 3 = Both
86	How often do you strictly control your children's consumption with respect to food children prefer but you may consider as unhealthy: such as sweets, chips?	1 = Never, I allow them to eat whatever they want 2 = Sometimes 3 = Regularly 4 = Always, every day
87	How often does the family go for fast food such as MacDonald's, KFC, Dominos, etc.?	1 = Never 2 = Sometimes (less than 4 times in a month) 3 = Regularly (more than 4 times in a month)
88	Does anyone in the household watch any cooking shows in order to learn new dishes?	0 = No 1 = Yes

264 Appendices

89	Does anyone in the household read any dietary/health magazine?	0 = No 1 = Yes
90	Can you identify any changes in your food consumption habits/preferences in the last 10 years? Has anything changed in terms of the types of food you buy? IF NO, GO TO QUESTION 92.	0 = No 1 = Yes
91	IF YES: Please explain what has changed in few words?	
92	How do you describe a healthy diet in just a few words?	

xv. Alcohol consumption		
93	Does anyone in the household drink alcohol? IF NO, GO TO QUESTION 103.	0 = No 1 = Yes
94	Are women in the household allowed to drink?	0 = No 1 = Yes
95	IF NO, can you explain why women cannot drink, in just a few words?	
96	Do you serve alcohol when you have guests?	0 = No 1 = Yes
97	How often does [Name] drink?	1 = Only in occasion, wedding, festivals 2 = Less than twice a month 3 = More than twice a month 4 = Often, most days 5 = Every day
98	How often does [Name] go to a bar?	1 = Never 2 = Less than twice a month 3 = More than twice a month 4 = Often, most days 5 = Every day
99	Approximately how much does [Name] spend on alcohol every week?	
100	What does [Name]'s favourite type of alcohol?	1 = Locally made alcohol 2 = Indian brand 3 = foreign brand 4 = Others
101	Are you aware of the danger of alcohol? IF NO, GO TO QUESTION 103.	0 = No 1 = Yes

102	Can you tell me in only few words about the danger of alcohol?	

xvi. Media and Social media and News		
103	Does anyone in the household have access to Internet?	0 = No 1 = Yes
104	Does anyone in the household use social media channels such as Facebook and Twitter?	0 = No 1 = Yes
105	Does anyone in the household follow news on newspaper? TICK AS APPLY	0 = No 1 = Yes, Regional 2 = Yes, National 3 = Yes, International 4 = 1 & 2 5 = 1 & 2 & 3
106	Does anyone in the household follow news on TV? TICK AS APPLY	0 = No 1 = Yes, Regional 2 = Yes, National 3 = Yes, International 4 = 1 & 2 5 = 1 & 2 & 3
107	Does anyone in the household follow news on radio? TICK AS APPLY	0 = No 1 = Yes, Regional 2 = Yes, National 3 = Yes, International 4 = 1 & 2 5 = 1 & 2 & 3
108	Does anyone in the household follow news online? TICK AS APPLY	0 = No 1 = Yes, Regional 2 = Yes, National 3 = Yes, International 4 = 1 & 2 5 = 1 & 2 & 3
109	What do you think is the purpose of TV?	1= Entertainment 2= Information 3= Time pass 4 = 1 and 2 or 3
110	Do female members follow any news?	0 = No 1 = Yes
111	What programme do female members usually follow?	

xvii. Clothes		
112	How do you describe your preferred clothes?	1 = Good value for money 2 = They reflect fashion and your awareness of brands 3 = Traditional 4 = Comfortable but clean 5 = Chic and stylish 6 = Do not care
113	And preferred clothes for your children?	1 = Good value for money 2 = They reflect fashion and your awareness of brands 3 = Traditional 4 = Comfortable but clean 5 = Chic and stylish 6 = Do not care
114	When you purchase your clothes what is the most important thing to consider?	1 = Cost 2 = Style and fashion 3 = Quality 4 = Brands 5 = Others Specify: __ __
115	Does [Name] know any foreign brands for clothes and shoes he/she likes to wear? This question is for young members.	

xviii. Political participations		
116	Are you familiar with the reservations policies? IF NO, GO TO QUESTION 122.	0 = No 1 = Yes
117	Do you think the government should continue the reservations policies? IF NO, GO TO QUESTION 119.	1 = No, I oppose reservations 2 = Yes, In both education and jobs 3 = Yes, but only in jobs 4 = Yes, but only in education
118	IF YES: Why do you think the reservations should be continued?	1= Reservations help reducing the caste discrimination in society 2 = Lower caste are poorer that is why they need reservation 3 = Others Specify: __ __

119	IF NO: Why do you think the reservations should be stopped?	1 = Because reservations don't reach the poor 2 = Because reserved category candidates qualify with lesser marks, while students with good marks outside reserved category cannot have access to jobs and education 3 = Reserved category candidates do not work hard 4 = Reservations are prone to fraud and corruption 5 = Reservations are misused for political gains 6 = Others Specify: __ __
120	What do you think the reservation should be based on?	1 = Reservations should be stopped 2 = Caste based 3 = Economic considerations 4 = Merit 5 = Both merit and economic considerations 6 = Reservations should only be given to rural areas 7 = Reservations should only be given to women
121	Do you think the government of India should extend the reservations to other castes?	1 = No 2 = Yes, to Marathas 3 = Yes, to Brahmins 4 = Yes, to Muslims 5 = More reservations to the caste the respondent is from 6 = Yes, to all castes 7 = Others (not mentioned here), Specify: __ __

xix. Voting behaviour		
122	Did you vote in the last Lok Sabha elections (2014)?	0 = No 1 = Yes
123	IF NO: What was the main reason you did not vote?	
124	IF YES: What of the following was the most important consideration for you when you voted in the last Lok Sabha election?	1 = Local Candidate 2 = Party 3 = Prime ministerial candidate of a party 4 = Other Specify: __ __
125	Which party did you vote for in the last Lok Sabha elections (2014)? And which party for the last state elections?	
126	Do you think your vote has any impact on how things are run in India?	0 = No 1 = Yes

268 Appendices

127	So far are you satisfied with the performance of the BJP government at the Centre and why? IF YES, GO TO QUESTION 129.	0 = No 1 = Yes
128	IF NO, what is your main reason for you dissatisfactions?	1 = Not caring about rural development 2 = Not caring about waste and rubbish collection 3 = Not caring about not environment and pollution 4 = Not caring quality of education 5 = Not caring about quality of health system 6 = Corruption 7 = Not caring about women safety 8 = Not caring about the poor 9 = Not caring about low agriculture market prices 10 = Inflation 11 = Others Specify: __ __
129	What is the single most important issue for you that you want this BJP government to focus on?	1 = Rural development 2 = Environment and pollution 3 = Waste and rubbish collection 4 = Quality education 5 = Quality health system 6 = Reservation extension 7 = Environment 8 = Eliminating corruption 9 = Increase agriculture market price 10 = Inflation 11 = Water 12 = Others Specify: __ __
130	Were you satisfied with the performance of the Congress-led UPA government at the Centre? IF YES, GO TO QUESTION 132.	0 = No 1 = Yes
131	IF NO, what was your main reason for you dissatisfactions?	1 = Not caring about rural development 2 = Not caring about waste and rubbish collection 3 = Not caring about not environment and pollution 4 = Not caring quality of education 5 = Not caring about quality of health system 6 = Corruption 7 = Not caring about women safety 8 = Not caring about the poor 9 = Not introducing right prices for agri products 10 = Inflation 11= Others Specify: __ __

Appendices 269

132	Are you traditionally supporter of a specific party? IF NO, GO TO QUESTION 134.	0 = No 1 = Yes
133	IF YES: Which party?	
134	Which state in India do you think is the most developed state?	
135	Why do you think this state is the most developed state in India?	1= Because of industrial development, good roads and facilities 2 = Good agricultural development 3= Good education facilities 4 = Good health facilities 5 = Less corruption 6 = Less poverty 7 = Cleanness 8 = Women safety 9 = Availability of employment 10 = Others Specify: __ __
136	What is the one quality you appreciate the most in your favourite politician?	1 = Honesty 2 = Delivering promises 3 = Caring about the poor 4 = Decisiveness 5 = Bravery 6 = Vision 7 = Caring about development 8 = Making India a powerful country 9 = Who does not engaged in corruptions 10 = Good control over gov. servants 11 = Creating employment 12 = Others Specify: __ __

xx. Confidence in institutions		
137	Rank (0 to 5) your confidence in the following:	0 = No confidence whatsoever 5 = Great deal of confidence)
A	Politicians to deliver their promises	
B	Police force to protect the community	
C	Village Panchayat to implement public projects	
D	Public schools to provide good education	
E	Private schools to provide good education	
F	Public hospitals to deliver good medical treatment	
G	Private hospitals to provide good medical treatment	

270 Appendices

H	Military to defend the boarders	
I	Banks to keep your money safe	
J	Newspaper for their transparency and truth telling	
K	Election Commission for election expense monitoring	

xxi. Desire and ambition
If you had an option to change your life, how would you change it in the following matters? This is an imaginary situation; please state your preference and desirable answers.

138	Where would you live?	1 = Same village 2 = Town 3 = Metro city 4 = Abroad 5 = Others, specify: __ __
139	In a few words tell me why?	
140	To what level would you have educated yourself?	1 = Up to class 5 2 = Up to class 10 3 = Higher secondary (class 12th) 4 = Graduate (bachelor's) 5 = Post-graduate (master's, PhD) 6 = Professional/higher research degrees
141	What level of education would you like to give to your children? 1 = Up to class 5 2 = Up to class 10 3 = Higher secondary (class 12th) 4 = Graduate (bachelor's) 5 = Post graduate (master's, PhD) 6 = Professional/higher research degrees	Male child ☐ Female child ☐
142	Where would you send your children to school? 1 = Same village 2 = Town 3 = Metro city 4 = Abroad	Male child ☐ Female child ☐
143	What kind of occupation would you choose for yourself?	
144	What occupation would you chose for your children?	Male child __ __ __ __ Female child __ __ __ __
145	What language would you speak at home?	1 = English 2 = Hindi 3 = Marathi 4 = Others Specify: __ __

146	What style of furniture would you buy for your house?	1 = Same as what we have now 2 = Simple and comfortable 3 = Chic and stylish and lavish 4 = Imported furniture, very expensive
147	Where would you go for your next vacation?	1 = Inside India 2 = Abroad
148	What kind of activities (leisure) would you do?	1 = Travelling inside India 2 = Travelling abroad 3 = Play sport like football or cricket 4 = Play musical instrument 5 = Go for movies and concerts 6 = Do arts and crafts such as paintings 7 = Read books 8 = Learn a new language 9 = Go to pilgrimage 10 = Others Specify: __ __
149	What do you think success in life depends on?	

	xxii. Self-perception and the middle class	
150	Have you heard of the term 'middle class' before? IF NO, GO TO QUESTIONS 152, 154 & 155.	0 = No 1 = Yes
151	Do you consider yourself as a middle class family?	0 = No 1 = Yes
152	How do you describe your household?	1 = Poor 2 = Lower middle class 3 = Middle middle class 4 = Upper middle class 5 = Rich
153	And what percentage of this village you think is middle class, poor, and rich?	__ __ Middle class __ __ Poor __ __ Rich
154	Are you better off or worse off than 10 years ago?	1 = Better off 2 = Worse off 3 = Same
155	Between the richest family and the poorest family in this village where do you sinuate yourself? Rank between 0 and 10 (0 if you think you are the poorest in the village, and 10 if you think you are the richest in the village).	

References

Abercrombie, N. and J. Urry (1983). *Capital, Labour and the Middle Classes*. London: George Allen and Unwin.

Adnan, Sh. (1985). 'Classical and Contemporary Approaches to Agrarian Capitalism'. *Economic and Political Weekly* 20 (30): 53–64.

Ahluwalia, M. S. (2011). 'Prospects and Policy Challenges in the Twelfth Plan'. *Economic and Political Weekly* 46 (21): 88–105.

Alesina, A. and R. Perotti (1996). 'Income Distribution, Political Instability and Investment'. *European Economic Review* 40 (6): 1203–28.

Ambedkar, B. R. (2013 [1936]). *Annihilation of Caste: The Annotated Critical Edition*, Edited by S. Anand. New Delhi: Navayana Publishing.

Appadurai, A. (1986). *The Social Life of Things: Commodities in Cultural Perspective*. Cambridge: Cambridge University Press.

——— (1996). *Modernity at Large: Cultural Dimensions of Globalization*. London: University of Minnesota Press.

Aslany, M. (2019). 'The Indian Middle Class, Its Size, and Urban–Rural Variations'. *Contemporary South Asia* 27 (2): 196–213.

Athreya, V., G. Böklin, G. Djurfeldt and S. Lindberg (1987). 'Identification of Agrarian Classes: A Methodological Essay with Empirical Material from South India'. *The Journal of Peasant Studies* 14 (2): 147–90.

Attwood, D. W. (1984). 'Capital and the Transformation of Agrarian Class Systems: Sugar Production in India'. In *Agrarian Power and Agricultural Productivity in South Asia*, ed. M. Desai, S. H. Rudolph and A. Rudra. Delhi: Oxford University Press, pp. 20–50.

Banerjee, A. and E. Duflo (2008). 'What Is Middle Class about the Middle Classes around the World?' *Journal of Economic Perspectives* 22 (2): 3–28.

Bardhan, P. (1998). *The Political Economy of Development in India*. New Delhi: Oxford University Press.

Baru, S. (2000). 'Economic Policy and Development of Capitalism in India: The Role of Regional Capitalists and Political Parties. In *Transforming India: Social and Political Dynamics of Democracy*, ed. F. R. Frankel, Z. Hasan, R. Bhargava and B. Arora. New Delhi: Oxford University Press, pp. 207–30.

Basile, E. (2009). 'The Institutional Embeddedness of Indian Rural Capitalism'. In *The Changing Identity of Rural India: A Socio-historic Analysis*, ed. E. Basile and I. Mukhopadhyay. New York: Anthem Press, pp. 31–62.

Baviskar, A. and R. Ray (2011). 'Introduction'. In *Elite and Everyman: The Cultural Politics of the Indian Middle Classes*, ed. A. Baviskar and R. Ray. New Delhi: Routledge, pp. 1–23.

Bayly, S. (2001). *Caste, Society and Politics in India from the Eighteenth Century to the Modern Age*. Cambridge: Cambridge University Press.

Bernstein, H. (2006). 'Is There an Agrarian Question in the 21st Century?' *Canadian Journal of Development Studies/Revue canadienne d'études du développement* 27 (4): 449–60.

Béteille, A. (1992). *The Backward Classes in Contemporary India*. New Delhi: Oxford University Press.

——— (1996). *Caste, Class, and Power: Changing Patterns of Stratification in Tajore Village* (2nd edn). New Delhi: Oxford University Press.

Birdsall, N. (2010). 'The (Indispensable) Middle Class in Developing Countries'. In *Equity and Growth in a Globalizing World*, ed. R. Kanbur and M. Spence. Washington DC: The World Bank (Commission on Growth and Development), pp. 157–87.

Birdsall, N., C. Graham and S. Pettinato (2000). 'Stuck in the Tunnel: Is Globalization Muddling the Middle Class?' *Brookings Institution, Center on Social and Economic Dynamics* (working paper), No. 14. Washington, DC: The Brookings Institution.

Bonnefond, C., M. Clément and F. Combarnous (2015). 'In Search of the Elusive Chinese Urban Middle Class: An Exploratory Analysis'. *Post-Communist Economies* 27 (1): 41–59.

Bourdieu, P. (1977). *Outline of a Theory of Practice*. Translated by Richard Nice. Cambridge: Cambridge University Press.

——— (1984). *Distinction: A Social Critique of the Judgement of Taste*. Translated by Richard Nice. Cambridge, MA: Harvard University Press.

——— (1986). 'The Forms of Capital'. In *Handbook of Theory and Research for the Sociology of Education*, ed. J. Richardson. Westport, DC: Greenwood Press, pp. 241–58.

——— (1987). 'What Makes a Social Class? On the Theoretical and Practical Existence of Groups'. *Berkeley Journal of Sociology* 32: 1–18.

——— (1988 [1984]). *Homo Academicus*. Cambridge: Polity Press.

——— (1990 [1984]). *The Logic of Practice*. Translated by Richard Nice. Stanford: Stanford University Press.

Bourdieu, P. and L. J. D. Wacquant (1992). *An Invitation to Reflexive Sociology*. Chicago: University of Chicago Press.

274   References

Breen, R. (2005). 'Foundations of a Neo-Weberian Class Analysis'. In *Approaches to Class Analysis*, ed. E. O. Wright. Cambridge: Cambridge University Press, pp. 31–50.

Breman, J. (1993). *Beyond Patronage and Exploitation: Changing Agrarian Relations in South Gujarat*. New Delhi: Oxford University Press.

——— (1996). *Footloose Labour: Working in India's Informal Economy*. Cambridge: Cambridge University Press.

Brosius, C. (2010). *India's Middle Class: New Forms of Urban Leisure, Consumption and Prosperity*. New Delhi: Routledge.

Burawoy, M. (2012). 'Theory and Practice: Marx Meets Bourdieu'. In *Conversations with Bourdieu: The Johannesburg Moment*, ed. K. Von Holdt and M. Burawoy. Johannesburg: Wits University Press, pp. 31–46.

Burkhauser, R. V., A. D., Crews, M. C. Daly and S. P. Jenkins (1996). *Income Mobility and the Middle Class (AEI Studies on Understanding Economic Inequality)*. Washington, DC: AEI Press.

Byres, T. J. (1981). 'The New Technology, Class Formation and Class Action in the Indian Countryside'. *The Journal of Peasant Studies* 8 (4): 405–454.

——— (1988). 'Charan Singh, 1902–87: An Assessment'. *The Journal of Peasant Studies* 15(2): 139–189.

Cavalcante, M. (2009). 'Income-based Estimates vs Consumption-based Estimates of Poverty: Evidence from Rural Tamil Nadu after Liberalization'. In *The Changing Identity of Rural India: A Socio-historic Analysis*, ed. E. Basile and I. Mukhopadhyay. New York: Anthem Press, pp. 113–48.

Chan, T. W. and J. H. Goldthorpe (2007). 'Class and Status: The Conceptual Distinction and Its Empirical Relevance'. *American Sociological Review* 72 (4): 512–32.

Chari, S. (2000). 'The Agrarian Origins of the Knitwear Industrial Cluster in Tiruppur, India'. *World Development* 28 (3): 579–99.

——— (2004). *Fraternal Capital: Peasant-Workers, Self-made Men, and Globalization in Provincial India*. Stanford: Stanford University Press.

Chatterjee, P. (1992). 'A Religion of Urban Domesticity: Sri Ramakrishna and the Calcutta Middle Class'. In *Subaltern Studies VII*, ed. P. Chatterjee and G. Pandey. New Delhi: Oxford University Press, pp. 40–68.

Chaurasia, R. S. (2004). *History of the Marathas*. New Delhi: Atlantic.

Chibber, V. (2006). 'On the Decline of Class Analysis in South Asian Studies'. *Critical Asian Studies* 38 (4): 375–87.

Chinnappa, B. N. (1977). 'Adoption of the New Technology in North Acrot District'. In *Green Revolution?* ed. B. H. Farmer. London: Palgrave Macmillan, pp. 92–123.

Clementi, F. and M. Gallegati (2005). 'Pareto's Law of Income Distribution: Evidence for Germany, the United Kingdom, and the United States'. In *Econophysics of Wealth Distributions*, ed. A. Chatterjee, S. Yarlagadda and B. K. Chakrabati. Berlin: Springer, pp. 3–14.

Colatei, D. and B. Harriss-White (2004). 'Social Stratification and Rural Households'. In *Rural India Facing the 21st Century: Essays on Long Term Village Change and Recent Development Policy*, ed. B. Harriss-White and S. Janakarajan. London: Anthem Press, pp. 115–59.

Commander, S. (1983). 'The Jajmani System in North India: An Examination of its Logic and Status across Two Centuries'. *Modern Asian Studies* 17 (2): 283–311.

Cox, O. C. (1950). 'Max Weber on Social Stratification: A Critique'. *American Sociological Review* 15 (2): 223–27.

Creswell, W. C. and V. L. Plano Clark (2007). *Designing and Conducting Mixed Methods Research*. California: SAGE.

——— (2011). *Designing and Conducting Mixed Methods Research*. California: SAGE.

Crompton, R. (1993). *Class and Stratification: An Introduction to Current Debates*. Cambridge, MA: Polity Press.

Crompton, R. and J. Gubby (1977). *Economy and Class Structure*. London: Macmillan.

Da Corta, L. and D. Venkateshwarlu (1999). 'Unfree Relations and the Feminisation of Agricultural Labour in Andhra Pradesh, 1970–95'. *The Journal of Peasant Studies* 26 (3): 71–139.

Dasgupta, R. (2014). *Capital: The Eruption of Delhi*. New York: The Penguin Press.

Davis, E. D. (2004). *Discipline and Development: Middle Classes and Prosperity in East Asia and Latin America*. Cambridge: Cambridge University Press.

Desai, S. and Dubey, A. (2011). 'Caste in 21st Century India: Competing Narratives'. *Economic and Political Weekly* 46 (11): 40–49.

Deshpande, G. P. (2009). *The World of Ideas in Modern Marathi*. New Delhi: Tulika Books.

Deshpande, S. (2003). *Contemporary India: A Sociological View*. New Delhi: Penguin Books.

Deshpande, R. and S. Palshikar (2008). 'Occupational Mobility: How much Does Caste Matter?' *Economic and Political Weekly* 43 (34): 61–70.

Devereux, S. and J. Hoddinott (1999). 'The Context of Fieldwork'. In *Fieldwork in Developing Countries*, ed. S. Devereux and J. Hoddinott. Colorado: Lynne Rienner Publishers, pp. 3–24.

Dhanagare, D. N. (1995). 'The Class Character and Politics of the Farmers' Movement in Maharashtra during the 1980s'. In *New Farmers' Movements in India*, ed. T. Brass. Essex: Frank Cass, pp. 72–94.

Dhar, P. (2004). 'Ramoshi'. In *People of India: Maharashtra*, Part 3, Vol. xxx, ed. K. S. Singh et al. Mumbai: Popular Prakashan Pvt. Ltd, pp. 1768–72.

Dirks, N. B. (2003). *Castes of Mind: Colonialism and the Making of Modern India*. New Delhi: Permanent Black.

Dobbin, Ch. (1972). *Urban Leadership in Western India: Politics and Communities in Bombay City 1840–1885*. New York: Oxford University Press.

Donner, H. (2008). *Domestic Goddesses: Maternity, Globalisation and Middle-Class Identity in Contemporary India*. Aldershot: Ashgate Publishing Limited.

——— (ed.) (2011). *Being Middle-class in India: A Way of Life*. Oxon: Routledge.

——— (2015). 'Bringing It All Back Home: Re-making Middle-Class Families in Neoliberal Kolkata'. In *Anthropologies of Class: Power, Practice, Inequality*, ed. J. Carrier and D. Kalb. Cambridge: Cambridge University Press, pp. 131–48.

Donner, H. and G. De Neve (2011). 'Introduction'. In *Being Middle-class in India: A Way of Life*, ed. H. Donner. Oxon: Routledge, pp. 1–22.

Douglas, M. and B. Isherwood (1979). *The World of Goods: Towards an Anthropology of Consumption*. New York: Routledge.

Dumont, L. (1970). *Homo Hierarchicus: The Caste System and Its Implications*. Translated by M. Sainsbury, L. Dumont and B. Gulati. London: Weidenfeld & Nicolson.

Easterly, W. (2001). 'The Middle Class Consensus and Economic Development'. *Journal of Economic Growth* 6 (4): 317–35.

Ehrenreich, B. and J. Ehrenreich (1977). 'The Professional-Managerial Class'. *Radical America* 11 (3): 7–32.

Emirbayer, M. (1997). 'Manifesto for a Relational Sociology'. *American Journal of Sociology* 103 (2): 281–317.

Ermini, L. and D. Hendry (1995). 'Log Income versus Linear Income: An Application of the Encompassing Principle'. Working Paper, Nuffield College, University of Oxford.

Everitt, B. S. et al. (2011). *Cluster Analysis* (5th edn). Sussex: John Wiley & Sons Ltd.

Fernandes, L. (2000). 'Restructuring the New Middle Class in Liberalizing India'. *Comparative Studies of South Asia, Africa and the Middle East* 20 (1 & 2): 88–112.

——— (2006). *India's New Middle Class: Democratic Politics in an Era of Economic Reform*. Minneapolis: University of Minnesota Press.

——— (2011). 'Hegemony and Inequality: Theoretical Reflections on India's 'New' Middle Class'. In *Elite and Everyman: The Cultural Politics of the Indian Middle Classes*, ed. A. Baviskar and R. Ray. New Delhi: Routledge, pp. 58–82.

Fernandes, L. and P. Heller (2006). 'Hegemonic Aspirations: New Middle Class Politics and India's Democracy in Comparative Perspective'. *Critical Asian Studies* 38 (4): 495–522.

Fine, B. and A. Saad-Filho (2004). *Marx's Capital*. London: Pluto Press.

References 277

Fink, A. (2009). *How to Conduct Surveys: A Step-by-Step Guide* (4th edn). London: SAGE Publications.

Frankfort-Nachmias, Ch. and D. Nachmias (2005). *Research Methods in the Social Sciences* (5th edn). London: Hodder Arnold.

Fuller, C. J. (1996). 'Introduction'. In *Caste Today*, ed. C. J. Fuller. New Delhi: Oxford University Press, pp. 1–31.

Ganguly-Scrase, R. and T. J. Scrase (2009). *Globalisation and the Middle Classes in India: The Social and Cultural Impact of Neoliberal Reforms*. London: Routledge.

Garchedi, G. (1977). *The Economic Identification of Social Classes*. London: Routledge and Kegan Paul.

Ghosal, R. K. (2002). 'Liberalisation and Occupational Diversification in Rural India'. In *Economic Liberalisation and Its Implications for Employment*, ed. A. Mathur and P. S. Raikhy. New Delhi: Deep and Deep Publications, pp. 218–38.

Gibbon, P. and M. Neocosmos (1985). 'Some Problems in the Political Economy of "African Socialism"'. In *Contradictions of Accumulation in Africa: Studies in Economy and State*, ed. H. Bernstein and B. K. Campbell. Beverly Hills, CA: Sage, pp. 153–206.

Giddens, A. (1973). *The Class Structure of the Advanced Societies*. London: Hutchinson.

——— (1981). *The Class Structure of the Advanced Societies*. London: Hutchinson.

——— (1995). 'The Growth of the New Middle Class'. In *The New Middle Classes: Life-styles, Status, Claims, and Political Orientations*, ed. Arthur J. Vidich. New York: New York University Press, pp. 103–29.

Goldthorpe, J. H. (1997). 'The "Goldthorpe" Class Schema: Some Observations on Conceptual and Operational Issues in Relation to the ESRC Review of Government Social Classifications'. In *Constructing Classes: Towards a New Social Classification for the UK*, ed. D. Rose and K. O'Reilly. Swindon: Economic and Social Research Council and Office for National Statistics, pp. 40–48.

Gramsci A. (1971). *Selections from the Prison Notebooks*. Edited and translated by Q. Hoare and G. Nowell-Smith. London: Lawrence and Wishart.

Gooptu, N. (2009). 'Neoliberal Subjectivity, Enterprise Culture and New Workplaces: Organised Retail and Shopping Malls in India'. *Economic and Political Weekly* 44 (22): 45–54.

Gouldner, A. W. (1979). *The Future of Intellectuals and the Rise of the New Class: A Frame of Reference, Theses, Conjectures, Arguments, and an Historical Perspective on the Role of Intellectuals and Intelligentsia in the International Class Contest of the Modern Era*. New York: Seabury Press.

Guha, R. (1982). 'On Some Aspects of Historiography of Colonial India'. In *Subaltern Studies I: Writings on South Asian History and Society*, ed. R. Guha. Delhi: Oxford University Press, pp. 1–9.

278 References

——— (ed.) (1982). *Subaltern Studies I: Writings on South Asian History and Society*. Delhi: Oxford University Press.

——— (2013). *Beyond Caste: Identity and Power in South Asia, Past and Present*. London, Boston: Brill.

Gupta, N. and K. Sharan (2004). 'Industrial Workers and the Formation of 'Working-Class Consciousness' in India'. *Sociological Bulletin* 53 (2): 238–50.

Guérin, I., A. Bhukhut, K. Marius-Gnanou and G. Venkatasubramanian (2009). 'Neo-bondage, Seasonal Migration, and Job Brokers: Cane Cutters in Tamil Nadu'. In *India's Unfree Workforce: Of Bondage Old and New*, ed. J. Breman, I. Guérin and A. Prakash. Delhi: Oxford University Press, pp. 233–58.

Hansen T. B. (1996). 'Recuperating Masculinity: Hindu Nationalism, Violence and the Exorcism of the Muslim "Other"'. *Critique of Social Anthropology* 16 (2): 321–43.

Harriss, J. (1991). 'Population, Employment, and Wages: A Comparative Study of North Arcot Villages, 1973–1983'. In *The Green Revolution Reconsidered: The Impact of High-Yielding Rice Varieties in South India*, ed. P. R. Hazell and C. Ramasamy. Baltimore and London: John Hopkins University Press, pp. 105–24.

——— (2006). 'Middle-Class Activism and the Politics of the Informal Working Class'. *Critical Asian Studies* 38 (4): 445–65.

——— (2012). 'Reflections on Caste and Class, Hierarchy and Dominance'. Seminar paper. Available at www.india-seminar.com/2012/633.htm.

Harriss-White, B. (1996). *A Political Economy of Agrarian Market in South India: Masters of the Countryside*. Delhi: Sage Publications.

——— (1999) *A Political Economy of Agrarian Market in South India: Masters of the Countryside*. Delhi: Sage Publications.

——— (2003). *India Working: Essays on Society and Economy*. Cambridge: Cambridge University Press.

——— (2008). *Rural Commercial Capital: Agricultural Markets in West Bengal*. New Delhi: Oxford University Press.

——— (2010). 'Local Capitalism and the Foodgrains Economy in Northern Tamil Nadu, 1973–2010'. MIDS (submitted for the Working Paper series), University of Oxford.

——— (2012). 'Capitalism and the Common Man: Peasants and Petty Production in Africa and South Asia'. *Agrarian South: Journal of Political Economy* 1 (2): 109–60.

——— (2015). 'Introduction: The Economic Dynamism of Middle India'. In *Middle India and Urban–Rural Development: Four Decades of Change*, ed. B. Harriss-White. New Delhi: Springer, pp. 1–28.

——— (2016). 'From Analysing "Filières Vivrieres" to Understanding Capital and Petty Production in Rural South India'. *Journal of Agrarian Change* 16 (3): 478–500.

Harriss-White, B. and J. Heyer (eds). (2010). *The Comparative Political Economy of Development: Africa and South Asia*. London and New York: Routledge.

Harriss-White, B. and S. Janakarajan (1997). 'From Green Revolution to Rural Industrial Revolution in South India'. *Economic and Political Weekly* 32 (25): 1469–77.

———— (2004). *Rural India Facing the 21st Century*. London: Anthem Press.

Harvey, D. (2015). *Seventeen Contradictions and the End of Capitalism*. London: Profile Books Ltd.

Hazell, P. R. and C. Ramasamy (eds). (1991). *The Green Revolution Reconsidered: The Impact of High-Yielding Rice Varieties in South India*. London: John Hopkins University Press.

Hennis, W. (2000). *Max Weber's Central Questions* (2nd edn). Translated by Keith Tribe. Berks: Threshold Press.

Hilton, P. R. (2005). *Statistics Explained* (2nd edn). London and New York: Routledge.

Islam, R. (ed.). (1987). *Rural Industrialisation and Employment in Asia*. New Delhi: ILO, Asian Employment Programme.

Jaffrelot, C. (2003). *India's Silent Revolution: The Rise of the Lower Castes in North Indian*. London: Hurst and Company.

———— (2005). *Dr. Ambedkar and Untouchability: Fighting the Indian Caste System*. New York: Columbia University Press.

———— (2007). *Hindu Nationalism: A Reader*. Ranikhet: Permanent Black.

Jaffrelot, C. and A. Kalaiyarasan (2017). 'Quota Is the Wrong Answer'. *Indian Express*, 3 May, Online edition. Available at http://indianexpress.com/article/opinion/columns/quota-is-the-wrong-answer-4637872/ (accessed 23 May 2017).

Jaffrelot, C. and P. van der Veer (2008). 'Introduction'. In *Patterns of Middle Class Consumption in India and China*, ed. C. Jaffrelot and P. van der Veer. New Delhi: SAGE Publication India Pvt. Ltd, pp. 11–34.

Jayaraj, D. (2004). 'Social Institutions and the Structural Transformation of the Non-Farm Economy'. In *Rural India Facing the 21st Century: Essays on Long Term Village Change and Recent Development Policy*, ed. B. Harriss-White and S. Janakarajan. London: Anthem Press, pp. 175–91.

Jayaram, N. (1996). 'Caste and Hinduism: Changing Protean Relationship'. In *Caste: Its Twentieth Century Avatar*, ed. M. N. Shrinivas. New Delhi: Viking, pp. 69–86.

Jeffrey, C. (1997). 'Richer Farmers and Agrarian Change in Meerut District, Uttar Pradesh, India'. *Environment and Planning A* 29 (12): 2113–27.

———— (2001). 'A Fist Is Stronger than Five Fingers: Caste and Dominance in Rural North India'. *Transactions of the Institute of British Geographers* 26 (2): 217–36.

280 References

——— (2008). 'Kicking Away the Ladder: Student Politics and the Making of an Indian Middle Class'. *Environment and Planning D: Society and Space* 26 (3): 517–36.

——— (2010a). *Timepass: Youth, Class, and the Politics of Waiting in India*. California: Stanford University Press.

——— (2010b). 'Kicking Away the Ladder: Student Politics and Making of an Indian Middle Class'. *Internationales Asienforum* 41 (1–2): 5–31.

Jeffrey, R. and P. Jeffrey (1997). *Population, Gender and Politics: Demographic Change in Rural North India*. Cambridge: Cambridge University Press.

Jeffrey, C., P. Jeffrey and R. Jeffery (2005). 'Reproducing Difference: Schooling, Jobs and Empowerment in Uttar Pradesh, India'. *World Development* 33 (12): 2085–101.

Jeffrey, R., P. Jeffrey and C. Jeffrey (2011). 'Are Rich Rural Jats Middle-Class?' In *Elite and Everyman: The Cultural Politics of the Indian Middle Classes*, ed. A. Baviskar and R. Ray. New Delhi: Routledge, pp. 140–63.

Jodhka, S. J. and A. Prakash (2016). *Oxford India Short Introductions: The Indian Middle Class*. New Delhi: Oxford University Press.

Joshi, S. (2001). *Fractured Modernity: Making of a Middle Class in Colonial North India*. New Delhi: Oxford University Press.

——— (2011). 'The Spectre of Comparisons: Studying the Middle Class of Colonial India'. In *Elite and Everyman: The Cultural Politics of the Indian Middle Classes*, ed. A. Baviskar and R. Ray. New Delhi: Routledge, pp. 83–107.

Kalecki, M. (1972). 'Social and Economic Aspects of "Intermediate Regimes"'. In *Selected Essays on the Economic Growth of the Socialist and the Mixed Economy*, ed. M. Kalecki. Cambridge: Cambridge University Press, pp. 162–70.

Konárd, G. and I. Szelenyi (1979). *The Intellectuals on the Road to Class Power*. New York: Harcourt, Brace Jovanovitch.

Krishna, A. (2007). 'Subjective Assessments, Participatory Methods and Poverty Dynamics: The Stages-of-Progress Method'. Chronic Poverty Research Centre, Working Paper No. 93.

Kulkarni, D. (2014). 'Demands for Quotas from New Groups Add to Maharashtra Government's Woes'. *DNA*, 10 February, Online edition. Available at http://www.dnaindia.com/mumbai/report-demands-for-quotas-from-new-groups-add-to-maharashtra-govt-s-woes-1960607 (accessed 23 June 2017).

Kunnath, G. (2012). *Rebels from the Mud Houses: Dalits and the Making of the Maoist Revolution in Bihar*. New Delhi: Social Science Press.

Lalvani, M. (2008). 'Sugar Co-Operative in Maharashtra: A Political Economy Perspective'. *The Journal of Development Studies* 44 (10): 1474–505.

Lele, J. (1982). *Elite Pluralism and Class Rule: Political Development in Maharashtra*. Bombay: Popular Prakashan.

——— (1990). 'Caste, Class and Dominance: Political Mobilization in Maharashtra'. In *Dominance and State Power in Modern India: Decline of a Social Order*, Vol. II, ed. F. R. Frankel and M. S. A. Rao. New Delhi: Oxford University Press, pp. 116–211.

Lerche, J. (1999). 'Politics of the Poor: Agricultural Labourers and Political Transformations in Uttar Pradesh'. In *Rural Labour Relations in India*, ed. T. J. Byres, K. Kapadia and J. Lerche. New York: Routledge, pp. 182–241.

——— (2010). 'From "Rural Labour" to "Classes of Labour": Class Fragmentation, Caste and Class Struggle at the Bottom of the Indian Labour Hierarchy'. In *The Comparative Political Economy of Development: Africa and South Asia*, ed. B. Harriss-White and J. Heyer. London: Routledge, pp. 66–87.

——— (2012). 'Labour Regulations and Labour Standards in India: Decent Work?' *Global Labour Journal* 3 (1): 16–39.

Lerche, J., A. Shah and B. Harriss-White (2013). 'Introduction: Agrarian Politics and Left Politics in India'. *Journal of Agrarian Change* 13 (3): 337–50.

Liechty, M. (2003). *Suitably Modern: Making Middle-Class Culture in a New Consumer Society*. Princeton: Princeton University Press.

Lindberg, S. (1995). '"New Farmers" Movements in India as Structural Response and Collective Identity Formation: The Cases of Shetkari Sanghatana and the BKU'. In *New Farmers' Movements in India*, ed. T. Brass. Essex: Frank Cass, pp. 95–125.

Löwith, K. (1993). *Max Weber and Karl Marx*. London: Routledge.

Macaulay, Hon'ble T. B. Minute, dated the 2 February 1835. Available at http://www.columbia.edu/itc/mealac/pritchett/00generallinks/macaulay/txt_minute_education_1835.html.

Madey, D. L. (1982). 'Some Benefits of Integrating Qualitative and Quantitative Methods in Program Evaluation, with Illustrations'. *Educational Evaluation and Policy Analysis* 4 (2): 223–36.

Mankekar, P. (1999). *Screening Culture, Viewing Politics: An Ethnography of Television, Womanhood, and Nation in Postcolonial India*. London: Duke University Press.

Marx, K. (1853). 'The British Rule in India'. *New-York Daily Tribune*, 25 June.

——— (1959). *Capital: A Critique of Political Economy, Vol. III, The Process of Capitalist Production as a Whole*. Edited by F. Engels. New York: International Publishers.

——— (1967). *Capital*, Vol. III. New York: International Publishers.

——— (1969 [1850]). *The Class Struggles in France, 1848–1850*. Selected Works, Vol. 1, Moscow: Progress Publishers.

——— (1978). *Capital: A Critique of Political Economy*, Vol. II. London: Penguin Books Ltd.

282 References

——— (1978 [1861–3]). *Theories of Surplus-Value*, Part II. London: Lawrence & Wishart, pp. 737–41.

——— (1996 [1887]). *Capital: A Critique of Political Economy, Vol. I: The Process of Production of Capital*. Translated by Samuel Moore and Edward Aveling. Moscow: Progress Publishers.

Marx, K. and F. Engels (1969 [1848]). *Manifesto of the Communist Party*. Translated by Samual Moore in cooperation with Frederick Engels, 1888. Marx/Engels Selected Works, Vol. I. Moscow: Progress Publishers, pp. 98–137.

——— (2008 [1848]). *The Communist Manifesto*, with an introduction by D. Harvey. London: Pluto Press.

Mawdsley, E. (2004). 'India's Middle Classes and the Environment'. *Development and Change* 35 (1): 79–103.

Mazzarella, W. (2003). *Shoveling Smoke: Advertising and Globalization in Contemporary India*. Durham: Duke University Press.

——— (2005). 'Middle Class'. In *South Asia Keywords*, ed. R. Dwyer. Available at https://www.soas.ac.uk/south-asia-institute/keywords/file24808.pdf.

McCartney, M. and B. Harriss-White (2000). 'The "Intermediate Regime" and "Intermediate Classes" Revisited: A Critical Political Economy of Indian Economic Development from 1980 to Hindutva'. QEH Working Paper Series, No. 34.

Mellor, J. W. (1976). *The New Economics of Growth: A Strategy for India and Developing World*. Ithaca: Cornell University Press.

——— (1989). 'Rural Employment Linkages through Agricultural Growth: Concepts, Issues and Questions'. In *The Balance between Industry and Agriculture in Economic Development: Proceedings of the Eighth World Congress of the International Economic Association*, Vol. 2, ed. J. G. Williamson and V. R. Panchamukhi. London: Sectors Proportions, Macmillan and International Economic Associations, pp. 306–19.

——— (1995). 'Introduction'. In *Agriculture on the Road to Industrialization*, ed. J. W. Mellor. Baltimore: John Hopkins University Press, pp. 1–22.

Meyer, C. and B. Birdsall (2012). 'New Estimates of India's Middle Class: Technical Note'. Centre for Global Development. Available at https://www.cgdev.org/doc/2012-10-29_MiddleClassIndia_TechnicalNote.pdf.

Miller, D. (1995). 'Consumption and Commodities'. *Annual Review of Anthropology* 24 (141): 141–61.

Ministry of Industry. (1963). *Development of Small Scale Industries in India: Prospects, Problems and Policies*. New Delhi: Government of India.

Ministry of Home Affairs (2011). 'Census Data'. Available at http://www.censusindia.gov.in/2011-Common/CensusData2011.html.

——— (2011). *District Census Handbook: Pune*. Available at http://www.censusindia. gov.in/2011census/dchb/2725_PART_B_DCHB_%20PUNE.pdf.

Misra, B. B. (1961). *The Indian Middle Classes: Their Growth in Modern Times*. New Delhi: Oxford University Press.

Mukherjee, R. (1999). 'Caste in Itself, Caste and Class, or Caste in Class'. *Economic and Political Weekly* 34 (27): 1759–61.

Mukhopadhyay, I. (2009). 'Identifying Livelihood in Rural India'. In *The Changing Identity of Rural India: A Socio-historic Analysis*, ed. E. Basile and I. Mukhopadhyay. New York: Anthem Press, pp. 15–30.

Nadarajah, S. (2005). 'Exponentiated Pareto Distributions'. *Statistics* 39 (3): 255–60.

Nadkarni, M. V. (1987). *Farmers' Movement in India*. New Delhi: Allied Publishers.

Nardo, M. et al. (2005). 'Handbook on Constructing Composite Indicators: Methodology and User Guide'. OECD Statistics Working Papers, 2005/03, Paris: OECD Publishing.

Nayab, D. E. (2011). 'Estimating the Middle Class in Pakistan'. *The Pakistan Development Review* 50 (1): 1–28.

NCAER. (2011). 'Indian Human Development Survey-II, A Public Use Database for Informed Policy (Survey Description)'. University of Maryland. Available at http://www.ihds.umd.edu/IHDS_papers/Brief%20of%20IHDS-II%20Survey. pdf.

Nehru, J. (1998 [1946]). *The Discovery of India*. New Delhi: Oxford University Press.

Ollman, B. (1979). *Social and Sexual Revolution: Essays on Marx and Reich*. Cambridge, MA: South End Press.

O'Hanlon, R. (1985). *Caste, Conflict and Ideology: Mahatma Jotirao Phule and Low Caste Protest in Nineteenth-Century Western India*. Cambridge: Cambridge University Press.

Onwuegbuzie, A. J. and N. L. Leech (2005). 'On Becoming a Pragmatic Researcher: The Importance of Combining Quantitative and Qualitative Research Methodologies'. *International Journal of Social Research Methodology* 8 (5): 375–87.

Parkin, F. (2002). *Max Weber* (rev. edn). New York: Routledge.

Parry, J. (2009). '"Sociological Marxism" in Central India: Polanyi, Gramsci, and the Case of the Unions'. In *Market and Society: The Great Transformation Today*, ed. C. Hann and K. Hart. Cambridge: Cambridge University Press, pp. 175–202.

——— (2013). 'Company and Contract Labour in a Central Indian Steel Plant'. *Economy and Society* 42 (3): 348–74.

Patil, R. (2000). 'Search for Identity among Dalit Middle Class in Maharashtra'. *Social Action* 50 (1): 70–9.

Patnaik, U. (1976). 'Class Differentiation within the Peasantry: An Approach to Analysis of Indian Agriculture'. *Economic and Political Weekly* 11 (39): A82–101.

284 References

——— (1987). *Peasant Class Differentiation: A Study in Method with Reference to Haryana*. Bombay: Oxford University Press.

Pattenden, J. (2011). 'Gatekeeping as Accumulation and Domination: Evidence from South India'. *Journal of Agrarian Change* 11 (2): 164–94.

——— (2016a). *Labour, State and Society in Rural India: A Class-Relational Approach*. Manchester: Manchester University Press.

——— (2016b). 'Working at the Margins of Global Production Networks: Local Labour Control Regimes and Rural-based Labourers in South India'. *Third World Quarterly* 37 (10): 1809–33.

Pawar, Sh. (2016). *On My Terms: From the Grassroots to the Corridors of Power*. New Delhi: Speaking Tiger Publishing.

Planning Commission, Government of India. (2008). *Eleventh Five-Year Plan (2007–2012): Agriculture, Rural Development, Industry, Services, and Physical Infrastructure*, Vol. III. New Delhi: Oxford University Press. Available at http://planningcommission.nic.in/plans/planrel/fiveyr/11th/11_v3/11th_vol3.pdf.

——— (2013). *Twelfth Five-Year Plan (2012–2017): Economic Sectors*, Vol. II. New Delhi: SAGE Publications, Available at http://planningcommission.nic.in/plans/planrel/fiveyr/12th/pdf/12fyp_vol2.pdf.

Poulantzas, N. (1975). *Classes in Contemporary Capitalism*. London: Verso.

Pressman, S. (2007). 'The Decline of the Middle Class: An International Perspective'. *Journal of Economic Issues* 41 (1): 181–200.

Prakash, A. (2015). *Dalit Capital: State, Markets and Civil Society in Urban India*. London: Routledge.

Prakash, G. (2000). 'Writing Post-orientalist Histories of the Third World: Perspectives from Indian Historiography'. In *Mapping Subaltern Studies and the Postcolonial*, ed. V. Chaturvedi. London: Verso, pp. 163–90.

Raj, K. N. (1973). 'The Politics and Economics of "Intermediate Regimes"'. *Economic and Political Weekly* 8 (27): 1189–98.

Rajagopal, A. (2001). 'Thinking about the New Middle Class: Gender, Advertising and Politics in an Age of Globalisation'. In *Signposts: Gender Issues in Post-Independence India*, ed. S. R. Rajeswari. New Brunswick: Rutgers University Press, pp. 57–99.

Rao, K. R. (2004). 'Sonar'. In *People of India: Maharashtra*, Part 3, Vol. xxx, ed. K. S. Singh et al. Mumbai: Anthropological Survey of India in Association with Popular Prakashan Pvt. Ltd, pp.1887–93.

Razavi, S. (1992). 'Agrarian Change and Gender Power: A Comparative Study in South Eastern Iran'. D. Phil. Thesis, Oxford University.

Reinhard, B. (1966). *Max Weber: An Intellectual Portrait*. London: Methuen.

Robinson, T. P. (2014). *Café Culture in Pune: Being Young and Middle Class in Urban India*. Oxford: Oxford University Press.

Rudolph, L. I. and Rudolph, S. H. (1987). *In Pursuit of Lakshmi: The Political Economy of the Indian State*. Chicago: The University of Chicago Press.

Rutten, M. (1995). *Farms and Factories: Social Profile of Large Farmers and Rural Industrialists in West India*. New Delhi: Oxford University Press.

Säävälä, M. (2001). 'Low Caste but Middle-Class: Some Religious Strategies for Middle-Class Identification in Hyderabad'. *Contributions to Indian Sociology* 35 (3): 293–318.

Said, E. (1988). 'Foreword' to *Selected Subaltern Studies*. pp. v–x.

Saith, A. (1992). *The Rural Non-farm Economy: Processes and Policies*. Geneva: ILO.

——— (2001). 'From Village Artisan to Industrial Clusters: Agendas and Policy Gaps in Indian Rural Industrialization'. *Journal of Agrarian Change* 1 (1): 81–123.

Sangari, K. (2002). *Politics of the Possible: Essays on Gender, History, Narratives, Colonial English*, London: Anthem Press.

Seekings, J. and N. Nattrass (2005). *Class, Race, and Inequality in South Africa*. Michigan: Yale University.

Sharma, K. L. (1999). *Social Inequality in India: Profiles of Caste, Class and Social Mobility*. Jaipur: Rawat Publications.

Sheth, D. L. (1999a). 'Secularisation of Caste and Making of New Middle Class'. *Economic and Political Weekly* 34(34/35): 2502–10.

——— (1999b). 'Caste and Class: Social Reality and Political Representations'. In *Contemporary India*, ed. V. A. Pai Panandiker and A. Nandy. New Delhi: Tata McGraw Hill, pp. 337–63.

Sridharan, E. (2004). 'The Growth and Sectorial Composition of India's Middle Class: Its Impact on the Politics of Economic Liberalization'. *India Review* 3 (4): 405–28.

——— (2011). 'The Growth and Sectoral Composition of India's Middle Classes: Their Impact on the Politics of Economic Liberalization. In *Elite and Everyman: The Cultural Politics of the Indian Middle Classes*, ed. A. Baviskar and R. Ray. New Delhi: Routledge, pp. 27–57.

Srinivasan, M. V. (2004). 'Time and Space: Intervillage Variation in the North Arcot Region and Its Dynamics, 1973–95'. In *Rural India Facing the 21st Century: Essays on Long Term Village Change and Recent Development Policy*, ed. B. Harriss-White and S. Janakarajan. London: Anthem Press, pp. 78–114.

——— (2016). 'Arni's Workforce: Segmentation Processes, Labour Market Mobility, Self-employment and Caste'. In *Middle India and Urban–Rural Development: Four Decades of Change*, ed. B. Harriss-White. New Delhi: Springer, pp. 65–96.

Shukla, R. (2010). *How India Earns, Spends and Saves: Unmasking the Real India*, New Delhi: SAGE and NCAER-CMCR.

286 References

Shukla, R. and R. Purosothaman (2008). *Market Information Survey.* New Delhi: National Council for Applied Economic Research.

Singh, K. S. et al. (eds). (2004). *People of India: Maharashtra,* Part 3, Vol. xxx. Mumbai: Popular Prakashan Pvt. Ltd.

Swartz, D. (1997). *Culture and Power: The Sociology of Pierre Bourdieu.* London: The University of Chicago Press.

Unni, J. (2000). *Sustainable Development and Social Security: The Role of the Non-Farm Sector.* New Delhi: Vikas Publishing House.

Upadhya, C. B. (1988). 'From Kulak to Capitalist: The Emergence of a New Business Community in Coastal Andhra Pradesh, India'. Unpublished PhD thesis, Yale University, New Haven.

Upadhya, C. (1997). 'Culture, Class and Entrepreneurship: A Case Study of Coastal Andhra Pradesh'. In *Small Business Entrepreneurs in Asia and Europe: Towards a Comparative Perspective,* ed. M. Rutten and C. Upadhya. New Delhi: Sage, pp. 47–80.

——— (2004). 'The Indian Middle Class in the New Economy: Corporate Culture and Strategy in the IT Industry'. In *Cultures and Technologies in Asia: The Paradigm Shifts,* ed. M. Vicziany. Clayton: Monash Asia Institute, Monash University Press.

——— (2008). 'Rewriting the Code: Software Professionals and the Reconstitution of Indian Middle Class Identity'. In *Patterns of Middle Class Consumption in India and China,* ed. C. Jaffrelot and P. van der Veer. New Delhi: Sage Publication India Pvt. Ltd, pp. 55–87.

——— (2011). 'Software and the New Middle Class in the New India'. In *Elite and Everyman: The Cultural Politics of the Indian Middle Classes,* ed. A. Baviskar and R. Ray. New Delhi: Routledge, pp. 167–92.

Varma, P. (1998). *The Great Indian Middle Class.* New Delhi: Viking.

——— (2015). *The New Middle Class.* New Delhi: Harpercollins India.

Vora, R. (2009). 'Maharashtra or Maratha Rashta?' In *Rise of the Plebeians? The Changing Face of the Indian Legislative Assemblies,* ed. C. Jaffrelot and S. Kumar. New Delhi: Routledge, pp. 215–44.

Wacquant, L. (1991). 'Making Class: The Middle Class(es) in Social Theory and Social Structure'. In *Bringing Class Back In: Contemporary and Historical Perspectives,* ed. S. G. McNall, R. F. Levine and R. Fantasia. Oxford: Westview Press, pp. 39–64.

Weber, M. (1930). *The Protestant Ethics and the Spirit of Capitalism.* Translated by T. Parsons. London: Brown University Books.

——— (1958). *The Religion of India: The Sociology of Hinduism and Buddhism.* Translated by Gerth, H. H. and D. Martindale. Glencoe, IL: The Free Press.

——— (1964). *The Theory of Social and Economic Organization*. Edited by Talcott Parsons. New York: The Free Press.

——— (1978). *Economy and Society: An Outline of Interpretative Sociology*. Edited by Guenther Roth and Claus Wittich. Berkeley: University of California Press.

——— (1991 [1948]). *From Max Weber: Essays in Sociology*. Translated by Gerth, H. H and C. W. Mills. Oxon: Routledge.

——— (2019). *Economy and Society: A New Translation*. Edited and translated by Keith Tribe. Cambridge, MA: Harvard University Press.

Weininger, E. B. (2005a). 'Pierre Bourdieu on Social Class and Symbolic Violence'. In *Approaches to Class Analysis*, ed. E. O. Wright. Cambridge: Cambridge University Press, pp. 116–65.

——— (2005b). 'Foundation of Pierre Bourdieu's Class Analysis'. In *Approaches to Class Analysis*, ed. E. O. Wright. Cambridge: Cambridge University Press, pp. 82–118.

van Wessel, M. (2004). 'Talking about Consumption: How an Indian Middle Class Dissociates from Middle Class-Life'. *Cultural Dynamics* 16 (1): 93–116.

Wright, E. O. (1980). 'Varieties of Marxist Conceptions of Class Structure'. *Politics & Society* 9 (3): 323–70.

——— (1985). *Classes*. London: Verso.

——— (1989). 'A General Framework for the Analysis of Class Structure'. In *The Debate on Classes*, ed. E. O. Wright et al. New York: Verso, pp. 3–46.

——— (1997). *Class Counts: Comparative Studies in Class Analysis*. Cambridge: Cambridge University Press.

——— (2009). 'Understanding Class: Towards and Integrated Analytical Approach'. *New Left Review* 60: 101–16.

Zhang, Q. F. (2015). 'Class Differentiation in Rural China: Dynamics of Accumulation, Commodification and State Intervention'. *Journal of Agrarian Change* 15 (3): 338–65.

Index

Adivasis, 63n5
advanced capitalist societies, 68
agrarian capitalism/agricultural capitalism, 76, 80
agrarian capitalist class/agricultural capitalists, 74, 87, 97, 110, 204
agrarian change, 4, 7, 39n8, 110
agrarian classes, 7, 81, 204
agricultural growth, 77
Agricultural Labour Days Hired-in (ALDH), 87
Agricultural Labour Days Sold-out (ALDS), 87
agricultural labourers, 44–45, 48, 52–53, 74–75, 87, 103, 128–29, 134, 148, 160n14, 161n28, 162n36, 186, 204, 207
allied agriculture, 22, 32, 78, 149, 213–15
Andhra Pradesh, 76, 98, 111n11
annual per capita income, 20–25, 31, 33, 154
artisans, 2, 22, 58–59, 68, 70, 78, 101, 111n4, 123–24, 149, 213–15
aspirational cultural class, 3
aspirations, 4, 6–7, 17, 37, 38n5, 115–16, 119n3, 143–44, 157, 161n29, 162n29, 165, 203–04, 207–08, 210
average landholding, 47, 51, 84, 86, 99, 227

backward caste groups. *See* Other Backward Classes (OBCs), Scheduled Castes (SCs), Scheduled Tribe (STs)
bara balutedar system, 146, 162n32

Bhandal Basti, 49–50
big capitalists, 69
Bourdieu, Pierre, 4–6, 21–22, 158, 164, 171, 203
Bourdieuian middle class, 200
Bourdieuian perspective, 61
  ambition and aspiration of middle classes, 181–84
  analysis of France's academic world, 162n29
  approach to social classes, 6–7, 164–65, 167, 170, 200, 208
  class and consumption, interpreting, 184–200
  coexistence of social fields, 209
  concept of distinction, 166–67, 170–78, 180–81, 184–85, 189, 206–10
  formation of rural middle classes, 8, 175–81
  habitus, 5, 166, 168–71, 206–09
  Indian middle class, 170–75, 207
  self-identified middle class, 176–81
  social and cultural capital, 12, 62, 169, 206, 208–09
  social reality, 208
  symbolic representation, 8
bourgeoisie, 2, 5, 67–69, 71–73, 111n3–4, 112n14, 119n3, 121, 167
Brahmins, 16, 56, 58, 123, 125, 148–49, 155–57, 213–17, 221–22, 227–32
bullock capitalists, 75

capital, 2–5, 7–9, 12, 14–16, 18, 27, 65, 68–69, 71, 73–76, 80–82, 84,

88–90, 93–94, 96–99, 101, 112n11,
113n22, 115, 118, 121–22, 125–26,
128, 132, 136, 143, 145, 156–58,
158n3, 161–62n29, 162n38, 166,
168–69, 171–73, 178–79, 182, 184,
202n33, 204, 206, 208–210, 227
productive, 2, 4–5, 8, 68–69, 71–72,
74, 76, 80, 84, 92, 96–97, 101,
103, 105–06, 117, 120–21, 128,
136, 142, 157, 158n3, 165, 200,
204–05, 209, 228
profit-making, 96–97
unproductive, 97
capital accumulation, 66, 73, 76, 84, 93,
111–12n11
capital conversion, 162n38
capitalism, 7, 67, 70–72, 77, 80, 123–25
agricultural, 76, 80
provincial, 76
regional, 76
capitalist class, 12, 66, 70–76, 81, 89, 91–
99, 101, 104–06, 111–12n11, 143,
158n3, 204, 206
capitalist farmers, 76, 112n14, 158n3, 204
capitalist market, 2
capitalist mode of production, 2, 67–68
capitalist societies, 67–68, 71, 126
advanced, 68
modern, 68
capital ownership, 74, 81, 89–90, 97, 102
caste. 3–4, 8, 15–16, 27, 31, 38n3, 41–46,
48–51, 53–58, 62–63n4, 63n8,
64n18, 81–82, 114n42, 115–16,
119n3, 122–28, 130, 142, 145–53,
155–57, 158n4–8, 159n8, 160n18,
162n31–32, 162n37, 163n39–42,
201n22, 207, 212–17, 220,231, 240,
258. *See also* Other Backward Classes
(OBCs), Scheduled Castes (SCs),
Scheduled Tribes (STs)
Dangar caste, 49, 53–54, 58, 92, 186
disparity in labour market, urban India,
212–13

forward, 148–49, 155–57, 213–16,
220–21, 223, 225–30
Gaurav caste, 177
impact of, 158n8
income differentiation, 156
income distribution, 216–21
Kunbi caste, 62n4
Lohar caste, 57–58, 162n32
Mahar caste, 48–49, 56–58, 158n8,
162n32
Mali caste, 51, 53–54, 57, 92, 94–95,
99, 103, 131–32, 180, 186
Mang/Matang caste, 57–58, 162n32
Maratha caste, 56, 62n4, 92, 94, 99,
153–54
Mulani caste, 58
occupational distribution, rural India,
149, 213–15
Ramoshi caste, 56
relationship between occupation and,
57–58, 127–28, 162n32
Shudra caste, 126
source of income, urban India, 213
upper, 15, 75, 127, 156, 161n31,
162n34, 163n42, 213, 226,
229–30
caste–class debate, in India, 125–28
caste compositions, 31, 41, 46, 63n8,
64n18, 116, 127, 147
of classes in rural Maharashtra, 229–30
of Rahatwade and Nandur, 55–58
of rural middle class, 34, 110, 122, 156–
58, 163n41–42, 181, 204
of urban middle class, 228–29
casual labourer/casual employment, 87, 90,
100–03, 107, 112n16, 132, 136,
139–40, 159n14, 160n14, 161n28,
207, 211
casual contract, 112, 139–40
Centre for the Study of Developing
Societies, CSDC-Lokniti, 26, 39n13,
127
Chambhar, 162n32

290　Index

Chibber, Vivek, 3
Chougula, 162n32
class-ambiguous transformations, 66, 110
class boundaries, 6–7, 61, 74, 145, 157–58,
　　167, 208
classes of labour, 66, 81–82, 90–91, 99–102,
　　104, 110, 112n16, 158n3, 204–06
class identity, 5, 12, 17–18, 61, 126, 159n8,
　　172, 204, 207
colonial middle class, 13–15
comfortable middle class, 28–35, 37–38,
　　157, 231
commercial capital, 113n22
commercial (or acquisition) classes, 115,
　　118–22, 136–37, 150, 210
Communist Manifesto (Marx), 70
consumer durables, ownership of, 21–22,
　　26–27, 40n16, 89, 94, 97
consumer goods, 18, 31, 33, 89, 96, 117–
　　18, 130, 144, 146, 150–52, 171–73,
　　176, 186, 198–200, 207, 229
consumption, 4, 8, 16–21, 26, 38, 70–71,
　　77, 112, 118, 126, 129, 132, 158,
　　161n27, 165, 170, 172–73, 176,
　　184–86, 192, 194, 198–200, 202,
　　207, 210, 227–30, 259, 262–64,
　　184–200
contemporary India, 62, 120, 125, 129
contested theory, 4
contestation in Indian society, 38n3
contradictory class locations, 4, 73
　　within class relations, 72–73
credentials, 5, 10n12, 18, 21, 26, 115, 118,
　　120–21, 128–29, 137, 142, 145,
　　161n29, 168, 184, 202n33, 204–05,
　　207, 210, 230
cultivation, 22, 32, 36, 47, 57–58, 78, 84,
　　92, 98, 103, 137–38, 149, 151–52,
　　213–15, 224–26, 234, 251–52
cultural capital, 3, 5, 12, 15, 62, 164,
　　168–69, 172–73, 178, 183–84, 202,
　　206, 208, 210
　　embodied, 168–69, 172

institutionalised, 168, 172
objectified, 168, 172

Dalit Basti, 48–49
Dalits, 63n5, 147, 154, 159n8, 181
developing countries, 1, 17, 39n13
　　middle class in, 11, 111n3
Dhangar Basti, 49
Dhangars, 49, 51, 53–54, 56–58, 92, 94, 99,
　　101, 103, 147–48, 150–52, 182, 186
Dhor, 162n32
distinction, 2, 5–6, 8, 10n15, 16, 18, 42,
　　48, 63, 71, 81, 122–24, 126, 139,
　　158n5, 162, 166–67, 170–76, 178,
　　180–81, 184–85, 189, 206–10
diversification, 4, 51, 203
　　economic, 65, 74, 76, 83, 111–12n11
　　non-farm, 76, 84, 87
　　rural livelihood, 76
domination, 5, 8, 44, 72–73, 209
dry land, 44, 51, 54, 84, 103, 109, 235, 251
Dudhane Basti, 49
Dumont, L., 125
Durkheim, Émile, 2, 166

economic capital, 5, 12, 15, 62, 69, 184,
　　202, 202n33, 209–10
economic liberalisation, 3, 8–9, 13, 15,
　　17–18, 66, 77–79, 170–72, 181,
　　203, 210
Economy and Society (Weber), 116–17, 120
education, 13–15, 17–19, 21, 26, 29, 31–
　　32, 40n16, 45, 58, 62n4, 65, 69, 89,
　　93–97, 107, 109–10, 115–21, 125,
　　127–29, 135–37, 139–40, 142–47,
　　150, 151–53, 156–57, 159n8, 161–
　　62n29, 163n38, 165–66, 168–73,
　　175–76, 178–84, 186, 189, 193–94,
　　198, 201n12, 202n33, 204–07,
　　209–10, 224–30
　　adult, 26, 150–53, 224–30
　　colonial-based English, 13–14
　　employment status and, 135–36, 139–40

English-medium, 13, 143, 162n38, 171, 176, 181, 183–85, 193–94, 207, 209

formal, 21, 26, 95, 112n13, 114, 120–21, 129, 137, 144

higher, 11, 26, 29, 32, 37, 45, 51, 54, 58, 82, 97, 109, 112, 128, 130, 135, 138, 143–45, 149, 156, 159, 161–62n29, 168, 194, 196, 202n33, 213, 217, 227, 231–32

161n29, 201n33

private, 19, 96, 145, 150, 179

proportion of total expenditure, 226

relationship between income and, 222–24

educational capital, 118, 121

educational institutions, 15, 17, 42, 145, 157

education index, 26

elites, 14–16, 116

Hindu, 15

Maratha, 43

rural, 9, 43, 210

embodied cultural capital, 172

employment status

caste and, 149, 213–15

class position and, 140

education and, 139–40

English-medium schooling, 13, 143, 162n38, 171, 176, 181, 183–85, 193–94, 207, 209

entrepreneurship, 15–16, 32, 38n3, 65, 76, 118, 120, 136–38, 159n7

ethnicity, 3, 158n5

ethnic segregation, 158n5

ethnocentrism, 6

exchange labour, 64, 89–90, 97, 99–100, 102

exploitation, 5, 8, 67, 72–74, 71–72, 80–81, 87–88, 104, 112–13n18, 142, 209, 97, 100, 208–09

exploitation-centred concept of class, 8, 72

exploitation of labour, 67, 73–74, 80–81, 87–88, 104, 142, 209

factories and enterprises, 16, 51–54, 60, 65, 69, 82–83, 93–96, 98, 101, 104, 107–10, 116, 118, 124, 129–32, 134, 139–44, 157, 159, 174, 179, 182–83, 192–94, 211–12

factory capitalism, 67

family labour, 64n17, 68, 80–82, 84, 88–90, 93, 95–103

farm-owning industrial working class, 74, 102–03

farm-owning skilled workers, 89, 91, 96–99, 102–06, 204

'field,' Bourdieu's notion of, 169, 172–73, 184, 209

forward castes, 148–49, 155–57, 213–17, 220–21, 223–32

Gāvāta (the main village), 48, 50, 53–54, 101, 129–30

gender, 3–4, 45, 81, 88, 98, 107, 157, 161, 167, 172, 207, 231, 243, 250

geographic and social identity, 48–50

Giddens, Anthony, 5, 10n18, 121

globalisation, 11, 18, 172

Gopal, 57

Gore Basti, 49

Green Revolution, 19, 39n8, 44, 66, 75–76, 79, 83, 112n14

Gujarat, 76

Gurav community, 53, 57–58, 162n32, 177

habitus, 5, 166, 168–71, 206–09

HDPI survey, 7, 10n22, 66, 78–79, 116, 149, 163n37, 214, 216

Hindu nationalist organisations, 171

Hindus, 15, 42, 58, 123

home ownership, 23, 33, 48, 52

Honar, 57

household income, 221–22, 228

annual, 39n9, 92, 94, 97, 99, 102–03, 159n14

distribution of, 137–39, 149, 155, 216–20

292   Index

sources of, 21–23, 31, 33, 36, 39n14, 52, 60, 63n10, 78–79, 113n36, 132, 135, 147, 160n15, 212–15
spending of, 184
Household Survey Questionnaire, 230
household surveys, 6, 60, 64n14, 67, 103, 107, 116, 153, 163n36, 165, 174, 230

identity
   class, 5, 12, 17–18, 61, 126, 159n8, 172, 204, 207
   geographic and social, 48–50
   religious, 15
   social and cultural, 3, 48, 111–12n11
income distribution, 116, 153–56, 163n40, 217–22, 229
income sources, 47, 59, 63n10, 73, 137–38, 140, 213–15
India Human Development Survey (IHDS-I and IHDS-II), 7, 10n22, 13, 20, 22–31, 33–37, 41, 66, 78–79, 116, 148–49, 154–57, 162n37, 212–13, 215–23
India Human Development Survey II (2011–12), 7
Indian political economy surveys, 7
Indira-era austerities, 17
industrial capitalism, 67
industrialisation, 4, 7–9, 17, 39n8, 45, 53, 62, 65–68, 76, 83, 95, 107, 110, 114–15, 119, 121, 124–25, 128, 130, 141, 145–46, 150, 157, 161n18, 194, 204–05, 210
   class differentiations due to, 65
   economic impact of caste system, 124–25
   employment opportunities, 69, 107
   formation of middle class and, 45
   impact of, 69, 83, 128, 130, 145, 194
   labour contractors and, 141
   local, 150
   price of land and, 95
   rural, 7, 17, 38n8, 65–67, 76, 83, 110, 119, 121, 157, 204–05

transformation in labour class, 69, 107, 115, 145–46
industrial labour contractors, 74, 93–95, 141
informational capital, 168, 178
institutionalised cultural capital, 172
intermediate classes, 2, 9n6, 70, 75
International Monetary Fund (IMF), 17
irrigated land, 48, 51–52, 84–86, 92, 94–96, 99, 101–06
irrigated landholding, 47

jajmani system, 83, 126–27
Jangam, 57–58
Joshi, 57

Kamble, 48
Kamble Basti, 48–49
Kanjarbhat, 57
kirana shop (grocery store), 48, 53
Koli, 56–57, 162n32
Kumbhar, 162n32
Kunbis, 42

labour, 2–5, 7–8, 10n12, 12, 14, 21–23, 27, 57, 60, 64n17, 65–74, 77, 80–83, 86–01, 103–04, 106–07, 109–10, 112n16, 112n18, 113n30, 114n42, 115–25, 127–28, 132, 135–36, 138–42, 145, 147–48, 159–60n14, 160n23, 161n28, 162n37, 179, 182, 204–07, 209–10, 212–13, 246, 249, 251
labour contractors, 52, 54, 74, 89, 93–95, 132, 138, 140–42, 179, 182, 212
labour-exploitation ratio, 80–81, 87–88, 97, 100, 104, 112, 142
labour markets, 5, 8, 10n12, 22, 27, 62, 74, 81, 88–89, 94, 115–22, 127–30, 132, 135–36, 140, 142, 145, 148–49, 153, 156, 161n28, 162n37, 173, 204–06, 209–10, 212–13
labour relations, 7–8, 60, 66, 80–81, 87–90, 99, 107, 110, 204
land ownership, distribution of, 48, 51–52, 68, 80, 84–86, 104, 150, 153, 225

Index   293

landowning capitalist class, 66, 89, 91–93, 96, 105–06, 158n3, 206

leisure activities, 170, 199

Licence Raj, 17

Lingayat, 57

livelihood changes, patterns of, 4, 12, 47, 60, 63n8, 65–67, 76, 78, 82, 84, 87, 100–02, 110, 150, 175, 205

Lohar caste, 57–58, 162n32

Lorenz curves, 155, 163n40

lower middle class, 28–35, 37–38, 157, 165, 175–76, 186, 188, 195–99, 231–32

lowest class, 28–29, 33–35, 157, 229–30

macroeconomic surveys, 66–67, 116

Maharashtra, 1, 6–7, 41–45, 54–58, 62n2–3, 76, 107–08, 112n14, 125, 128, 146, 161n31, 162n32, 163n42, 181, 204, 232. *See also* Nandur; Rahatwade

Maratha dominance, 42

Nomadic Tribes (NT-C) in, 56, 58

rural middle classes in, 204–07, 229–30

Shetkari Sanghatana farmers' movement, 43

sugar cooperatives of, 43

Mahars, 48–49, 56–58, 159n8, 162n32

Malis, 51, 53–54, 57, 92, 94–95, 99, 103, 131–32, 180, 186

Mang/Matang caste, 57–58, 162n32

manual labouring households, 22–23, 30–31, 34–35, 39n14, 40n16, 60–61, 64n17, 68–69, 72, 78, 87, 118–20, 122, 135–36, 139, 147–48, 153, 157, 158n3, 170, 175, 178–81, 195–98, 206, 209, 230

Maratha-led anti-Brahmin movement, 42

Marathas, 42, 46, 48–50, 54, 56–57, 62n2, 62n4, 84, 92, 94, 99, 103, 147–48, 150–54, 178–79, 182

class division among, 153

dominance of, 42–44

in Nandur, 58

population, 42

of Rahatwade, 47, 57, 153–54

marketable capital, 5, 122, 132, 136, 157, 206

market situation, 5–6, 117, 119, 209

Marx, Karl, 2, 4–8, 9n4, 21, 65, 67–71, 83, 101, 103–04, 110n1, 111n2, 112n7, 116–120, 123, 158, 164, 167, 170, 174, 203–09

criticism of, 68

Das Kapital, 67–69

Marxist analysis, 3, 22, 186

capitalist mode of production, 67

class categorisation in rural India, 80–82 (*see also* Nandur; Rahatwade)

classes, notion of, 66–71, 110, 114n42, 115, 118

historical materialism, 116

idea of Indian villages, 83

labouring classes, 103–09

officials, 68

ownership, notion of, 8, 66, 69, 72, 80–81, 84–85, 88–90, 97, 103–04, 110, 204–05

owners of means of production (*bourgeoisie*), 67

petty bourgeoisie, 68

physicians, 68

problem of conceptualising middle class, 71–74

rural middle class, 204–05

workers (*proletariat*), definition, 67

means of production, 8, 19, 22, 42, 45, 66–67, 72–75, 80, 84, 89, 93, 95, 97, 99, 109–10, 116–17, 204–05

Ricardo's views, 111n2

merchants' capital, 113n22

middle class, 1, 163n42

ambition and aspiration of, 181–84

caste composition of, 127, 156–58, 158n8

colonial, 13–15

consumption practices, 26–27, 184–200

294 Index

definition, 39n13
economic liberalisation policies and, 17
elite, 14, 16
households, 59–62
in India, 19–23
Jeffrey's argument on formations, 38n6
lifestyle, 26–27
lower, 28–35, 37–38, 38n6, 157, 165,
  186, 188, 195–99, 229–30,
  175–76
new, 17–19
post-independence, 13, 15–16, 19,
  42–43, 126–27
post-liberalisation, 17–18
property ownership, 120–21, 175–76
in relation to position of women, 180
self-sufficiency of, 83, 176–77, 179–80,
  207
status, 7, 17, 19, 37–38, 46, 58–59, 61,
  98, 111n4, 115–16, 119, 122–27,
  135–36, 139, 157, 158n1,
  158n4–5, 159n8, 161–62, 166,
  168, 172–75, 178–79, 183, 185,
  199–201, 227–28
straddling, 66, 89, 96–97, 102, 104,
  204–05
upper, 28–32, 34–38, 157, 165, 171,
  175–78, 182, 189, 191, 195–99,
  229–30
middle-class-ness, 6, 8, 21–22, 175–76,
  178, 207, 209–10
middle middle class, 164–65, 174–76, 178,
  186, 189–91, 195–99, 262
migration, 4, 54, 63n9, 77, 107–08, 146
  inward migration, 51, 63n9
mode of production, 2, 67–68
modern capitalist society, 68
modernisation, 2
Mordara Basti, 50
Mulani caste, 57–58, 99, 130
Muslims, 15, 46–47, 49, 53–54, 56–58, 85,
  99, 147–48, 151–52, 177

Naik, 162n32
Nandur, 6, 8, 10n21, 41–42, 45–46, 51–58,
  60–61, 63–65, 74, 77–79, 81–97,
  99–110, 113n20, 113n22–32,
  113n34, 113n39–41, 115–16,
  127–39, 141–146, 148–152, 156,
  159n9–11, 161n16–17, 161n19–
  21, 161n24–26, 161n28–29,
  162–63n32–34, 163n39, 165, 173,
  177, 179–80, 182, 186–90, 194,
  201n8–11, 201n17–18, 201n20,
  201n23–27, 202n29, 202n32,
  202n38, 204–07, 210
average landholding, 51, 86, 99
caste composition of, 55–58
castes of, 145–56
categorising classes in, 82–84
classification of households in, 91
communication devices possession, 197
domestic appliance possession, 196
economic classes, 88–90
family engagement in agriculture, 88
farm-owning industrial working class,
  66, 74, 89, 91, 96–97, 102–06,
  204
farm-owning skilled workers, 66, 90–91,
  96–97, 102, 104–06, 204
interior design of 'living rooms' in, 8,
  165, 176, 186, 189, 198–200
labour contractors, 140–42
land and home ownership and access to
  basic amenities in, 52
land distribution in, 84–86
landless labouring class, 104
landowning capitalist class, 92
manual labouring households in, 60
map of, 55
middle-class formation in, 122, 135–37
net hired labour days, 87
new capitalist class, 94
non-farm activities in, 79
non-farm occupations in, 211–12
non-labouring households, 61

occupational classes in, 137–40
occupational patterns in, 161n28
petty commodity producers (PCPs),
99–100
physical structure of, 53–55
process of industrialisation in, 115, 121
rural middle classes, 116, 156–58
self-identified middle-class households,
174, 176, 178–79, 188, 191
skills, education and qualifications of
individuals, 142–45, 161n29
social classes, 165
social media use in, 198
social relations in, 81
socio-economic characteristics of,
128–34
sofa set possession, 199
use of outside labour, 87
vehicle ownership, 195
water supply in, 93
Nav Buddha, 48–49, 56–58
Nehru, J., 14, 16, 75
    Gandhian–Nehruvian idealism, 16
    Nehruvian socialism, 16, 17
neo-Marxists, 71–74
Net Agricultural Labour Days (NALD),
87–91, 93, 96–97, 99–100, 103–06
new capitalist class, 66, 89, 91, 93–96, 99,
104–06, 143, 158n3, 206
new social movements, 9n11
Nhawi, 162n32
Nomadic Tribes (NT-C), 46, 56–58
non-agricultural labourers, 94, 96
non-labouring households, 22–23, 27–31,
34–35, 39n14, 60–61, 87, 90–91,
97, 99, 102, 105–06, 129–30, 135,
139, 144, 148, 153–54, 163n39,
194–98, 209
    categorisation, 2011–2012, 28–29
non-property capital, 118, 121

objectified cultural capital, 172
officials, Marx's view, 68

organised business, 22, 32, 78, 149, 213–15
Other Backward Classes (OBCs), 42, 46,
62n4, 103, 223
    income distributions, 155, 213–15
    occupational distribution among, 149,
214
    in rural India, 157
    in rural Maharashtra, 49, 51, 53, 56–58,
99, 103, 147–48
    socio-economic variables, 151–52,
225–27
    in urban India, 229–30

Parits (Dhobis), 57–58, 162n32
peasantry/peasantries, 2, 42, 44, 67–69,
74–75, 77, 81, 111n7, 112n14, 120,
124
    poor peasants, 77, 81
    rich peasants, 81
    upper middle peasants, 100
petty bourgeoisie, 2, 68, 71–73, 111n3–4,
119n3, 121
petty commodity producers (PCPs), 2, 59,
65–66, 82, 89, 99–101, 204–05
physical capital, 69, 73, 89
physicians, Marx's view, 68
political economy, 3, 7, 19, 41, 62n2, 68,
70, 74, 110, 210
poor class, 16, 37, 77, 81, 130–31, 150,
154–55, 158n8, 162n36, 164–65,
170, 174–81, 193–99
post-independence middle class, 15–17
postcolonial, 2–3
postmodernism, 3
poststructuralism, 3
poverty lines, 20, 23–24, 39n10, 40n16
Prakash, Gyan, 3
private school, 143, 163n38, 176, 182–83,
185, 201n12, 243, 253, 260
productive capital, 4–5, 68–69, 80, 96, 128,
157, 209
profit-making capital, 96–97
proletariats, 2, 5, 67, 69, 111n7, 167

296   Index

property classes, 115, 117–18, 120, 158n3
  negatively privileged, 118, 158n3
  positively privileged, 118, 158n3
property market, 117, 120, 135–36
property ownership, 117, 120–21, 175–76
provincial capitalism, 76

Rahatwade, 1, 6, 8, 10n21, 41–42, 44–58,
    60–61, 62n4, 63n9, 64n11–12,
    64n17–18, 65–66, 74, 77–79, 81–
    88, 90–94, 96–97, 99–100, 102–05,
    107–10, 113n22–24, 113n28–29,
    113n34, 115–16, 127–30, 132, 134–
    39, 141–42, 144–50, 153–54, 156,
    161n22, 161n28–29, 162–63n32,
    163n35, 163n39, 165, 173–176,
    178–79, 182, 188, 191, 193–200,
    201n12–17, 213n19–20, 201n28,
    202n30, 202n35–37, 202n40,
    202n43, 194, 204–07, 210–11
  average landholding, 47, 84, 99
  caste composition of, 55–58
  castes of, 56, 145–56
  categorising classes in, 82–84
  classification of households in, 91
  communication devices possession, 197
  domestic appliance possession, 196
  economic classes, 88–90
  family engagement in agriculture, 88
  farm-owning industrial working class,
    102–03
  farm-owning skilled workers, 96–97, 99
  interior design of 'living rooms' in, 8,
    165, 176, 186, 189, 198–200, 207
  labour contractors, 140–42
  land and home ownership and access to
    basic amenities in, 48
  land distribution in, 84–86
  landless labouring class, 104
  landowning capitalist class, 92
  manual labouring households in, 60
  map of, 49–50
  middle-class formation in, 122, 135–37

  net hired labour days, 87
  new capitalist class, 94
  non-farm activities in, 79
  non-farm occupations in, 211–12
  non-labouring households, 61
  occupational classes in, 137–40
  occupational patterns in, 161n28
  petty commodity producers (PCPs),
    99–100
  physical structure of, 48–51
  process of industrialisation in, 115, 121
  residence of Dalit agricultural labouring
    family in, 188
  rural middle classes, 116, 156–58
  self-identified middle-class households,
    174, 176, 178–79, 191
  skills, education and qualifications of
    individuals, 142–45, 161n29
  social classes, 165
  social media use in, 198
  social relations in, 81
  socio-economic characteristics of, 64,
    128–34
  sofa set possession, 199
  use of outside labour, 87
  vehicle ownership, 195
  water supply in, 93
Ramoshis, 56–57
regional capitalism, 76
regional capitalists, 76
religion, 58, 114n42, 124–25, 169
religious identity, 15
rich class, 155, 165, 174–81, 193–99
rich Dalits, 154
rich farmers/rich peasants, 19, 75, 81,
    112n13–14, 121
rich Marathas, 43, 154
rotational employment, 132, 139–40
rural capitalism, 7, 76
rural capitalist class, 75–76, 111n11
rural class formation, 38n8, 41, 66, 74, 122
rural economy, 4, 9, 77, 79, 112n18, 203,
    210

rural industrialisation, 7, 39n8, 65, 76, 83, 110, 119, 204–05
rural middle class, 34–36
rural non-farm sector, 77–78
rural societies, 1–2, 126

Said, Edward, 3
salaried employment, 12, 22, 31–32, 36–37, 63n10, 72, 78, 121, 149, 159n14, 160, 213–14, 228, 230
    approximate annual income from, 137–39, 159n14
    caste population engaged in, 149, 213–15
    changes in household income, 78, 213
    growth in, 78
    as main source of household income, 31–32, 36
    middle class, 31–32, 36–37, 59
    over representation, 31, 36–37
    SC households in rural India, 149, 214
    in upper caste groups, 213
Scheduled Castes (SCs), 44, 46, 58, 103, 155–57, 207, 212–17, 220–21, 223–30
    access to reservations, 149
    average annual income, 216, 220–21, 223
    in Borate Basti, 54
    clusters of villages, 45
    in Gāvāta, 53
    landless, 53, 86, 134
    landowning households, 53, 84
    level of adult education, 225
    livelihood of, 145, 147–49, 152, 213–14
    low work participation rates, 45
    in Nandur, 57, 94, 148, 150, 152, 156
    occupational distribution among, 214–15
    in Rahatwade, 10, 46, 48–51, 54, 56, 58, 60–61, 63–65, 74, 78, 82–88, 90–94, 96–100, 102–05, 107, 113n20, 113n22–24, 113n28, 115–16, 127–29, 132, 134–39,

141–42, 145–51, 153–54, 156, 161n28–29, 163n29, 165, 173–74, 178–79, 182, 188, 191, 193–96, 198, 200, 205–06, 211
    in rural Maharashtra, 56, 229–30
    salaried employment, 149
    socio-economic indicators, 225–28
    status in caste hierarchy, 58
    in urban India, 225–29
Scheduled Tribes (STs), 45–46, 54, 84, 145, 147–52, 155, 207, 217, 221
    access to educational institutions, 157
    access to reservations, 156
    average annual income, 216, 220–21, 223
    income distribution, 156
    landless households, 150
    landowning, 150
    livelihood, 156, 212–15
    in Nandur, 57–58
    occupational distribution among, 214
    in Rahatwade, 56, 84–85
    in rural Maharashtra, 56, 229–30
    socio-economic indicators, 225–28
    source of household income, 149
    status in caste hierarchy, 58
    in urban India, 225–29
second lowest class, 28–29, 33–35, 157, 229–32
self-identified middle classes, 7, 37–38, 41, 59, 61, 150, 165, 170, 173–82, 184, 186, 188–91, 194–95, 197–99, 207, 209–10
self-perpetuating class, 15
Simmel, Georg, 2
simple polarisation of class structure, 5, 71
small-scale industries, 12, 16–17, 19, 75–77, 93, 101, 212
    dairy production business, 148
    sugarcane farming, 95, 98
social and cultural identity, 111n11
social capital, 5, 12, 15, 62, 161–62n29, 173, 182, 184, 208–10

298 Index

social classes, 4, 6, 68, 115, 119–20, 164–
  70, 174, 181, 200, 201n33
social identity, 3, 48
social networks, 21, 27, 29, 33, 115, 117–
  21, 128, 140–42, 145–46, 150–53,
  156, 162n29, 184, 210, 222–30
social relations of production, 88, 204
Sonar, 57–58, 162n32
South Asian studies, 3
state, 2, 9, 11–16, 19, 42–43, 58–59, 62,
  68, 74–75, 77, 89, 91–92, 95–97,
  111n7, 112n13–14, 114n42, 121,
  125, 159n7, 168, 203, 210
status, 7, 17, 19, 31, 36–38, 42–43, 46,
  50–51, 58–59, 61, 98, 116, 119,
  122–27, 135–36, 139, 157, 158n4,
  158n8, 161n27, 161n29, 166, 168,
  172–75, 178–79, 183, 185, 199–
  200, 208, 225, 227, 230
straddling middle class, 66, 89, 96–97, 102,
  104, 204–05
strata, 69–70, 104, 121, 222–24
stratification, 9, 41, 44–48, 59–62, 70,
  87, 90, 115–16, 122–23, 145–46,
  158n1, 168, 207, 210
subaltern, 2–3, 9n7
surplus accumulation, 208–09
Sutar, 162n32

Tamil Nadu, 44, 76, 112n18, 128
Tönnies, Ferdinand, 2
trade liberalisation, 17

unproductive class, 5, 68, 70–72, 110
upper castes, 15, 75, 127, 156, 161n31,
  162n34, 163n42, 213, 226, 229–30
upper class, 28–30, 33–35, 156–57,
  163n42, 171, 229–30
upper middle class, 28–32, 34–38, 157,
  165, 171, 175–78, 182, 189, 191,
  195–99, 229–30
upward mobility, 119, 161n29
urban middle-class labour market, 212–13

Vadar, 57

Wacquant, Loïc, 5
wage, 12, 44, 59–60, 63n10, 64n16–17,
  67–69, 71–74, 78–79, 81–82,
  88–89, 93–94, 101–03, 105–06,
  111n12, 118, 121, 124, 128, 131,
  136, 145, 148–50, 153, 156, 160,
  163n36, 179, 181, 209, 212–13,
  230, 249–51
wage labourers, 22–23, 31, 59, 60, 63n10,
  64n16, 67–68, 74, 78–79, 82, 93,
  101, 105–06, 131, 136, 145, 148–
  50, 153, 156, 159n14, 160, 164n16,
  179, 181, 209, 213–14
Washington Consensus, 17
Weber, Max, 2, 4–6, 8, 21, 164, 167–68,
  170, 174, 203, 208, 210, 223, 225.
  See also Weberian perspectives
Weberian perspectives
  caste composition, 127, 156–58
  castes as status groups, 122–25
  castes of Rahatwade and Nandur,
    145–56
  categorisation of classes, 22, 115–20
  criticism of Marx, 119, 202
  distinction between caste and ethnicity,
    158n5
  distinction between classes and status
    groups, 122
  education, 142–45
  idea of status ranking, 126
  'life chances', conception of, 8, 117, 142,
    145, 156, 208–10
  middle classes, 1, 5–6, 8–9, 9n1–2,
    11–14, 18, 21, 26, 28, 31–35,
    37, 68–71, 87, 91, 110, 120–22,
    127, 135–37, 143, 147, 150,
    156, 161n27, 179–80, 186, 200,
    205–06
  occupational patterns in Rahatwade and
    Nandur, 135–40